Contacting the Author

Email: jerry@honeycutt.com

On the Web: http://www.honeycutt.com

Important System Policies

HKEY_CURRENT_USER\Software\Microsoft\Windows\CurrentVersion\Policies contains all the policies you see in the following table. Each section heading indicates ~~~ you set it. To set a policy, set its DWORD value to 0x00000001. To clear ~~~ 0x00000000.

VALUE	POLICY
\EXPLORER	
NoSaveSettings	Don't save settings at exit
NoActiveDesktop	Disable Active Desktop
NoActiveDesktopChanges	Do not allow changes to Active Desktop
NoInternetIcon	Hide Internet Explorer icon
NoNetHood	Hide Network Neighborhood icon
NoDesktop	Hide all desktop items
NoFavoritesMenu	Remove Favorites menu from Start Menu
NoFind	Remove Find menu from Start Menu
NoRun	Remove Run menu from Start Menu
NoSetActiveDesktop	Remove the Active Desktop item from the Settings menu
NoChangeStartMenu	Disable drag and drop context menus on Start Menu
NoFolderOptions	Remove the Folder Options menu item from Settings menu
NoRecentDocsMenu	Remove Documents menu from Start Menu
NoRecentDocsHistory	Do not keep history of recently opened documents
ClearRecentDocsOnExit	Clear history of recently opened documents
NoLogoff	Disable Logoff option on Start Menu
NoClose	Disable Shut Down command
NoSetFolders	Disable changes to Printers and Control Panel Settings
NoSetTaskbar	Disable Changes to Taskbar and Start Menu Settings
NoTrayContextMenu	Disable context menu for Taskbar
NoStartMenuSubFolders	Hide custom Programs folders
ClassicShell	Enable Classic Shell
NoFileMenu	Disable File menu in Shell folders
NoViewContextMenu	Disable context menu in shell folders
EnforceShellExtensionSecurity	Only allow approved Shell extensions
LinkResolveIgnoreLinkInfo	Do not track Shell shortcuts during roaming
NoDrives	Hide Floppy Drives in My Computer
NoNetConnectDisconnect	Disable net connections/disconnections
NoPrinterTabs	Hide General and Details tabs in Printer Properties
NoDeletePrinter	Disable Deletion of Printers
NoAddPrinter	Disable Addition of Printers
RestrictRun	Run only specified Windows applications
\ACTIVEDESKTOP	
NoComponents	Disable ALL desktop items
NoAddingComponents	Disable adding ANY desktop items
NoDeletingComponents	Disable deleting ANY desktop items
NoEditingComponents	Disable editing ANY desktop items
NoClosingComponents	Disable closing ANY desktop items
NoHTMLWallPaper	No HTML Wallpaper
NoChangingWallPaper	Disable changing wallpaper
NoCloseDragDropBands	Disable dragging, dropping and closing ALL toolbars
NoMovingBands	Disable resizing ALL toolbars
\WINOLDAPP	
NoRealMode	Do not allow computer to restart in MS-DOS mode
Disabled	Disable MS-DOS prompt

SAMS

Teach Yourself

The Windows Registry®

in 24 Hours

D0890475

VALUE	POLICY
\SYSTEM	
DisableRegistryTools	Disable Registry editing tools
NoDispCPL	Disable Display Control Panel
NoDispBackgroundPage	Hide Background page
NoDispScrSavPage	Hide Screen Saver page
NoDispAppearancePage	Hide Appearance page
NoDispSettingsPage	Hide Settings page
NoSecCPL	Disable Passwords Control Panel
NoPwdPage	Hide Change Passwords page
NoAdminPage	Hide Remote Administration page
NoProfilePage	Hide User Profiles page
NoDevMgrPage	Hide Device Manager page
NoConfigPage	Hide Hardware Profiles page
NoFileSysPage	Hide File System button
NoVirtMemPage	Hide Virtual Memory button
\NETWORK	
NoNetSetup	Disable Network Control Panel
NoNetSetupIDPage	Hide Identification Page
NoNetSetupSecurityPage	Hide Access Page
NoEntireNetwork	No 'Entire Network' in Network Neighborhood
NoWorkgroupContents	No workgroup contents in Network Neighborhood

Significant Class Identifiers

FOLDER	CLASS IDENTIFIERS
ActiveX Cache Folder	{88C6C381-2E85-11D0-94DE-444553540000}
Briefcase	{85BBD920-42A0-1069-A2E4-08002B30309D}
Control Panel	{21EC2020-3AEA-1069-A2DD-08002B30309D}
Dial-Up Networking	{992CFFA0-F557-101A-88EC-00DD010CCC48}
Internet Cache...	{7BD29E00-76C1-11CF-9DD0-00A0C9034933}
Internet Explorer	{FBF23B42-E3F0-101B-8488-00AA003E56F8}
Infrared Recipient	{00435ae0-bffb-11cf-a9d8-00aa00423596}
My Computer	{20D04FE0-3AEA-1069-A2D8-08002B30309D}
My Documents	{450D8FBA-AD25-11D0-98A8-0800361B1103}
Network Neighborhood	{208D2C60-3AEA-1069-A2D7-08002B30309D}
Printers	{2227A280-3AEA-1069-A2DE-08002B30309D}
Recycle Bin	{645FF040-5081-101B-9F08-00AA002F954E}
Scheduled Tasks	{D6277990-4C6A-11CF-8D87-00AA0060F5BF}
Shell Favorite...	{1A9BA3A0-143A-11CF-8350-444553540000}
Subscription Folder	{F5175861-2688-11d0-9C5E-00AA00A45957}
The Internet	{3DC7A020-0ACD-11CF-A9BB-00AA004AE837}
URL History Folder	{FF393560-C2A7-11CF-BFF4-444553540000}

TASK	STATEMENT
DELREG SECTION	
To remove a key	*HKEY, Subkey*
To remove a value	*HKEY, Subkey, ValueName*
ADDREG SECTION	
To add a key	*HKEY, Subkey*
To add a string	*HKEY, Subkey, ValueName, 0, "String"*
To add a binary	*HKEY, Subkey, ValueName, 1, XX, XX,...*
To add a DWORD	*HKEY, Subkey, ValueName, 0x10001, XX, XX, XX, XX*
To set default	*HKEY, Subkey,, 0, "String"*

Jerry Honeycutt, Jr.

SAMS
Teach Yourself
the Windows®
Registry
in 24 Hours

SAMS

201 West 103rd Street, Indianapolis, Indiana, 46290

Sams Teach Yourself the Windows® Registry in 24 Hours

Copyright © 1999 by Sams Publishing

International Standard Book Number: 0-672-31552-1

Library of Congress Catalog Card Number: 98-89208

Printed in the United States of America

First Printing: April, 1999

02 01 00 99   4 3 2 1

Trademarks

Warning and Disclaimer

EXECUTIVE EDITOR
Christopher Will

ACQUISITIONS EDITOR
Tracy M. Williams

DEVELOPMENT EDITOR
Faithe Wempen

MANAGING EDITOR
Brice Gosnell

PROJECT EDITOR
Kevin Laseau

COPY EDITOR
JoAnna Kremer

INDEXER
Johnna VanHoose

PROOFREADER
Billy Fields

TECHNICAL EDITORS
Joey Kulakowski
Dave Navarro

INTERIOR DESIGN
Gary Adair

COVER DESIGN
Aren Howell

LAYOUT TECHNICIANS
Brian Borders
Susan Geiselman
Mark Walchle

Contents at a Glance

Contents

Dedication

This one is for Jody and Verby.

Acknowledgments

To do a book right takes a lot of time and a lot of effort from a lot of people. Some of those people deserve special mention. Otherwise, make sure you flip over a few pages to see a full list of the people who contributed to this book. In particular, I'd like to thank Tracy Williams for her patience. Faithe Wempen's development expertise and Dave Navarro's and Joey Kulakowski's technical expertise were significant as well.

About the Author

Jerry Honeycutt provides business-oriented technical leadership to the end-user and Internet community as well as the software development industry. Companies such as the Travelers, IBM, Nielsen North America, IRM, Howard Systems International, and NCR have benefited from his expertise. Jerry continues to serve a variety of organizations through independent consulting, speaking, training, and so on.

Jerry is a leading author in the Internet and operating system categories. He is the author of 20 other books through various publishers, including *Windows 98 Registry Handbook: A Guide for Power Users*. Most of Jerry's books are sold internationally and have been translated into a variety of languages. He has been printed in *Computer Language* magazine and is a regular speaker at Windows World, Comdex, and other industry trade shows on topics related to software development, the Windows product family, and the Internet. He also writes a bimonthly column for *Frisco Style Magazine*. Jerry also maintains a Web site at http://www.honeycutt.com, where he speaks to a variety of issues confronting all readers, individual and corporate.

Tell Us What You Think!

As the reader of this book, *you* are our most important critic and commentator. We value your opinion and want to know what we're doing right, what we could do better, what areas you'd like to see us publish in, and any other words of wisdom you're willing to pass our way.

As an Associate Publisher for the Operating Systems team at Macmillan Computer Publishing, I welcome your comments. You can fax, email, or write me directly to let me know what you did or didn't like about this book[md]as well as what we can do to make our books stronger.

Please note that I cannot help you with technical problems related to the topic of this book, and that due to the high volume of mail I receive, I might not be able to reply to every message.

When you write, please be sure to include this book's title and author as well as your name and phone or fax number. I will carefully review your comments and share them with the author and editors who worked on the book.

Fax: 317.581.4663

Email: lowop@mcp.com

Mail: Associate Publisher
          Sams Publishing
          201 West 103rd Street
          Indianapolis, IN 46290 USA

Introduction

The Registry contains most of the configuration data that is used by Windows 95 and Windows 98. It's the central repository for your configuration data, tying all the different parts of the operating system together so that it operates seamlessly. One of the biggest technologies that is made possible by the Registry is Plug and Play. It also provides a central location to store all configuration data, which is a great improvement over the plethora of INI files that Windows 3.1 programs use.

Other advantages of the Registry over INI files are less spectacular[md]but equally important. The Registry allows applications to integrate with the operating system, for instance, making it tough to determine where the operating system ends and the application begins.

As a tool, the Registry is useful to two types of users. Administrators gain the most from the Registry, using it as a remote administration tool. Power users use the Registry to customize their computers and to make their friends say, "Wow! I didn't know you could do that."

What's New for Windows 98?

Outwardly, Microsoft has made few changes to the Windows 98 Registry. The organization is roughly the same as with Windows 95, but it does contain a number of new settings. The Registry Editor is unchanged. Most of the changes to the Registry are technological:

- The Registry uses less memory, allowing Windows 98 to start faster, and providing an across-the-board performance improvement.
- Microsoft has improved the Registry's caching so that looking up values takes less time. This is another across-the-board performance improvement.
- Windows 98 automatically detects a variety of Registry errors and repairs them. You're less likely to see Registry errors when you start the computer.
- Windows 98 includes a new backup and repair utility that does for the Registry what ScanDisk does for the file system.

This book covers both the Windows 95 and Windows 98 Registry, pointing out any differences along the way.

What You're Going to Learn

The simple goal of this book is to make you an expert. By the time you finish reading this book, you'll know as much, or more, about the Windows 95 and Windows 98 Registry as anyone else on your block.

You're going to learn what's in the Registry, for example. You'll learn about how the operating system organizes data in the Registry and what types of data you find there. Using that information, you also learn how to customize the operating system to suit your needs. Do you want examples? You can customize any file's shortcut menu. You can change the icons that appear on the Start menu. You can customize how the operating system behaves. The possibilities are endless, and this book gets you going with some of the most useful customizations that I've found.

This book also teaches you how to protect the Registry. It's the weak link in your computer's configuration because all the operating system's configuration data is in the Registry. It makes sense to take good care of it, eh? The most important part of that process is to back up the Registry on a regular basis. You also learn several different ways to protect yourself while working in the Registry.

Some of the hours in this book are for administrators. If that describes you, you're in luck. You learn how to enable remote administration, you learn how to administer multiple users, and you learn how to take serious control of the desktops in your organization and control what users can and can't do.

The last few hours in this book help you fix errors in the Registry and application errors that are caused by the Registry. Not only do you learn about the techniques and tools that are available for troubleshooting, you also learn about the different error messages that result from Registry errors—and what to do about them.

First Things First

Before you get too excited about all the possibilities, you must learn some basics. You need to learn what technologies the Registry enables; you must learn the overall organization of the Registry; and, more importantly, you need to learn the terminology that is used to describe various parts of the Registry. Therefore, without delaying any further, I recommend that you get started with Hour 1, "Understanding the Registry."

I've made every effort to make sure that the material in this book is under-standable. Still, the Registry is a complex topic that's difficult to describe in terms that everyone, everywhere can understand. If I've left you with unanswered questions, please feel free to contact me. My email address is jerry@honeycutt.com.

PART I
The Registry

Hour

Hour 1

Understanding the Registry

Microsoft calls the Windows Registry the central repository for configuration data. I prefer to think of it as simply the *configuration database*. Indeed, the Registry is a database—a hierarchical database. This means that data is stored in a hierarchy, much like an outline or a company's organizational chart. There is little or no relationship between data in one branch of the database and data in another branch unless a relationship was explicitly created by the data stored in it. This organization just brings a measure of structure to all the data so that you can locate it easily using a simple notation that's similar to paths in the MS-DOS file system.

Each bit of data in the database is stored as an *order pair* with a name and a value. This is similar to the way that a bank associates an account number (the name) with an account balance (the value).

The Registry serves dozens of innovative purposes, allowing features that were difficult—at best—to implement in previous versions of Windows to work smoothly. It keeps track of the software you install on the computer and how each program interrelates.

With few exceptions, all 32-bit Windows programs store their configuration data as well as your preferences in the Registry, whereas most 16-bit Windows programs and MS-DOS programs don't—they favor the outdated INI files (text files that 16-bit Windows use to store configuration data) instead. The Registry contains the computer's hardware configuration, which includes Plug and Play devices with their automatic configuration and legacy devices. It allows the operating system to keep multiple hardware configurations and multiple users with individual preferences. It allows programs to extend the desktop with such items as shortcut menus and property sheets. It supports remote administration via the network. And the list goes on…

After finishing this hour, you'll have a good feeling for the Registry. You learn about the following topics:

- New Registry features in Windows 98
- What the Registry means to users and administrators
- How Windows stores the Registry on the hard disk
- What tools you can use to work with the Registry

What's New for Windows 98

Outwardly, little has changed in the Registry between Windows 95 and Windows 98. The organization is the same; the Registry Editor is the same; the Application Programming Interface (API) looks the same.

The underlying code is new, though. Microsoft optimized it, improving the overall performance of the operating system ever so slightly. The API now uses less real and protected mode memory. It also has improved caching. Both improvements make access to the Registry easier and allow the operating system to start faster.

Real mode and protected mode are two different modes in which a processor can address memory. In real mode, programs aren't protected from one another, and they're limited to 1MB of memory using 16-bit segmented addresses. In protected mode, the processor protects each program's address space, and each program can access up to 4GB of memory using 32-bit linear addresses.

The Windows 98 Registry is also a bit more reliable than the one in Windows 95. This isn't due to changes in the Registry itself—it's the operating system. The operating system automatically watches for errors in the Registry, and if it detects a problem, it uses Registry Checker to scan and fix the problem. It also uses Registry Checker to automatically back up the Registry once a day. The Registry Checker is new to Windows 98, combining a number of different tools for which you had to look elsewhere before. You can use it to back up the Registry, scan and fix problems in the Registry, and optimize the Registry so that it requires less disk space.

The single biggest Registry-related improvement in Windows 98 is the Registry Checker. This utility makes backing up, fixing, and optimizing the Registry easier. More importantly, its automatic daily backups ensure that you'll always have a working configuration. You'll learn more about this utility in Hour 3, "Backing Up/Restoring the Registry." Hour 22, "Fixing Errors in the Registry," shows you how to use Registry Checker to scan for and fix errors in the Registry.

A BED OF ROSES IT ISN'T

The Registry isn't a bed of roses. Most of the problems people have with it result from a lack of readily-available information. Microsoft scarcely says a word about the Registry, forgetting that the Registry is a powerful tool when placed in the right hands. Windows Help provides a few short lines on using the Registry Editor. The *Microsoft Windows 98 Resource Kit,* published by Microsoft Press, does say a bit more in a handful of pages dedicated to the Registry, but it leaves you with plenty of unanswered questions: How do I optimize the Registry? How do I distribute Registry updates in a user's login script? How do I import DWORD values via an INF file? How do I customize Windows? How do I use the Registry to eliminate the operating system's irritating features?

Misinformation knows few boundaries. Following is my favorite example: Windows 98 has an error message that says that you must reinstall the operating system, when actually freeing up a few megabytes for a backup copy of the Registry takes care of the problem. Microsoft is infamous for stating that the Registry makes the operating system easier to use and maintain, but they leave you in the dark when common problems occur, such as a corrupted Registry, a haywire file association, or a corrupted hardware configuration. When these problems occur, the operating system is anything but easy to use if you don't know how to fix the problems in the Registry. Given that I use more than *400* pages to adequately explain the Registry, I suppose I can't fault Microsoft for not making the same information available.

What the Registry Means to You

With all this mumbo jumbo about the technological advantages of the Registry, you might feel a bit left out. What does the Registry do for you? This book discusses that very topic. You can customize the heck out of Windows. You can make the user interface snappier, add commands to shortcut menus, slim down the Start menu, and so on. Hours 14–16 describe an abundance of customizations that you can use to make Windows fit your needs.

Mastering the Registry enables you to prevent configuration problems by backing it up. Because the Registry contains the whole of the computer's configuration, making a backup copy of the Registry protects your computer's entire configuration. Hour 3 discusses backing up and restoring the Registry in detail.

Sometimes restoring a backup copy of the Registry isn't the best idea because you might lose any configuration changes that have been made since your last backup. In such cases, you can fix a variety of common problems, the solutions to which are rooted in the Registry. The biggest example is a file association that's gone awry; that's easy to fix in the Registry. Other examples include fixing broken property sheets or replacing commands that are missing from shortcut menus. Hour 23, "Fixing Program Errors via the Registry," discusses this in greater detail.

Administrators get the best deal when it comes to the Registry because it enables remote administration. In other words, the administrator can sit at his computer and edit settings on a remote computer. It even enables the administrator to control what the user can do, and where and when the user can do it. Hours 19–21 describe how to enable remote administration and how to take control of the workstations on your network.

> The one word that describes what understanding the Registry means to you is *control*. You control the computer's configuration. You control whether the computer succumbs to some silly configuration error. Learning about the Registry is similar to learning how to give your car a tune-up.

Registry Files on Disk: .dat

Windows stores the entire contents of the Registry in two files: System.dat and User.dat. These are binary files that you can't view using a text editor, as you can with INI files. Windows also turns on the read-only, system, and hidden attributes of System.dat and User.dat so that you can't accidentally replace, change, or delete them. System.dat contains computer-specific configuration data, and User.dat contains user-specific data.

Take a look; both files are in C:\Windows. You must show hidden and system files in order to see them; to do so from Windows Explorer, choose View, Folder Options, and then choose Show All Files on the View tab.

The location of User.dat is different on a computer that has user profiles enabled. When you enable user profiles, Windows creates a new system folder called C:\Windows\Profiles, under which you'll find a folder for each user who logs on to the machine. Each user's profile folder contains an individual copy of User.dat (and many other files and folders). You'll still find a User.dat file in C:\Windows, which Windows uses as the default for new users. Just remember that you see C:\Windows\Profiles*Name* for each user who logs on to that computer. Hour 20, "Administering Multiple Users with Profiles," shows you how to enable profiles and what other files and folders you find within each user's profile folder.

> Profiles enable multiple users to log on to a single computer with their own familiar settings (Start menu, desktop, and so on). You enable profiles using the Enable Multiusers Settings Wizard, which you access by opening Users in the Control Panel. Alternatively, you can open the Passwords icon in the Control Panel and use the Passwords Properties dialog box.

One other file, Config.pol, affects the settings that you see in the Registry—but it's not actually part of the Registry. Unlike System.dat and User.dat, Config.pol is an optional part of the Windows configuration. Open a policy template in the System Policy editor, choose the settings that you want to enforce, save the results to Config.pol, and place this file on the network. When a user logs on to a Windows computer, the operating system applies any settings it finds in Config.pol to the user's Registry. There is little a user can do to circumvent the settings you put in this file, as long as he logs on to the network, so it's a good way to enforce restrictions throughout the network. Hour 21, "Controlling the Desktop via System Policies," shows where on the network you place this file.

The following list summarizes the files that comprise the Registry:

- **User.dat**—The following list describes how Windows determines the folder from which it loads User.dat:
  - **C:\Windows**—Windows always loads User.dat into the Registry from this folder and uses it for the default user, even if profiles are enabled. This means that the operating system loads two different User.dat files simultaneously if you use profiles.
  - **C:\Windows\Profiles*Name***—Windows loads User.dat from this folder if profiles are enabled and the operating system doesn't find a more recent User.dat file in the user's network home folder.
  - **\\Server*Home* or \\Server*Mailfolder***—Windows loads User.dat from the network server if the user has a home folder and a profile in it that's more current than the files in C:\Windows\Profiles*Name*.

- **System.dat**—For the most part, Windows always loads System.dat from C:\Windows. If you're using a diskless workstation, the operating system might load System.dat from the network, but this situation is so rare that it is not discussed in this book.
- **Config.pol**—Windows loads Config.pol from two different places, depending on which network server is designated as the primary network logon:
  - The Client for Microsoft Networks looks for Config.pol in \\Server\Netlogon.
  - The Client for NetWare Networks looks for Config.pol in SYS:PUBLIC.

Two files that existed in Windows 95 are not part of Windows 98. System.da0 and User.da0 were backup copies of the Registry that Windows 95 made every time the operating system started successfully. Because Windows 98 uses Registry Checker to make backup copies in CAB files, these DA0 files are no longer necessary.

REGISTRY TERMINOLOGY

The following Registry terminology might come in handy:

- **Registry** Physically, the Registry is the two files System.dat and User.dat. Logically, the Registry is the configuration data that you see in the Registry Editor.
- **Registry Editor** The program you use to edit the Registry. It shows the Registry as a single unit even though Windows stores the Registry in two files.
- **HKEY** Windows divides the Registry into six sections called HKEY_*Name*. Programmers know that HKEY means *handle* to a *key*. Another name for these is *root key*. In an outline, these are the very top levels.
- **key** Similar to a folder in Windows Explorer. It can contain additional folders and one or more values. Think of a key as sections within an outline.
- **subkey** A *child* that appears underneath another key, the *parent*. This concept is similar to folders and subfolders in Windows Explorer. Subkeys are similar to subsections in an outline.
- **branch** Represents a particular subkey and everything it contains. A branch can start at the very top of the Registry, but it usually describes a key and all its contents. In an outline, a branch is a section and everything that appears below it.
- **value entry** An order pair with a name and a value. Value entries are analogous to files in Windows Explorer.
- **default value** Every key has a default value that might or might not contain data. The default value in each key is called (Default) in the Registry Editor.

1

Your Choice of Registry Tools

You use a variety of tools to work with the Registry. Some types of tools are required, and others are just niceties. A registry editor is a must-have. You use it to change values in the Registry. You can use the Registry Editor that comes with Windows, or you can use a third-party registry editor such as the Norton Registry Editor or the ShellWizard Registry Editor.

Tools of the non-required variety include customization utilities and troubleshooting tools. Customization utilities are programs that help you make changes to the Registry via a well-defined user interface, which typically uses checkboxes to enable or disable options. An example is Tweak UI, which you'll learn about in Hour 8, "Using Microsoft's Tweak UI." Hour 8 also discusses dozens of other programs. Troubleshooting tools include programs that help you fix the Registry after it gets screwed up. These include programs such as Norton WinDoctor, which fixes a whole host of common Registry problems, and REGCLEAN, which fixes problems that are specific to several Microsoft products.

You'll learn about a huge variety of Registry tools in this book. The following sections give you a brief overview of most of them. This book takes a definitive position, though, and recommends some specific programs that you need to include in your toolbox. Following is your shopping list:

- **ConfigSafe**—Has a good reputation. It locks your configuration in a safe place so that you can restore any portion of it if things go wrong.

- **Norton Utilities**—Comes with two really great Registry programs, Norton Registry Editor and Norton WinDoctor, and one average program called Norton Registry Tracker.

- **Registry Monitor**—Enables you to watch what's going on in the Registry in real time. In other words, you can observe changes to the Registry as they occur. The best part is that Registry Monitor is free.

- **Registry Checker**—Comes with Windows 98. It is the best program to use for automatically backing up and restoring the Registry and fixing the most common problems with the Registry.

Often, the best tools for the job aren't programs at all; they're scripts and INF, and REG files. You use these files to specify changes to the Registry. When you run, install, or import these files, the operating system implements the changes that you describe in the file. These are particularly hard-working tools for administrators because they enable the administrator to distribute changes to users all across the network.

Registry Editor

The Registry Editor comes with Windows; you'll learn about the Editor in Hour 4, "Editing the Registry with REGEDIT." This program enables you to make the usual types of changes; you can add and remove keys and values, change values, or export entire branches of the Registry to a REG file and then import that REG file at a later time.

The Registry Editor is good enough to tackle most jobs, and it's relatively bug-free, but it lacks the advanced features that power users require. My biggest beef with the Registry Editor is that opening the Registry to the same key repeatedly is inconvenient. You must navigate to that same location by opening each parent key and click, click, click, until you finally reach the target. Other Registry Editors, such as Norton Registry Editor, solve this problem by enabling you to bookmark keys and then return to them by choosing the name from a menu. Other features that are missing include the capability to undo changes you make, to search and replace values, to make shortcuts to branches within the Registry, and to back up the Registry from within the editor. The Norton Registry Editor has all these capabilities.

Norton Utilities

If you intend to become a certified Registry guru, you must have Norton Utilities. It fills all the voids left by the Registry tools that come with Windows. You read about Norton Registry Editor in the preceding section and now know that it provides all the advanced features that a guru-in-training needs.

It has a few other Registry programs, too, that make the entire suite megabyte-worthy. Norton Rescue helps you start the computer in the event of system failure. It can even help you recover from startup problems that are caused by Registry errors. Registry Tracker isn't the sharpest program in the suite, but it does help you track changes to the Registry. Other programs, such as ConfigSafe, are better at this task. One of the most useful programs in the Norton suite is Norton WinDoctor, which helps you fix a whole host of Registry problems, including orphans. Finally, Norton Optimization Wizard helps you optimize the Registry, both logically and physically, with the aim of improving your computer's performance.

You can purchase Norton Utilities from any computer retailer. You can even get it from most consumer electronics stores, such as Best Buy and Circuit City. If you want more immediate gratification, download an evaluation copy from http://www.symantec.com or order a copy from http://www.software.net.

You will learn about the tools that come with Norton Utilities in the following hours:

- Hour 3 discusses recovering a system with Norton Rescue.
- Hour 4 shows you how to use Norton Registry Editor.
- Hour 22 shows you how to repair the Registry using Norton WinDoctor.
- Hour 17, "Tracking Registry Changes," describes how to use Norton Registry Tracker to uncover changes to the Registry.

Registry Monitor

Registry Monitor is a freeware program that you use to monitor changes to the Registry as they occur. It gives you insight into how the operating system and other programs use the Registry. You can monitor Windows Explorer's Registry access as you open the Folder Options dialog box to see where the program stores each option in the Registry. If you're curious about the changes that a setup program makes to the Registry, monitor the setup program and filter Registry Monitor's output so that it displays only changes. You learn about this program in Hour 9, "Trying Other Registry Programs."

Registry Checker

Registry Checker comes with Windows 98. Finally, Microsoft ships a useful Registry program with the operating system! This program fulfills several purposes:

- Backs up and restores the Registry
- Scans and fixes a variety of Registry errors
- Optimizes unused space in the Registry

The best part about Registry Checker is that it largely does its own thing. Windows 98 starts Registry Checker every time you boot the operating system. Registry Checker then backs up the Registry to CAB files (compressed archive files) that you find in C:\Windows\Sysbckup. It also scans the Registry for errors. If it finds any, Windows 98 restarts the computer in MS-DOS mode and runs Registry Checker to automatically restore a good backup copy of the Registry or to fix those errors. You learn about Registry Checker in Hour 3 and Hour 22.

ConfigSafe

ConfigSafe periodically makes a backup copy of your configuration. Each backup is called a *snapshot*; each snapshot contains any portion of your configuration that you specify.

You can compare any two snapshots, and ConfigSafe neatly displays the differences. Did you install a program on Wednesday? Compare snapshots taken on Tuesday and Thursday to figure out what changed. You can also compare any snapshot to your current configuration. If you find a change that doesn't sit well with you, or if your computer isn't working correctly, compare your current configuration to the most recent snapshot and restore the original settings to fix the problem. You learn about this program in Hour 17.

> ConfigSafe isn't a substitute for Registry Checker, and vice versa. ConfigSafe is more like a version control system for your configuration, enabling you to undo individual changes to your configuration. Registry Checker can restore an entire backup of the Registry but not individual settings. ConfigSafe can't repair a broken Registry, but Registry Checker can fix common problems.

REGCLEAN

REGCLEAN is a freeware utility from Microsoft that repairs a number of problems that are common to Microsoft products. This utility isn't nearly as useful as Norton WinDoctor, but it serves the needs of many users. You learn about this program in Hour 22.

Tweak UI

The one customization utility you need to install is Microsoft Tweak UI. Microsoft developers built this tool to help users use the most popular customizations without actually having to edit the Registry. This program didn't come with Windows 95; you had to download it from the Internet. It does come with Windows 98. You learn about Tweak UI in Hour 8.

Microsoft Windows 98 Resource Kit

The *Microsoft Windows 98 Resource Kit,* published by Microsoft, comes with three MS-DOS Registry utilities that aren't available on the Windows 98 CD-ROM. Look in \Reskit\Registry. The *Microsoft Windows 95 Resource Kit*, also published by Microsoft, provides similar utilities.

1

Compreg.exe enables you to compare branches from two different Registries and list the differences. For example, you can compare a branch in the local Registry to the same branch in a remote Registry, and locate differences that might help you solve a problem. Reg.exe provides a plethora of functions in a neatly wrapped MS-DOS program. You can query, add, update, delete, copy, save, back up, restore, load, and unload keys and values. Srchreg.exe enables you to search for keys, value names, and value data in the Registry. It displays each item it finds, but it doesn't allow you to replace values.

Other Files and Programs

Hour 9 describes dozens of shareware Registry programs you can use to edit, customize, and troubleshoot the Registry. Some of them are terrific programs, but others aren't worth the money the author is asking. One good example of a shareware Registry program is ShellWizard's Registry Editor. If you don't already own Norton Utilities, ShellWizard's editor is close competition for Norton's Registry Editor. It has most of the same features, and then some. (For example, you can record notes for each Registry key.) I prefer Norton Registry Editor because ShellWizard's editor is a bit buggy, but if you don't already have the utilities, ShellWizard's Registry Editor is a good alternative.

 One shareware Registry program deserves special mention for administrators: It's called Multi-Remote Registry Change, and it doesn't get enough notice, which is too bad. This is a great product that enables an administrator to change a Registry value across any number of computers on the network. You can't beat convenience like this when you need a quick fix.

Three important types of files you need to add to your arsenal aren't programs; they're scripts, INF files, and REG files. Windows 98 includes the Windows Scripting Host, an interpreter that understands JavaScript and VBScript script files and allows those scripts to access the object model exposed by the Windows operating system. Internet Explorer 4 or greater adds the Windows Scripting Host to Windows 95. INF and REG files are very similar. They both enable you to script changes to the Registry. You can use INF files to add, remove, and change values. The notation is simple and easy to write. REG files enable you only to add and change values, not remove them. They're also not as clean to write as INF files, but you can easily create them by exporting branches from within the Registry Editor.

All three types of files have the benefit of being easy to distribute via the network. You can post them to a Web site and enable users to launch them. You can email them to a user for the same purpose. You can also put them in the user's login script so that the operating system automatically launches them. Hour 18, "Scripting Changes to the Registry," shows you how to distribute these files using all three methods. Distributing INF files via login scripts is a bit more complicated than just launching scripts or REG files, so pay close attention to the advice in Hour 18 regarding Rundll32.exe.

Summary

The Registry is where Windows stores most of its configuration data. It's a hierarchical database that, when viewed in the Registry Editor, looks like a huge outline. Each section of the Registry has a name and is called a Registry key. Each value entry in the Registry has a name and value.

Windows stores the Registry in two different files. System.dat contains the machine-specific hardware and software settings. User.dat contains the user-specific settings. The operating system stores System.dat in \Windows. It stores User.dat in \Windows if user profiles aren't enabled or in \Windows\Profiles*Username* if user profiles are enabled.

The tools you use to access the Registry are varied. Windows comes with Registry Editor, and Windows 98 provides a new utility called Registry Checker. This book introduces you to a variety of other useful Registry programs, too, which include a handful of tools that come with Norton Utilities.

Q&A

Q Can I restore a User.da0 or System.da0 from Windows 95 in Windows 98?

A NO! The differences between each Registry are subtle, but they're enough to prevent them from being compatible. Trying to restore a Windows 95 Registry in Windows 98 renders the computer useless until you either restore the Windows 98 Registry or reinstall the operating system.

Q Why does Windows store the Registry in two separate files?

A Some settings don't change no matter who logs on to the computer. These are called per-machine settings and the operating system can safely store them in a single file. Other settings change from user to user, and those settings are easier to manage when they're stored in separate files for each user. Thus, Windows stores machine-specific settings separately from user-specific settings, and it stores each user's settings separately from every other user.

Q **What happened to System.da0 and User.da0 in Windows 98? Is there any way to make the operating system create these files?**

A Windows 98 no longer requires these files because it uses Registry Checker to back up the Registry. If you still want to create these files each time the operating system starts, add two lines to Autoexec.bat that copies System.dat to System.da0 and User.dat to User.da0.

Workshop

The following quiz will help your understanding of the topics discussed in this hour.

Quiz

1. True or false? The Windows Registry is organized like a table, with rows and columns.

2. True or false? Windows stores the Registry in three files: System.dat, User.dat, and Group.dat.

3. Which of the following files are part of the Registry?

   a. User.dat

   b. Registry.dat

   c. System.dat

   d. Winreg.dat

   e. Both a and c

   f. Both a and d

4. A Registry key is most like which of the following?

   a. A car key

   b. A password

   c. A folder

5. Which of the following programs do you get to know well if you're going to work with the Windows 98 Registry?

   a. More Properties

   b. Registry Editor

   c. Regedt32.exe

   d. Registry Checker

   e. Both b and d

   f. Both c and d

Answers to Quiz Questions

1. False

   The Windows Registry is organized more like an outline.

2. False

   There isn't a file called Group.dat.

3. e

   User.dat and System.dat are the primary files that comprise the Registry. Another file that might make up the Registry is called Config.pol.

4. c

   Registry keys are more similar to folders. In fact, they look just like folders in the Registry Editor.

5. e

   Windows 98 provides Registry Editor and Registry Checker. These are the essential programs for working with the Registry. Other programs make the experience a bit more pleasant, however. Note that Regedt32.exe is the Registry editor that comes with Windows NT.

PART II

Working with the Registry

Hour

HOUR 2

Looking Inside the Registry

Before setting out to edit the Registry, familiarize yourself with its terminology and organization. Doing so ensures that you won't get lost when working through the remaining hours of this book. To that end, this hour teaches you the following:

- Terminology: key, subkey, value, and so on
- Where different types of values are in the Registry
- How INI files fit into the overall scheme of things

Getting to know what's in the Registry and how it's organized gives you more confidence in working with it. If you know what types of things you're going to see in the Registry, you aren't going to be surprised when you finally do open it in the Registry Editor. For example, if you know how the Registry is organized, you'll know right where to go when you are told to open HKEY_LOCAL_MACHINE\Software in the Registry Editor.

Keys, Subkeys, Values, and Other Bits

Figure 2.1 shows how the Windows Registry looks in the Registry Editor. In the left pane, called the *Key pane,* you see all the Registry's folders. At the top, you see My Computer. This represents the local computer, whose Registry you're viewing. When viewing a remote computer in the Registry Editor, you see an additional item at the same level as My Computer, which has the same name as the remote computer.

Value entry name

FIGURE 2.1

The Registry Editor is a simple program that packs a lot of power, providing access to the entire configuration.

Registry keys

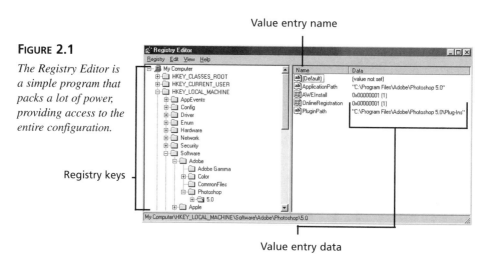

Value entry data

Under My Computer, you see a number of folders organized somewhat like an outline or an upside-down tree. Each folder in the Key pane is called a *key*. Again, keys are analogous to folders in Windows Explorer. As such, they can contain any number of subfolders, called *subkeys*. Subkeys can contain more subkeys, and so on. You see subkeys in Registry Editor's Key pane, so don't look for them in the right pane. If you need to know whether a key contains subkeys, look for a plus or minus sign next to the key's name. Note that the six keys you see directly under My Computer are called *root keys*. Key names can be any combination of alphabetic, numeric, or symbol characters (except backslashes) and spaces. If all this seems a bit much to remember, occasionally refer to the sidebar called "Registry Terminology" in Hour 1, "Understanding the Registry," to refresh your memory.

In this book, the terms *key* and *subkey* are used interchangeably. In particular, the first time a reference is made to a *child key*, or a key underneath the key that is being discussed, it is called a subkey. From then on, it is referred to simply as a key. Also, in most cases throughout this book, the discussion is started by presenting the fully qualified key name, starting from the root key. When the path to a subkey is obvious based on the context, its name is used.

In Registry Editor's right pane, called the *Contents pane,* you see all the configuration data for the selected key. Each key, besides containing any number of subkeys, can contain any number of value entries. *Value entries*—sometimes just called *values*—are analogous to files in Windows Explorer. Each value entry has three parts:

- **Name**—Each name can be any combination of alphabetic, numeric, and symbol characters, including spaces. You can't use backslashes. The name uniquely identifies the value entry within a key. You might find the same name used in other Registry keys, but not within the same key.
- **Data type**—Whereas INI files store only string configuration data, the Registry stores a variety of different types in a value entry. Table 2.1 describes the types of data that you'll find in the Windows Registry.
- **Data**—Value data can be up to 64KB in size in Windows 98. An important concept that you need to understand is that of an *empty value entry*—there's no such thing. If Windows or some other program has never assigned a value to a value entry, the value entry contains the *null* value. This is very different from assigning an empty string to a value entry, which is a string of characters that just happens to be of zero length.

TABLE 2.1   REGISTRY DATA TYPES

Type	Example	Description
String	`"Hello World"`	Text. Words. Phrases. The Registry always displays strings within quotation marks.
Binary	F03D990000BC	Binary values of unlimited size represented as hexadecimal. They're similar to DWORDs except that they're not limited to 4 bytes.
DWORD	0x12345678	32-bit binary values in hexadecimal format (double words). The Registry displays DWORDs as 8-digit hexadecimal numbers.

Every key contains at least one value entry, called (Default). In this book it is usually just called the default value for a key. The default value is always a string value. Windows provides it for compatibility with the Windows 3.1 Registry and older 16-bit applications. In many cases, the default value is null. In other cases, when a program needs to store only one value, the default value entry is the only data stored in that key.

Value entries associate a value with a name. This makes them an *ordered pair*. Every value also has a data type that indicates whether the value is a string, binary, or DWORD value.

REGISTRY PATHS

You must get acquainted with the notation used in this book (and other sources) to describe the location of a value in the Registry. It's called a *path,* and is similar to file paths in the MS-DOS file system.

Remember that the Registry is a hierarchical database. You can therefore describe the location of any value by showing its path as follows: *key1\key2\key3*. This means open *key1*, and then, underneath that, open *key2*, followed by *key3*. An example is regfile\shell\open, which means to open the key called regfile, open its subkey called shell, and then open shell's subkey called open. A *fully qualified path* always starts with the root key so that you can find the value that is relative to the top of the Registry.

The value's name is never given as part of the path. It's always named separately, as follows: "Open MyValue in HKEY_LOCAL_MACHINE\MyKey" or "Open HKEY_LOCAL_MACHINE\MyKey and change MyValue to Howdy." When discussing a key's default value entry, you'll see something such as the following: "Change the default value of MyKey" or "Open MyKey and change the default value to Howdy."

Registry Organization and Content

You find six root keys in the Windows Registry (as shown in Figure 2.1). Windows stores HKEY_LOCAL_MACHINE in System.dat and each branch of HKEY_USERS in the appropriate User.dat file. You learn about these keys in detail in Hours 10–13.

The remaining root keys are aliases. *Aliases* are shortcuts to branches within HKEY_LOCAL_MACHINE or HKEY_USERS that make accessing a particular set of configuration data easier. For instance, HKEY_CURRENT_USER is an alias for HKEY_USERS*Name*, where *Name* represents the username of the current user. This branch contains all the user's settings. An alias for HKEY_LOCAL_MACHINE\Software\Classes is HKEY_CLASSES_ROOT, which makes it easier to access file associations in the Registry. Think of an alias as containing a temporary copy of a branch in either HKEY_LOCAL_MACHINE or HKEY_USERS. If you change a value in the alias, the original branch reflects that change. The opposite applies, too. Figure 2.2 illustrates this concept.

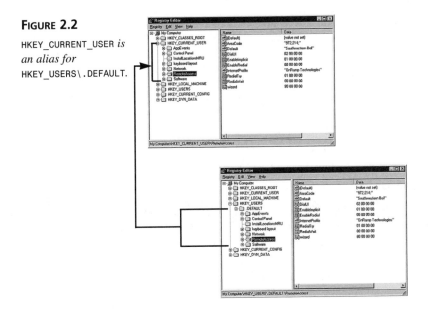

FIGURE 2.2

HKEY_CURRENT_USER *is an alias for* HKEY_USERS\.DEFAULT.

Throughout the discussions that follow, keep in mind that the Windows 95 and Windows 98 Registries are only slightly different. In a few rare cases, you'll read about settings that are unique to Windows 98; these settings are pointed out to you.

HKEY_USERS

HKEY_USERS contains all the user-specific configuration data for the computer. Under this root key, you find one or two keys. If you see a single subkey called .DEFAULT, profiles are not enabled on the computer, and Windows loads .DEFAULT from the User.dat file in C:\Windows. If you see two subkeys, one is .DEFAULT and the other is *Username*, where *Username* is the name of the current user. Again, .DEFAULT comes from the User.dat file in C:\Windows, whereas *Username* comes from either the User.dat file found in C:\Windows\Profiles*Username*, or from the user's home folder on the network.

The following list describes the subkeys that are typically found under each subkey of HKEY_USERS:

- **AppEvents**—This subkey associates the sounds that Windows produces with events generated by the operating system and other programs. You'll find subkeys called EventLabels, which describes each sound event, and Schemes\Apps, which assigns sound files to each event.

- **Control Panel**—This subkey contains settings that the user can change using the Control Panel, such as Display and Accessibility options. Many of the settings in Control Panel were migrated from the Windows 3.1 Win.ini and Control.ini files.

- **InstallLocationsMRU**—This tiny subkey contains the last several paths from which you've installed Windows components. That is, every time you open the Add/Remove Programs Properties dialog box from the Control Panel and click Have Disk on the Windows Setup tab to install an extension, Windows records the path of the INF file in InstallLocationsMRU.

- **Keyboard Layout**—This subkey defines the language used for the current keyboard layout. You change these values in the Keyboard icon in the Control Panel.

- **Network**—Windows stores persistent network connections in HKEY_CURRENT_USER\Network\Persistent. Each subkey represents a mapped drive letter (D, E, F, and so on). Under each drive letter's subkey, you'll find a handful of value entries that describe the connection, such as Provider Name, RemotePath, and UserName.

- **Software**—Software is by far the most interesting subkey in this branch. It contains software settings that are specific to each user. Windows stores each user's desktop preferences under this subkey. In addition, each program installed on the computer installs user-specific preferences in this subkey. This subkey is organized just like the similarly named subkey in HKEY_LOCAL_MACHINE.

> The Registry has an order of precedence. Often, Windows and other programs store duplicate data in both HKEY_USERS and HKEY_LOCAL_MACHINE. In such cases, the configuration data stored in HKEY_USERS has precedence over the data stored in HKEY_LOCAL_MACHINE. Windows does this so that individual user preferences override computer-specific settings.

WINDOWS VERSUS WINDOWS NT

The Windows and Windows NT Registries are identical where it counts: file associations and software settings. In other words, HKEY_CLASSES_ROOT and the Software branches of HKEY_LOCAL_MACHINE and HKEY_CURRENT_USER are organized the same in both operating systems.

The Registries are radically different, however, when you look at the binary files on disk. The NT Registry stores HKEY_LOCAL_MACHINE in separate files called *hive files,* one for each subkey of HKEY_LOCAL_MACHINE, which you find in \Winnt\System32\Config. Furthermore, each user's configuration is in Ntuser.dat rather than in User.dat. Given that Windows

NT's file system is secure, you can't copy or remove these files while the operating system is running—so backing up the Registry isn't a simple matter of copying the files.

Security is another difference between the two Registries. Whereas Windows has none, the Windows NT Registry does have security, which enables the administrator to control exactly which keys and values a user can access. Furthermore, the administrator can audit the user's usage of the Registry to see what he's been doing.

The Windows NT Registry is different in a variety of other ways, too. It supports more data types than the Windows Registry. The organization of hardware data is different in the NT Registry, owing to the fact that NT doesn't fully support the Plug and Play specification. NT also comes with its own Registry Editor, Regedt32, in addition to the Registry Editor you see in Windows.

2

HKEY_LOCAL_MACHINE

HKEY_LOCAL_MACHINE contains configuration data that describes the hardware and software installed on the computer, such as device drivers, security data, and computer-specific software settings such as uninstall information. This information is specific to the computer itself rather than to any one user who logs on to it. Thus, the operating system uses the settings stored in HKEY_LOCAL_MACHINE regardless of who logs on to the computer.

The following list describes the contents of each subkey immediately under HKEY_LOCAL_MACHINE:

- **Config**—This subkey contains information about multiple hardware configurations for the computer, also known as *hardware profiles*. It contains groups of individual hardware settings from which Windows can choose automatically, or that you can choose when you start the computer. Each subkey under HKEY_LOCAL_MACHINE\Config (numbered 0001, 0002, and so on) represents an individual hardware profile. HKEY_LOCAL_MACHINE\System\CurrentControlSet\ Control\IDConfigDB contains the name and identifier of the hardware profile that Windows is currently using.

- **Enum**—This subkey contains information about each device installed on the computer. Each subkey under Enum represents a particular type of bus (BIOS, ESDI, PCI, PCMCIA, SCSI, and so on). Under each hardware class, you'll find one or more subkeys that in turn contain subkeys that identify a single piece of hardware. The organization of this branch and its contents depends largely on the devices you install on the computer and how the manufacturer organizes its settings.

- **Hardware**—Windows doesn't do much with this subkey. It exists to provide compatibility with Windows NT.

- **Network**—This subkey contains information about the user who is currently logged on to the computer. Each time a user logs on to the computer, Windows stores details about the current network session, such as the user's logon name, in `Network\Logon`.

- **Security**—This subkey contains information about the computer's network security provider, administrative shares (for remote administration), and public shares. Windows keeps track of all open network connections that other users have on your computer in `Security\Access`; you find a single subkey for each connection.

- **Software**—This and the next subkey are the heart and soul of `HKEY_LOCAL_MACHINE`. Programs store settings that are specific to the computer in this subkey. These programs store their settings in branches such as `HKEY_LOCAL_MACHINE\Software\CompanyName\ProductName\Version`, where *CompanyName* is the name of the company, *ProductName* is the name of the product, and *Version* is the current version number of the product. You find many Windows-specific settings in this subkey, too, under `Software\Microsoft\Windows\CurrentVersion`.

- **System**—Windows maintains *control sets,* each of which determines exactly which device drivers and services the operating system loads and how it configures them when it starts. For example, a control set provides the various parameters that Windows needs when it starts, such as the computer's network name and the current hardware profile. A control set also controls which device drivers and file systems Windows loads, and it provides the parameters that Windows needs in order to configure each driver. Windows 98 extends the information stored in this part of the Registry beyond Windows 95.

The single largest branch in the Registry is `HKEY_LOCAL_MACHINE\Software\Classes`. This subkey describes all the associations between documents and programs, as well as information about *Component Object Model* (*COM*) classes, and is therefore very large. You can also get to this branch through the alias `HKEY_CLASSES_ROOT`.

THE WINDOWS CONFIGURATION MANAGER

The Configuration Manager is at the heart of Plug and Play. It is responsible for managing the configuration process on the computer. It identifies each bus on your computer (PCI, SCSI, ISA) and all the devices on each bus. It notes the configuration of each device, making sure that each device is using unique resources (IRQ, I/O address).

The Configuration Manager uses three key components to make all this happen: *bus enumerators, arbitrators,* and *device drivers.* Following is a summary of the purpose of each component:

- **Bus enumerators**—These are responsible for building the *hardware tree.* They query each device or each device driver for configuration information.

- **Arbitrators**—These assign resources to each device in the hardware tree. That is, they dole out IRQs, I/O addresses, and so on to each device, resolving conflicts as they arise.

- **Device drivers**—The Configuration Manager loads a device driver for each device in the hardware tree and communicates the device's configuration to the driver.

Aliases: `HKEY_CURRENT_USER` and So On

Even though the Registry Editor shows six root keys, there are really only two: `HKEY_LOCAL_MACHINE` and `HKEY_USERS`. As you have already learned, the remaining root keys are aliases that refer to branches within the other two root keys. In other words, aliases are a bit like shortcuts in Explorer: If you change a value in one of the aliases, that value is actually changed in the original location.

Table 2.2 lists each alias and the branch to which it points. `HKEY_CLASSES_ROOT` points to a branch within `HKEY_LOCAL_MACHINE` that contains the associations between file extensions and programs. `HKEY_CURRENT_USER` points to the subkey of `HKEY_USERS` that belongs to the current user; without user profiles, it always points to `HKEY_USER\.DEFAULT`. `HKEY_CURRENT_CONFIG` is an alias for `HKEY_LOCAL_MACHINE\Config\Profile`, where *Profile* is `0001`, `0002`, and so on. It contains the computer's current hardware configuration.

TABLE 2.2   ALIASES IN THE REGISTRY

Alias	Branch
HKEY_CLASSES_ROOT	HKEY_LOCAL_MACHINE\ Software\Classes
HKEY_CURRENT_USER	HKEY_USERS*Username*
HKEY_CURRENT_CONFIG	HKEY_LOCAL_MACHINE\ Config*Profile*

HKEY_DYN_DATA isn't actually an alias. It's a dynamic key that contains dynamic information about the current status of the computer. As with aliases, this root key isn't stored to disk; the operating system rebuilds it every time you restart the computer.

When you export the Registry to a REG file, the file contains HKEY_LOCAL_MACHINE and HKEY_USERS. It doesn't contain entries from the four remaining aliases because exporting an alias is redundant.

ABBREVIATIONS FOR ROOT KEYS

You'll frequently see abbreviations for the root keys used in many publications. These abbreviations are not used in this book, so the Registry paths you see here more closely match what you see in the Registry Editor. The following table describes the abbreviations that are commonly used for each root key:

Abbreviation	Root Key	Alias For
HKCR	HKEY_CLASSES_ROOT	HKEY_LOCAL_MACHINE\Software\Classes
HKCU	HKEY_CURRENT_USER	HKEY_USERS*Username*
HKLM	HKEY_LOCAL_MACHINE	
HKU	HKEY_USERS	
HKCC	HKEY_CURRENT_CONFIG	HKEY_LOCAL_MACHINE\Config*Profile*
HKDD	HKEY_DYN_DATA	

The Role of INI Files in Windows

Remember INI files? Windows isn't quite finished with them. When I search my hard disk for INI files, I find 54—and that's after a clean installation and after installing a handful of 32-bit applications such as Microsoft Office. The operating system still uses Win.ini and System.ini, too. Some of those settings are duplicated in the Registry, and are provided in the INI files only for compatibility with applications that require them.

Recall that INI files are text files that you can edit with Notepad. In fact, Windows associates INI files with Notepad so that you can easily open them for editing. Open Win.ini in Notepad, and you'll see something similar to Listing 2.1. An INI file is separated into sections, with each section name appearing between brackets. In Listing 2.1, for example, [windows] and [Desktop] are sections. Following each section name you see a number of items, each with a name and a value separated by an equal sign. As with the Registry, this is an ordered pair that allows a program to retrieve the value from the INI file by providing the value's name in addition to the name of the section that contains it.

LISTING 2.1 WIN.INI

```
[windows]
load=
run=
NullPort=None
device=HP LaserJet 5,PCL5EMS,\\SERVER\LaserJet

[Desktop]
Wallpaper=(None)
TileWallpaper=1
WallpaperStyle=0
Pattern=(None)
```

Two INI files are of special interest. Win.ini typically contains data used to specify user preferences: desktop settings, wallpaper, and so on. Windows now stores these values in the Registry, but the operating system still reflects these settings in Win.ini for compatibility with old Windows applications.

System.ini contains system settings. The [boot] section contains drivers that Windows needs when it starts. The [386Enh] section loads any virtual device drivers that the operating system requires when it starts. This section is smaller than it was in previous versions of Windows because the operating system loads most of its VXD files from the \Iosubsys and \Vmm32 folders within C:\Windows\System, eliminating the need to explicitly list these files in System.ini. Note that if Windows recognizes a device when you upgrade, it removes that device's settings from System.ini and stores them in the Registry. Otherwise, it might leave those settings in System.ini.

INI FILES IN WINDOWS

INI files serve the same purpose as the Registry. Unlike the Registry, which contains settings from the operating system and a variety of applications, each INI file is unique to a single application. Remember, too, that keys in the Registry can contain subkeys and values. The sections in an INI file can contain only values, however; they can't contain subsections. A common work-around for this problem, used by clever programmers, is to have an item within a section that points to a different INI file.

Windows keeps a variety of other INI files, in addition to System.ini and Win.ini, and uses them partially. When an INI file doesn't contain all the settings that you expect or that it used to contain in previous versions of Windows, assume that those settings are now in the Registry. Even if you do see settings in an INI file, assume that the operating system reflects all or a portion of its contents in the Registry.

Summary

The Registry has two different elements that you need to understand. Keys are similar to folders and contain additional keys, called subkeys, and value entries. Value entries have a name and an associated piece of data. All this data is organized much like an outline, with each section being a key.

HKEY_USERS has a single subkey called .default (if user profiles aren't enabled), and that subkey contains the per-user settings for the current user. If user profiles are enabled, HKEY_USERS contains an additional subkey that's named for the user's logon name. This subkey contains the user's per-user settings if profiles are enabled. HKEY_LOCAL_MACHINE contains per-machine settings. These are hardware and software settings that don't change from user to user.

Other subkeys that you see in the Registry are actually aliases to other branches within HKEY_USERS or HKEY_LOCAL_MACHINE. HKEY_CURRENT_USER is actually HKEY_USERS*Username*, for example, where *Username* is either .default or the name of the current user.

Q&A

Q Which portion of the Registry contains the most interesting customizations?

A About 80 percent of all the customizations you read about in this book are performed in HKEY_CLASSES_ROOT. This is the branch that controls which actions users can perform on which files. Hour 14, "Files and Folders," is dedicated to these types of customizations.

Q I don't understand hexadecimal notation. How can I convert a hexadecimal number into something that I can understand?

A Use Calculator in Scientific Mode. On the Start menu, point to Programs, Accessories, and click Calculator. Choose Scientific from the View menu.

Workshop

The following quiz will enhance your understanding of the topics discussed in this hour.

Quiz

1. Which of the following is part of a value entry?

    a. Data Type

    b. Declaration

    c. Memory Area

    d. Label

2. Which of the following is not a data type supported for value entries in Windows?

    a. DWORD

    b. Binary

    c. Character

    d. String

3. True or false? Registry paths are similar to file paths.

4. True or false? HKEY_CURRENT_USER and HKEY_LOCAL_MACHINE are the only two real Registry keys.

5. True or false? HKEY_CLASSES_ROOT and HKEY_LOCAL_MACHINE\Software\Classes are the same thing.

Answers to Quiz Questions

1. a

    The three parts of a value entry are its name, data type, and value.

2. c

    The three types of data supported by the Windows Registry are DWORD, Binary, and String.

3. True

    Registry paths are similar to file paths. In fact, you specify both using the same notation.

4. False

    The three *real* Registry keys are HKEY_USERS and HKEY_LOCAL_MACHINE. HKEY_CUR-RENT_USER is an alias for the subkey of HKEY_USERS

5. True

    HKEY_CLASSES_ROOT is an alias.

HOUR 3

Backing Up/Restoring the Registry

All users have two different backup needs: the quick, intermittent backup that ensures that the system can be repaired if an immediate task goes wrong, and the occasional full system backup that preserves the entire system for recovery in the event of total failure. This hour doesn't discuss the latter; it focuses on the periodic backups. More specifically, this hour focuses on intermittent backups of the Registry that ensure that the user can recover from problems such as an errant setup program, a configuration error, or a bad customization.

The only thing that Windows 98 users need to know about in making intermittent backup copies of the Registry is the new Windows 98 utility called Registry Checker, which you'll learn about in the following section. This is a big improvement over the Registry backup utilities provided in Windows 95. In most cases, it works in the background so silently that you don't even know it's doing its job. Registry Checker makes regular, daily backups of the Registry. If you want to be more cautious, you can force Registry Checker to make additional backup copies of the Registry before you make a significant configuration change.

Aside from using Registry Checker in Windows 98, this hour teaches you a variety of other backup techniques:

- Copying System.dat and User.dat in Windows Explorer
- Using the Registry Editor to export the Registry
- Back up the Registry using Microsoft Backup
- Back up using the Emergency Repair Utility
- Use the Norton Utilities Rescue Disk
- Restore System.1st—as a last resort

> If you want to store backup copies of the Registry somewhere other than your computer's disk, you might need to consider the alternative backup methods in this hour. You can copy the Registry files to a network drive, for example, or use Norton's Repair Disk to create a backup copy of the Registry on a ZIP disk.

The Backup Plan

Following is a backup plan that you can use to make sure that you always have a good backup copy of the Registry available. It takes into account both of the backup types mentioned at the beginning of this hour (full and intermittent). Follow this plan and alter it to suit your needs:

1. Allow Registry Checker to make its daily backups. If nothing else, you can always revert to the previous day's Registry backup, and you'll lose only the configuration changes that you've made in the last day.

2. Force Registry Checker to make a Registry backup before you make any significant change to your configuration. This includes installing new programs, adding new hardware, or trying out one of the customization tips you'll learn in Hours 14–16.

3. Use a backup program such as Microsoft Backup, or a network backup agent such as Cheyenne, to make full system backups on a regular basis—weekly if possible. Remember to back up any changed files on a more regular basis, such as once a day.

System.da0 and User.da0

Windows 95 creates a backup copy of the Registry each time you start the operating system, successfully or not. It copies System.dat to System.da0 and User.dat to User.da0. Windows 98, on the other hand, does not create these files.

If you're certain that Windows 95 hasn't replaced either backup file with a corrupt Registry, you can restore these files. You might be certain of this fact if you haven't restarted Windows 95 since the Registry became corrupt. Copy System.da0 over System.dat and User.da0 over User.dat. The section "Windows Explorer," later in this hour, shows how to restore these files using Windows Explorer.

Easy Backups with Registry Checker

Windows 98 doesn't copy the Registry to .dao files when you start the operating system; instead, it provides a program called Registry Checker.

Windows 98 actually provides two different versions of Registry Checker: a Windows version and a DOS-based version. The Windows version, with the filename Scanregw.exe, scans the Registry for errors but doesn't fix them. It also determines whether the Registry requires optimization, but doesn't perform the optimization itself. Finally, it backs up the Registry files to CAB files that are found in \Windows\Sysbckup. You'll read more about CAB files later.

If SCANREGW detects an error or determines that the Registry must be optimized to remove unused space, it prompts you to restart the computer. The DOS-based version, with the filename Scanreg.exe (without the *w*), attempts to fix the Registry. It tries to restore the previous backup first, repairing the Registry only if it can't find a good backup. If SCANREGW determines that the Registry requires optimization, SCANREG optimizes the Registry the next time you start Windows 98. This is a bit much to remember; look at Table 3.1, which summarizes all this information so that you can remember the differences between SCANREGW and SCANREG.

TABLE 3.1   SCANREGW VERSUS SCANREG

Feature	SCANREGW	SCANREG
Operating environment	Windows	MS-DOS
Runs automatically	Yes	Yes, if problem detected
Backs up the Registry	Yes	Yes
Compresses backups	Yes	No

continues

TABLE 3.1 CONTINUED

Feature	SCANREGW	SCANREG
Repairs the Registry	No	Yes
Restores the Registry	No	Yes
Runs in Safe Mode	Yes	No
Scans the Registry	Yes	Yes

SCANREGW and SCANREG support similar command-line options, all of which are listed in Table 3.2. /backup and /comment work in both versions of Registry Checker. /opt, /restore and /fix are available only with SCANREG. /autorun and /scanonly are available only with SCANREGW.

TABLE 3.2 SCANREGW AND SCANREG COMMAND LINES

Switch	Description
/autoru	Automatically scans the Registry, but backs it up only once a day. You see this switch used in the Run key of HKEY_LOCAL_MACHINE.
/backup	Backs up the Registry without prompting the user. Backups are stored in CAB files that are found in \Windows\Sysbckup.
"/comment=x"	Associates a comment with the backup. Use this switch with /backup and be sure to enclose the entire switch in quotation marks.
/fix	Repairs the Registry.
/opt	Stands for "optimize." Compresses unused space.
/restore	Enables you to choose from a list of backup configurations that you can restore.
/scanonly	Scans the Registry and returns an error code that you can test from within a batch file. It doesn't back up or repair the Registry.

For more information about using Registry Checker to repair the Registry, see Hour 22, "Fixing Errors in the Registry." Hour 6, "Reducing the Size of the Registry," describes how to use Registry Checker to optimize the Registry.

CREATE A STARTUP DISK

If you're in a pinch and can't start Windows, you'll be very glad that you created a startup disk. This disk gets your computer going when it won't start from the hard drive. You'll also find a handful of utilities on the startup disk that you can possibly use to fix your computer. It doesn't contain the Registry files, however, so don't create the startup disk as a substitute for doing a Registry backup. Following are the steps used to create the startup disk:

1. Open the Add/Remove Programs icon in the Control Panel.

2. Click the Startup Disk tab in the Add/Remove Programs Properties dialog box.

3. Click the Create Disk button and follow the onscreen instructions. Windows probably asks you for the CD-ROM (or diskettes).

4. After Windows finishes creating your startup disk, click OK to close the Add/Remove Programs Properties dialog box.

5. Label your Emergency Startup Disk and keep it in a safe place just in case you encounter problems starting Windows.

Windows 98 puts CD-ROM drivers on the startup disk, but not network drivers. Double-check to make sure that the CD-ROM drivers that the operating system puts on the disk do indeed provide access to your CD-ROM drive. To do so, boot using the startup disk and, when prompted, choose to start with CD-ROM support. When the DOS prompt appears, try to access a disk in the CD-ROM drive. If you can't access the CD-ROM drive using the startup disk, try installing the drivers that came with the computer's CD-ROM drive. The vendor should have provided a disk to install the driver's SYS file in Config.sys and load MSCDEX.EXE in Autoexec.bat.

If you need access to the network when you start from the startup disk, copy the 16-bit network drivers to the disk and edit the Config.sys and Autoexec.bat files using Notepad.exe so that they load properly. You won't usually find the 16-bit drivers on the hard disk, so copy them from the disk that your vendor provides with the network interface card. Better yet, get the appropriate network drivers from the network administrator.

3

Backing Up the Registry

Windows 98 automatically backs up the Registry for you. It uses the Windows-based Registry Checker, SCANREGW, once each day to back up the Registry to a CAB file that it puts in C:\Windows\Sysbckup, a hidden folder. The first backup is named RB000.cab, the second is RB001.cab, and so on. The file with the highest number is the most recent backup file; thus, RB004.cab is more recent than RB002.cab. This folder also might contain dozens of other configuration files that the operating system copies to this folder when a setup program replaces them with more recent versions. Right-click one of the CAB files, presumably the most recent, and choose View to examine its contents. You'll find four files: System.dat, System.ini, User.dat, and Win.ini. As described in the section "Configuring Registry Checker," you can also specify additional files to back up into each CAB file. After you open a CAB file in Windows Explorer, you can drag any file from the CAB file to any folder on the computer. You can restore Win.ini, for instance, by dragging it from an open CAB file to C:\Windows.

By default, Windows Registry Checker keeps only five copies of the Registry, but you can increase that number by changing the MaxBackupCopies entry in Scanreg.ini to a higher number—perhaps 10. It is strongly recommended that you do so because many configuration errors can go for days without detection, and if you have only five days' worth of backup copies, you're out of luck.

You can also force Registry Checker to make additional backup copies of the Registry even if it has already made its daily backup:

1. Run Scanregw.exe. You find it in C:\Windows. You can start it quickly by choosing Run on the Start menu, typing scanregw, and pressing Enter. After scanning the Registry for errors, it asks you if you want to make another backup of the Registry.

2. Click Yes. Windows Registry Checker backs up the Registry to another CAB file and displays a dialog box telling you that it's finished.

3. Click OK to close the Windows Registry Checker.

Restoring the Registry

You can't restore a backup using the Windows-based version of Registry Checker. You must use the DOS version, Scanreg.exe, which you find in C:\Windows\Command:

1. Start Windows in MS-DOS mode. To do so, select Command Prompt Only from Windows 98's boot menu, or choose Start, Shut Down, Restart in MS-DOS mode, and then press Enter.

2. Type scanreg /restore at the command prompt and press Enter to start Registry Checker.

3. Select a backup from the list provided. Registry Checker displays the date, status, and filename of each backup. Ideally, pick the most recent backup. If you know it doesn't work, pick the next most recent backup.

4. Press Enter. Registry Checker restores the backup to your computer.

5. Press Enter to restart your computer.

 Registry Checker does the same thing as Microsoft's CFGBACK, a utility that came with Windows 95, but it does a better job. CFGBACK didn't work well—Microsoft even warned users not to use it.

Configuring Registry Checker

Both versions of Registry Checker, SCANREGW and SCANREG, load settings from Scanreg.ini. Table 3.3 describes the settings that you can change in this file. The most interesting settings include `MaxBackupCopies` and `Files`. `MaxBackupCopies` controls the number of backups that Registry Checker keeps; the first backup is the first one to be deleted. The default value for this setting is 5, which is a bit small if you want to make sure that you can always recover from configuration problems. Sometimes you can go several days before noticing that Windows 98 has a problem. By then, Registry Checker has already replaced the last good backup copy of your configuration with a broken copy.

TABLE 3.3   SETTINGS IN SCANREG.INI

Setting	Description
`Backup=[0¦1]`	Specifies whether to run SCANREGW to back up the Registry each time Windows 98 starts. The default value is 1, meaning that Registry Checker backs up the Registry once each day.
	0 = don't run SCANREGW at startup
	1 = Run SCANREGW at startup
`Optimize=[0¦1]`	Specifies whether to automatically optimize the Registry. The default value is 1, meaning that Registry Checker optimizes the Registry as required.
	0 = Don't automatically optimize
	1 = Automatically optimize
`MaxBackupCopies=x`	Specifies the maximum number of backup copies to make of the Registry each time Windows 98 starts. The default value is 5, meaning that Registry Checker keeps only five backup copies. Possible values are 0–99.
`BackupDirectory=x`	Specifies the location in which to store the CAB files containing the configuration backup. The default value is \Windows\Sysbckup. If you use this setting, you must provide a full path starting from the root folder.
`Files=[code,]f1,f2`	Specifies additional files to include in the configuration backup. You can include this setting as many times as required. Table 3.4 describes the directory codes that you can use for code.

`Files` enables you to specify additional configuration files that you want to include in each backup. By default, Registry Checker backs up System.ini and Win.ini, but what if you want to include Protocol.ini or Autoexec.bat? The syntax looks like the following:

`Files=[dir code,]file1,file2,file3`

dir code is one of the codes listed in Table 3.4. These codes indicate the location of the configuration file. Note that code 31 is useful only if you're using Registry Checker on a computer with compressed volumes. To back up Protocol.ini from \Windows, for example, write a line like the following:

```
Files=10,protocol.ini
```

You can include more than one file in each statement, with each separated by a comma.

TABLE 3.4 VALUES FOR `dir` code

Code	Directory	Example
10	Windows installation folder	\Windows
11	Windows system folder	\Windows\System
30	Boot drive	C:\
31	Boot host folder	H:\

Alternative Methods for Manual Backups

Windows Registry Checker is the preferred method for backing up the Registry. You really don't need to use any other method to safely back up and restore the Registry. There are alternative methods that might better suit your needs, however:

- Windows Explorer
- Registry Editor
- Microsoft Backup
- Emergency Repair Utility

You'll learn about each of these methods in the following sections.

Not one of these methods is suitable for a regular, daily backup of the Registry. They do have special purposes, however. Backing up the Registry files using Windows Explorer or batch files isn't really suitable for any purpose, considering how easy it is to back up with the Registry Checker, but they are included in this hour for the sake of completeness. Backing up the Registry using Microsoft Backup is suitable when you're backing up your complete system. Backing up a Registry branch using the Registry Editor is suitable when you're working in a specific portion of the Registry. The Emergency Repair Utility does almost the same thing as Registry Checker, but gets the job done a bit sloppier.

Even though several alternative methods for backing up the Registry are presented here, don't ever consider replacing Registry Checker with them if you're using Windows 98. Registry Checker is the most effective way to safeguard your computer's configuration—don't throw it out in exchange for inferior methods.

Windows Explorer

The absolute easiest way to back up the contents of the Registry is to copy the files that contain the Registry to a safe place. You can even do this in Windows Explorer:

1. Create a folder on your computer to hold the backup copy of the Registry: C:\Windows\Registry.

2. Make sure that you can view hidden files in Windows Explorer. Select View, Folder Options; then click the View tab, select Show all files, and click OK.

3. Copy System.dat from C:\Windows to the backup folder. Copy User.dat from C:\Windows or your profile folder to the backup folder.

4. Don't forget to restore Windows Explorer so that it hides system files. Choose View, Options; then click the View tab, select Do not show hidden or system files, and click OK.

If you'd rather do this more or less automatically, create a batch file that does the same thing. Then, all you have to do is execute the batch file to copy System.dat and User.dat to a safe place. The following batch file copies both files (System.dat and User.dat):

```
xcopy %WinDir%\system.dat %WinDir%\Registry\ /H /R
xcopy %WinDir%\user.dat %WinDir%\Registry\ /H /R
```

It uses the xcopy command with the /H and /R switches. The /H switch copies files with hidden and system attributes. You use this switch in lieu of changing the files' attributes with the attrib command. The /R switch replaces read-only files. That way, xcopy can write over previous backup copies of the Registry. %WinDir% expands to the location of your Windows folder when the batch file runs. This file can be found on my Web site, http://www.honeycutt.com, in a file called Backup.bat.

Some programs make backup copies of the Registry files when you install them. Norton Utilities copies the Registry files to System.nu3 and User.nu3, for instance, and other programs perform similar tasks. You can locate all these backup files by showing hidden files in Windows Explorer and then searching the root and Windows folders for any files that begin with *System* or *User*. If you don't have a good backup copy of the Registry handy, one of these backups might make a suitable replacement.

To restore a backup copy of the Registry that you made using Windows Explorer or the batch file you just read about, follow these steps:

1. Make sure that you can view hidden files in Windows Explorer. Choose View, Folder Options; then click the View tab, select Show all files, and click OK.

2. Copy your backup copy of System.dat to C:\Windows. Copy User.dat to C:\Windows or to your profile folder.

3. Don't forget to restore Windows Explorer so that it hides system files. Choose View, Folder Options; then click the View tab, select Do not show hidden or system files, and click OK.

4. Restart your computer.

You can create a batch file that automatically restores your backup copies of System.dat and User.dat. Then all you have to do is execute the batch file to restore them. The following batch file restores your backup files:

```
Xcopy %WinDir%\Registry\System.dat %WinDir%\System.dat /R /H
Xcopy %WinDir%\Registry\User.dat %WinDir%\User.dat /R /H
```

This backup uses the xcopy command with the /H and /R switches, which you learned about earlier in this section. The /H switch copies hidden and system files, and the /R switch replaces read-only files. That way, xcopy can overwrite the current System.dat and User.dat files. %WinDir% expands to the location of your Windows folder when the batch file runs. This batch file can be found on my Web site, http://www.honeycutt.com, in a file called Restore.bat.

If you configured Windows to use user profiles, you'll need to tweak the batch files to make them pick up the correct User.dat file. In particular, you need to change the second line of both batch files so that they copy these files to and from your profile folder rather than the Windows folder. You can also enhance this batch file so that it copies User.dat for all users on the computer by copying the second line for each user, making sure to copy each user's User.dat file into a separate folder.

For more information about the files that comprise the Registry, see Hour 1, "Understanding the Registry." Hour 20, "Administering Multiple Users with Profiles," describes the contents of each profile folder.

WHEN TO DO A MANUAL BACKUP

Most folks don't back up the Registry when they need to. Because doing so is easy, consider backing up the Registry at the following events:

- Immediately after installing Windows
- Before installing or removing any program
- Before making a significant change to your configuration, such as adding new devices
- Before changing policies via the System Policy Editor that might lock you out of the Registry
- Before editing the Registry with any tool

3

Registry Editor

As you'll learn in Hour 4, "Editing the Registry with REGEDIT," you can export any portion of the Registry into a REG file. In the Windows-based Registry Editor, choose Registry, Export Registry File. Using the real mode Registry Editor, type

```
REGEDIT [/L:system] [/R:user] /E filename
```

at the command prompt and press Enter. *system* is the path and filename of the System.dat file, *user* is the path and filename of the User.dat file, and *filename* is the path and filename of the REG file. With a full backup copy of the Registry in a REG file, you can import it into the Registry at a later time. You can't import a REG file containing the entire Registry while Windows is running, however, because the Registry Editor can't replace keys that are open. You need to start your computer in MS-DOS mode and then use the Registry Editor in real mode to import the Registry:

1. Start Windows in MS-DOS mode. To do so, select Command Prompt Only from Windows' boot menu, or choose Start, Shut Down, and then select Restart in MS-DOS mode, and press Enter.

2. Type the following at the command prompt:

```
regedit /L:system /R:user /C regfile
```

system is the path and filename of System.dat. *user* is the path and filename of User.dat. Normally, this points to the User.dat file in C:\Windows, but if you're using profiles, this might point to a User.dat file within a profile folder in

C:\Windows\Profiles. /C instructs the real mode Registry Editor to replace the entire Registry with the contents of *regfile*, which is the filename of the REG file containing the backup.

3. Restart your computer.

Don't rely on a REG file as your only backup. Microsoft reports problems such as Windows not correctly updating all Registry data when you restore a backup using this method. The best use of a REG file is backing up a portion of the Registry in which you're making changes. That way, if something goes awry, you can easily restore that branch by importing the REG file.

Norton Registry Editor has a backup feature. To use it, choose File, Backup Entire Registry. Note that this feature does nothing more than export the entire Registry to a REG file, and you can do this easily (and faster, too) with the Registry Editor. You can try using Norton Registry Editor's archive feature, but this feature archives the Registry into a proprietary format that other programs, including Windows 98, can't read. Thus, using the archive feature for Registry backups isn't a good idea.

Microsoft Backup

Windows comes with a backup utility that you can use as part of your regular backup strategy. Setup doesn't install it by default, but you can use the Add/Remove Programs Properties dialog box in the Control Panel to install it. After you install it, choose Start, Programs, Accessories, System Tools, Backup to run it in Windows 98. By default, Microsoft Backup doesn't back up the Registry, but you can set it to do so. Follow these steps before starting the backup, which are the same in either operating system:

1. Choose Job, Options to display the Backup Job Options dialog box (shown in Figure 3.1), and click the Advanced tab.

2. Select Back up Windows Registry.

3. Click OK to save your changes.

4. Continue performing your backup as normal.

FIGURE 3.1

By default, Microsoft Backup doesn't back up the Registry.

3

As you do when backing up the Registry using Microsoft Backup, you must specifically configure the program to restore the Registry:

1. Choose Job, Options and click the Advanced tab.

2. Select Restore the Registry.

3. Click OK to save your changes.

4. Continue restoring the backup as usual.

> Using Microsoft Backup to back up and restore the Registry is a method better suited to a full backup. In other words, if you restore the Registry from a backup tape, also restore the entire system from the same tape. Doing so ensures that the files on your computer match the settings found in the Registry. If you restore just the Registry from an older tape, chances are that your computer won't work properly because the configuration data in the Registry doesn't match the remaining files on your computer.

Emergency Repair Utility

The *Emergency Repair Utility (ERU)* is a tool that you can use to back up important configuration files. You can't back up to a floppy disk, which is ERU's default choice, because the configuration files usually won't fit on a floppy. By default, ERU backs up the following files (but you can change the list, as you'll learn later in this section):

- Autoexec.bat
- Command.com

- Config.sys
- Io.sys
- Msdos.sys
- Protocol.ini
- System.dat
- System.ini
- User.dat
- Win.ini

Unlike Windows 95, Windows 98 doesn't include ERU. You can find it on the CD-ROM that comes with the *Microsoft Windows 98 Resource Kit,* published by Microsoft, in the following path: `\Tools\Misc\Eru`. You can also download it from the following URL and run it to unzip the files: `http://www.microsoft.com/windows/download/eruzip.exe`. Copy all four files to a folder on your computer, and then add a shortcut to your Start menu by dragging Eru.exe onto the Start button.

After copying ERU to your computer, use the following steps to back up your configuration files, including the Registry:

1. Start ERU by choosing it from the Start menu or double-clicking Eru.exe in Windows Explorer.
2. Click Next after ERU appears. You see a dialog box in which you can choose between backing up to a floppy or to another folder.
3. Choose Drive A: if you want to back up your configuration files to disk, or choose Other Directory to back up your configuration files to another folder on your hard drive. Click Next to continue.
4. If you're backing up your configuration files to another folder on your computer, type the path of the folder in the space provided. Then click Next to continue. Otherwise, insert a formatted disk in drive A: and click OK to continue. You see a list of files that ERU is backing up, as shown in Figure 3.2.
5. Click Next. ERU backs up your configuration files to the destination you chose.
6. ERU displays a dialog box that explains how to restore your configuration in the event that something bad happens. Click OK to close the dialog box.

FIGURE 3.2

Click Custom to change the files that ERU includes in the backup.

 You can add files to the list that ERU backs up. Open Eru.inf in your favorite text editor (Notepad, perhaps) and follow the instructions that you see at the top of the file.

3

To restore your configuration using the backup files created by ERU, follow these steps:

1. Start your computer in MS-DOS mode.
2. Change to the folder to which you backed up your configuration files. If you backed up your configuration files to a disk, put it in the drive, and change to it.
3. Run Erd.exe. It's mixed in with all the backup copies of your configuration files.
4. Select the files that you want to recover. Highlight a configuration file using the arrow keys, and press the Enter key to select it.
5. After you've selected the configuration files that you want to recover, select Start Recovery, and then press the Enter key.

Norton Utilities Rescue Disk

Norton's Repair Disk is better than Windows 98's startup disk because it includes more useful utilities across more disks, and it makes a backup copy of the Registry. *Basic Rescue* is a set of floppy disks that it creates. You use the first one in the set to start your PC, and the others to fix problems. Repair Disk can also back up the files to a ZIP disk and create a bootable floppy disk that you can use to start the computer and access the ZIP drive. This is called *Zip Rescue*.

Start Repair Disk by choosing Start, Programs, Norton Utilities, Rescue Disk. Click Options to specify additional files that you want the program to include on your rescue disk set. This opens the Options dialog box, which enables you to view the files that are to be included on the disks, including their original locations and their destinations. Click

Create to make a new rescue disk set, or click Update to update an existing set. Make sure that you keep your rescue disk set current. If you allow the disk set to get out of date, it is of no use to you at all. Norton System Doctor has an indicator that alerts you when it thinks your configuration has changed enough to warrant updating the disk set.

> Norton's Rescue Disk can get your computer up and running in the event of a disaster. It makes backup copies of all the important files that are required to start the computer, including the Registry. If things go awry, put the first disk of the rescue disk set in drive A: and restart the computer.

Following is a list of the information that Rescue Disk puts on each rescue disk set:

- Config.sys
- Autoexec.bat
- Msdos.sys
- Autoexec.dos
- Config.dos
- CMOS Information
- Boot Record Information
- Partition Information
- Registry Backup
- Rescue.exe
- Rescued.hlp
- Diskedit.exe
- Ndd.exe
- Format.com
- Sys.com
- Fdisk.exe
- Unerase.exe
- Unformat.exe

INI files are what's missing from the default rescue disk set that Rescue Disk creates. In particular, it doesn't back up Win.ini or System.ini. Add these and other important INI files by clicking the Options button in Rescue Disk's main window.

At the time that this book was written, the Rescue Disk program that comes with Norton Utilities doesn't work properly with Windows 98. The operating system reports a compatibility problem when you run Rescue Disk, saying that the Zip Rescue feature doesn't work. If you continue running the program, Rescue Disk reports the same compatibility problem but enables you to go ahead and create a Basic Rescue. You can expect Symantec to update this program, however. You can check for the update by opening LiveUpdate from the Control Panel. Follow the onscreen instructions to update your copy of Norton Utilities with the latest software from Symantec's Web site.

3

System.1st as a Last Resort

If all else fails, you'll find one more backup copy of the Registry on your computer. System.1st is a read-only, hidden system file in the root folder of your boot drive. This is a backup copy of System.dat that Windows made after you successfully installed and started the operating system. It doesn't contain any custom settings, nor does it include any information added by the programs you've installed. This file just gets your computer running again if all else fails. Read Hour 22 before you give up and restore System.1st.

Use the following steps to restore System.1st:

1. Start your computer in MS-DOS mode.

2. Copy your C:\System.1st to C:\Windows\System.dat. In other words, type

   ```
   Xcopy C:\system.1st C:\windows\system.dat /H /R
   ```

   at the command prompt, and press Enter.

3. Restart your computer.

Use this method as a last resort only. All the configuration changes you've made to your computer since you first installed Windows are gone after you restore this file.

Summary

Windows 95 automatically backs up the Registry each time you start the operating system. It copies System.dat to System.da0 and User.dat to User.da0.

Windows 98 doesn't copy the Registry to DA0 files, but it makes backup copies of the registry through the Registry Checker. Registry Checker automatically backs up the Registry to CAB files that you find in \Windows\Sysbckup. You can use the Windows-based Registry Checker, SCANREGW, to back up the Registry, and you can use the MS-DOS-based Registry Checker, SCANREG, to both back up and restore the Registry.

You can use a variety of alternative methods to backup the Registry. Copy System.dat and User.dat to a safe place using Windows Explorer. Export the Registry to a REG file using the Registry Editor. Back up the Registry using Microsoft Backup.

Q&A

Q Aside from backing up the Registry, what else can I do with Registry Checker?

A Registry Checker does far more than back up the Registry. You can use it to optimize the Registry, removing unused space. You can also use it to scan the Registry for errors and repair them. Both features are only available in SCANREG, however, not SCANREGW.

Q Can I use Registry Checker in Windows 95?

A Shucks, no. Registry Checker checks the operating system's version to make sure that you're using it on Windows 98. Hour 16, "Other Customizations," describes how to spoof the version and enable you to attempt to run Registry Checker in Windows 95.

Q I tried using Xcopy as described in this chapter, but it says that I used invalid parameters.

A You are probably using OSR-1, the original release of Windows 95. Windows 95 OSR-2 and Windows 98 support the command-line options described in this hour.

Workshop

The following quiz will enhance your understanding of the topics discussed in this hour.

Quiz

1. True or false? Windows 98 copies System.dat to System.da0 and User.dat to User.da0.

2. Which of the following describes how to restore the Registry using Registry Checker:

    a. Use SCANREG in Windows

    b. Use SCANREGW in Windows

    c. Use SCANREG in MS-DOS

    d. Use SCANREGW in MS-DOS

    e. Both b and c

3. True or False? Copying System.dat and User.dat are the safest ways to back up the Registry.

Answers to Quiz Questions

1. False

    Windows 95 backs up the Registry to these files, but Windows 98 uses Registry Checker.

2. C

    Only the MS-DOS-based version of Registry Checker, SCANREG, can restore the Registry. You must run SCANREG in MS-DOS mode.

3. This is a trick question. In Windows 95, copying System.dat and User.dat are the only way to quickly back up the Registry. In Windows 98, Registry Checker is the safest way to back up the Registry.

HOUR 4

Editing the Registry with REGEDIT

Microsoft's attitude regarding the Registry Editor is that if you don't know about it, you'll never miss it. Setup doesn't copy a Registry Editor shortcut to the Start menu when you install Windows, and Microsoft doesn't tell you much about it. For that matter, you'll find barely a handful of help screens in the operating system that describe how to use the Registry Editor, and the *Microsoft Windows 98 Resource Kit* contains only one chapter to describe the entire Registry. It's probably just as well, though. Microsoft wants to prevent inexperienced users from accidentally harming their computer systems by tampering with the Registry, so they don't provide any encouragement by over-documenting it.

Administrators and power users can't avoid the Registry Editor, however; it's your window into the computer's configuration, enabling you to fix many problems and to customize Windows in a variety of ways. You use the Registry Editor to customize a desktop object's icon, for example, and you can use it to customize a file's shortcut menu. Many of the solutions in Microsoft's Knowledge Base also require you use the Registry Editor to make subtle changes to the computer's configuration.

The Registry Editor is a powerful but simple program. It doesn't have a toolbar; its menus are fairly straightforward. It displays the organization of the Registry on the left side of the window and the actual configuration data on the right side—not too complicated. You will learn how to use this program in this hour. You will also learn a variety of helpful tips that come from my own agonizing experiences with the Registry Editor. You will learn how to perform the following tasks in this hour:

- Starting the Registry Editor in Windows
- Navigating the Registry Editor's two panes
- Performing various actions on keys and values
- Using a better editor: Norton Registry Editor

If you think that the Registry Editor sounds too simplistic, you might consider using one of the alternative Registry editors you'll learn about in this hour. The Norton Registry Editor comes with Norton Utilities and offers a variety of enhancements over the Registry Editor. The ShellWizard Registry Editor is a shareware editor that provides even more features than the Norton Registry Editor.

Starting the Registry Editor

The Registry Editor isn't on your Start menu, but it is in your Windows folder. Its filename is Regedit.exe. Choose Start, Programs, Run; then type regedit, and press Enter. Because the Windows folder is usually in the PATH environment variable, you don't have to specify a path on the command line. You can also drag Regedit.exe from your Windows folder to the Start button to create a shortcut for it. If you're using the Microsoft Management Console that comes with the *Microsoft Windows 98 Resource Kit*, published by Microsoft Press, consider adding the Registry Editor to the snap-ins that are already shown, keeping all your administrative tools in one convenient place.

If you don't find Regedit.exe in \Windows and you installed Windows from shared source files on the network, the administrator might have prevented the Setup program from copying it to your computer. You can ask the administrator for a copy of the program, or you can extract it from Win98_42.cab, which you find on the Windows 98 CD-ROM in \Win98. If you don't find Regedit.exe in Win98_42.cab, search for the file using the technique discussed in Hour 23, "Fixing Program Errors via the Registry." Right-click the CAB file and choose View to open the CAB file in a folder, and then drag the file from the CAB file to \Windows. Again, the administrator can prevent you from gaining access to the Registry using the System Policy Editor; in this case you see a message that says Registry editing has been disabled by your administrator when you try to open the Registry Editor. If you want to use the Registry Editor to change values in the Registry, you'll have to plead your case to the administrator for permission to change the Registry.

Is the Registry safe from tampering? No, it's not. In Hour 21, "Controlling the Desktop via System Policies," you'll learn how to prevent a user from starting the Registry Editor. This policy requires the cooperation of the Registry editing program, however. The Registry Editor cooperates; other programs probably won't. What's more, even if you prevent access to the Registry editing tools by using system policies, the user can still modify it by creating and importing a REG or INF file. Furthermore, even if a clever administrator removes the association between REG files and the Registry Editor, users can still merge a REG file by typing `regedit filename` at the command prompt. Therefore, you can never be sure that the Registry is safe from tampering.

For more information about gaining access to the Registry when system policies prevent it, see Hour 16, "Other Customizations." Hour 21 discusses how to protect Windows as well as the Registry. In particular, you learn about a policy called Disable Registry Editing Tools.

4

Getting Around the Registry Editor

Figure 4.1 shows how the Registry Editor looks when you open it on your desktop. You see the Registry Editor's menu bar across the top of the window and its status line across the bottom. The status line displays the fully qualified path of the selected Registry key. By now, you are already familiar with the controls in the Registry Editor's title bar.

Within the window, you see two panes, which the Registry Editor separates by a divider that you can drag to change the size of either pane. The left pane contains the Registry's hierarchy, and the right pane displays the value entries for the selected Registry key. Throughout this book, the left pane is called the *Key* pane and the right pane the *Contents* pane. The following sections describe the contents of each pane in more detail.

If the left pane isn't big enough for you to easily tell which key is selected, look at the Registry Editor's status bar to see the key's fully qualified name. You can also drag the divider to the right to make the left pane bigger.

Registry Hierarchy

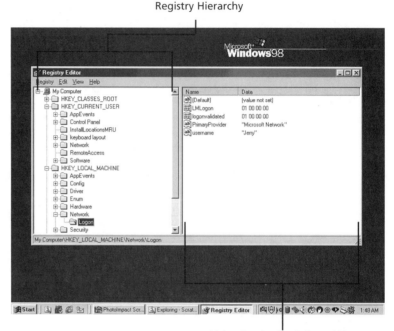

FIGURE 4.1

*The left pane of the
Registry Editor works
much like the left pane
of Windows Explorer.*

Value Entries for Selected Key

The Key Pane: Registry Organization

The Key pane shows the organization of the Registry—its hierarchy. Even though
Windows stores the Registry in two files, System.dat and User.dat, the Registry Editor
displays the entire Registry as one logical unit. When you update a key in the Registry
Editor, it automatically updates the appropriate Registry file, storing changes to
HKEY_USERS in User.dat and changes to HKEY_LOCAL_MACHINE in System.dat. However,
the location of User.dat varies, depending on whether you enable user profiles on the
computer (as you learned in Hour 1, "Understanding the Registry").

The first entry is My Computer. It contains several root keys that the Registry Editor
represents as folders. Each root key contains subkeys, which are also represented as
folders. Click the plus sign (+) to expand a branch, or click a minus sign (–) to
collapse a branch. If you'd rather use the keyboard, you can use the keystrokes listed in
Table 4.1 to move around the Registry Editor. These key combinations are often the
quickest way to navigate because you don't flop around with the mouse. You can
collapse an entire branch by pressing the left-arrow, for example, and then press the
left-arrow again to select the parent key.

TABLE 4.1 REGEDIT KEYSTROKES

Key	Description
	Searching
Ctrl+F	Searches the Registry.
F3	Repeats the previous search.
	Miscellaneous
F1	Displays online help.
F2	Renames the selected key or value.
F5	Refreshes the Registry Editor's contents.
F10	Opens the Registry Editor's main menu.
Shift+F10	Displays the context menu (right-click) for the selected key or value.
Alt+F4	Closes the Registry Editor.
	Navigation
Keypad +	Expands the selected folder one level.
Keypad -	Collapses the selected folder one level.
Keypad *	Expands all levels of the selected folder.
Up arrow	Selects the previous open key.
Down arrow	Selects the next open key.
Right arrow	Expands the selected key if it's collapsed; otherwise, selects the first subkey.
Left arrow	Collapses the selected key if it's expanded; otherwise, selects the parent key.
Home	Selects the first entry in the outline.
End	Selects the last open key in the outline.
Page Up	Moves up one screen in the list.
Page Down	Moves down one screen in the list.
F6	Toggles between the Key and Contents panes.
Tab	Toggles between the Key and Contents panes.

4

If you don't want the Registry Editor to "remember" which subkeys are open below a folder after you collapse it, press F5 to refresh it. If you collapse a branch and then expand it, for instance, the Registry Editor restores the branch as it was before you collapsed it. If you want to expand a key so that you see only the subkeys immediately below it, press F5 before expanding it.

The Contents Pane: Value Entries for the Selected Key

The Contents pane shows the value entries for the key that you've selected in the Key pane. Each row in the Contents pane represents a single value entry. The Name column contains the value's name. The Data column contains the actual value data for each. You can resize each column by dragging the divider you see between each heading.

The first value entry is always (Default). This is a string value entry that represents the default value for that Registry key. You learned about default value entries in Hour 2, "Looking Inside the Registry." All Registry keys contain this value entry, but some keys don't contain any additional value entries. Aside from (Default), therefore, each key can contain zero or more value entries that have both a name and data. To edit any value entry, double-click its name in the Contents pane. Note also that you can right-click any key or value name to open a shortcut menu, from which you can choose a variety of commands.

Notice that different value entries in the Contents pane of the Registry Editor window have different icons. These icons represent the different types of data that the Registry can store, as described in Table 4.2. The first row represents string value entries, and the second represents DWORD and binary value entries.

TABLE 4.2   ICONS REPRESENTING DATA TYPES

Icon	Description
ab	String values that you can read (text)
011	Binary values (hexadecimal strings or DWORDs)

Working with Keys and Values

The following sections show you how to use the Registry Editor to search for, add, change, and delete configuration data. You'll also find tips for doing all these things as safely as possible. Some of these sections contain real-world examples so that you can exercise what you learn. Before you continue, however, remember the following advice:

- Back up the Registry before you change it.
- Make sure that you have a plan for making changes so that you can fix any problems you encounter.

The plan involves making sure that you can get out of a bad situation if one arises. You can do this by setting up a situation in which you can restore a value's original data if necessary, whether you deleted or changed it. Exporting the key is one approach; copying a value's data to the Clipboard is sometimes a simpler method. Continue reading this hour to learn about both.

Searching the Registry

When you search the Registry, the Registry Editor looks for keys, value names, and value data that matches the text for which you're searching. It scans the name of each key, the name of each value entry, and the actual data from each value entry for a match. You can use the search feature to find entries relating to a specific product, to find all the entries that contain a reference to a file on your computer, or to locate entries related to a particular hardware device. Use the following steps to search the Registry for keys, value names, and value data that contain a particular string:

1. Select Edit, Find. The Registry Editor displays the dialog box shown in Figure 4.2.

FIGURE 4.2

Deselect the parts of the Registry in which you don't want REGEDIT to search: Keys, Values, and Data.

2. Type the text for which you want to search. If you're searching for a number in a string value entry, try both the decimal and hexadecimal notations because both formats are common in the Registry.

3. Click Find Next; the Registry Editor searches for a match. This can sometimes take quite a while—up to several minutes on slower machines. If the Registry Editor finds a matching key, it selects that key in the left pane. If the Registry Editor finds a matching value entry, it opens the key that contains it in the left pane and selects the value entry in the right pane.

4. If the result isn't exactly what you had in mind, press F3 to continue searching. When the Registry Editor reaches the bottom of the Registry, it displays a dialog box telling you that it has finished searching.

You can hasten the Registry Editor's search if you know which portion of the Registry contains the string you're searching for: keys, value entry names, or value entry data. As was just mentioned, deselect Keys, Values, or Data if you don't think the Registry Editor will find the string in one or more of those places. If you're pretty certain that the string for which you're searching is in a value entry's name, for example, deselect Keys and Data to limit the Registry Editor to value entry names, thus speeding up the search.

Neither the Registry Editor nor the Norton Registry Editor provides the capability to search binary and DWORD value entry data. You can't simply search for 0x000000001 and expect the Registry Editor to find any matching DWORD values. You can still locate these values, however, by exporting the Registry to a text file and searching the text file with your favorite editor. See the later section "Importing and Exporting Registry Entries" to learn how to export the Registry to a REG file. What you need to know is how those values look in a REG file so you can search for them using a text editor. The following table shows you the format of each type in the REG file. For example, if you are searching for the DWORD value 0xA0B0C0D0, search the REG file for dword:A0B0C0D0. If you are searching for the binary value 05 20 59 02 14 65, search the REG file for the string hex:05,20,59,02,14,65.

Type	Shown in Registry Editor	Format in Exported REG File
DWORD	0x00000054	dword:00000054
Binary	A0 00 00 00	hex:a0,00,00,00

Incremental searching makes it easier to locate an exposed key in the Registry Editor window, which is particularly valuable when you are trying to locate a subkey in HKEY_CLASSES_ROOT, a monstrous branch of the Registry. If you click anywhere in the Registry Editor's Key pane and start typing the name of a Registry key, the Registry Editor selects the key that best matches what you've typed thus far. For example, expand HKEY_CLASSES_ROOT. Then press ., and REGEDIT selects .386; press b, and it selects .bat; press m, and it selects .bmp. Note that if you pause between keystrokes, the Registry Editor starts the *incremental search* over with the next keystroke.

TECHNIQUES FOR SEARCHING THE REGISTRY

After using the Registry Editor for a time, you can probably predict where to find a certain key or value. With that knowledge, you can position the cursor somewhere near where you think you'll find the item, and then use the Search feature to find it. This takes much less time than searching the entire Registry for the item.

Consider the following example: If you're searching for a file extension, open HKEY_CLASSES_ROOT and do an incremental search to locate it faster. Note that you can locate the *program identifier* associated with a file extension, which defines the commands available for the file, by looking at the file extension's default value entry.

Finding a program's configuration data is straightforward, too, because most programs store the same types of configuration data in the same places. You find the program's file associations in HKEY_CLASSES_ROOT. The program probably stores configuration data in \Software*Vendor**AppName**Version* under HKEY_LOCAL_MACHINE and HKEY_CURRENT_USER, where *Vendor* is the name of the company that produced the software, *AppName* is the name of the application, and *Version* is the version number of the program or CurrentVersion.

Remember that computer-specific data goes in HKEY_LOCAL_MACHINE, whereas user-specific data goes in HKEY_CURRENT_USER. Use that information to your advantage. If you're relatively certain that the data you're searching for is computer-specific, select HKEY_LOCAL_MACHINE before beginning the search. For example, you search for any information about a particular device in this root key. Otherwise, if you're certain the data is user-specific, select HKEY_CURRENT_USER before beginning the search.

Renaming a Key or Value Entry

Renaming a key or value entry in the Registry Editor works much like renaming a file in Windows Explorer, except that you can't rename it by clicking the name. Instead, select the key or value name that you want to rename, choose Edit, Rename, type over the name to change it, and press Enter. Alternatively, select the name and press F2, and then type over the name and press Enter.

Renaming a key or value entry has practical value. It's a good way to hide a key or value entry prior to permanently deleting it. Hiding the item under some obscure name has the same effect as removing it. If things go awry, however, you can restore the item's original name to undelete it. For example, assume that you want to remove the IsShortcut value entry from the lnkfile program identifier, which prevents Windows from displaying the shortcut overlay on shortcuts. Instead of deleting the value, rename it to something such as MyIsShortcut to test the change. Then permanently remove MyIsshortcut after you're satisfied that everything works OK.

Changing a Key or Value Entry

To change a value entry, double-click its name or select it and choose Edit, Modify. Then change the value and click OK to save your changes.

Recall from Hour 2 that a value entry can be a string, DWORD, or binary data. Thus, when you change a value entry, the Registry Editor presents a different dialog box, depending on the type of data stored in the value. Figures 4.3, 4.4, and 4.5 show you the

4

dialog boxes for String, DWORD, and binary values, respectively. Here's the rundown on each one:

- **String**—Editing a string value entry is uneventful. You type the new string in the Edit String dialog box, shown in Figure 4.3. Remember, though, that you don't add the quotation marks that the Registry Editor displays around a string value. They appear automatically. You must still add any quotation marks that you want to embed in the string, however.

FIGURE 4.3

The Edit String dialog box shows you the original data before you start editing.

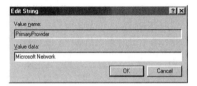

- **DWORD**—The Registry Editor presents the Edit DWORD Value dialog box, shown in Figure 4.4, when you double-click a DWORD value in the Contents pane. If you know the hexadecimal value, type it in the space provided. Otherwise, select Decimal and type the value in decimal notation.

FIGURE 4.4

Choose Decimal if your hexadecimal math is a bit rusty. The Registry Editor converts the value to binary.

- **Binary**—Figure 4.5 shows the Edit Binary Value dialog box, which the Registry Editor presents when you double-click a binary value in the Contents pane. You can type each hexadecimal byte on the left side of this dialog box, or you can type ASCII characters from the keyboard on the right side. To choose the side in which you want to type, click that area of the dialog box.

 Use a bit of caution when changing a value. The later sidebar titled "Protecting Yourself from Errant Edits" provides some good tips for backing up the portion of the Registry in which you're working. Doing so helps you recover from any problems that your edits might cause. The best tip that can be offered regarding editing a value is to make a backup copy of it by giving the original value an obscure name. Then add a new value that has the original name and value. If things go awry, you can remove the new value and restore the original from the backup.

Edit hexadecimal bytes

FIGURE 4.5

You can use the Windows calculator (in Scientific mode) to convert decimal values to hexadecimal values for use with this dialog box.

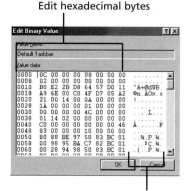

Edit ASCII characters

The following example shows you how to change the text you see below the Recycle Bin icon on your desktop. You can make it a bit more personal, for example, by changing it to something such as "Jerry's Trashcan." Use the following steps to change the text below your Recycle Bin:

1. Open HKEY_CLASSES_ROOT\CLSID\{645FF040-5081-101B-9F08-00AA002F954E} in the Registry Editor.

2. In the Contents pane, double-click the default value entry, (Default).

3. In the Edit String dialog box, type the text you want to see below the Recycle Bin icon on your desktop.

4. Click OK to save your changes, and minimize the Registry Editor so that you can see the desktop.

5. Click any open area of the desktop and press F5. This causes the desktop to refresh itself.

Changes that you make to the Registry might not be reflected immediately in Windows or the programs that are currently running. The only way to make sure is to restart Windows or log off and back on again after closing the Registry Editor. In particular, if you change a value in

HKEY_LOCAL_MACHINE, you might have to restart the computer in order for the change to take effect. If you change a value in HKEY_USERS, you might have to log off and back on again in order for the change to take effect.

Creating a Key or Value Entry

Creating a new key or value entry is generally harmless and useless—unless, of course, you know for sure that either the operating system or another program will actually use your new key. For example, the Microsoft Knowledge Base might instruct you to create a new Registry key to fix a problem.

When you create a new key, the Registry Editor creates a key called New Key #1 and highlights the name so that you can rename it. When you create a new value entry, the Registry Editor creates a value called New Value #1, and it highlights the name so that you can rename it. The Registry Editor sets the initial value of a new value entry to a null string for string values, a null binary string for binary values, or zero for DWORD values. You must change the value as described in the preceding section to set its value.

To create new key or value entry, do one of the following:

- **New Key**—Select an existing key under which you want your new subkey to appear. Select Edit, New, Key; then type the name of your key, and press Enter.

- **New Value**—Select an existing key under which you want your new value entry to appear. Select Edit, New and then choose String Value, Binary Value, or DWORD Value. Type the name of your new value entry and press Enter. You can edit your key as described in the preceding section.

TECHNIQUES USING THE CLIPBOARD

When using the Registry Editor, use the Clipboard to make your job easier. You can copy to and paste from the Clipboard whenever you edit a name or data, for example. Thus, consider the following different ways to use the Clipboard in the Registry Editor:

- To copy the fully qualified name of a Registry key to the Clipboard, select the key and choose Edit, Copy Key Name.

- To copy a value entry's data to the Clipboard, open the value entry for editing, select the data, and press Ctrl+C to copy the data to the Clipboard.

- To paste data from the Clipboard into a value entry, open the value entry for editing, select the data that you want to replace, and press Ctrl+V.

- To copy a key or value entry's name to the Clipboard, right-click the item in the Registry Editor, choose Rename, and press Ctrl+C.

> The second item in the list tells you how to copy a value entry's data to the Clipboard. Use this to back up a value entry before changing it. Copy the value's data to the Clipboard and paste that data into a new bogus value entry. If you want to restore the original value, copy the backup data to the Clipboard and paste it into the value.

Deleting a Key or Value Entry

Be very careful about deleting keys and value entries from the Registry. You can easily prevent Windows from working properly if you carelessly delete configuration data. To remove a key or value entry, follow these steps:

1. Highlight the key or value you want to delete.

2. Press Delete. The Registry Editor prompts you to confirm that you want to delete the item.

3. Click Yes to delete the key or value.

> Before deleting a key, give it an obscure name such as MyDeletedKey. This hides it from Windows and your applications. Restart your computer and test things. If everything works, go ahead and permanently delete the key.

4

Printing a Key

Some people think that printing the Registry is useful as a backup or for reading the Registry to better understand it. Considering that a full printout of the entire Registry might occupy hundreds of pages, and keeping in mind that you can't import a printout back into the Registry, this position is nonsense.

Printing a small subkey does have merit, however, for two reasons. First, it serves as a useful backup when you're working within a small portion of the Registry. You can restore the original data if you mess things up. Second, it is sometimes helpful to print a small portion of the Registry that you need as a reference when working in another part of the Registry. This is particularly true because you can't open two copies of the Registry Editor to view two portions of the Registry at the same time.

To print a branch, select it in the Key pane, choose Registry, Print, and click OK. The Registry Editor sends the print job to the spooler. The resulting output looks similar to a REG file, as shown in Listing 4.1. Note that the format of each value is slightly different from a REG file, however. The Registry Editor doesn't put quotation marks around string values, for instance. It also doesn't prefix a binary value with the string hex:. The most notable difference is that it writes DWORD values as binary values, reversing the bytes as required in a Little Endian architecture (see Hour 18, "Scripting Changes to the Registry"). The following table describes how the Registry Editor formats each data type when it prints it:

Type	Shown in Registry Editor	Format in Printed Output
String	"This is a string"	This is a string
DWORD	0x00000054	54,00,00,00
Binary	A0 00 00 00 01 23 A0,00,00,00,01,23	

LISTING 4.1 REGISTRY EDITOR PRINTER OUTPUT

```
[HKEY_CURRENT_USER\Control Panel\Desktop]
DragFullWindows=1
FontSmoothing=1
UserPreferencemask=a0,00,00,00
ScreenSaveUsePassword=00,00,00,00
SmoothScroll=01,00,00,00
MenuShowDelay=400

[HKEY_CURRENT_USER\Control Panel\Desktop\WindowMetrics]
MenuWidth=-270
MenuHeight=-270
MinAnimate=0
Shell Icon Size=32
IconTitleWrap=0
test=01,00,00,00

[HKEY_CURRENT_USER\Control Panel\Desktop\WindowsMetrics]
MinAnimate=1
```

Using the Norton Registry Editor

Hour 1 gave you an overview of the different Registry tools you can use. One of those tools, the Norton Registry Editor, comes with Symantec's Norton Utilities and is a much more powerful editor than the one that comes with Windows. Take a look at Figure 4.6. The Key and Contents panes are similar to the Registry Editor. The primary differences are that the Norton Registry Editor uses different icons to represent string, binary, and DWORD value entries in the Contents pane.

Contents pane

FIGURE 4.6

*Click one of the tabs in
the output area to see
the results of Norton
Registry Editor's
unique features.*

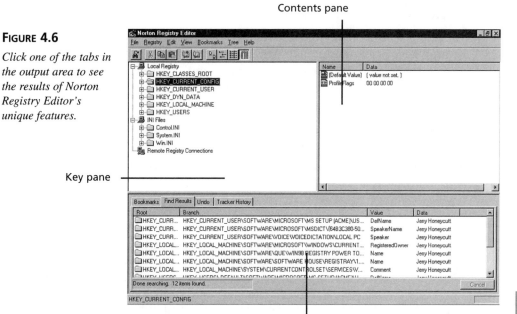

Key pane

Output area

In the Key pane, you'll notice some new entries at the top of the outline. `Local
Registry` is the same as `My Computer` in the Registry Editor. `INI Files` contains an
entry for each INI file that the Norton Registry Editor is tracking. In this manner, the
Norton Registry Editor enables you to work with INI files as if they were part of the
Registry. The last entry at the top of the outline is `Remote Registry Connections`,
which contains an entry for each remote Registry to which you connect.

The bottom pane is unique to the Norton Registry Editor. It provides output from a
number of different features. Click each tab to work with Bookmarks, Find Results, and
Undo, for instance. You'll learn more about each of these features in the following
sections, which describe what makes the Norton Registry Editor different from the
Registry Editor.

To use the Norton Registry Editor, you must first install Norton Utilities as
described in Hour 1. An evaluation version of Norton Utilities is available
from Symantec's Web site, http://www.symantec.com, or you can purchase
the retail version at your local computer store. After you've installed Norton
Utilities, start the Norton Registry Editor by choosing Start, Programs,
Norton Utilities, Norton Registry Editor.

Find

The Find feature provided by the Norton Registry Editor is far more powerful than the Registry Editor—and quicker, too. Press Ctrl+F to open the Find dialog box, and type the text for which you're searching in the space provided. If you click the Advanced tab, you can limit the search to specific branches in the Registry or to specific portions such as key names, value names, or value data.

The best part of this feature is that it lists in the Find Results tab all the matches that it finds, all at once (see Figure 4.6). Double-click any line in the Find Results tab to open it in the editor's Key pane. This enables you to move randomly through all the matches without having to start the search over again if you missed the value for which you were searching.

 The Norton Registry Editor has a search-and-replace feature that you can use to scan the Registry for specific strings and replace them with other text. Press Ctrl+R, type the text that you want to replace in the Find What box, and type the text with which you want to replace it in the Replace Where box. As with the Norton Registry Editor's Find feature, you can limit the search-and-replace to specific root keys in the Registry, as well as to specific portions of its anatomy, by clicking the Advanced tab and filling in the information.

Bookmarks

In the Norton Registry Editor, bookmarks work much like they work in a Web browser. They enable you to bookmark a certain Registry key, move to another portion of the Registry hierarchy, and return to the bookmarked key with just a few mouse clicks.

Right-click any key in the Key pane of the Norton Registry Editor, and choose Bookmark This. You see the bookmarked key on the Bookmarks tab of the output area, as shown in Figure 4.7. Explore other portions of the Registry. When you're ready to return to the bookmarked key, double-click its name on the Bookmarks tab of the output area. Note that you can bookmark as many keys as you want because navigating the Bookmarks tab is easy.

FIGURE 4.7

The Bookmarks tab organizes bookmarks by root key.

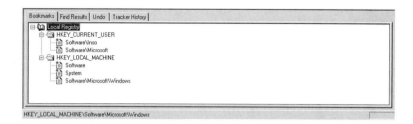

 The Norton Registry Editor supports shortcuts. It treats shortcuts like aliases. In other words, when you create a shortcut for a key, the Norton Registry Editor creates a root key for it that enables you to navigate to that particular branch from the top of the hierarchy. Create a shortcut to the key called `HKEY_LOCAL_MACHINE\Software\Microsoft\Windows`, for example, and you'll see a new root key by that name that gives you quick access to the entire branch. To create a shortcut, right-click any key and choose Make Shortcut.

Safety Features

The Undo tab of the output area contains a list of all the changes you've made using the Norton Registry Editor. You can undo any change by right-clicking it in the Undo tab and choosing Undo. Alternatively, press Ctrl+Z to undo changes in reverse order. That is, pressing Ctrl+Z undoes the most recent change, pressing Ctrl+Z again undoes the change before that, and so on.

One safety feature is the Read Only feature. It enables you to explore the Registry all you want without fear of messing things up. If you choose Registry, Read Only, you can't change anything in the Registry. To enable changes, choose Registry, Read Only again to remove the checkmark next to the command.

 Probably the nicest feature of the Norton Registry Editor is its online help, which is more extensive than the help that comes with the Registry Editor. Use this resource to learn more about the unique features found in the Norton Registry Editor and as a refresher when you forget the purpose of certain portions of the Registry.

Summary

The Registry Editor is your window into the Registry. You use it to add keys and values, remove keys and values, change values, and search the Registry. Windows uses the exact same Registry Editor.

A variety of other registry editors provide more capabilities. Norton Registry Editor and the ShellWizard Registry Editor enable users to bookmark keys, for example. Both registry editors have more powerful search features than the Windows Registry Editor.

Q&A

Q I don't see all the columns in the Contents pane of the Registry Editor. How do I restore them?

A To reset Registry Editor's view, remove the View value from
`HKEY_CURRENT_USER\Software\Microsoft\Windows\CurrentVersion\Applets`
`\Regedit`.

Q Can I edit backup copies of the Registry?

A Yes and no. You can't edit a backup copy of the Registry using Registry Editor. However, you can make rudimentary changes to a backup copy using the real-mode Registry Editor (command-line version). You specify the location of the System.dat and User.dat files on its command line.

Workshop

The following quiz will enhance your understanding of the topics discussed in this hour.

Quiz

1. Which of the following are not method(s) you can use to start the Registry Editor?

    a. Type `Regedit.exe` in the Run dialog box.

    b. Type `Regedit.exe` at the MS-DOS command prompt.

    c. Click Registry Editor on the System Information utility's Tools menu.

    d. On the Start menu, point to Programs, followed by Accessories and System Tools; then, click Registry Editor.

    e. Both b and c

    f. Both c and d

2. Which of the following methods are not methods that you can use to locate data in the Registry?

    a. Incremental search

    b. Press Ctrl+F and type the search text

    c. On the Start menu, point to Find and then click Find in the Registry

3. True or false? Renaming a Registry key or value is the best way to test its deletion.

4. What does the error message `Registry editing has been disabled by your administrator` mean?

    a. The administrator has removed the Registry Editor from your computer.

    b. The administrator has set the read only attribute of System.dat and User.dat so that you can't edit the Registry.

    c. The administrator has set a policy that prevents you from editing the Registry.

Answers to Quiz Questions

1. f

    You can start Regedit.exe both from Windows and from the MS-DOS command prompt.

2. d

    There isn't a command called Find in the Registry.

3. True

    Rename a key or value to an obscure value so that you can test what might happen if you deleted it.

4. c

    Administrators set the Disable registry editing tools policy to prevent you from using the Registry Editor.

4

Hour 5

Importing/Exporting the Registry

REG files are a text file version of all or portions of the Registry. They look similar to INI files, with which you're probably already familiar.

Windows supports importing from and exporting to REG files. Although this might seem to be an activity in which you have no interest, hang around long enough to let me change your mind.

In this hour, you learn two different methods for importing and exporting the Registry:

- You learn how to do these tasks from within the graphical Registry Editor, which is useful for quick and easy backups.
- You also learn how to do these tasks from the real-mode Registry Editor. Doing so is also useful from backups, particularly from within batch files, but it is more useful for optimizing the Registry (as described in the next hour, "Reducing the Size of the Registry").

Importing and Exporting Registry Entries

Exporting the Registry creates a text file with a REG extension, which you can edit using any text editor. This file contains all the information required to describe the keys and values in the exported branch.

Up to this point, you've used the Registry Editor to work with the Registry. You can also export the Registry to a REG file and edit it using a text editor such as WordPad. (The file is too big for Notepad). Just make sure you save the file as a text file and not as a word processor file (such as a DOC file). If you export the Registry to a REG file, you can use the editor's search-and-replace features to make massive changes to it. Be careful doing this, however, because you can inadvertently change a value that you didn't mean to change. Then you can import the REG file with all its changes by right-clicking it and choosing Merge.

Aside from editing the Registry with a text editor, exporting the Registry to a text file has a more practical purpose. You can export as a backup any branch of the Registry in which you're making many changes. If you get confused, or if changes get out of hand, you can import that file back into the Registry to restore your settings. You can also export a key or a branch that contains a useful Registry hack. Then you can share that REG file with other people so that they can implement the same hack by importing the REG file you provide (all they have to do is double-click the file).

Exporting to a REG File

To export your entire Registry—or just a specific branch—follow these steps:

1. Select the key in the Key pane that represents the branch that you want to export.

2. Choose Registry, Export Registry File. The Registry Editor displays the dialog box shown in Figure 5.1.

FIGURE 5.1

If you don't type a file extension, REGEDIT uses the default file extension (REG).

3. If you're exporting the entire Registry, select All. Otherwise, choose Selected branch. The Registry Editor automatically fills in the key that you selected in step 1.

4. Type the filename into which you want to export the Registry in the File name box, and then click Save.

 Make sure that you use clear 8.3 filenames for the REG files you export. Clear names help you find these files at the MS-DOS command prompt, and 8.3 filenames help make sure that you can easily specify the name to the real mode Registry Editor on the command line. See the section "Using the Real Mode Registry Editor," later in this hour, for more information.

Importing a REG File

In Windows Explorer, right-click a REG file and choose Merge. Windows updates your Registry with the contents of the REG file, replacing existing items and adding new ones. When you merge a REG file into the Registry, Windows doesn't remove keys and value entries that exist in the Registry but not in the REG file. As an alternative to merging a REG file from Windows Explorer, you can import a REG file from within the Registry Editor using the following steps:

1. Choose Registry, Import Registry File. The Registry Editor displays the Import Registry File dialog box.

2. Type the path and filename of the REG file in the space provided, or browse your hard disk to locate it.

3. Click Open. The Registry Editor imports the REG file, displaying a message that says `Information in` *`filename`* `has been successfully entered into the registry`.

Be careful not to double-click a REG file unless you want to merge it with the Registry. Merge is the default command for REG files. Note that you can change the default command for REG files, as described in Hour 15, "Menus and Windows." You can also use a file extension other than REG for exported Registry files, which prevents the user from accidentally merging them. Furthermore, consider storing all your REG files in their own folder, as well, so that you're more inclined to be careful when working with files in that folder.

5

You must remember that importing a REG file only replaces or adds keys
and values to the Registry. This action never removes a key or value that's in
the Registry but not in the REG file. If you want to do this sort of thing,
remove the key that you want to replace from the Registry and then import
the REG file.

Reading a REG File

The resulting file looks very much like a classic INI file. Open the REG file in Notepad
by right-clicking it and choosing Edit (Notepad offers to open the file in WordPad if it's
larger than 64KB). The first line always contains REGEDIT4, which identifies the file as a
Registry file. The remainder of the file contains the keys and value entries that the
Registry Editor exported.

Listing 5.1 shows how a REG file looks. The file is split into multiple sections, with each
Registry key in its own section. The name of the key appears between brackets, and it is
the fully qualified name of that key in the Registry file. In other words, you see the entire
name of the branch, including the name of the root key. Each value entry for a key is
listed in that key's section. The value entry's name is in quotation marks, except for
default value entries, which the Registry Editor represents with the at sign (@). The value
entry's data looks different depending on its type, as shown in Table 5.1.

LISTING 5.1   A SAMPLE REG FILE

```
REGEDIT4

[HKEY_CURRENT_USER\Control Panel\Desktop]
"DragFullWindows"="1"
"FontSmoothing"="1"
"wallpaper"=""
"TileWallpaper"="0"
"UserPreferencemask"=hex:a0,00,00,00
"WallpaperStyle"="0"
"ScreenSaveLowPowerActive"="1"
"ScreenSavePowerOffActive"="0"
"ScreenSaveActive"="0"
"ScreenSaveTimeOut"="60"
"ScreenSaveUsePassword"=dword:00000000
"SmoothScroll"=hex:01,00,00,00
"WheelScrollLines"="3"
"Pattern"=""
"DragWidth"="2"
"DragHeight"="2"
```

```
"DoubleClickWidth"="4"
"DoubleClickHeight"="4"
"HungAppTimeout"="inget"
"WaitToKillAppTimeout"="inget"
"CoolSwitchRows"="inget"
"CoolSwitchColumns"="inget"
"MenuShowDelay"="400"
"test"=dword:00000054

[HKEY_CURRENT_USER\Control Panel\Desktop\ResourceLocale]
@="00000409"

[HKEY_CURRENT_USER\Control Panel\Desktop\WindowsMetrics]
"MinAnimate"="1"
```

TABLE 5.1   FORMATS FOR STRING, DWORD, AND HEX DATA

Type	Example
String	`"This is a string value"`
DWORD	`DWORD:00000001`
HEX	`HEX:FF 00 FF 00 FF 00 FF 00 FF 00 FF 00`

For more information about REG files, see Hour 18, "Scripting Changes to the Registry." In this hour, you learn about the contents of REG files in much greater detail, including how to build them by hand.

5

PROTECTING YOURSELF FROM ERRANT EDITS

It can't be stressed enough how important it is to protect yourself while making changes to the Registry. You can restore Registry Checker's most recent backup, but more-immediate and less-drastic solutions are available. Create a backup copy of a value before changing it, for example, by creating a backup value entry and naming it whatever you want. Then copy the original value to the Clipboard and paste it to the backup value entry.

If you're working with a number of values within a key or even an entire branch, export the branch to a REG file before making changes. If things go wrong, import the REG file to restore the original settings. You can replace the mangled branch by removing it before importing the REG file. If you can't even start Windows, import the REG file from the MS-DOS command line as described in the next section.

Using the Real Mode Registry Editor

The Registry Editor provides several command-line arguments that you can use to automatically import from and export to REG files. To use the command line options, choose Start, Run, and then type `regedit` followed by any of the options that you want to use; then press Enter.

The Registry Editor runs as a real mode MS-DOS application, which means that you can run it when the computer is running in MS-DOS mode. Don't confuse yourself thinking that there are two different versions of the Registry Editor, one for Windows and one for real mode because there aren't. It's the same executable file that runs in two different modes. To run the Registry Editor in real mode, start the computer in MS-DOS mode from the boot menu or by choosing Restart in MS-DOS mode from the Shut Down Windows dialog box. Then type `regedit` at the command prompt, followed by any command line arguments, and press Enter.

You can use the real mode Registry Editor to recover from problems when Windows doesn't start properly. The command-line arguments enable you to remove keys and import REG files. You can even use the real mode Registry Editor to replace the entire Registry using a REG file you created as a backup. Hour 3, "Backing Up/Restoring the Registry," contains more information about backing up the Registry with REG files.

The Registry Editor's command line has four different forms; you will learn more about each of the forms in the following sections. This list describes the command line and each of its arguments as reported by the Registry Editor:

LISTING 5.2 COMMAND LINES

```
REGEDIT [/L:system] [/R:user] filename1

REGEDIT [/L:system] [/R:user] /C filename2

REGEDIT [/L:system] [/R:user] /E filename3 [regpath1]

REGEDIT [/L:system] [/R:user] /D regpath2
```

The following table explains each of the arguments in the preceding listing.

Argument	Function
/L:system	Specifies the location of the System.dat file.
/R:user	Specifies the location of the User.dat file.
filename1	Specifies the files to be imported into the Registry.

Argument	Function
/C filename2	Specifies the file from which to create the Registry.
/E filename3	Specifies the file to which to export the Registry.
regpath1	Specifies the starting Registry key from which to export. (Defaults to exporting the entire Registry.)
/D regpath2	Specifies the Registry key to be deleted.

The Emergency Startup Disk contains Regedit.exe, which is the same file that you run when you launch the Registry Editor in Windows. When you boot the startup disk and run this program, you're running the Registry Editor in real mode.

REGEDIT [/L:*system*] [/R:*user*] *filename1*

Use this form of the Registry Editor's command line to import one or more REG files into the Registry. /L specifies the location of System.dat and /R specifies the location of User.dat. Both of these arguments are optional, enabling you to specify locations other than the default. You must use the /R argument if you enable user profiles on the computer, for example, to specify the actual location of the user's User.dat file. The Registry Editor imports each of the files it finds on the remainder of the command line.

REGEDIT [/L:*system*] [/R:*user*] /C *filename2*

This is the scariest form of the Registry Editor's command line. /C replaces the entire contents of the Registry with the contents of *filename2*. This is handy, however, if you've exported the entire Registry as a backup and you need to restore it using the real mode Registry Editor.

5

The Registry Editor sometimes reports an error that says Error accessing the Registry: The file may not be complete or Unable to open Registry (14) - System.dat when you try to import the Registry using the /c argument. Due to a known problem in the real mode Registry Editor, you might get this error message when you try to import very large REG files using the /c switch. Microsoft acknowledges this problem but hasn't yet provided a solution. If you can start the Registry Editor in Windows, that's the best alternative. Otherwise, consider splitting the REG file into multiple sections, editing as necessary, and importing each one into the Registry.

REGEDIT [/L:*system*] [/R:*user*] /E *filename3* [*regpath1*]

Use this form of the Registry Editor's command line to export the entire Registry, or just a specific branch of the Registry, to a REG file. /L and /R work as you read in the previous sections. /E specifies the name of the file into which you want to export the Registry. *regpath1* is the fully qualified name of the key that you want to export, including all its subkeys. If you want to export the entire Registry, leave out *regpath1*.

> Create a shortcut that contains the preceding command line so that you can back up a portion of the Registry by double-clicking the shortcut. You'll want to change the name of the REG file and branch to something useful, though. Then, using the Registry Editor command lines that you learn about in this hour, you can restore this file in MS-DOS mode or within the Windows GUI.

REGEDIT [/L:*system*] [/R:*user*] /D *regpath2*

This form of the Registry Editor's command line removes a key from the Registry files indicated by /L and /R. *regpath2* is the fully qualified name of the key that you want to remove, including all its subkeys. This command line can be destructive if you don't use it carefully. Consider exporting the branch you're removing to create a backup before actually removing it.

Summary

The simplest way to export portions of the Registry is to select the Registry key that you want to export and then click Export Registry File on the Registry menu. Alternatively, you can use the real mode Registry Editor's /e command-line option.

Certainly the easiest way to import a REG file is to double-click the REG file in Windows Explorer. You can also click Import Registry File on the Registry Editor's Registry menu, or you can use the real mode Registry editor.

In either case, exporting all or portions of the Registry is a great way to make quick backups. If you're editing a particular branch the Registry, export that branch to a REG file before making your changes. Other uses for REG files include the following:

- Export the entire contents of the Registry to a REG file and then replace the entire contents of the Registry with that REG file.

- Export all or portions of the Registry before and after running a program that makes a change to the Registry. Then, compare each version in a text comparison utility so that you can discover how the program changes the Registry.

Q&A

Q Can I use a REG file exported from one version of Windows in any other version of Windows?

A Well, the Registry Editor in each version of Windows certainly enables you to do this. Doing so isn't a very good idea, however, because each version of Windows has a different Registry—and each is incompatible with the other.

Q The real mode Registry Editor's command-line options seem a bit too complex. Are there any alternatives?

A Yes. The *Windows 98 Resource Kit*, published by Microsoft Press, provides a handful of real mode utilities that make short work of editing the Registry from the MS-DOS command prompt.

Workshop

The following quiz will enhance your understanding of the topics discussed in this hour.

Quiz

1. True or false? You can replace the contents of the Registry with a REG file using the Windows-based Registry Editor.

2. Assume you're importing a REG file containing a key called MyKey. What happens if MyKey contains a value called MyValue in the Registry, but MyKey in the REG file doesn't exist?

   a. Nothing.

   b. MyValue is removed from the Registry.

   c. MyValue is flagged for removal.

   d. MyValue's datatype is changed to DWORD.

3. Which of the following must always begin a REG file?

   a. REGEDIT followed by a blank line

   b. REGEDIT4 followed by two blank lines

   c. REGEDIT4 followed by a blank line

   d. REGEDT4 followed by a blank line

5

4. Which of the following command-line options replaces the Registry with the contents of a REG file?

    a. /c

    b. /e

    c. /d

Answers to Quiz Questions

1. False

   The real mode Registry Editor is the only version that's capable of replacing the Registry with the contents of a REG file because the Registry is in use while Windows is running.

2. a

   Importing a REG file only replaces or adds keys to the Registry; this action does not remove keys and values that are present in the Registry but absent from the REG file.

3. c

   All REG files begin with REGEDIT4 followed by a single blank line.

4. a

   The /c command line option replaces the Registry with the contents of the REG file specified on the command line.

HOUR **6**

Reducing the Size of the Registry

Over time, the Registry ends up with a lot of wasted space. As programs remove keys from the Registry, the operating system doesn't automatically reclaim that space. You need to periodically reclaim all that unused space. Doing so doesn't make the Registry work any faster, but it does recover a good amount of disk space.

In this brief hour, you're going to learn the following:

- How to optimize the Registry, and reclaim all that unused space.
- How to optimize the disk so that all the parts of the Registry are stored contiguously, a process that does indeed make the Registry faster.

Compressing the Registry

Registry Checker, only available in Windows 98, has an undocumented feature that enables you to optimize the Registry. Registry Checker compresses the Registry whenever it detects that it has more than 500KB of dead space, making the file smaller and slightly faster to access. To get an idea of the amount of space you can save by compressing the Registry, take a look at the following table. In this example, doing so compressed more than 100KB out of System.dat but didn't save any space in User.dat. Your results might vary, depending on the amount of unused space in each file.

File	Before	After
System.dat	1,740,832	1,630,240
User.dat	221,216	221,216

You can force Registry Checker to optimize the Registry using the /opt command line option. This works only with the DOS-based version of Registry Checker, SCANREG. Remember also that you can't run the DOS-based version in Windows, so you must boot the computer to MS-DOS mode. Use the following steps to optimize the Registry:

1. Start the computer in MS-DOS mode. To do so, choose Command Prompt Only from the boot menu, or choose Start, Shut Down. Then select Restart in MS-DOS mode and click OK.

2. Type scanreg /opt at the command prompt. SCANREG runs but doesn't report its progress; it just exits to the command prompt.

Optimizing the Registry for Performance and Space

With Windows 95, compressing the Registry was a formidable task that involved the following steps:

1. Exporting the Registry to a REG file.

2. Importing the Registry using the /c switch, which caused the Registry Editor to replace the entire contents of the Registry with the contents of the REG file you exported in step 1.

Windows 98 provides an alternative, however: Registry Checker. You learned how to compress the Registry using the Registry Checker earlier in this hour. You can also use Norton Optimization Wizard in Windows 95 and Windows 98, which does a better job of compressing the Registry than the Registry Checker does. The following instructions pertain to Norton Utilities 3.0:

1. Launch Norton Optimization Wizard. Choose Start, Programs, Norton Utilities, Norton Optimization Wizard.

2. Skip to the Optimize Your Registry page of the wizard. Select Optimize my Registry and click Next.

3. Click Reboot. Norton Optimization Wizard optimizes the Registry and restarts Windows. Make sure that you don't have any applications open on the desktop when you click Reboot.

> Size Doesn't Matter. Compressing the Registry so that the files are smaller doesn't improve Windows's performance appreciably. The only real benefit of compressing the Registry is that backing up the Registry is quicker, and requires less space.

Defragmenting the Disk

In an ideal world, every portion of every file would be stored on the hard disk contiguously. *Fragmentation* occurs when the file system can't find a contiguous area on the disk in which to store the entire file, so it puts a portion of the file in one location, another portion in another location, and so on. The *file allocation table* (FAT) helps the file system put the file back together again by indicating the series of *clusters,* in order, that contain all the file's pieces.

Fragmentation adversely affects the Registry. The Registry is big, and it is one of the most-used files on the hard disk. Given that the operating system relies on it so heavily, you'll notice a performance penalty if the Registry becomes severely fragmented.

Windows includes a utility called Disk Defragmenter to defragment files on the hard disk. It doesn't defragment system files, however, so it skips the Registry. Windows doesn't enable you to remove the system attribute from these files, either, or you could do so before running Disk Defragmenter. Norton Speed Disk (see Figure 6.1) does optimize the Registry, though, as well as the Windows swap file. You launch it by choosing Start, Programs, Norton Utilities, Speed Disk. You can customize Speed Disk by clicking Properties and then choosing Options.

6

Figure 6.1

*Norton Speed Disk
defragments the space
occupied by the
Registry; Windows's
Disk Defragmenter
does not.*

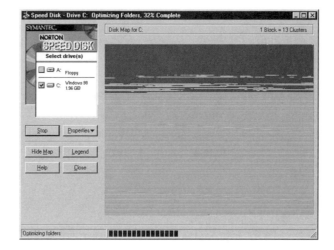

Removing File Types You Don't Use

Windows installs a large number of file types that most users never use. Removing
unused file types doesn't save a lot of space in the Registry, but it *does* tidy things up a
bit and help make navigating HKEY_CLASSES_ROOT a bit easier. The best way to remove
unused file types from the Registry is to use the Folder Options dialog box in Windows
Explorer:

1. Choose View, Folder Options. You see the Folder Options dialog box.
2. Click the File Types tab to see a list of registered file types.
3. Remove each file type that you no longer require. Do so by highlighting the file
   type in the list and clicking Remove. The File type details area describes the file
   type so that you can figure out which program opens it.
4. Confirm that you want to remove the file type.

If you have a number of file types that refer to programs that you removed from the computer, you have orphans in the Registry. The next section describes how to remove
orphaned Registry keys in a more or less automatic manner.

Removing Orphans from the Registry

Orphans are Registry keys that point to nonexistent files or other nonexistent Registry
keys. They occur when programs don't clean up after themselves or when you manually
remove a program from the computer. Uninstall programs don't always remove all the
application's Registry settings, for instance, leaving values that point to missing files.

Vendors such as Microsoft think that they're doing you a favor by leaving these orphans; when you reinstall the program, it can use your previous configuration.

In most cases, nothing bad happens as a result of orphans; they just clutter up the Registry and waste a small bit of space. In other cases, orphans wreak havoc with your computer system:

- If a program leaves a key in `PropertySheetHandlers` that points to a missing DLL, the property sheet for that object might not work correctly.
- If a program leaves a reference to a device driver after removing the device driver from the disk, Windows reports an error when it starts.

REGCLEAN, which you learn about in Hour 22, "Fixing Errors in the Registry," can fix a small number of orphans related specifically to Windows and Microsoft Office, but it doesn't go as far as Norton WinDoctor. WinDoctor checks for orphans in all portions of the Registry, including `HKEY_CLASSES_ROOT`, `Application Paths`, `Run`, `VxD`, and much more. The best part is that Norton WinDoctor detects when an orphan points to a file or folder that you moved and fixes the value accordingly. Don't confuse WinDoctor with System Doctor. System Doctor monitors your computer in real time, whereas WinDoctor proactively probes your computer, looking for and fixing problems. Here's how to use it to repair orphans in the Registry:

1. Start Norton WinDoctor. Choose Start, Programs, Norton Utilities, Norton WinDoctor.
2. Choose Perform All Norton WinDoctor Tests (Recommended) and click Next.
3. Click Next after Norton WinDoctor finishes scanning for errors, and then click Finish. Norton WinDoctor displays a list of the errors it found, as shown in Figure 6.2.
4. Double-click each item in the list to repair it.

Norton WinDoctor doesn't remove orphans that point to removable drives or network volumes. It assumes that these files are temporarily unavailable but that they might be available again at a later time. If you want to remove these orphans, you must replace step 2 in the preceding instructions with the following: Choose Let me choose which tests to run, click Analysis Agents in the following window, and deselect Ignore missing files on removable drives and UNC paths.

6

FIGURE 6.2

Norton WinDoctor is the best utility for repairing the contents of the Registry and finding orphans.

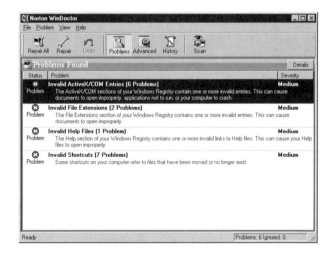

Summary

In Windows 98, you use the MS-DOS-based Registry Checker's /opt command line option to optimize the Registry, removing unused space. The command line looks like the following: scanreg /opt.

Windows 95 users can't rely on Registry Checker. They can export the entire contents of the Registry to a REG file, however, and then replace the Registry with that REG file by exporting it using the real-mode Registry Editor. They can also use Norton's Optimization Wizard, which automates the same process.

Defragmenting the disk is the only way to actually improve the Registry's performance. You can't use the Windows Defrag utility, however, because it won't defragment system files. You can use Norton Speed Disk to defragment the Registry.

Q&A

Q The Registry Checker's /opt command line option seems so useful, so why is it undocumented?

A The idea behind this command-line option is that Windows 98 can automatically use the option whenever it detects an overabundance of unused space, about 500KB, in the Registry. You don't have to wait for the Registry to become so bloated, however, before you optimize the Registry.

Q Why does System.dat usually have so much more unclaimed space than User.dat?

A Windows is always writing values to and removing values from HKEY_LOCAL_MACHINE. On the other hand, most per-user settings aren't removed after they're created in the Registry.

Q What do I do if I see an error message that says, Windows found an error in your system files and was unable to fix the problem. You will need to install Windows to a new directory.

A Don't panic. Although this error message can indicate a serious problem, make sure that you have enough disk space for Registry Checker to store a backup copy of your configuration. Registry Checker erroneously displays this message if it doesn't have enough disk space to create the CAB file containing your configuration backup, which is usually less than 5MB.

Workshop

The following quiz will enhance your understanding of the topics discussed in this hour.

Quiz

1. True or false? The Windows-based version of Registry Checker, SCANREGW, can optimize the Registry.

2. Which of the following optimization methods are the most similar?

    a. Exporting the Registry to a REG file, and then replacing the Registry with its contents.

    b. Using Registry Checker's /opt command line option.

    c. Using the Norton Optimization Wizard.

    d. Using Norton Speed Disk to optimize the Registry.

3. Which of the following are the preferred methods for removing orphan values from the Registry?

    a. Registry Checker

    b. Norton WinDoctor

    c. Norton Optimization Wizard

    d. REGCLEAN

6

Answers to Quiz Questions

1. False

   Only SCANREG can optimize the Registry; SCANREGW can't.

2. a is similar to c

   Norton Optimization Wizard exports the Registry to a REG file, restarts the computer to MS-DOS, and then replaces the Registry with the contents of the REG file.

3. b

   Norton WinDoctor is the most thorough utility for removing orphaned values from the Registry.

Hour 7

Taking the Necessary Precautions

Windows is hot. Therefore, the amount of information and programs that
becomes available each day is staggering. If you don't want to wait for the
next Windows super book or next month's magazine (they're three months
out of date anyway), you have to go online to get that information. You can
get a lot of it through commercial online services such as CompuServe,
America Online, or The Microsoft Network. However, you'll find more variety, and potentially more useful information, on the Internet. More specifically, look at

- Mailing lists
- UseNet Newsgroups
- World Wide Web

That's where this hour comes in. It points you to some of the best resources
on the Internet for Windows information, help, and programs. Keep in mind
that there are hundreds of Internet sites for each site that you find in this
hour. Most of them aren't included here because they contain nothing more

than links to the other sites. The result is an empty Web of Windows pages, all linked together, that contain nothing but useless links.

Mailing Lists

The Windows 98 Give-and-Take List (WIN98-L) is one of the only collaborative mailing lists for Windows 98. As such, it's very popular. You can subscribe to this list by sending a message to `listserv@peach.ease.lsoft.com` with the text SUBSCRIBE WIN98-L in the body of the message. If the traffic on this list becomes too much for your inbox, subscribe to the digest version, which sends you one or two messages a day containing all the posts to that point. To subscribe to the digest version of WIN98-L, send a message to `listserv@peach.ease.lsoft.com` with the text SET WIN98-L DIGEST in the body of the message. Do this after subscribing to the list.

> The Windows 95 Give-and-Take List is still active and has four times more subscribers than the Windows 98 Give-and-Take List. You're more likely to get your questions answered on the Windows 95 list until more people move to the Windows 98 list. To use the Windows 95 list, replace WIN98-L with WIN95-L in all the instructions you see in this section. To subscribe to the Windows 95 list, for example, send a message containing the text SUBSCRIBE WIN95-L to `listserv@peach.ease.lsoft.com`.

Windows Magazine maintains a number of useful mailing lists, none of which are collaborative. They are more like newsletters. Open `http://winweb.winmag.com/listserv`, and choose between any of the following lists to which you can subscribe on the Web site:

- **LangaList**—This periodic list strives to keep you informed of what Fred Langa is up to, including his columns and his independent ventures.
- **New Products**—A weekly email describing three of the hottest products for that week.
- **Tip of the Day**—Mails you hints and tips Monday through Friday. Many of these tips are rather simple, though, so this list might irritate you.
- **Win Letter**—*Windows* magazine describes this list as containing "inside information, undocumented tips, secret shortcuts, cool trivia…directly from *Windows* magazine Editor Mike Elgan."
- **Windows 98**—A regular email containing tips and information about Windows 98.

- **WinList**—Mails you a list of *Windows* magazine's favorite hardware and software once a month.
- **Windows Magazine Online Update**—A daily email describing the news and features that you'll find on the *Windows* magazine Web site that day.

Microsoft also offers a number of valuable mailing lists. These are not give-and-take lists; they're more like newsletters that keep you up-to-date on Microsoft technologies. You subscribe to them from Microsoft's homepage. Go to `http://www.microsoft.com`, and click Free Newsletters to go to Microsoft's Personal Information Center. Follow the onscreen instructions to subscribe to any of the following lists:

- **MSDNFlash**—A biweekly newsletter for developers.
- **Windows Technology News**—A biweekly newsletter for technical professionals responsible for deploying and supporting Windows products.
- **BackOffice News**—A weekly newsletter about Microsoft BackOffice.
- **Exploring Windows**—A biweekly newsletter for home and business users that contains tips and tricks.
- **Insider's Update**—A monthly newsletter that contains inside information about Microsoft's products.
- **Microsoft: This Week!**—A weekly newsletter that contains general information about Microsoft.
- **Microsoft Technical Support Alerts—Developer Products**—Posted as needed, this newsletter informs you of support alerts for Microsoft's developer products.
- **Microsoft Technical Support Alerts—BackOffice**—Posted as needed, this newsletter informs you of support alerts for Microsoft BackOffice.
- **Microsoft Technical Support Alerts—Windows**—Posted as needed, this newsletter informs you of support alerts for the Windows family of products.
- **MCP News Flash**—A bimonthly newsletter with announcements and schedule updates regarding Microsoft's certification program.
- **Training and Certification News**—A monthly newsletter containing information about the latest training and certification programs at Microsoft.

The list of newsletters that Microsoft offers changes on a regular basis. Visit the Personal Information Center regularly to see what newsletters are available.

7

Usenet Newsgroups

Usenet newsgroups are bulletin boards on the Internet. People from all over the world post messages to these newsgroups for other people to read. You use a newsreader, such as Outlook Express, to read messages on the newsgroups and to post your own messages.

Because there are a variety of newsgroups for Windows 98, you can rely on the newsgroups for peer support. You can post a question and receive an answer in short order. You can also search Usenet to see if someone has already answered your question. Look in each of the following hierarchies for additional Windows 98 newsgroups:

- `alt.windows95`
- `comp.os.ms-windows.`
- `microsoft.public.inetexplorer.`
- `microsoft.public.win98.`
- `microsoft.public.win32.`

A handful of Usenet newsgroups tend to contain the lion's share of Registry discussions. These groups include the following:

- `alt.windows95`
- `microsoft.public.win95.general.discussion`
- `symantec.support.win95.nortonutilities.general`
- `microsoft.public.win98.pre-release`

Often, the most valuable information about Windows 98 comes from other users, rather than from the support lines at companies such as Microsoft. In fact, you can bet that in most cases someone has already answered your question; you just have to find that answer.

How? Use DejaNews.

DejaNews is a free Web site that works much like Yahoo! or Infoseek. You can use it to search Usenet for messages containing keywords that you specify. Go to `http://www.dejanews.com`, type keywords in the space provided, and click Find. DejaNews displays a list of articles that match your query. Subject lines that begin with `RE:` are the best messages to view because they contain replies to questions.

You can also use DejaNews to locate newsgroups in which people discuss a particular topic. Open DejaNews and click Interest Finder. In the space provided, type keywords describing the topic, and then click Find. DejaNews displays a list of matching newsgroups, sorted top to bottom by relevance.

Don't ever underestimate the value of this resource. Any time I have a problem with Windows, the first place I search is DejaNews. I get real-world solutions that are frequently better than those given by Microsoft's online support—and I can almost always get solutions to problems that I never find at Microsoft's site.

World Wide Web

The explosive growth of Windows-related Web pages is evident if you search for the keyword *Windows* using one of the many available Web search tools. You can find thousands of Web pages dedicated to Windows, some from corporations such as Microsoft and Symantec. Many more are published by individuals who want to make their mark on the world by sharing what they know about Windows. One caveat, however, is that the vast majority of these sites are worthless; you must sift through the dirt to find gold. The remainder of this hour helps you do that by recommending some of the best Windows-related Web sites on the Internet.

> Visit my Web site at `http://www.honeycutt.com`. It contains white papers, information about my other books, and more.

By the time you get this book, plenty of new sites will have sprung up, and you can find them using the search string *Windows 98* with one of the following search tools:

AltaVista	`http://www.altavista.digital.com`
Excite	`http://www.excite.com`
Infoseek	`http://www.infoseek.com`
Lycos	`http://www.lycos.com`
Yahoo!	`http://www.yahoo.com`

Aside from using the search term *Windows 98,* you can use more specific keywords to find Registry-related sites. Try using the keywords *Windows 98 Registry,* for instance. You can also search using keywords that you'd expect to find on a Web page about the Registry: `HKEY_LOCAL_MACHINE`, `HKLM`, `HKCU`, `value entry`, `subkey`, `DWORD`, and so on.

7

www.cmpnet.com

CMP is a large publisher that is responsible for dozens of magazines. To their credit, they publish *BYTE, LAN Times, Windows* magazine, and more. You can find links to each magazine and a number of related Web sites at the bottom of CMP's home page. You can also find a large site dedicated to Windows 98 at `http://cmpnet.com/win98`. This site includes information about the new user interface, upgrading, and more.

www.cnet.com

CNET is a leader on the Web. They have sites for everything imaginable, including a download site, an online software store, a news site, and so on. Within CNET's site, you'll find a list of the most frequently asked questions about Windows 98. The URL for this site is `http://www.cnet.com/Content/Features/Techno/Win98`. Following are some examples of the questions you'll find:

- What's new in Windows 98?
- Can it run all my software?
- Can it run faster than Windows 95?
- Should I upgrade to Windows NT instead?
- Can I still use Netscape Navigator?
- Can I uninstall Internet Explorer?
- What comes after Windows 98?

www.worldowindows.com

Frank Condron provides a Windows 98 site that's even better than its predecessor. It includes information about software updates, tips, and more. The most useful aspect of this site is the list of updated drivers. Look here for device drivers before trying to find drivers at the manufacturer's Web site.

www.creativelement.com

As the name "Windows 98 Annoyances" implies, this site is dedicated to all the annoying features in Windows 98. The authors of this site don't just gripe about them; they offer solutions. If you're having trouble with networking in Windows 98, for instance, you can find information that might help you. This Web site cuts to the core of some of the most irritating features in Windows 98. You can find the Windows 98-specific content at `http://www.creativelement.com/win98`.

www.hotfiles.com

The Ziff-Davis Software Library is the best collection of shareware and freeware on the Internet. It contains thousands of files that you can download and has a plethora of features that make finding and downloading files much easier. This site reviews and rates each of the programs so that you know exactly what you're getting before you start downloading.

www.imaginations.com

Hosted by Imaginations Web, this site contains the ubiquitous Registry FAQ, which contains the most frequently asked questions about the Windows Registry. It's at `http://www.imaginations.com/regfaq`. Although there is nothing in this FAQ that you won't find in this book, it's a handy reference to keep around.

www.mcp.com

Macmillan's site contains information about all the books it publishes. It also offers online versions of the most popular titles and a number of resource centers that contain value-added information.

www.microsoft.com

Microsoft's Web site contains an amazing amount of information about its products, services, plans, job opportunities, and more. Not bad for a company that almost completely missed the Internet a few years back! You'll learn more about Microsoft's offerings later in this hour. You can find information specific to Windows 98 at `http://www.microsoft.com/windows/windows98`.

support.microsoft.com

You learn how to use Microsoft Online Support later in this hour. This is the authoritative place to look for solutions to problems you're having with Windows 98 or any other Microsoft product.

netpropensity.com

This Web site provides useful information about Windows 98—its features, shareware programs, and so on. This site also offers access to chat rooms, newsgroups, and mailing lists. You can find Windows 98-specific content at `http://netpropensity.com/windows98`.

7

www.windowscentral.com

WindowsCentral contains a plethora of Windows 98 information. It claims to have more than "10,000 pages of premium Windows information," containing news, tips, downloads, and much more. Click Features to see a valuable list of how-to articles, special reports, and editorial opinions by industry leaders. This Web site, in addition to the others published by My Desktop Network, promises to show real leadership on the Web.

www.winmag.com

Windows magazine provides more information about Windows 98 than even Microsoft does at this point. `http://www.winmag.com/win98` provides numerous customization tips, news, white papers, and other bits of technical information. Click Inside Windows 98 to learn about the new features in Windows 98. Of all the Web sites dedicated to Windows 98, this is one of my favorites.

www.zdnet.com

Ziff-Davis provides reviews, tips, and other resources for Windows 98 users. The best part of this site is that it has very useful articles about using and abusing the operating system. For example, it has several articles that help you determine whether you need to upgrade to Windows 98. The Windows 98-specific content is buried at `http://www.zdnet.com/products/windows/98.html`. This site also offers several newsletters for Windows users.

Microsoft Support Online

Microsoft's Support Online contains thousands of articles that provide information about a specific problem. Support Online was called the Knowledge Base in its previous incarnation. Each article describes a problem's symptoms, causes, resolution, and—sometimes—status. For example, you might learn that the reason your desktop redraws so slowly is because the video driver has a bug that you can repair by changing a setting in the Registry.

Go to `http://support.microsoft.com` to find Microsoft's Support Online. Select a product from My search is about, type keywords that describe the problem in My question is, and click Find. Support Online returns a list of articles that match your query.

> In Windows 98, you can also access Support Online by choosing Start, Settings, Windows Update. Then click Technical Support.

Microsoft TechNet

Microsoft TechNet is a resource for professionals who are in a position to support Microsoft products such as Windows 98 and NT. It's a CD-ROM that Microsoft distributes to subscribers on a monthly basis. It contains information you need to plan your projects, execute your plans, and solve problems. Here's what you'll find on the CD-ROM:

- Technical information, such as product evaluations and implementation guides
- The Microsoft Knowledge Base, which contains answers to more than 50,000 technical questions
- Microsoft Resource Kits for products such as Windows, Microsoft Office, and Microsoft Mail
- Conference notes taken from trade shows such as Tech-Ed and DevCon
- Updated drivers and patches, which contain the latest files in the Microsoft Software Library

To subscribe to Microsoft TechNet, call (800) 344-2121. The cost is $299 for a single user and $39.95 for each additional user. You can get a server-unlimited user license for $699.

Microsoft Developer Network

Microsoft Developer Network (MSDN) is similar to TechNet, except that it's for Windows developers. Like TechNet, you subscribe to MSDN to receive quarterly updates. Unlike TechNet, MSDN has different subscriptions, depending on how many goodies you need (and can afford):

- **Library**—The Library subscription gets you the Development Library, which is a CD-ROM that contains more than 1.5GB of documentation, articles, samples, and the Developer Knowledge Database. You also get the Developer Network News and a discount on Microsoft Press books. It costs $199 per year.
- **Professional**—The Professional subscription gets you everything in the Library subscription, as well as the Development Platform, which is a set of CD-ROMs that contain all the software development and device driver kits, Windows and Windows NT Workstation operating systems, and premium shipments of important system releases. The professional subscription is $499 per year.

7

- **Enterprise**—The Enterprise subscription gets you everything in the Professional subscription, plus the BackOffice Test Platform, which contains the latest server components of Microsoft BackOffice. The enterprise subscription is $1,499 per year.

- **Universal**—The Universal subscription is the ultimate subscription level. It contains everything in the Enterprise level, as well as all the Microsoft Visual Tools (Visual Basic and Visual C++, for example), Microsoft Office products, and upcoming development tools. The Universal subscription costs $2,499 per year.

> Microsoft publishes a free version of the Developer Library Online. You register to use the MSDN Online Library at http://www.microsoft.com/msdn; follow the onscreen instructions. After you've registered, you can proceed directly to the Developer Library Online by going to http://premium.microsoft.com/msdn/library.

You can subscribe to the Microsoft Developer Network by calling (800) 759-5474. Note that if you already subscribe to one of the subscription levels, Microsoft offers a reasonable upgrade fee to one of the higher levels.

Microsoft FastTips

Microsoft FastTips is a free, automated service that you can use to get answers to some of the more common problems that Microsoft has recorded. You call FastTips, provide your fax number, and order an item, and FastTips faxes you the article. Call the number listed in Table 7.1 that most closely matches the type of information you need.

TABLE 7.1 FastTips 800 Numbers

Type of Information You Need	Number to Call
Desktop applications	(800) 936-4100
Personal operating systems	(800) 936-4200
Development tools and products	(800) 936-4300
Business systems	(800) 936-4400

> Get a FastTips Map before you use this service so that you can more easily find your way around. Call one of the numbers listed in Table 7.1, and then follow the prompts until you're offered a FastTips map.

Microsoft Windows 98 Readme Files

The Windows 98 CD-ROM comes with a number of text files that contain additional information about Windows 98. The Windows 95 CD-ROM contains comparable text files. Instead of a Readme.txt file, you find several text files in \Windows that cover specific topics, as shown in Table 7.2:

TABLE 7.2 FILES AND THEIR TOPICS

Filename	Topics
Cdaccess.txt	Generic CD-ROM driver
Config.txt	Config.sys file
Display.txt	Display and monitor settings
Exchange.txt	Microsoft Exchange
Extra.txt	Various information and tips
Faq.txt	Frequently asked questions
General.txt	General issues, known bugs, and so on
Hardware.txt	Hardware compatibility
Ie4.txt	Internet Explorer 4.0
Infrared.txt	Windows 98's infrared support
Internet.txt	Internet Explorer 4.0
Javadbg.txt	Debugging information for Java
License.txt	End-user license agreement
Mouse.txt	Mouse and keyboard information
Msdosdrv.txt	MS-DOS device drivers
Msimn.txt	Microsoft Outlook Express
Msn.txt	Microsoft Network
Msnver.txt	Microsoft Network version information
Netmeet.txt	NetMeeting
Network.txt	Windows 98 networking support
Printers.txt	Printer information
Pws.txt	Personal Web Server
Relnotes.doc	Windows 98 release notes
Services.txt	Online services provided in Windows 98
Setup.txt	Windows 98 Setup

7

continues

TABLE 7.2   CONTINUED

Filename	Topics
Support.txt	Product support information
Testps.txt	PostScript test file
Tips.txt	Tips and tricks for Windows 98

Microsoft Downloadable Files

Microsoft provides a list of download sites at `http://support.microsoft.com/support/downloads`. Each of the following sites contains updated drivers, software updates, and additional free downloads:

- BackOffice
- Desktop Publishing
- Development Tools
- Games and Kids' Products
- Microsoft Hardware
- Microsoft Internet Explorer
- Microsoft Office
- Microsoft Windows
- Microsoft Works
- MS-DOS
- Online Products and Services
- Personal Finance
- Reference and Research
- Service Packs
- Windows NT Server and Workstation
- Additional Downloads

Microsoft Support

Microsoft offers a variety of support services that are provided by a staff of engineers, consultants, and other professionals, as shown in Table 7.3:

TABLE 7.3   MICROSOFT SUPPORT SERVICES

Service	Phone Number	Description
Consulting	(800) 426-9400	Microsoft consultants who help you design and implement business systems.
Solution Provider	(800) 765-7768	Independent certified consultants who help you with implementation and maintenance.
Product Support	(206) 637-7098	Free technical support for the first 90 days of using Windows 98. $2 per minute with a $25 limit after that. The time period begins with your first call.

 Support.txt in \Windows contains a full list of Microsoft support resources, including contact information, pricing, and so on.

Summary

Learning the Registry is difficult enough, but you can make it easier if you use the Internet's resources wisely. The best Web site for you to become comfortable with is Microsoft Online Support. This Web site answers most users' questions and describes how to solve a variety of problems, many of which have solutions that are rooted in the Registry.

Q&A

Q Where can I go to discuss the Registry with other users?

A Check my Web site at http://www.honeycutt.com. You'll find a mailing list dedicated to the Registry, and you can sign up by filling in a simple form.

Q How do I find other Web sites dedicated to the Registry?

A Use one of the popular search engines. http://www.infoseek.com and http://www.yahoo.com are examples. Use keywords such as *Registry* and *Windows*. You can find Registry related sites that provide good details by searching for actual root key names: HKEY_LOCAL_MACHINE or HKLM, for example. If you're searching for a Registry solution to a specific problem, be sure to include a few keywords that describe the problem. For example, if you think that the Registry can help you fix a problem with a video adapter, try using the keywords *registry*, *video adapter*, and HKEY_LOCAL_MACHINE.

7

Workshop

The following quiz will enhance your understanding of the topics discussed in this hour.

Quiz

1. Which of the following online resources cannot help you immediately solve problems in Windows?

    a. `http://support.microsoft.com`

    b. `http://www.support.com`

    c. `http://www.dejanews.com`

2. Which of the following is my Web site?

    a. `http://www.writer.com`

    b. `http://www.jerryhoneycutt.com`

    c. `http://www.honeycutt.com`

3. If all else fails, which of the following options do you use to find help with the Registry?

    a. Toss the computer out of the window.

    b. Remove Windows and use another operating system.

    c. Content me at `jerry@honeycutt.com`.

Answers to Quiz Questions

1. b

   I have no comment about `http://www.support.com`, and you must visit this Web site to understand why.

2. c

   Visit this Web site to learn more.

3. c

Please don't throw the computer out the window. Do feel free to content me with your questions about the Registry. I might not always be able to answer your questions, but I do guarantee a reply.

7

PART III

Using Third-Party Registry Programs

Hour

HOUR **8**

Using Microsoft's Tweak UI

According to Brian Livingston in the November 6, 1995, issue of *InfoWorld* magazine, "Tweak UI gives you control over a fistful of Win95 user-interface options that previously required messy editing of your Registry database." Likewise, Edward Mendelson said in the May 14, 1996, issue of *PC Magazine*, "Microsoft Corp.'s Power Toys make Windows 95 more convenient, customizable, and powerful than you ever imagined—and won't cost you anything except for the connect time to download them from the company's Web site."

The Tweak UI utility supports a large number of the customizations that you learn about in Hours 14–16, which means that you can get the same benefits from these customizations without risking human error in the Registry. Tweak UI isn't the only program that does this for you, however. You learn about many more customization programs in Hour 9, "Trying Other Registry Programs."

In this hour, you learn about the following topics:

- Installing Tweak UI and Power Toys
- Checking for a newer version of Tweak UI
- Using Tweak UI to customize your computer

Installing Tweak UI

Prior to Windows 98, Tweak UI was a free, unsupported utility from Microsoft that was part of Power Toys, a collection of must-have utilities for power users. You had to download it from Microsoft's Web site because it didn't come with Windows 95. You can still download the Windows 95 version, a process you'll learn about later in this hour. Microsoft updated Tweak UI for Windows 98, though, and included it on the CD-ROM. To install Tweak UI, right-click Tweakui.inf in the \Tools\Reskit\Powertoy folder of the CD-ROM, and choose Install. Windows 98 copies the required files to the computer and displays online help with an overview of how to use Tweak UI. Close the help document to finish installing Tweak UI.

Tweakui.inf describes the values that Windows 98 writes to the Registry. These values include uninstall information so that you can easily remove Tweak UI using the Add/Remove Programs Properties dialog box. This INF file also describes the files that Windows 98 copies to the computer:

- Tweakui.cpl is a Control Panel extension that Windows 98 copies to \Windows\System.
- Tweakui.hlp and Tweakui.cnt are help files that Windows 98 copies to \Windows\Help.

Checking for Newer Versions of Tweak UI

The current version of Tweak UI is 1.25, but Microsoft occasionally updates it. To find out which version of Tweak UI you're using, right-click Tweakui.cpl in \Windows\System, choose Properties, and click the Version tab; the file version number is at the top of the dialog box. Although you might find updates to Tweak UI using Windows Update, Microsoft's download site is always a sure thing: http://www.microsoft.com/windows/downloads. Select Windows 98 (select Windows 95 for the other version) from the first drop-down list, select Power Toys & Kernel Toys from the second list, and then click Go. If the version that is available at the Web site is a later version than the one you're using, download and install it. You can also compare the modification date given at the Web site with the modification date of Tweakui.cpl in \Windows\System.

You can download Tweak UI by itself, or you can download it as part of Microsoft Power Toys. Power Toys is a must-have collection of utilities for Windows 95; however, their value is questionable in Windows 98. Here are some of its tools:

- **CabView**—Enables you to view and extract the contents of CAB files. This utility is no longer required in Windows 98, however, because Windows 98 includes this feature. Open a CAB file in Windows Explorer by right-clicking it and choosing View.

- **CD AutoPlay Extender**—Enables you to control the Windows AutoPlay feature. It enables you to configure a CD-ROM to start automatically even though the disk doesn't have an Autorun.inf file.

- **FlexiCD**—Enables you to control musical CD-ROMs from the Windows status area, located on the right side of the taskbar.

- **QuickRes**—Enables you to change screen resolution and color depth via an icon on the status area. This utility isn't useful in Windows 98, however, because Windows 98 includes this feature. You can configure it using the Display Properties dialog box.

- **Round Clock**—Uses a good old-fashioned round clock that looks similar to the old analog windup clocks.

- **Telephone Location Selector**—A must for road warriors. It enables you choose your dialing location from the status area.

- **Xmouse 1.2**—Enables you to bring a window to the foreground by moving your mouse over it. This utility isn't useful in Windows 98 because Windows 98 includes a Registry setting that enables you to configure the same functionality. These settings are now available in the Windows 98 version of Tweak UI.

- **Command Prompt Here 1.1**—When you right-click any folder and choose DOS Prompt Here, Windows opens an MS-DOS window with that folder set as the current working directory. You don't have to have Power Toys to set this up, however, as you will learn in Hour 15, "Menus and Windows."

- **Contents Menu**—Displays the entire contents of a folder as a submenu of its shortcut menu.

- **Desktop Menu**—Displays the entire contents of the desktop as a submenu that you pop up from the Windows 98 status area, which is on the taskbar.

- **Explore from Here**—If you right-click any folder and choose Explore from Here, Windows 98 opens a new Explorer window with that folder at the top, as described in Hour 15.

- **Find X 1.2**—Uses a number of extensions to the Start menu's Find submenu.

- **Send to X 1.2**—Right-click any file or folder, choose Send To, and choose from a variety of new locations where you can send that object. The two most useful locations include Any Folder, which enables you to browse for a folder, and Clipboard as Name, which sends the name of the file or folder to the Clipboard.

- **Shortcut Target Menu 1.2**—Enables you to open the shortcut menu of a shortcut's target object without actually locating the target object on the computer. This is particularly useful for shortcuts on the desktop.

To obtain Power Toys, download it from `http://www.microsoft.com/windows/downloads`. Select Windows 98 (select Windows 95 for the other version) from the first drop-down list, select Power Toys & Kernel Toys from the second list, and then click Go. Download the file Powertoys.exe into an empty scratch folder. You must do this because it contains a large number of compressed files and you have to clean up the file droppings yourself. Decompress the file by launching it in Windows Explorer, making sure to launch it from within the scratch folder. Install each Power Toy individually by right-clicking its INF file and clicking Install.

If you're having trouble accessing Microsoft's Web site, you can download Tweak UI from just about any shareware site. For example, try `http://www.hotfiles.com`, which is a Ziff-Davis site, or `http://www.winfiles.com`.

Using Tweak UI to Customize Windows

The Windows 95 and Windows 98 versions of Tweak UI are different. The Windows 98 version has additional tabs and a few additional options on the preexisting tabs. This section describes how to use Tweak UI in Windows 98, but you can also follow these instructions for the Windows 95 version—just keep in mind that you won't see all these features in the Windows 95 version.

When you double-click the Tweak UI icon in the Control Panel, you see the window shown in Figure 8.1. Click one of the tabs to set options related to its name (click the left and right arrow buttons to scroll through the list of tabs). Here's a description of what you find on each tab:

- **Mouse**—Contains settings to adjust the mouse's sensitivity.

- **General**—Changes the behavior of individual windows, the location of special folders, and the default search engine used by Internet Explorer 4.0.

8

- **Explorer**—Changes the overlay displayed on the bottom-left corner of shortcuts, what happens when Windows starts, and various other settings, such as whether Windows remembers open Explorer windows and their positions between sessions.

- **IE4**—Changes a variety of advanced settings for customizing how Internet Explorer 4.0 looks and feels.

- **Desktop**—Adds or removes special icons to or from the desktop. You can also create special icons as a file, which enables you to put them on the Start menu—or anywhere else, for that matter.

- **My Computer**—Enables or disables specific drive letters in the My Computer folder.

- **Control Panel**—Enables or disables specific applets in the Control Panel folder.

- **Network**—Automatically logs on to the network without providing a username and password.

- **New**—Creates new templates that appear on the New menu when you right-click a folder and choose New.

- **Add/Remove**—Edits the list of programs that appear in the Add/Remove Programs Properties dialog box.

- **Boot**—Changes a variety of boot options that are defined in the Msdos.sys file.

- **Repair**—Fixes various aspects of the operating system, including desktop icons and the Fonts folder.

- **Paranoia**—Clears various history lists each time you log on to the computer, such as the Run MRU list, documents MRU list, and Find Files MRU list. This tab also provides a variety of methods for covering your tracks so that prying eyes can't see what you've been up to.

FIGURE 8.1

Tweak UI uses a tabbed dialog box similar to the other property sheets that you find in the Control Panel.

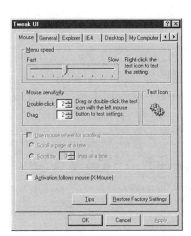

Click the Tips button on the Mouse tab to open Tweak UI's help. Also, you can restore the original factory settings for the Mouse, Explorer, and Boot tabs by clicking the Restore Factory Settings button on those tabs.

Customizing How the Mouse Works

You can change the Windows mouse settings on the Mouse tab of Tweak UI. This tab hasn't changed since the original version of Tweak UI that Microsoft provided for Windows 95. Note that all the values that you find on this tab are in HKEY_CURRENT_USER\Control Panel\Desktop; thus, any subkeys you learn about in this section start there.

Menu speed controls the span of time before a menu automatically follows the mouse pointer. Drag the slider to the left to make menus follow faster, or drag it to the right to make them follow slower. Right-click Test Icon to test this setting. Tweak UI writes this value to MenuShowDelay, a string value containing a delay time in milliseconds (400ms is the default).

Mouse sensitivity has two options. First, Double-click determines how close together two mouse clicks must be before Windows considers them a double-click. Drag determines how far the mouse pointer must move with the button held down before Windows recognizes that you're dragging an object. Both values are in pixels, but Tweak UI stores the first as half-pixels in the Registry. Tweak UI stores these values in the following string value entries:

- DoubleClickWidth
- DoubleClickHeight
- DragWidth
- DragHeight

Activation follows mouse (X-Mouse) prevents you from having to click a background window to bring it forward because windows automatically come forward as you move the mouse over them. Windows reads this value from UserPreferenceMask, which is a binary value whose bits indicate a variety of user preferences. For more information, see Hour 12, "HKEY_USERS/HKEY_CURRENT_USER."

Controlling the Behavior of Individual Windows

The General tab, shown in Figure 8.2, contains a variety of settings that control how Windows 98 looks and where it locates special shell folders. Effects contains a number of self-explanatory options that control how Windows 98 looks, all of which are checkboxes that you enable or disable:

- Window animation
- Smooth scrolling
- Beep on errors
- Menu animation
- Combo box animation
- List box animation
- Menu underlines
- X-mouse AutoRaise
- Mouse hot tracking effects
- Show Windows version on desktop

FIGURE 8.2

The middle portion of this tab enables you to relocate the Windows shell folders. You'll learn more about this in the next section.

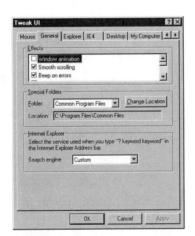

Look in HKEY_CURRENT_USER\Control Panel\Desktop for all the following values, which are set by the options that were listed previously:

- PaintDesktopVersion
- UserPreferenceMask
- SmoothScroll
- WindowMetrics\MinAnimate
- Sound\Beep

Specifying the Location of Special System Folders

You can change the location of special shell folders in the middle of the General tab. Select the name of the folder whose location you want to change from the Folder box. Then click Change Location, select a folder on the disk, and click OK. Tweak UI enables you to change the location of any shell folder defined in the `Software\Microsoft\Windows\CurrentVersion\Explorer\Shell Folders` branch of either `HKEY_LOCAL_MACHINE` or `HKEY_CURRENT_USER`. Following are some typical examples of the folders you find in this list:

Name	Default Location
Common Program Files	C:\Program Files\Common
Desktop	C:\Windows\Desktop
Document Templates	C:\Windows\ShellNew
Favorites	C:\Windows\Favorites
My Documents	C:\My Documents
Program Files	C:\Program Files
Programs	C:\Windows\Start Menu\Programs
Recent Documents	C:\Windows\Recent
Send To	C:\Windows\SendTo
Start Menu	C:\Windows\Start Menu
Startup	C:\Windows\Start Menu\Programs\Startup

 Changing the location of a shell folder using Tweak UI doesn't actually move the current shell folder—it just points Windows to a different folder for that purpose. You must move the contents of the original folder to the new one if you want to keep it.

Controlling the Appearance and Name of Shortcuts

Windows displays a small square icon in the bottom-left corner of each shortcut you create. This icon is called an *overlay*. When you create a shortcut to a document, for instance, Windows combines the original icon with the overlay so that you can readily identify it as a shortcut to the document rather than the document itself.

You can choose which icon Windows uses for that overlay, or even choose not to use an overlay at all. Open the Explorer tab of Tweak UI, shown in Figure 8.3, and select Arrow, Light arrow, None, or Custom. If you choose None, you can't distinguish between shortcuts and documents unless you open the icon's property sheet. If you choose Custom, Tweak UI displays a dialog box that you use to browse the computer for an icon that you want to use as the overlay. Note that Tweak UI changes the following values to reflect the setting you chose:

```
HKEY_LOCAL_MACHINE\Software\Microsoft\Windows\
➥CurrentVersion\explorer\Shell Icons
```

```
HKEY_CURRENT_USER\Software\Microsoft\Windows\
➥CurrentVersion\explorer\link
```

FIGURE 8.3

The icons on the right side of this tab show you how a shortcut looks after you change this setting.

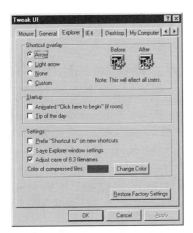

Aside from choosing an overlay to use for shortcuts, you can also prevent Windows from prefixing the words *Shortcut to* to each shortcut's filename. Disable Prefix "Shortcut to" on new shortcuts. You don't need to worry about duplicate filenames, by the way, because shortcuts use the LNK file extension and the original document keeps its own file extension.

Windows 95 was known to misbehave when you disabled the shortcut overlay. Although I haven't confirmed this problem in Windows 98, revert this setting to its original value if you start experiencing bizarre problems after changing it.

Specifying What Happens When Windows Starts

By default, each time you start Windows, it displays the tip of the day. You probably disabled this feature straightaway right after you installed Windows, however. The Explorer tab, shown earlier (in Figure 8.3), enables you to restore this setting if you did disable it. Select Tip of the day. Show in
`HKEY_CURRENT_USER\Software\Microsoft\Windows\CurrentVersion\explorer\Tips`
contains this setting.

Windows also displays a bouncing message on the taskbar each time it starts that says `Click here to begin` (if there is enough room on the taskbar). If this message annoys you, deselect Animated "Click here to begin" on the Explorer tab. Windows retrieves this setting from `NoStartBanner` in
`HKEY_CURRENT_USERS\Software\Microsoft\Windows\CurrentVersion\Policies\Explorer`.

Saving Open Windows and Locations Between Sessions

Windows remembers certain information about your desktop between sessions. Each time you start Windows, for example, it restores any Explorer windows that you left open when you shut it down. This includes single-pane folder windows and Internet Explorer. It also remembers the location of each Explorer window. Because every window has the same name, Windows remembers the position of each window in stacking order. In other words, it remembers the position of the first, second, and third Explorer windows.

To prevent Windows from saving these settings between sessions, disable Save Explorer window settings in the Explorer tab of Tweak UI (shown earlier in Figure 8.3). Tweak UI writes this setting to the Registry a value of
`HKEY_CURRENT_USER\Software\Microsoft\Windows\CurrentVersion\Policies\Explorer\` called `NoSaveSettings`.

One option is to arrange your Explorer windows just the way you want them, reboot, and then disable Save Explorer window settings in Tweak UI. A better option is to use a shareware product called EzDesk, which gives you complete control over your desktop's layout. You can download EzDesk from `http://members.aol.com/EzDesk95/index.html`.

Setting Advanced Options for Internet Explorer 4.0

On the IE4 tab, shown in Figure 8.4, Tweak UI contains a variety of settings that control the look and feel of Internet Explorer 4.0. These settings are self-explanatory:

- Active desktop enabled
- Add new documents to Documents on Start Menu
- Allow changes to Active Desktop
- Allow Logoff
- Clear document, run, typed-URL history on exit
- Detect accidental double-clicks
- IE4 enabled
- Show Documents on Start menu
- Show Favorites on Start menu

FIGURE 8.4

You can set all these values on the IE4 tab of Tweak UI in the System Policy Editor.

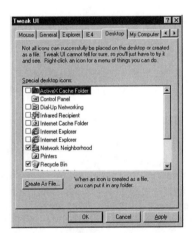

What's not self-explanatory is where in the Registry Windows stores these settings. All the value entries described in Table 8.1 are in the Registry under `HKEY_CURRENT_USER\Software\Microsoft\Windows\CurrentVersion\Policies\Explorer`.

TABLE 8.1 TWEAK UI SETTINGS IN THE REGISTRY

Setting	Registry Value
Active desktop enabled	`NoActiveDesktop`
Add new documents to Documents on Start menu	`NoRecentDocsHistory`
Allow changes to Active Desktop	`NoActiveDesktopChanges`
Allow Logoff	`NoLogoff`
Clear document, run, typed-URL history on exit	`ClearRecentDocsOnExit`
IE4 enabled	`ClassicShell`
Show Documents on Start menu	`NoRecentDocsMenu`
Show Favorites on Start menu	`NoFavoritesMenu`
Show Internet icon on desktop	`NoInternetIcon`

The one exception is Detect accidental double-clicks, which is found in `UseDoubleClickTimer` under `HKEY_CURRENT_USER\Software\Microsoft\Windows\CurrentVersion\Explorer\Advanced`.

ATTENTION: ADMINISTRATORS

A question I frequently receive from readers is how to lock down the Start menu as well as the desktop. Windows 95 didn't provide much help in removing some of the menu commands, such as Find and Documents, from the Start menu.

Windows 98 does contain Registry entries that enable you to control this menu, and you can set those values using Tweak UI. Better still, you can change those values for an individual user, a group of users, or a group of machines using the System Policy Editor, as described in Hour 21, "Controlling the Desktop via System Policies." In that hour, you'll learn how to distribute policies via both Microsoft and Novell networks that enable you to remove submenus from the Start menu and special icons from the desktop.

The best part is that it's not easy for a user to override your policies. Because Windows 98 enforces policies as the user logs on to the network, the user must be quite knowledgeable about Windows to circumvent these settings.

8

Controlling Which Shell Icons are on the Desktop

A typical desktop includes the My Computer, Recycle Bin, Network Neighborhood, and Internet Explorer icons—and possibly more. Although there is little you can do to remove the My Computer icon from the desktop (it's hard-coded into the operating system), Windows enables you to control the remaining icons.

Tweak UI is the simplest method for adding or removing shell icons to or from the desktop. The Desktop tab, shown in Figure 8.5, contains a list of all the icons you can put on the desktop. Some of the icons you see in this list are absolutely meaningless on the desktop—ActiveX Cache Folder, for example. The following icons *are* useful on the desktop, however, and you learn more about them in Hour 10, "HKEY_CLASSES_ROOT." You can remove any of the icons in the list from the desktop:

Name	Class Identifier
Control Panel	{21EC2020-3AEA-1069-A2DD-08002B30309D}
Dial-Up Networking	{992CFFA0-F557-101A-88EC-00DD010CCC48}
Internet Explorer	{871C5380-42A0-1069-A2EA-08002B30309D}
Recycle Bin	{645FF040-5081-101B-9F08-00AA002F954E}
Microsoft Outlook	{00020D75-0000-0000-C000-000000000046}
Network Neighborhood	{208D2C60-3AEA-1069-A2D7-08002B30309D}
Printers	{2227A280-3AEA-1069-A2DE-08002B30309D}
Scheduled Tasks	{D6277990-4C6A-11CF-8D87-00AA0060F5BF}

FIGURE 8.5

You can't add objects that don't have a checkmark next to their names to the desktop as an object.

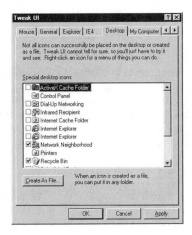

You can work with shell icons in two different ways:

- **As an object in the desktop's name space**—To add a shell icon to the desktop as an object, select the checkbox next to it. Deselect an icon's checkbox to remove the icon from the desktop. When you add an icon to the desktop's name space, you don't see a file in the \Windows\Desktop folder. Tweak UI adds the icon's class identifier to HKEY_LOCAL_MACHINE\Software\Microsoft\Windows\ CurrentVersion\explorer\Desktop\NameSpace instead.

- **As a file or folder located anywhere**—To add a shell icon to any folder on the computer, select the icon in the list and click Create As File. Select the folder in which you want to create the icon, and click Save. Note that Tweak UI creates files for some icons and folders for others. In particular, it creates the Control Panel and Printers icons as folders. To remove a shell icon as a file or folder, simply delete it within Windows Explorer.

When you try to remove Network Neighborhood using Tweak UI, you see a message that says Removing the Network Neighborhood from the desktop has additional consequences which are not obvious. In a nutshell, after removing the Network Neighborhood icon from the desktop, you can't use UNC paths, which look like \\Server\Resource, to access resources on the network. You'll have to map directly to those resources instead. Removing this icon also prevents Direct Cable Connection from displaying the contents of the host computer properly.

Enabling and Disabling Specific Drive Letters

Tweak UI enables you to easily disable specific drive letters in My Computer. Although this does prevent drives from showing up in My Computer or Windows Explorer, it doesn't prevent those same drives from showing up in the Save As and Open dialog boxes; therefore, don't look at this as a way to prevent users from copying files to a floppy disk. If that's your requirement, disable the floppy drive in the PC's BIOS.

To enable or disable specific drive letters, open Tweak UI's My Computer tab, shown in Figure 8.6. To disable a drive, deselect the checkmark next to it. To enable a drive, select the checkmark.

How Tweak UI stores these settings in the Registry deserves a brief explanation. Windows uses each bit of a 32-bit value to indicate whether a drive is enabled or disabled. The first bit corresponds to drive A, the second bit corresponds to B, and so on. Thus, in the binary value 1010, drives B and D are disabled because the second and fourth bits are 1. Note that Tweak UI stores this DWORD value as a binary value, so when you look at it in the Registry, you must reverse the order of the bytes. If you see 06 00 00 00 in the Registry, reverse the order of the bytes to 00 00 00 06. Then examine each bit to determine which drives are disabled. To find this value, look in `NoDrives` under `HKEY_CURRENT_USER\Software\Microsoft\Windows\CurrentVersion\Policies\Explorer`.

If binary values confuse you, Hour 12 has a sidebar called "Bit Masks for the Binary-Illiterate" that will show you how to convert binary to and from decimal notation.

FIGURE 8.6

The My Computer tab helps reduce clutter in the My Computer folder or in Windows Explorer, but don't rely on it as a security measure.

Enabling and Disabling Specific Control Panel Icons

Just like you can disable individual drive letters in My Computer, you can disable individual Control Panel icons. Open the Control Panel tab, shown in Figure 8.7. To enable a Control Panel icon, select the checkmark next to it. To disable an icon, deselect the checkmark next to it.

Do not rely on this as a security measure, however, because the user can easily restore the icon. When you disable a Control Panel icon, Tweak UI adds a line to the [don't load] section of Control.ini that disables the icon. It has the format `filename=no:` `main.cpl=no`, for example.

An alternative method of disabling a specific Control Panel icon is to simply remove its corresponding CPL file from \Windows\System.

FIGURE 8.7

Tweak UI shows you the filename and title of each icon.

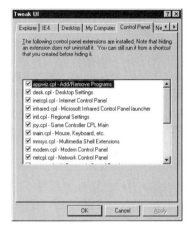

Logging on Automatically

If you aren't logging on to a network, or if you're logging on to a network where security isn't a concern, you can avoid typing your username and password every time you start Windows 98.

 Tweak UI doesn't encrypt your password when you use this feature. It's stored in the Registry as plain text that can be read by anyone.

Go to the Network tab of Tweak UI, shown in Figure 8.8, and select Log on automatically at system startup. Then type your username and password in the spaces provided. Tweak UI configures automatic logon in the Registry under
HKEY_LOCAL_MACHINE\Software\Microsoft\Windows\CurrentVersion\Winlogon:

- AutoAdminLogon contains a logical value that enables or disables this feature.
- DefaultPassword contains the readable text password that you typed in the Network tab.
- DefaultUserName contains the username that you provided.

FIGURE 8.8

Even though Tweak UI doesn't display your password in this dialog box, it doesn't encrypt your password in the Registry.

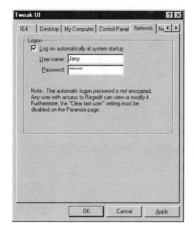

Adding New Templates to the New Menu

If you right-click any open area in a folder and choose New, you see a list of file types that you can create from a template. Rename the file, and open it in the associated program to edit it. Windows gets the items on the New menu from the Registry. It looks in HKEY_CLASSES_ROOT for any extension that contains a ShellNew subkey. When it finds one, it adds it to the New menu. Some ShellNew subkeys refer to an additional template file in \Windows\Templates that Windows uses to create the new file.

Tweak UI enables you to define additional templates that you'll see on the New menu. In every case, you create a template from a file that you build and drag it onto the New tab, shown in Figure 8.9. Tweak UI copies the file to \Windows\Templates and adds the ShellNew subkey to the file's extension under HKEY_CLASSES_ROOT.

FIGURE 8.9

Tweak UI enables you to permanently remove or temporarily hide file types from the New menu.

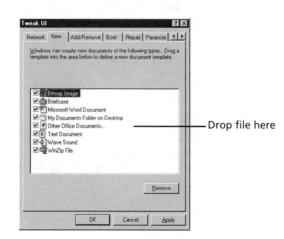

Drop file here

There are two ways to remove a type from the New menu:

- If you deselect the checkbox next to the file type, Tweak UI merely hides the file's ShellNew subkey so that it no longer appears on the menu. You can restore it by reselecting the checkbox.
- Select the file type and click Remove. This permanently removes the file type from the New menu and removes the type's ShellNew subkey.

Editing the Add/Remove Programs Properties List

Windows displays a list of programs that you can remove automatically in the Add/Remove Programs Properties dialog box. If you manually remove a program, the entry for that program still appears in the list. On the flip side, if an application has an uninstall program but it doesn't appear in the list, you can add it. Just remember that editing this list doesn't actually change the programs on your disk. In other words, removing an item from this list doesn't remove the program, just its uninstall information.

Open Tweak UI's Add/Remove tab, shown in Figure 8.10. Then you can carry out the following tasks:

- **To remove a program from the list**—Select the program you want to remove, and click Remove. Confirm the operation.
- **To add a program to the list**—Click New. Provide a description and the path to the uninstall program, and click OK to save your changes.
- **To change a program in the list**—Click Edit. Change the description and path, and click OK to save your changes.

FIGURE 8.10

Removing an item from this list doesn't remove the program from your computer.

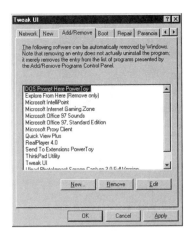

8

Windows stores uninstall information in the Registry at
`HKEY_LOCAL_MACHINE\Software\Microsoft\Windows\CurrentVersion\Uninstall`. For
each application, you'll find two values. `DisplayName` corresponds to what Tweak UI
calls Description. `UninstallString` corresponds to Command in Tweak UI.

> Removing an item from the Add/Remove Programs Properties dialog box is a
> decent way to keep users from removing programs. Although you can edit
> this list at the user's computer using Tweak UI, you're better off distributing
> an INF file (as described in Hour 18, "Scripting Changes to the Registry") or
> editing the user's Registry remotely (as described in Hour 19, "Enabling
> Remote Administration").

Setting Boot Options (Msdos.sys)

Msdos.sys, a text file that you find in the root folder of the boot disk, contains a number
of options that control how Windows starts. You can boot directly to an MS-DOS command prompt, for example, rather than to the Windows user interface.

The *Microsoft Windows 98 Resource Kit,* published by Microsoft Press, and the
Microsoft Windows 95 Resource Kit each contain a complete description of the options
that are available in Msdos.sys. However, Tweak UI enables you change many of these
options on the Boot tab, shown in Figure 8.11, as described here:

- **Function keys available**—Determines whether or not you can use keys such as F4
  and F8 to change how Windows starts.

- **Start GUI automatically**—Determines whether Windows starts to the MS-DOS
  command prompt or to the graphical user interface.

- **Display splash screen while booting**—Determines whether you see the Windows
  animated splash screen as the operating system boots.

- **Allow F4 to boot previous operating system**—Enables or disables the dual-boot
  capability. This must be enabled if you want to start the previous system.

- **Autorun Scandisk**—Determines whether Windows never runs Scandisk when it
  starts, runs Scandisk only after prompting the user, or always runs Scandisk when
  it starts.

- **Always show boot menu**—Enables you to make sure that Windows always displays the boot menu every time it starts. If you're not quick enough at pressing F8
  to display the boot menu, enable this option.

- **Continue booting after *xx* seconds**—Specifies the amount of time that must pass
  before Windows continues booting, accepting the default boot menu selection.

FIGURE 8.11

*If things get out of
hand, click Restore
Factory Settings to
return Msdos.sys to its
original condition.*

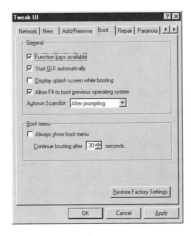

This Tweak UI tab doesn't affect the Registry at all. It writes all its changes to Msdos.sys
instead. To help you make sense out of the values it writes to this entry, Table 8.2
describes the items it changes.

TABLE 8.2 TWEAK UI SETTINGS IN THE REGISTRY

Tweak UI Setting	Msdos.sys Setting
Function keys available	BootKeys=
Start GUI automatically	BootGUI=
Display splash screen while booting	Logo=
Allow F4 to boot previous operating system	BootMulti=
Autorun Scandisk	AutoScan=
Always show boot menu	BootMenu=
Continue booting after *xx* seconds	BootMenuDelay=

Repairing Icons, System Files, and More

Tweak UI's Repair tab, shown in Figure 8.12, provides the capability to fix a variety of
common problems in Windows 98. Select the item that you want to repair from the drop-
down list, and click Repair Now. The following options are self-explanatory:

- Rebuild Icons
- Repair Associations

- Repair font Folder
- Repair Regedit
- Repair System Files
- Repair Temporary Internet Files
- Repair URL History

FIGURE 8.12

In the middle of this tab, Tweak UI provides a description of the repair option you've selected.

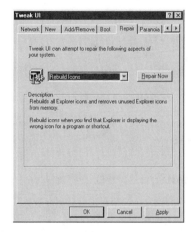

Keeping Your Activities Private

If you're uncomfortable with the fact that other people using your computer can come along and see everything you've been doing, you need to check out Tweak UI's Paranoia tab, shown in Figure 8.13. It provides a good measure of privacy by clearing Windows 98's MRU (Most Recently Used) lists each time the operating system starts. The options you see in the Covering Your Tracks list are self-explanatory:

- Clear Document history at logon
- Clear Find Computer history at logon
- Clear Find Files history at logon
- Clear Internet Explorer history at logon
- Clear Last User at logon
- Clear Network Connection history at logon
- Clear Run history at logon
- Clear Telnet history at logon

FIGURE 8.13

Tweak UI's Paranoia tab.

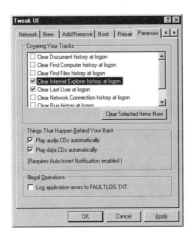

TweakUI implements these settings through the following three Registry keys:

- HKEY_LOCAL_MACHINE\Software\Microsoft\Windows\
  CurrentVersion\Winlogon\DontDisplayLastUserName

- HKEY_LOCAL_MACHINE\Software\Microsoft\Windows\
  CurrentVersion\Applets\TweakUI\1

- HKEY_CURRENT_USER\Software\Microsoft\Windows\
  CurrentVersion\Explorer\RecentDocs

This tab also keeps you from embarrassing yourself, thanks to Windows 98's AutoPlay feature. If you've ever had a game CD-ROM start automatically, blaring loud music to the entire office, you know what I'm talking about. Prevent audio CDs from starting automatically upon insertion by deselecting Play audio CDs automatically. Prevent CD-ROMs from starting automatically by deselecting Play data CDs automatically. Windows 98 retrieves these settings from HKEY_CLASSES_ROOT\AudioCD\Shell\(default) and HKEY_CURRENT_USER\Software\Microsoft\Windows\CurrentVersion\Policies\Explorer\NoDriveTypeAutorun.

Summary

Microsoft's Tweak UI is the ultimate program to use for customizing how Windows looks and works. Microsoft has two versions of this program, one for Windows 95 and one for Windows 98. You can download the Windows 95 version from Microsoft's Web

8

site, or any other shareware site; the Windows 98 version comes on the Windows 98 CD-ROM.

Q&A

Q Can I use the Windows 98 version of Tweak UI in Windows 95 or vice versa?

A No and, well, a half-hearted yes. Tweak UI checks to make sure that it's running in the appropriate operating system. Hour 16, "Other Customizations," does describe a method for concealing the operating system's true version, however, which allows the Windows 98 version of Tweak UI to run in Windows 95. Just keep in mind that Windows 95 doesn't support all the settings that the Windows 98 version of Tweak UI supports, and I haven't tested this scenario enough to warn you against any eminent dangers.

Q What are some alternative locations where I can download Tweak UI?

A The two best locations from which to download Tweak UI are `http://www.hotfiles.com` and `http://www.shareware.com`.

Workshop

The following quiz will enhance your understanding of the topics discussed in this hour.

Quiz

1. Which of the following best describes how to install Tweak UI after unzipping the files you downloaded?

    a. Run Setup.exe

    b. Right-click Tweakui.inf and choose Install.

    c. Run Install.exe

    d. Right-click Tweakui.inf and choose Setup.

2. True or false? Tweak UI is a safer method for implementation than the customizations you learn about in Hours 14–16.

3. True or false? Tweak UI is the best way to administer certain settings for computers on the network.

Answers to Quiz Questions

1. b

   Right-click Tweakui.inf and choose Install.

2. True

   Most certainly. Tweak UI removes the factor of human error from the task of editing the Registry.

3. False

   Tweak UI isn't the best method for administering users. It doesn't support remote administration, for one thing. It's a good way to experiment with the Registry, however. Then, you can implement those settings using remote administration.

Hour **9**

Trying Other Registry Programs

This hour describes some of the best programs outside of Windows that you can use to both edit the Registry and customize Windows. The first few sections describe what I consider the best-of-breed. The section "Other Registry Programs" provides an overview of more than a dozen additional shareware programs that you might want to evaluate. You can download them from the Web sites that are given with the descriptions.

Of all the Registry programs you can download, a serious power user needs three types: a good Registry editor, a good customization utility, and a good monitoring program. The best shareware Registry editor I've found is ShellWizard's Registry Editor. It's much better than the Windows Registry Editor and its features go beyond what the Norton Registry Editor provides. You'll learn more about it soon. The best customization utility, other than Tweak UI, is More Properties. It provides similar features to Tweak UI or any other customization utility, but uses those features better. By far the best program for monitoring Registry access is Regmon (Registry Monitor), which you'll also learn about in this hour.

The Windows NT and Windows Resource Kits contain additional Registry utilities that are worthwhile, particularly for the administrator. Many of the Registry programs in the Windows NT resource kit work with Windows.

More Properties

Following is some information on More Properties:

Cost:	Freeware
Vendor:	Imaginary Software
Address:	http://www.imaginary.co.za/mp20

More Properties is one of the most popular shareware customization utilities on the Internet. With more than 82,000 downloads and a four-star-out-of-five rating, you can't go wrong. This utility enables you perform the following tasks and more:

- Change Explorer's Save on exit settings.
- Change the colors used in Windows Help.
- Change the menu delay.
- Change the Recycle Bin.
- Clear the Run and Document histories at startup.
- Customize shell icons, including the Start button.
- Customize Tip of the day messages.
- Customize Windows Explorer's shortcut menus.
- Enable AutoRun for drive types other than CD-ROM.
- Enable or disable individual drives.
- Enable or disable smooth scrolling.
- Enable or disable window animation.
- Hide desktop icons, including Network Neighborhood.
- Optimize the Maximum Transmission Unit settings.
- Rename and relocate shell folders.
- Update the Windows license information.

Figure 9.1 shows More Properties open on the desktop. It looks more like the System Policy Editor than Tweak UI, but it has many of the same features that are found in Tweak UI. Click the tab containing the setting that you want to change, and expand the outline to expose the settings. Most settings have a checkbox that you enable or disable. Other settings have a small icon next to them indicating that, if you select the setting, you can edit its value at the bottom of the window.

FIGURE 9.1

More Properties looks a bit like the System Policy Editor.

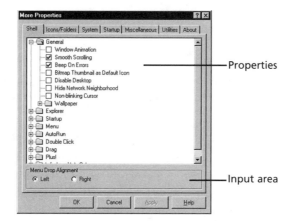

Properties

Input area

9

Follow the instructions that you find at the bottom of Imaginary Software's Web page to download and install More Properties. You can download two different installation files: full setup and lite setup. Use the full setup, which is 1.7MB, if you don't have the Visual Basic runtime libraries installed on your computer. Otherwise, download the 351KB lite setup, which doesn't include the runtime libraries.

Sometimes More Properties does not start or reports a missing DLL or other system file. More Properties requires several runtime files from Visual Basic. Windows 98 comes with all the files required to run More Properties. If you do have problems or are using Windows 95, however, make sure that the following files exist on your computer, and double-check to make sure that you're using the most recent version: Comctrl32.ocx, Mfc40.dll, Msvcrt40.dll, Olepro32.dll, Vb40032.dll, Ven2232.olb, Stdole2.tlb, Msvbvm50.dll, Msvcirt.dll, Msvcrt.dll, and Regsvr32.exe. You can download these files from Imaginary Software.

Because very little has changed between Windows 98 and Windows 95 with regard to the Windows Registry, most Windows 95 Registry programs work just fine in Windows 98. In fact, the lion's share of the programs you'll read about in this hour were written for Windows 95.

Norton Utilities

Following is some information on Norton Utilities:

Cost: Free evaluation

Vendor: Symantec Corporation

Address: `http://www.symantec.com`

Norton Utilities comes with two useful Registry programs which, if you already own and use Norton Utilities, make a handy addition to your Registry toolkit.

The two utilities include Norton Registry Editor and Norton Registry Tracker. The Norton Registry Editor provides similar features to ShellWizard's Registry Editor. Registry Tracker does similar work to ConfigSafe, which you'll learn about in Hour 17, "Tracking Registry Changes," but it does so in real-time. The problem with Registry Tracker is that if you try to use it to its full potential, it grinds your computer to a halt because the program is so slow, making the simplest tasks painfully time-consuming.

Registry Search & Replace

Following is some information on the Registry Search & Replace:

Cost: Shareware, $20

Vendor: Stephen J. Hoek

Address: `http://www.hotfiles.com`

Registry Search & Replace is a familiar utility that you can use to automatically locate and change entries in the Registry. Windows Notepad has a search-and-replace feature, as do WordPad and Microsoft Word. Registry Search & Replace is a bit more complicated, however, because it works with the Windows Registry. Following is an overview of its features:

- **Search for any string of characters**— You can restrict the search to values or data, as well as to certain types of data and certain root keys. This utility can't search for both values and data at the same time, however.

- **Use Registry Search & Replace with remote computers**—Both computers must be configured to use the Remote Registry Search, as described in Hour 19, "Enabling Remote Administration."

- **Matching with Registry Search & Replace**—For each match that Registry Search & Replace finds, have it prompt you for a replacement, automatically replace the matching string with another string, or just display the matching entry.

As far as I can tell, the author no longer maintains this utility. His Web site is no longer available, and the download file hasn't changed since 1996. Regardless, you can still download this utility from ZDNet's Software Library at `http://www.hotfiles.com`. Even though the author has in all likelihood abandoned this program, it's still useful and worth considering.

> Registry Search & Replace can make sweeping changes to the Registry, which you might not be prepared to make. Therefore, always perform a search first to make sure you know what it's going to change. After confirming what will change, do a full search-and-replace. Alternatively, you can have Registry Search & Replace confirm each change before it makes the change.

9

Regmon

Following is some information on Regmon:

Cost:	Freeware
Vendor:	Systems Internals
Address:	`http://www.sysinternals.com/regmon.htm`

Regmon is a very popular download on the Ziff-Davis Software Library. It has more than 36,000 downloads and a five-star-out-of-five rating. Regmon is an extremely powerful utility that enables you to watch Registry access in real-time, as shown in Figure 9.2. This means that you can see every value read from and written to the Registry as the operation happens. Regmon does this with little impact on the computer's performance. Regmon enables you to filter the list by process, Registry path, or type of access. If you're interested in viewing the values that Windows Explorer reads, for instance, limit Regmon to read-only access from Windows Explorer. Following are some additional notes on how to use Regmon:

- **To search the log for specific information**—Choose Search, Find. Type the text for which you're searching, and click Find Next.

- **To see a truncated path or value**—Right-click it. You'll see a small window displaying the entire item. You'll use this feature frequently because many Registry branches are too large to fit in the small column provided by Regmon.

- **To filter the information that Regmon displays**—Choose Events, Filter. Then provide the following values:

Value	Description
Process	The name of the process that you want to watch. You can specify only one. The best way to figure out the name of the process is to observe the entries that Regmon logs. An asterisk (*) is a wildcard that stands for all processes.
Path Include	The Registry path to include in the filter, starting from the top. An asterisk (*) is a wildcard that stands for all Registry paths.
Path Exclude	A Registry path to exclude from the filter, starting from the top.
History Depth	The maximum number of lines that Regmon will display in the History window. The first lines in are the first lines out.
Log Reads	Indicates whether to include read access in the log. Reads include any operation that retrieves data from the Registry, such as iterating a branch or reading a value entry.
Log Writes	Indicates whether to include write access in the log. Writes include any operations that change the Registry, such as creating a new key or writing to a value entry.
Log Success	Indicates whether to include successful read or write accesses.
Log Errors	Indicates whether to include unsuccessful read or write accesses.

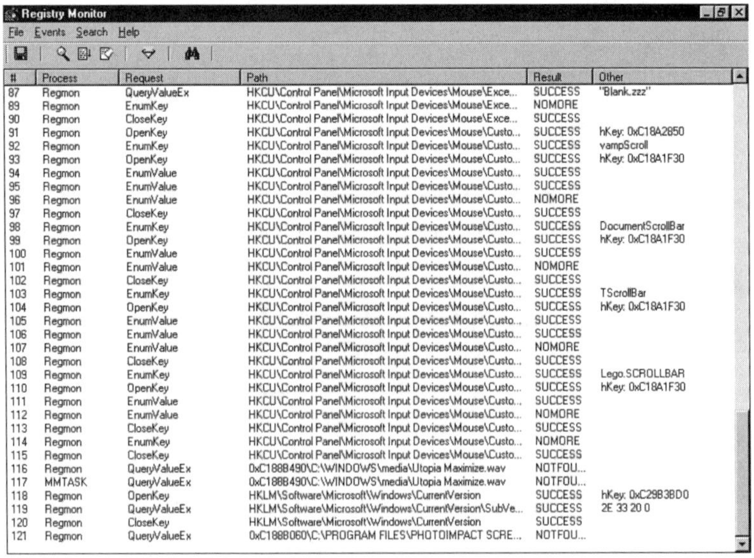

FIGURE 9.2

If Regmon truncates any key or value in the window, right-click it to see the whole string in a popup window.

Regmon is a quick download and is easy to install. Follow the instructions you find at the bottom of the Web page to download the 32KB installation file. It doesn't include a setup program, so you must unzip Regmon.zip into any folder and drag Regmon.exe to the Start menu if you want a shortcut. If you're interested in seeing how Regmon works, download the source code, too. See Hour 17 to learn more about using Regmon to track down changes to the Registry. This hour also describes a program called ConfigSafe that monitors changes to the Registry over a longer period of time than Regmon.

ShellWizard Pro

Following is some information on ShellWizard Pro:

Cost:	Shareware, $20
Vendor:	ShellWizard
Address:	`http://www.shellwizard.com`

ShellWizard Pro provides features that are similar to the other Registry customization programs, but it has a different user interface, as shown in Figure 9.3. Instead of a tabbed dialog box, it uses the wizard concept to walk you step-by-step through customizing the computer. Power users will most likely find the user interface annoying, but basic-to-intermediate users will appreciate the extra bit of help. You can preview changes before actually making them permanent. ShellWizard Pro contains extensive, well-built online help and Experts that provide guidance as you work.

FIGURE 9.3

ShellWizard Pro follows Microsoft's guidelines for building wizards; therefore, it meshes well with Windows

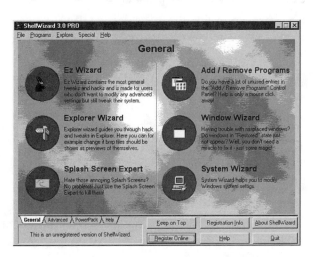

As shown in Figure 9.3, ShellWizard Pro has four tabs: General, Advanced, PowerPack, and Help. The General tab contains buttons for most of the typical settings found in utilities such as Tweak UI and More Properties. The Advanced tab provides the Startup Wizard to edit the Run and Run Once keys in the Registry, enabling you to control which programs start when you boot Windows. The PowerPack tab provides access to ShellWizard Pro's other utilities, including the following:

- **Program Doctor**—Helps you determine which DLL files a program is missing from the computer. If you've ever seen the message Required DLL file is missing, this utility can save you time.
- **Sfx Explorer**—Provides access to Microsoft's CAB files. You don't need this utility in Windows 98, however, because it is built into Windows Explorer.
- **Explorer Extension**—Adds additional features to Windows Explorer. This utility lives on the taskbar's status area, next to the clock. It provides quick access to folders, windows, and the Run dialog box.
- **File Split**—Enables you to split large files so that you can copy them to a floppy disk and rejoin them later.

ShellWizard Pro is at http://www.shellwizard.com. It's not available via the Ziff-Davis Software Library. Click Download under ShellWizard and follow the onscreen instructions. To install ShellWizard Pro, execute the file you downloaded.

ShellWizard Registry Editor

Following is some information about ShellWizard Registry Editor:

Cost:	Shareware, $30
Vendor:	ShellWizard
Address:	http://www.shellwizard.com

ShellWizard Registry Editor, shown in Figure 9.4, blows the heck out of the Windows Registry Editor. It offers all the same features but goes much further. It's easier to use, provides more useful information, and makes navigating the Registry easier. It includes the following features:

- Supports copy and paste.
- Provides awesome navigation via bookmarks, which work much like bookmarks in a Web browser.
- Offers a very fast search capability.
- SmartTips tell you about each class identifier.

- Provides a description, which you see in the bottom pane of the window, of many Registry keys.

- Includes a powerful macro language for writing complex scripts to add, change, or remove data.

FIGURE 9.4

Notice the additional menu commands that the Windows doesn't provide, and the bottom pane, which describes the selected Registry key.

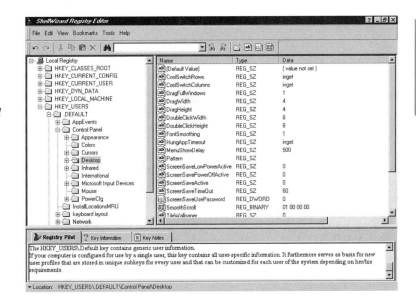

Open `http://www.shellwizard.com` and click Download under ShellWizard Registry Editor. This program is not available on the Ziff-Davis Software Library. Follow the onscreen instructions to finish downloading it. To install the ShellWizard Registry Editor, execute the file you downloaded.

If you already have Norton Utilities, don't pay for ShellWizard Registry Editor. Even though ShellWizard Registry Editor is better in many circumstances, the features of the two are quite similar.

Other Registry Programs

The following sections describe a number of additional Registry programs that have a following. Each section provides a price, vendor, address, and brief description. These shareware programs are listed in alphabetical order, with no regard given to the usefulness, popularity, or any other quality. In some cases, I've noted when a certain program has become hugely popular or when the Ziff-Davis Software Library gives the program an exceptionally high rating.

> You can download all the programs you read about in this hour from Ziff-Davis's Software Library at http://www.hotfiles.com. Another good site for downloading system utilities is http://www.danworld.com.

Associate File Utility

Following is some information about Associate File Utility:

Cost:	Shareware, $12
Vendor:	CT Software
Address:	http://members.aol.com/ron2222

The Associate File Utility makes associating file extensions with applications easier than it is with Windows Explorer: Simply provide the extension and the path to the application. It also enables you to define specific commands such as editing, printing, and so on. It's hardly worth the $12 registration fee, however.

Config97

Following is some information about Config97:

Cost:	Shareware, $10
Vendor:	Springer Software
Address:	http://members.tripod.com/~SpringerSoftware/Config97.htm

Config97 displays certain configuration information from the Registry. Although it repeats functionality provided by Windows 98, it offers a single location to access everything. This utility isn't really worth the $10 registration fee, considering that Windows 98 now provides the System Information utilities, which do the same thing.

JumpToRegKey

Following is some information about JumpToRegKey:

Cost:	Shareware, $15.95
Vendor:	PACT ONE Software
Address:	http://www.pact1.com

This utility doesn't have many downloads, but the Ziff-Davis Software Library gives it five stars out of five. It is definitely useful, creating shortcuts to specific Registry keys that you can put on the desktop. Double-click the shortcut, and JumpToRegKey opens the Registry Editor with that particular key highlighted. You can also choose a Registry key from an icon on the status area, which is on the right side of the taskbar.

Multi-Remote Registry Change

Following is some information about Multi-Remote Registry Change:

Cost:	Shareware, $25
Vendor:	Greg Eytcheson
Address:	http://www54.pair.com/eytch

Multi-Remote Registry Change isn't very popular and is an exceptionally large download file. It is probably more popular among administrators, however, because it does something that no other utility does: It enables you to change a Registry value on any number of remote computers, all at the same time. Select the computers to change from the list, and specify the key and value that you want to change.

RegChk

Following is some information about RegChk:

Cost:	Freeware
Vendor:	Ron Thompson
Address:	http://www.sageinst.com/regchk

RegChk looks in the Registry for references to files that no longer exist. It generates a report, enabling you to clean up the Registry on your own. Nifty.

Regfind

Following is some information about Regfind:

Cost:	Freeware
Vendor:	Intellisoft, Inc.
Address:	http://www.hotfiles.com

You use Regfind to search the Registry. It's good for locating problems such as value entries containing data from deleted programs. Because I didn't find the author's Web site, I'm referring you to the Ziff-Davis Software Library to download this file.

9

RegisTray

Following is some information about RegisTray:

Cost: Shareware

Vendor: Software House

Address: http://www.hotfiles.com

RegisTray enables you to customize features in Windows that you can't through the normal interface.

Registry Editor Extensions

Following is some information about Registry Editor Extensions:

Cost: Freeware

Vendor: DC Software Design

Address: http://www.hotfiles.com

Registry Editor Extensions adds a number of new features to the Registry Editor. For example, it adds a combo box that acts like the history list that you use in a Web browser. If you're using ShellWizard Registry Editor or Norton Registry Editor, you don't need this utility.

RegMonEx

Following is some information about RegMonEx:

Cost: Freeware

Vendor: Jan Sultan

Address: http://www.hotfiles.com

RegMonEx monitors each call to the Registry API. It includes the name of the program making the call, the Registry key, the result, and any values retrieved from the Registry. RegMonEx provides a filter, such as Regmon.

If you have to choose between RegMonEx and Regmon, choose Regmon. RegMonEx is an extension to RegMon's original source code that was created by a programmer other than the original authors. RegMonEx is a bit clumsy compared to RegMon because it adds more complexity and doesn't always get the job done. RegMonEx has more-advanced filtering capabilities, but using them can test your patience.

RegRepair 2000

Following is some information about RegRepair 2000:

Cost: Shareware, $29.95

Vendor: Easy Desk Software

Address: `http://members.aol.com/wcguy06`

RegRepair 2000 has more than 10,000 downloads from the Ziff-Davis Software Library and a five-star-out-of-five rating. It helps you fix pesky IOS errors and repairs files that failed to load, as noted in Bootlog.txt. It automatically scans Bootlog.txt for errors and tries to fix them. Note that this program backs up the Registry, but you don't need this feature if you're using Windows 98 because Windows 98 does an admirable job of that all by itself.

RegTune 98

Following is some information about RegTune 98:

Cost: Shareware, $35

Vendor: Ashish Computer Systems

Address: `http://www.ashishsystems.com`

RegTune 98 helps you change security settings in Windows. You can hide drivers, for instance, or manage passwords, Start menu submenus, and more. This program leaves holes that enable the user to reverse the settings that an administrator might configure, so don't rely on it if tight security is a must.

RegView for Windows 95

Following is some information about RegView for Windows 95:

Cost: Shareware, $39

Vendor: Vincent Chiu

Address: `http://www.xnet.com/~vchiu`

RegView looks and feels similar to the Windows Registry Editor, but it provides a few new features. It has a better search feature and enables you to perform a search and replace. It can compare the current Registry to the latest backup you've made using its backup feature.

If you're in the market for a new Registry Editor, consider using the ShellWizard Registry Editor, described earlier in this hour.

SecLOCK

Following is some information about SecLOCK:

Cost:	Freeware
Vendor:	CMSystems
Address:	http://www.strebersdorf.ac.at/CMSystems/CMSystems.html

SecLOCK helps you lock down the Windows desktop. It works with user profiles, enables you to set up restrictions similar to the System Policy Editor, hide desktop icons, remove submenus from the Start menu, and more. You can use it in lieu of the System Policy Editor. (Note that Tweak UI provides many of these features.) This is a German program that's roughly translated into English, but you will have no problems understanding the prompts.

Set Me Up 98

Following is some information about Set Me Up 98:

Cost:	Shareware
Vendor:	Omniquad
Address:	http://www.omniquad.com

Omniquad's Set Me Up 98 is clunky compared to the other Registry and customization tools (it suffers from diseases common to Visual Basic programs), but it offers features not found anywhere else. You can change how individual folders look by creating custom Desktop.ini files, for instance. Use your own splash screens for when Windows starts or shuts down. You can even customize Internet Explorer 4.0 options that are not available through the traditional user interface.

StartEd

Following is some information about StartEd:

Cost:	Shareware, $15
Vendor:	Thomas Reimann
Address:	http://www.alberts.com/authorpages/00014860/prod_687.htm

With a five-star-out-of-five rating and a whopping 21,000 downloads, this program must have something going for it. It enables you to control what programs Windows starts using the Run, Run Once, and RunServices keys in the Registry. The primary purpose of this utility is to avoid editing these keys using the Registry Editor. You can even add your own programs to the Run key instead of adding them to the Startup group of the Start menu. You must be the judge as to whether this simple program is worth the cost, considering that the StartUp Manager, described next, is free.

StartUp Manager

Following is some information about StartUp Manager:

Cost:	Freeware
Vendor:	Daniel Hofman
Address:	http://www.hotfiles.com

The StartUp Manager enables you to edit the Run, Run Once, Run Services, and Run Services Once Registry keys, as well as Win.ini's Run and Load entries. It helps you understand why a program might start when Windows starts and you don't see it in the Startup group. It's also a good alternative to adding programs to the startup group.

> You find the Run and Run Once keys in both the HKEY_LOCAL_MACHINE and HKEY_CURRENT_USER branches of the Registry. The difference is that items in the former start before the user logs on to Windows, and items in the latter start after the user logs on to Windows.

Tip Editor

Following is some information about Tip Editor:

Cost:	Freeware
Vendor:	Jelsoft Enterprises
Address:	http://www.hotfiles.com

Use Tip Editor to edit the tips that are displayed when Windows starts. It's a great way to add tips, export them to a REG file, and distribute them to a larger user base. Hour 18, "Scripting Changes to the Registry," describes how to write scripts that automatically change the Registry.

TweakDUN

Following is some information about TweakDUN:

Cost:	Shareware, $15
Vendor:	Patterson Design Systems
Address:	`http://pattersondesigns.com/tweakdun/`

TweakDUN gets a rating of five-stars-out-of-five and has more than 25,000 downloads from the Ziff-Davis Software Library. You use it to tune up your TCP/IP settings to improve the performance of your Internet connection. In particular, TweakDUN adjusts the size of certain packets and buffers to limit fragmenting. Furthermore, it can optimize these settings so that they work better with your ISP. You can easily change these settings yourself using the Registry Editor, but no other program provides the convenient user interface that TweakDUN provides, and no other program can detect the appropriate settings to use.

Win-eXpose-Registry

Following is some information about Win-eXpose-Registry:

Cost:	Shareware, $29
Vendor:	Shetef Solutions Ltd.
Address:	`http://www.shetef.com`

Use Win-eXpose-Registry to trace and monitor access to the Windows Registry.

WinHacker95

Following is some information about WinHacker95:

Cost:	Shareware, $17.95
Vendor:	Wedge Software
Address:	`http://www.wedgesoftware.com`

WinHacker 95 is the granddaddy of shareware Registry customization tools; however, it hasn't improved much since the original version, and it certainly doesn't meet the bar set by Tweak UI and More Properties, both described earlier in this hour. It offers all the basic settings, most of which are described in Hours 14–16. If you're looking for an alternative to Tweak UI and More Properties, however, download WinHacker95 from Wedge Software's Web site.

WinRescue 98

Following is some information about WinRescue 98:

Cost:	Shareware, $19.95
Vendor:	Super Win Software
Address:	`http://members.aol.com/evanetten`

9

The Ziff-Davis Software Library gives this popular program a five-star-out-of-five rating. It allows for preventative maintenance to recover from the inevitable crashes. It backs up important configuration files, as well as the Startup menu, desktop, Favorites folder, Recent folder, and many others. It compresses these backups into zip files.

WinTweak

Following is some information about WinTweak:

Cost:	Shareware, $8
Vendor:	Gooch Computer Services
Address:	`http://www.hotfiles.com`

WinTweak enables you to customize Internet Explorer 4.0. You can change default mail and news folders; remove Documents, Favorites, Find, and Run from the Start menu; change search pages; and more.

Summary

Dozens of shareware, freeware, and commercial programs are available to edit and otherwise manage the Registry. This hour described the ones available as of this writing, but you need to frequently check shareware sites such as `http://www.hotfiles.com` for newer stuff.

If you're serious about mastering the Registry, make sure that you have at least one of the following three types of programs: a good editor, customization utility, and monitor. The editor that comes with Windows is OK, but you can do better with Norton Registry Editor or ShellWizard Registry Editor. Tweak UI is probably the single best customization utility. The best Registry monitor I've found is Regmon.

Q&A

Q **Does the popularity of a shareware Registry program really say much about the program itself?**

A Absolutely. The program doesn't have more downloads than any other program because it's worse than the rest. Word of mouth about great programs spreads like wildfire on the Internet. The best programs generally have the most downloads.

Q **Some of the shareware programs in this hour are written by programmers in other countries. Is it safe to register these programs, or am I likely to have all sorts of interesting charges on my credit card?**

A It's generally safe. I've registered many of the programs in this hour, many in other countries, without any problems. The only thing worth mentioning is that when you register a program with some international shareware programs, the charge can take several months to actually hit your credit card. Note also that although some programs work in other countries, they use shareware registration services that are in the United States.

Q **Do Windows 95 Registry programs work in Windows 98?**

A In 99 percent of all cases, yes. The Registry just hasn't changed that much between each version of Windows.

Workshop

The following quiz will enhance your understanding of the topics discussed in this hour.

Quiz

1. True or false? More Properties is a customization utility that's similar to Tweak UI.

2. Which of the following are alternatives to the Windows Registry Editor?

    a. ShellWizard Registry Editor

    b. Que's Registry Editor

    c. Regedt32.exe from Windows NT

    d. Norton Registry Editor

    e. Both a and c

    f. Both a and d

3. True or false? You need to register a shareware program if you decide to continue using it beyond its evaluation period.

Answers to Quiz Questions

1. True

   More Properties has features that are similar to those of Tweak UI, but it presents them more like the System Policy Editor.

2. f

   The two alternatives to Registry Editor that this hour described were ShellWizard and Norton Registry Editors.

3. True

   Shareware authors make their living from people who register software. If people don't register, shareware authors don't make money, and shareware ceases to be available.

9

PART IV
Exploring the Registry

Hour

HOUR 10

HKEY_CLASSES_ROOT

Hour 2, "Looking Inside the Registry," discussed *aliases*. HKEY_CLASSES_ROOT is an alias for HKEY_LOCAL_MACHINE\Software\ CLASSES. That means that any change you make to HKEY_CLASSES_ROOT is actually made in \CLASSES. Likewise, HKEY_CLASSES_ROOT reflects any changes you make in \CLASSES. The pragmatic reason that this alias exists is for backward compatibility with Windows 3.1. Yes, Windows 3.1 did have a Registry, which it used for OLE, DDE, and related settings. As far as you're concerned, though, HKEY_CLASSES_ROOT just makes getting to this information quicker because you don't have to click your way to \CLASSES.

HKEY_CLASSES_ROOT is the single largest branch in the Registry. On a test computer, I found that this branch contained more than 50 percent of the Registry's data. You can verify this fact yourself by exporting HKEY_CLASSES_ROOT to a REG file called Classes.reg and exporting the entire Registry to another REG file called All.reg. Divide the file size of Classes.reg by the file size of All.reg to figure out how much of the Registry is HKEY_CLASSES_ROOT. In my case, Classes.reg was 2.69 MB and All.reg was 5.23 MB.

The Bigger Picture

HKEY_CLASSES_ROOT contains thousands upon thousands of keys and values that associate file extensions with programs, define *Component Object Model* (*COM*) classes, and much more. If you look closely at this branch, you'll notice two different types of subkeys. The subkeys toward the top, with the exception of the * subkey, are called *filename extension subkeys,* and they all begin with a period. They look like normal MS-DOS file extensions: .*ext.* They can contain any number of characters. Examples are .bat, .doc, and .html. * and the subkeys toward the bottom of HKEY_CLASSES_ROOT are *class definition subkeys,* and they include program identifiers and class identifiers:

- **Program identifiers**—Subkeys in HKEY_CLASSES_ROOT that define the actions that a program can perform on a file. Examples are batfile, docfile, and inifile. Some program identifiers also associate a program with a COM class. These are similar to aliases that make accessing a class easier. Examples are Word.Document.8 and Excel.Sheet.8.

- **Class identifiers**—Uniquely identify a COM class such as an ActiveX control. HKEY_CLASSES_ROOT\CLSID contains all the class identifiers. Each class identifier is a globally unique 16-byte number. An example is {3B7C8860-D78F-101B-B9B5-04021C009402}. Windows uses class identifiers extensively.

You'll learn much more about filename extension subkeys and class definitions in the following sections. The section titled "Miscellaneous Subkeys in HKEY_CLASSES_ROOT" describes a number of subkeys that you frequently find under both types of keys.

When you install Windows, it registers a large number of filename extension and class definition subkeys. Also, most applications register filename extensions and class definitions during installation.

Some programs store user preferences in HKEY_CLASSES_ROOT. It might seem odd to see \Software\Progressive Networks\RealAudio Player in this branch, for instance, but its presence is not necessarily an error. Some vendors, such as Progressive Networks, must create programs that work in both Windows 3.1 and Windows. In order to do that, the vendor writes its configuration data to HKEY_CLASSES_ROOT, the only root key that Windows 3.1 provides. In other words, *just live with it.*

Filename Extension Subkeys

Any time Windows accesses a file, whether it's to open the file or to display information about it in Windows Explorer, the operating system looks up the file's extension under HKEY_CLASSES_ROOT. If you open a DOC file, for example, Windows looks up .doc. The filename extension subkey doesn't contain enough information to tell the operating system much about the file, however, so the operating system looks in the filename extension's default value entry for the name of a program identifier, a class definition subkey, that contains more information. Look up the default value in .dll and you'll see that DLL files are associated with dllfile. You find the program identifier's subkey in the same place as the file extension: under HKEY_CLASSES_ROOT. Figure 10.1 illustrates the relationship by showing how AVI files are associated with the avifile program identifier via the .avi file extension subkey.

FIGURE 10.1

AVI files are associated with the avifile *file type via the* .avi *file extension subkey.*

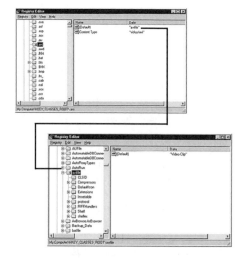

Microsoft really cleaned up the filename extension subkeys for Windows 98. In a fresh installation of Windows 98, the only subkeys you find under a filename extension are shellex and ShellNew. shellex describes shell extensions for that particular filename extension. An example is a context menu handler that adds additional items to a file's shortcut menu, which you display by right-clicking the file in Windows Explorer. In Windows 95, filename extension subkeys contained a strange mix of various DefaultIcon, shell, shellex, and ShellNew subkeys, most of which are more appropriate under class definition subkeys. If you upgrade to Windows 98, you're left with all this clutter in the Registry. Don't forget, too, that many Windows 98 applications add these

10

subkeys to the filename extension key when you install them. Even though these subkeys might be misplaced under a file extension rather than in a class definition, they still work for that particular file extension.

> All you need to remember about filename extension subkeys is that they are under HKEY_CLASSES_ROOT, that they look like .*ext* (where *ext* is a valid file extension), and that their default value points to one of the program identifiers that are also defined in HKEY_CLASSES_ROOT.

CONTENT TYPE

Typically, the only value you see in a filename extension subkey is Content Type. This value associates the file extension with a *Multipurpose Internet Mail Extensions* (*MIME*) type, a standard for specifying data types on the Internet.

A MIME type specifies the type of content embedded in a Web page or contained in a mail message's attachments. Sometimes the server provides the MIME type of the data it's transmitting, and other times the MIME type is embedded in the document itself. You might think that the server and document can just specify a file extension, but recall that the Internet is platform-neutral. This means that the Internet must support a wide variety of platforms, each of which might have different conventions for naming files.

MIME types look like *type/subtype*. *Type* is usually something such as application, audio, image, or text. application specifies that the data is raw and doesn't fit into one of the other MIME types. audio, image, and text speak for themselves. *subtype* can vary, but there are standards. A subtype for text might be plain or rich, for example, which specifies that the content is either plain text or richly formatted text. A type or subtype that begins with x- means that it's a private MIME type that isn't standardized. Just because a MIME type isn't standardized doesn't mean it's not in popular use.

The later section "MIME Types" contains more information about how Windows uses Content Type. You'll also learn how the operating system cross-references MIME types so that looking them up is quicker than searching each individual filename extension subkey.

Class Definition Subkeys

Class definition subkeys define a particular type of document or object. It might be a file type, which a program can open for editing, printing, and so on. It might be a COM class such as a compound document or ActiveX control.

Class definition subkeys come in two flavors. Program identifiers, which are associated with a filename extension subkey via the extension's default value entry, describe a program and the actions it can perform on a file. You'll learn about program identifiers in the following section. A class identifier uniquely identifies a COM class, which can generate objects such as a system folder. Familiar terms associated with COM classes are *object, module,* and *component.* ActiveX and OLE are related technologies that are actually part of COM.

You'll learn about each type of class definition in the following sections. You'll also learn about HKEY_CLASSES_ROOT\MIME, a database that makes cross-referencing a MIME type with a file extension quicker, in "MIME Types." You'll learn about a variety of subkeys that you might find under class definition keys in "Miscellaneous Subkeys in HKEY_CLASSES_ROOT."

If the word *COM* throws you, you might know it better as ActiveX or OLE (Object Linking and Embedding). I'll straighten these terms out for you: COM is Microsoft's technology for allowing applications to interoperate. COM technologies include ActiveX Controls and much more. ActiveX controls are COM objects that are designed for distribution via Web pages. OLE, on the other hand, strictly refers to Windows's *Object Linking and Embedding* capabilities, and you'll only see this term used when referring to *OLE drag and drop* or *embedded OLE objects.*

10

Program Identifiers

Flexibility is the reason that Windows splits information between filename extensions and program identifiers. The operating system can store all the information it needs in a filename extension, but doing so leaves the operating system incapable of handling anything but a one-to-one relationship between a file extension and a program. Some documents can have more than one file extension, for instance, as is the case with HTM and HTML files and JPG and JPEG files. Some programs can open more than one file extension, too. For example, Microsoft Word can open DOC, DOT, RTF, and other files. The organization of filename extensions and program identifiers allows the operating system to handle all these cases.

Recall that each filename extension's default value entry refers to a program identifier under HKEY_CLASSES_ROOT. The default value entry for .bat is batfile, for example. Look in HKEY_CLASSES_ROOT\batfile, and you see the information that the operating system requires to open, edit, and print BAT files. Given the way in which the Registry organizes this information, you can associate many different filename extensions with a single program, but you can't associate many different programs with a single file extension.

The following list shows you several examples of how a filename extension subkey's default value relates it to a program identifier:

Filename Extension Subkey	File Type/Default Value
.avi	avifile
.dll	dllfile
.exe	exefile
.htm	htmlfile
.lnk	lnkfile
.reg	regfile
.txt	txtfile

Each program identifier can have a number of different values. The default value entry usually contains a plain-English description of the program and the files it can open. You see this description when you view a file's details in Windows Explorer.

The mere presence of AlwaysShowExt, a string value, indicates whether Windows Explorer always displays the file's extension in a folder, regardless of Hide file extensions for known file types on the View tab of Windows Explorer's Folder Options dialog box. NeverShowExt, another string value, does the opposite. The presence of IsShortcut indicates whether the file is a shortcut and whether the operating system is to display the shortcut overlay on top of the file's icon. Table 10.1 summarizes these values, as well as EditFlags, another common value in most program identifiers. This is a 4-byte binary value that indicates how much editing you're allowed to do in the File Types tab of Windows Explorer's Folder Options dialog box, shown in Figure 10.2. The following list describes the bits that are used in this 32-bit value; just remember to count the bits from right to left, starting from 0.

Bit	Hex	Description
8	00 00 01 00	Clear Confirm open after download
16	00 01 00 00	Disable Description of type
17	00 02 00 00	Disable Change Icon button
18	00 04 00 00	Disable the Set Default button
20	00 10 00 00	Disable Application used to…
21	00 20 00 00	Disable Use DDE checkbox

Bit	Hex	Description
23	00 80 00 00	Disable Content Type (MIME)
24	01 00 00 00	Don't display in Registered file types
25	02 00 00 00	Do display in Registered file types
27	08 00 00 00	Disable the Edit on File Types tab
28	10 00 00 00	Disable the Remove on File Types tab
29	20 00 00 00	Disable the New button
30	40 00 00 00	Disable the Edit button
31	80 00 00 00	Disable the Remove button

TABLE 10.1 COMMON VALUES FOR FILE TYPES

Value	Type	Description
AlwaysShowExt	String	The presence of this value indicates that Windows Explorer is always to display the filename extension in a folder.
NeverShowExt	String	The presence of this value indicates that Windows Explorer is never to display the filename extension in a folder.
IsShortcut	String	The presence of this value indicates that the file represents a shortcut, and the operating system displays the shortcut overlay on top of the file's icon.
EditFlags	Binary	Contains flags that determine how much editing the user can do in the File Types tab of Windows Explorer's Folder Options dialog box.

Program identifiers are also an alternative method for identifying COM classes. You'll learn about COM classes in the later section "COM Class Identifiers." Sometimes known as a *progid,* a program identifier allows a program to refer to a class without using the nasty class identifiers. Contrast looking up a class under CLSID using {00020906-0000-0000-C000-000000000046} versus looking up the same class under HKEY_CLASSES_ROOT using Word.Document.8. The latter makes more sense. In this manner, you can think of program identifiers as aliases.

Program identifiers that represent COM classes are specified using a standard notation: *vendor.component.version.* An example is Microsoft.Word.8. You'll notice that in the

Registry they look more like Word.Document.8, which deviates a bit from the standard notation. Regardless, you can also recognize this type of program identifier in one of two ways:

- The name is separated into parts by periods (.).
- Program identifiers that represent a COM class always have a subkey called CLSID, which refers to a class identifier in HKEY_CLASSES_ROOT\CLSID.

FIGURE 10.2

Choose View, Folder Options from Windows Explorer, and click the File Types tab to view these dialogs.

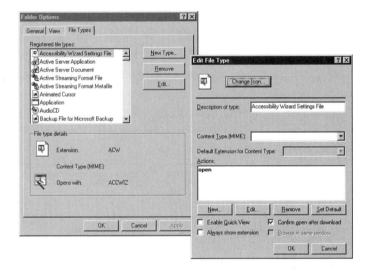

Program identifiers save the programmer from having to know a class's identifier. The programmer can instead use one of the operating system's functions that translate a program identifier into a class identifier, and vice versa. Note that because the program identifier uses some combination of the vendor or application name, component name, and version, there is little chance that two different applications will try to create the same program identifier.

CLSID

Because a program identifier can refer to a COM class, it must have a way to link itself to a class identifier—it does. Each program identifier can have a subkey called CLSID whose default value entry is the class identifier of a COM class.

You'll notice that the primary perpetrator of program identifiers is Microsoft. Just about every Microsoft Office product that you install creates several program identifiers.

CurVer

Imagine the following scenario: An application depends on a class labeled Word.Document.8. Later, the user installs an upgrade that changes the program identifier to Word.Document.9. The application can no longer find the class that it needs because the program identifier to which it refers is missing. The solution is *version-independent program identifiers*.

Some program identifiers leave out the version number on the end of their name: *vendor.component*. Examples are Excel.Sheet and Word.Document. These are called version-independent program identifiers. They allow an application to refer to a class without explicitly specifying a version number in the program identifier. A version-independent program identifier always has a subkey called CurVer. The default value of CurVer is the complete program identifier, including the current version.

Now change the scenario so that it uses version-independent program identifiers. An application refers to Word.Document, whose CurVer subkey's default value is set to Word.Document.8. When the user installs the upgrade, the application changes the default value entry of CurVer in Word.Document so that it refers to the new program identifier called Word.Document.9. The user got his upgrade, and the application can still find its object.

Two subkeys are common in both program and class identifiers: Insertable and NotInsertable. The mere presence of a subkey called Insertable indicates that the class appears on the Object dialog box of any application that supports it. You open the Object dialog box by choosing Insert, Object from the application. The presence of NotInsertable indicates that the class does not appear in the Object dialog box.

COM Class Identifiers

COM class identifiers are similar to Social Security numbers that uniquely identify people. They identify a COM class using a unique number called a *globally unique identifier*

(GUID). A program called Guidgen.exe, which comes with Visual C++ and the WIN32 SDK, generates this number. Don't let `HKEY_CLASSES_ROOT\CLSID`, the location of all the class identifiers in the Registry, daunt you. Each GUID is really nothing more than a class's Social Security number. Notice that all these class identifiers have the same peculiar format. They're 16-byte hexadecimal numbers separated into 8-, 4-, 4-, 4-, and 12-digit sections by a hyphen, with curly brackets surrounding the whole mess:

`{XXXXXXXX-XXXX-XXXX-XXXX-XXXXXXXXXXXX}`

The default value entry for a class identifier describes the class. In most cases, you see a plain-English description of the class. `Microsoft Excel Chart`, `HTML Thumbnail Extractor`, and `Desktop Task` are examples. In other cases, you see nothing, which leaves you wondering what the class represents. In those cases, you can search the Registry for references to the class identifier. The reference to the class is usually enough to tell you what it does. If you find a class identifier with no name, here are some techniques for uncovering its purpose:

- **Search the Registry for the class identifier**—The location in which the class identifier is used might tell you the class's purpose.
- **Look for a subkey called `ProgID`**—This is a link to a related program identifier in `HKEY_CLASSES_ROOT`. The program identifier might provide additional information about the class.
- **Look in each of the class identifier's subkeys for a reference to a DLL or other file**—View the file's properties by right-clicking it and choosing Properties. Frequently, the Version tab gives you a brief description of the file, indicating its purpose.

Class identifiers don't usually contain values. They are defined by their subkeys, as you'll learn in the following sections. One exception is a value called `InfoTip`. You commonly find this value entry in classes that create user interface objects, special system folders, and so on. Windows Explorer displays the contents of `InfoTip` in a small yellow box, also known as a ToolTip, when the user hovers the mouse pointer over the object. This is an additional way in which the operating system provides help to the user. When you hover the mouse pointer over My Computer on the desktop, for example, you see a tip that reads `Displays the contents of your computer`. Adding `InfoTip` to classes that don't already define this value doesn't seem to do much good. You can customize `InfoTip` for classes that do include it, however.

> Any time you see a GUID elsewhere in the Registry, you can almost always find a matching class identifier in CLSID. Exceptions do exist, however. Sometimes programs use a GUID to uniquely name subkeys or values in other parts of the Registry. These don't lead to class identifiers, but they look similar to them.

GENERATING CLASS IDENTIFIERS: GUIDGEN.EXE

Programmers use a program called Guidgen.exe, which comes with Visual C++ and the WIN32 SDK, to generate GUIDs. Microsoft guarantees that each GUID generated by Guidgen.exe is globally unique. That is, the program generates a new 16-byte integer GUID every time it runs—no matter how many times it runs.

It does so using a complex algorithm that uses a combination of data. The current date and time are in the GUID. The clock sequence on the computer is in there. An IEEE machine identifier, which Guidgen.exe gets from the network card if it is available, is in there. If the computer doesn't have a network card, Guidgen.exe generates a machine identifier from extremely variable machine data. This quote from the Microsoft Developer Network Library explains it all: "The chance of [Guidgen.exe] generating duplicate GUIDs...is about the same as two random atoms in the universe colliding to form a small California avocado mated to a New York City sewer rat."

ShellFolder

If you see ShellFolder underneath a class identifier, it has a single value called attributes. attributes indicates the built-in commands that Windows Explorer displays on the object's shortcut menu. attributes is a 4-byte binary value with each bit representing a flag that enables or disables a specific command. Table 10.2 describes the bits used by Windows. Setting a particular bit to 0 disables the command, whereas setting it to 1 enables the command. Remember that you count bits right to left in a binary value, so bit 0 is the first bit on the right, bit 1 is the second bit on the right, and so on. Because the Registry shows attributes as a hexadecimal value, you must convert it to binary to figure out which commands are enabled. Work with this value in binary until you're ready to change attributes, and then convert it to hexadecimal.

Here's a real-world example: The attributes value for the Internet Explorer icon is 72000000 in hexadecimal, which is 01110010000000000000000000000000 in binary. Counting from right to left, bits 25, 28, 29, and 30 are 1s. Thus, Windows displays the Cut, Rename, Delete, and Properties commands on the Internet Explorer icon's shortcut menu. You can remove the Cut command from the shortcut menu by turning off bit 25, which leaves you with a hexadecimal value of 70000000.

TABLE 10.2 BITS IN THE attributes VALUE

Bit Number	Command
30	Properties
29	Delete
28	Rename
25	Cut
24	Copy
16	Paste
5	Open and Explore for the Recycle Bin

Hour 14, "Files and Folders," shows you how to use ShellFolder to make shortcut menus look the way you want them to.

LocalServer and LocalServer32

The default values of the subkeys called LocalServer and LocalServer32 specify the path of an EXE that implements the server application. LocalServer specifies a 16-bit server application, whereas LocalServer32 specifies a 32-bit server application. Local servers run in their own address space.

InprocServer and InprocServer32

The default values of the subkeys called InprocServer and InprocServer32 specify the path of a DLL file that implements the server. InprocServer specifies a 16-bit server, whereas LocalServer32 specifies a 32-bit server. In-process servers run in the client process's address space.

If an in-process server is multithreaded, you see an additional value entry called ThreadingModel. This value can be one of the following:

- **Apartment**—This represents the *apartment threading model*. Each object exists in only a single thread.

- **Both**—An object can exist in a single thread, as with apartment threading, or it can exist in multiple threads of a single process—*free threading*.

InprocHandler and InprocHandler32

The default values of the subkeys called InprocHandler and InprocHandler32 specify the path of a DLL file that handles objects that are defined by the class identifier. InprocHandler specifies a 16-bit handler, whereas InprocHandler32 specifies a 32-bit handler. In-process handlers work in conjunction with local or in-process servers. You'll notice that this value almost always contains Ole32.dll, which provides COM functionality to the operating system and other applications.

The difference between in-process and local servers is the address space in which they run. In-process servers run in the host application's address space. Local servers run in their own address space. In-process servers perform better but can crash the client application. Local servers perform worse than in-process servers do, but they don't affect the host application if they crash.

ProgID

Earlier in this hour, you learned that a program identifier can be an alias for a class. Each program identifier can contain a subkey called `CLSID` whose default value contains the class identifier of the associated class. Each class identifier also contains a reference to its matching program identifier, if it exists, in a subkey called `ProgID`. The default value entry of `ProgID` is the program identifier or the version-independent program identifier.

MIME Types

In the earlier section called "Filename Extension Subkeys," you learned how the operating system associates a MIME type with a variety of file extensions. These file extensions contain a value called `Content Type`, which defines the MIME type that is associated with that extension. When a client program such as Internet Explorer or Outlook Express Mail needs to associate a program with a bit of data, it searches for the MIME type in the Registry. The search yields a file extension that in turn yields information about the program used to display and edit the data.

Windows doesn't examine each and every filename extension subkey for a matching `Content Type` value, however, because doing so makes the whole process pathetically slow. It looks up the MIME type in `HKEY_CLASSES_ROOT\MIME\Database\Content Type` instead. This key contains a subkey for each MIME type that is registered in the Registry. `Content Type\MimeType` contains a value called `Extension` that associates the MIME type with a file extension. `Content Type\Text/Plain` contains information about the `Text/Plain` MIME type, for example, and `Extension` contains `.txt`, which associates the `Text/Plain` MIME type with the TXT file extension. The `Extension` value entry for `Content Type\image/gif` contains `.gif`, which associates the `image/gif` MIME type with the GIF file extension.

Underneath some MIME types, you see a subkey called `Bits`. This subkey contains terrific information about the header that begins each type of file. Each value entry—the first being `0`, the second being `1`, and so on—in `Bits` defines a possible file header that identifies a file matching the MIME type.

The first 32-bit DWORD specifies the length of the file header. The next *n* bytes, where *n* is the length of the file header, appear to be a mask that determines which bits of the header to check. This portion is almost always `FF FF FF FF ...`, indicating that the operating system is to check every bit of the file header. The next *n* bytes, up to the end of the binary value entry, are the actual file header.

If the operating system encounters a file with an unknown MIME type or file extension, it can sometimes identify the file's MIME type by comparing its header to the values in `Bits`. Likewise, the operating system can test a file's header against the values in `Bits` to make sure that the file is valid. You see `02 00 00 00 FF FF 42 4D` in the value entry called `0`, found under `MIME\Database\Content Type\image/bmp\Bits`, a subkey of `HKEY_CLASSES_ROOT`. This indicates that a BMP file's header has two bytes, `42 4D`, and every bit in each of those bytes is significant. Sure enough, if you view a BMP file in a hex editor, the file starts with `42 4D`.

Miscellaneous Subkeys in HKEY_CLASSES_ROOT

Filename extensions and class definitions can contain a number of subkeys that define how they look and behave. It's more common for class definitions to contain such subkeys as `shell` and `DefaultIcon`, but these subkeys are still valid under filename extensions. `shellex` and `ShellNew` subkeys are more common under filename extensions, however.

The following sections describe the most common subkeys. Following is an overview of each:

- `shell`—Defines commands that appear on the shortcut menu of the file or object.
- `shellex`—Defines shell extensions for the file or object, such as extensions to the property sheet or shortcut menu.
- `ShellNew`—Defines a template for a new empty file with a particular file extension that the user creates by right-clicking a folder and choosing New.
- `DefaultIcon`—Defines an icon for the file or object.

shell

When you right-click a file or object in Windows Explorer, it displays a shortcut menu. Some of the items on the shortcut menu are built into the operating system (Shell32.dll); these appear at the bottom of the menu. You learned how to control these options in the earlier section "`ShellFolder`." Other items come from class definitions such as

Unknown or *, both of which you'll learn about later in this hour. The remaining items are at the top of the shortcut menu and come from the shell subkey of the class definition. HKEY_CLASSES_ROOT\txtfile\shell defines the items that you see at the top of a TXT file's shortcut menu, for example. In some unlikely cases, a filename extension key might have a shell subkey, too, which adds items to the file's shortcut menu only if the filename extension subkey is not connected to a program identifier by the subkey's default value entry. All this is a bit much to swallow, so look at the following generalization about how Windows Explorer builds the shortcut menu after the user right-clicks a file:

1. Windows notes the file's extension and looks up that extension in HKEY_CLASSES_ROOT.

2. Windows notes the default value entry of the filename extension subkey, which is the associated program identifier. If this value is empty, the operating system looks for a shell subkey in the filename extension key and adds those commands to the top of the shortcut menu. Otherwise, the operating system adds any commands it finds in the program identifier's shell subkey to the top of the shortcut menu.

3. Windows adds any commands it finds in the * and AllFilessystemObjects keys' shell subkey to the middle of the shortcut menu. For example, if you've installed WinZip, you'll see a command for it on every file's shortcut menu; this command comes from the * key. These are commands that apply to all files and all file system objects on the computer.

4. Windows adds any built-in commands to the bottom of the shortcut menu. These are defined in Shell32.dll.

Verbs

Each subkey under shell is a verb. A verb shows action in the user interface just as it does in the English language. "Open Readme.txt," "Edit Budget.xls," and "Print Picture.bmp" all represent examples of verb phrases that contain an action and a direct object. The actions are open, edit, and print. The direct objects are Readme.txt, Budget.xls, and Picture.bmp. The user completes one of these verb phrases by right-clicking a file, which supplies the direct object, and then choosing one of the commands on the menu, which supplies the verb. In the Registry, verbs have simple, arbitrary names such as open, edit, and print. The default value of shell indicates which verb defines the default command on the menu. Thus, if a shell key has two subkeys, open and edit, and the shell key's default value is open, the shortcut menu starts with the commands Open and Edit, and Open is the default choice. If the user clicks the file in the single-click user interface or double-clicks the file in the double-click interface, Windows opens the file using the command that is defined in shell\open.

> Microsoft documentation refers to some verbs as *canonical verbs*. If you look in the dictionary, you'll discover that *canonical* means official, sanctioned, or approved. open, openas, print, find, and explore are recognized by and built into the operating system and are therefore canonical verbs. Canonical verbs are localized by the Windows, so the operating system always uses the appropriate language when displaying them on a menu.

The default value of each verb contains the text that Windows displays on the shortcut menu. If the default value is blank, the operating system takes the text for the menu item from Shell32.dll—if the verb is canonical—or from the verb's name. Find, Open, Open With, and Print are canonical, so the operating system looks to Shell32.dll for the shortcut menu's text if the default value of the verb is empty. If the operating system uses the verb's name, it uses it verbatim, without capitalizing it or adding a hot key to it. The operating system does maintain the capitalization you use in the verb's default value, and you can indicate a hot key by prefixing the letter with an ampersand (&). Following are examples of how different values look on a shortcut menu:

In the Registry	On the Shortcut menu
open	open
&Open	Open
open in Wordpad	open in Wordpad
open in &Wordpad	open in Wordpad

Commands

Underneath each verb, you see a single subkey called command whose default value defines the command line that Windows executes when you choose that command from the shortcut menu. The command line for different verbs varies. In some cases, you see only the path and filename of the program, allowing the operating system to affix the file or object's name to the end of the command.

In most cases, however, you see commands that explicitly include the file or object's name in the command line using the %1 placeholder. Windows substitutes the file or object for %1 when it executes the command. Using %1 becomes particularly important when the command line contains switches and you must include the filename in a specific location: for example, myprog /p /k "%1" /s. In cases where the program has trouble with long filenames that include spaces, probably because the program is expecting multiple filenames or options on the command line, you see %1 surrounded by quotes: `"%1"`. This ensures that the program sees the entire filename as a single unit, for example `filename with spaces.txt` rather than individual chunks of text, such as `filename`, `with`, and `spaces.txt`.

Some command lines launch Rundll.exe or Rundll32.exe. This might seem kind of odd when you look at the command line for `cplfile\open`, which opens a dialog box in the Control Panel. Some programs aren't EXE files, though; they're DLL files, and the operating system provides Rundll.exe and Rundll32.exe to launch a specific function within a DLL file. The command line looks similar to the following: `rundll.exe` *`filename,function options`*. *filename* is the name of the DLL file, and *function* is the name of the function within the DLL to execute. The remainder of the command line contains options that Rundll.exe passes to the function.

> Some command lines contain nothing but `%1`. Recall that Windows replaces `%1` with the filename when the operating system executes the command. A command line that contains nothing but `%1` treats the file as a program, launching it as a new process. You see this in `scrfile` and `exefile`, for example.

Hour 15, "Menus and Windows," describes how to put the information you learn in this section to practical use. You learn how to add, change, and remove items on the shortcut menu.

THE LEAST YOU NEED TO KNOW

All you need to remember about `shell` subkeys is described here:

```
HKEY_CLASSES_ROOT\Name
    shell
        (default) = default
        verb
            (default) = Name
            command
                (default) = command
```

Name is a filename extension subkey or program identifier. *default* is the name of one the subkeys under `shell` (the verbs), and it identifies the default command on the shortcut menu. *verb* is an arbitrary name, and *Name* is the text that the operating system displays on the shortcut menu for that command. The operating system maintains the text's capitalization, and an ampersand (&) precedes a hot key. *command* is the command line that the operating system executes when you choose the command from the shortcut menu.

10

shellex

The term *shell extension* is almost—but not quite—self-explanatory. A shell extension enhances the user interface beyond its normal capabilities. A shell extension can add a tab to a property sheet, add commands to a shortcut menu, or provide an alternative means for a user to browse the contents of a folder. Other shell extensions provide icons for a file or object, add features to the Windows drag-and-drop functionality, and more. You know you're dealing with a shell extension when you see something called a *handler,* which is a 32-bit in-process server. A *property sheet handler* is a shell extension that adds tabs to a property sheet, for example, and an *icon handler* is a shell extension that supplies icons for an object. Windows supports a variety of shell extensions:

- **Context menu handlers**—Add items to a shortcut menu, which the user opens by right-clicking a file or object.
- **Drag handlers**—Provide drag-and-drop support to a file or object.
- **Drop handlers**—Provide support for additional commands when the user drops a file or object.
- **Icon handlers**—Supply icons for a file or object.
- **Property sheet handlers**—Add new tabs to a file or object's property sheet, which you display by right-clicking it and choosing Properties.
- **Copy-hook handlers**—Extend the copy, move, delete, or rename operations for a file or object.

Windows defines shell extensions for a filename extension or class definition in its shellex subkey. shellex is usually devoid of values, deriving its meaning from its subkeys instead. A handful of filename extension subkeys contain shellex, extending the shell just for that particular file extension. shellex is more common under class definitions, however, extending the shell for all file extensions belonging to an application or for a particular class. shellex has different subkeys, depending on the types of shell extension registered in it:

- ContextMenuHandlers
- CopyHookHandlers
- DataHandler
- DragDropHandlers
- DropHandler
- ExtShellFolderViews
- IconHandler
- PropertySheetHandlers

The format of each subkey, shellex\handler, can differ a bit. First, the default value of handler might contain a class identifier that implements that particular handler. A typical example is shellex\IconHandler with its default value entry set to the class identifier of a COM class that can supply icons for that particular file or object. Second, handler might contain a subkey whose name is the class identifier of a COM class, and its default value entry is the plain-English name of the handler. Last, handler might contain a subkey whose name is a plain-English name, and its default value entry is the class identifier of a COM class. You'll find all these formats in the Registry; they all work equally well.

Some subkeys under shellex have unintelligible names that look similar to GUIDs. They are, in fact, GUIDs, but you won't find them defined in HKEY_CLASSES_ROOT\CLSID. That is, they aren't class identifiers. These unknown GUIDs just represent another type of shell extension, or handler, that extends a filename extension or class definition. Most of these oddities are due to Internet Explorer 4.0, and they represent the first wrinkle in an otherwise flawless design. In a typical installation of Windows 98, I found the following subkeys under shellex, whose default value entries don't refer to an actual class definition under CLSID:

10

- **{BB2E617C-0920-11d1-9A0B-00C04FC2D6C1}**—Contains the GUID of a thumbnail extractor. It's common in the shellex subkeys of images because Windows Explorer can display a thumbnail of images when you view a folder as a Web page.

- **{00021500-0000-0000-C000-000000000046}**—Contains the GUID of an InfoTip handler. An InfoTip handler displays help text in a yellow box when the user hovers the mouse pointer over the object.

- **{000214EE-0000-0000-C000-000000000046}**—Contains the GUID of a shortcut handler for Internet shortcuts. Four other shellex subkeys also refer to shortcut handlers: {000214F9-0000-0000-C000-000000000046}, {00021500-0000-0000-C000-000000000046}, {CABB0DA0-DA57-11CF-9974-0020AFD79762}, and {FBF23B80-E3F0-101B-8488-00AA003E56F8}.

- **{D4029EC0-0920-11d1-9A0B-00C04FC2D6C1}**—Contains the GUID of a channel handler.

ExtShellFolderView IS AN ODD BIRD

ExtShellFolderView is a subkey that you frequently see under the shellex subkey of folders and classes that act as folders. It's an odd key that contains handlers for displaying a folder as a Web page. In every case, ExtShellFolderView contains a single subkey called {5984FFE0-28D4-11CF-AE66-08002B2E1262}. You don't find this GUID in HKEY_CLASSES_ROOT\CLSID, though, which means that this GUID isn't a class identifier.

Discovering how the operating system uses `ExtShellFolderView` took a bit more digging than just looking in `CLSID`. I used Registry Monitor, a utility you'll learn about in Hour 17, "Tracking Registry Changes," to see what happens when I display a folder as a Web page:

1. Windows Explorer opens `shellex\ExtShellFolderView` in the class definition subkey. If you're viewing a folder, for example, Explorer opens `shellex\ExtShellFolderView` underneath `HKEY_CLASSES_ROOT\folder`.

2. Windows Explorer enumerates each subkey of `ExtShellFolderView` and makes a note of its name. It also looks for a value called `PersistMoniker` in each subkey, which contains the path to the HTML file that Windows Explorer uses to draw the folder.

3. Windows Explorer displays the folder using the HTML file that it found in `PersistMoniker`.

`{5984FFE0-28D4-11CF-AE66-08002B2E1262}`, which is the subkey that Windows Explorer finds in step 2, is an arbitrary GUID. You can rename this subkey to any valid GUID; the operating system still finds `PersistMoniker`. The only special significance that this GUID might have is that Windows 98 creates an identical subkey under `HKEY_LOCAL_MACHINE\Software\Microsoft\Windows\CurrentVersion\ExtShellViews`, which describes the view's menu command, as Web Page, on Windows Explorer's View menu.

ShellNew

Right-click any folder and choose New to display a menu of new documents that you can create in the folder. This is a quick way to create a new document. You can then open the new document to edit its contents. If the associated program identifier has a verb called `new`, Windows automatically opens the file using the command line specified in `new\command`.

Windows builds this menu of templates by examining each filename extension subkey in the Registry to see if it has a `ShellNew` subkey. This process is why the New menu sometimes takes so long to display. `ShellNew` defines a template for the file extension. If Windows finds a `ShellNew` subkey, the operating system looks up the program identifier that is associated with it and displays a description of the file type on the New menu. Four different methods are available for specifying a template within `ShellNew`. Each method involves adding a different value entry to the filename extension's `ShellNew` subkey:

- **Command**—This string value entry indicates the command line to execute to create the new file.

- **NullFile**—This empty string value entry indicates that the new file is completely empty.

- **FileName**—This string value indicates the filename of a particular template file for which the operating system looks in \Windows\Shellnew.

- **Data**—This is a binary value whose contents Windows uses to create the new file when the user chooses it from the New menu. Windows just copies the bytes from this value entry directly into the file.

> These three terms are similar, but they mean different things in the Registry. Shell defines commands that you can perform on a file or object. ShellEx defines shell extensions that enhance how you interact with the object. ShellNew defines a template so that you can easily create a new file of a particular type in a folder.

Hour 15 provides step-by-step instructions for customizing the New menu using ShellNew.

DefaultIcon

All filename extension and class definition keys support the DefaultIcon subkey, which defines the icon for a file or object. You also see this icon used in folders, on an application's title bar, on the Start menu, and so on.

The default value entry of DefaultIcon specifies the location of the icon that Windows Explorer displays for the file. Icons come from EXE, DLL, RES, ICO, and other files. ICO, BMP, and similar files contain a single icon; you specify them by giving the path and filename of the image file. EXE, DLL, and RES files can contain any number of icons. You reference a particular icon in such files using the icon's index, starting from 0. The first icon is 0, the second is 1, and so on. You specify an icon in an EXE, DLL, or RES file by giving the file's path and filename, followed by the icon's index, as follows: *path,index*. *path* is the full path and filename of the file, and *index* is the index of the icon in the file.

There is one more convention you need to be aware of. Windows enables a programmer to assign a fixed identifier to each icon. This identifier is usually called a *resource ID*. The resource ID is any arbitrary integer value, such as 1037. It provides an easier way for the programmer to reference an exact icon without having to figure out the icon's index. The programmer can assign the integer value to a symbol and then use that symbol in the code. You can also specify an icon using its resource ID, assuming that you know it, by writing a line like the following: *path,-resource*. *path* is the full path and filename of the file, and *resource* is the icon's resource ID. The following list shows you an example of both methods for specifying the location of an icon:

- **Index**—C:\Windows\System\Shell32.dll,9
- **Resource ID**—C:\Windows\System\Shell32.dll,-37

If you see %1 in DefaultIcon, the icon handler provides the icon. Look for a subkey under shellex called iconhandler, which you learned about earlier in this hour. This shell extension supplies the icon specified by the %1 in DefaultIcon. If you don't find an icon handler for the class, the file is probably an image, so Windows Explorer uses a scaled-down copy of the file's contents as the icon.

 Windows doesn't even look at DefaultIcon if it finds the item's icon in the icon cache, Shelliconcache. You'll learn how to work with this file in Hour 14.

Significant Class Definitions

Many class definitions look like txtfile, docfile, and regfile. These define programs such as a text editor, word processor, or Registry Editor. Other class definitions have names such as * and folder. These don't define a particular program; they define special-purpose classes and classes for special types of objects. These aren't usually associated with a file extension or COM class. Windows just knows to look for them by name.

The following sections describe the most interesting of these special class definitions. If you don't find an explanation in this hour for a class definition that appears to have a special purpose, you can almost always figure out its purpose by examining its contents. If that doesn't help, use a program such as Registry Monitor to see what types of files and objects access that class definition.

*

Windows applies the contents of HKEY_CLASSES_ROOT* to every file on the computer. Usually the first subkey of HKEY_CLASSES_ROOT, * is a wildcard. Keep in mind that this is not a filename extension, contrary to what you might have read elsewhere. It's a class definition with all the features of any other class definition subkey.

* usually has a single subkey called shellex that leads to two other subkeys. ContextMenuHandlers adds additional items to every file's shortcut menu. An example is a handler that adds Update to a file's shortcut menu when the file is in a briefcase.

PropertySheetHandlers adds additional tabs to every file's property sheet, which you open by right-clicking the file and choosing Properties.

Unknown

When you right-click a file for which Windows Explorer doesn't find a matching file-name extension, the operating system uses the Unknown class definition to build the file's shortcut menu. Unknown\shell typically contains a single verb called openas, which adds the Open With option to the file's shortcut menu. You can add additional verbs to Unknown to provide additional commands for unknown files. Consider adding a verb that opens an unknown file in Notepad, for instance, which enables you to easily open any unregistered file in Notepad. This is a handy feature considering the variety of file extensions that vendors use to name Readme files: Read.me, Readme.txt, Readme.doc, Readme.1st, and so on.

AllFilesystemObjects

AllFilesystemObjects is a special class that applies to every object in the file system, including removable drives, folders, and files. By default, the only thing that this class does is add the Send To menu to each removable drive, folder, and file's shortcut menu.

Directory, Drive, and Folder

Directory, Drive, and Folder are similar class definitions. They extend the user interface for directories, drives, and folders. The distinction lies in which class the operating system uses when you work with different types of folders:

Folder Type	Example	Class Definitions
System folders	Control Panel	Folder
Drives	C:\	Drive and Folder
Normal folders	C:\Windows	Directory and Folder

A folder is any container that you can open and browse. This includes normal file system folders and special system folders. Windows provides a number of system folders. Examples include the Control Panel, Dial-Up Networking, Microsoft Network, My Computer, Network Neighborhood, Printers, and Recycle Bin folders.

AudioCD

Windows uses this class definition for audio CDs. It adds the Play option to an audio CD's shortcut menu.

AutoRun

When you insert a data CD into the CD-ROM drive, Windows copies several values from the Autorun.inf file in the disk's root folder, if it exists, to AutoRun. Listing 10.1 shows an example of a typical Autorun.inf file. Windows puts the value assigned to icon in the default value of the DefaultIcon subkey. It puts the value assigned to open in the default value AutoRun\num\Shell\AutoRun\command, where num is 0 if the disk is in drive A, 1 if it's in drive B, 2 if it's in drive C, and so on. Windows automatically executes the program that is indicated in the disk's AutoRun\Command subkey after the user inserts the disk. The user can also right-click the disk in Windows Explorer and choose AutoPlay, defined by the verb Shell\AutoRun.

LISTING 10.1   A TYPICAL AUTORUN.INF FILE

```
[autorun]
open=autorun.exe
icon=autorun.ico
```

In order for AutoRun to work properly, Auto insert notification must be enabled on the Settings tab of the CD-ROM drive's property sheet. Open the Device Manger from the Control Panel, double-click the CD-ROM drive to open its property sheet, and click the Settings tab. Enable Auto insert notification, and close the drive's property sheet and the Device Manager to save your changes.

regfile

regfile is a plain old program identifier. So what's it doing here? I mention it because the Registry Editor has an annoying habit of automatically importing REG files when you double-click them.

The default command for a REG file is to merge the file's contents into the Registry. If you accidentally double-click the file, thinking that you're going to edit it, you'll make a mistake. You can avoid this mistake by changing the default command for a REG file. To do so, change the default value of `regfile\shell` to `edit`, which then makes `regfile\shell\edit` the default command on the shortcut menu.

Significant COM Class Identifiers

Some classes have special significance. These are primarily classes that Windows adds to the namespaces of the desktop and the My Computer folder. The following table provides the names and class identifiers of these significant classes:

Folder	Class Identifier
ActiveX Cache Folder	{88C6C381-2E85-11D0-94DE-444553540000}
Briefcase	{85BBD920-42A0-1069-A2E4-08002B30309D}
Control Panel	{21EC2020-3AEA-1069-A2DD-08002B30309D}
Dial-Up Networking	{992CFFA0-F557-101A-88EC-00DD010CCC48}
Infrared Recipient	{00435ae0-bffb-11cf-a9d8-00aa00423596}
Internet Cache…	{7BD29E00-76C1-11CF-9DD0-00A0C9034933}
Internet Explorer	{FBF23B42-E3F0-101B-8488-00AA003E56F8}
My Computer	{20D04FE0-3AEA-1069-A2D8-08002B30309D}
My Documents	{450D8FBA-AD25-11D0-98A8-0800361B1103}
Network Neighborhood	{208D2C60-3AEA-1069-A2D7-08002B30309D}
Printers	{2227A280-3AEA-1069-A2DE-08002B30309D}
Recycle Bin	{645FF040-5081-101B-9F08-00AA002F954E}
Scheduled Tasks	{D6277990-4C6A-11CF-8D87-00AA0060F5BF}
Shell Favorite…	{1A9BA3A0-143A-11CF-8350-444553540000}
Subscription Folder	{F5175861-2688-11d0-9C5E-00AA00A45957}
The Internet	{3DC7A020-0ACD-11CF-A9BB-00AA004AE837}
URL History Folder	{FF393560-C2A7-11CF-BFF4-444553540000}

The best way to search for special class identifiers (those that you can insert into the desktop's namespace) is to search CLSID for any keys that contain a subkey called ExtShellFoldersView. Doing so uncovers only those shell folders that can actually display content in a folder.

10

> **GUIDs in Memory**
>
> The binary representation of a GUID in memory is a bit different than the string defini-
> tion you see in the Registry. The first four bytes are stored as a DWORD, so the bytes are
> reversed. (See Hour 18, "Scripting Changes to the Registry," to learn how the computer
> stores DWORD values in memory.) The next four bytes are stored as two words, again
> with their bytes reversed. The remaining bytes are stored as single bytes, so the order is
> not reversed. Thus, when you're looking for {5984FFE0-28D4-11CF-AE66-08002B2E1262} in
> memory, you're actually looking for a binary string such as
> `e0,ff,84,59,d4,28,cf,11,ae,66,08,00,2b,2e,12,62`.
>
> This is good information to know if you're trying to track down how Windows is using a
> particular class identifier. You find class identifiers referenced in a surprisingly large num-
> ber of binary value entries. These aren't obvious until you export the entire Registry to a
> REG file and start examining each binary value. After doing so, you start to see patterns
> emerge. Therefore, if you're trying to figure out how the operating system uses a partic-
> ular class identifier, search a complete REG file for the binary representation of it. A REG
> file might split a large binary value across multiple lines, by the way, so search for a por-
> tion of the GUID. In the preceding example, searching for `D4,28` (remember that the fifth
> and sixth bytes are stored as a single word with the bytes reversed) yields the desired
> result.

Summary

HKEY_CLASSES_ROOT is an alias for HKEY_LOCAL_MACHINE\Software\Classes. It contains
the settings that associate programs with the different types of files that they can open.
Immediately beneath this key, you find two different types of subkeys. File extension
subkeys associate a particular file extension with a class definition, the second type of
subkey. The name of a file extension subkey looks like *.ext*.

Class definition subkeys come in two different flavors. Program identifiers are subkeys
that define the actions that a program can perform on a file. Typical program identifiers
look like batfile or Word.Document.8. One of a program identifier's primary tasks is to
define the command line that's executed for each item on the file's shortcut menu. They
also associate a program with each COM class. Class identifiers uniquely identify a
COM class. You find all class identifiers in HKEY_CLASSES_ROOT\CLSID, each of which
looks like {3B7C8860-D78F-101B-B9B5-04021C009402}.

Q&A

Q **How do I open a DOC file in two different programs, Microsoft Word and WordPad, but I don't want to have to use the Open With dialog.**

A Find the class definition associated with DOC files by looking up the default value entry of HKEY_LOCASSES_ROOT\ .doc in the Registry; then, add a new command to the class definition's shell subkey that opens the file in the other program. You can choose between either program on the file's shortcut menu.

Q **The New menu has so many items on it that it takes forever for Windows to display it. Can I remove some of the items from this menu so that it displays faster?**

A Yes, you can, but be sure to remove only those items that you don't want to use. To remove them, search the Registry for all subkeys named ShellNew; then, if you don't want to create new files of that type by using the New menu, remove the ShellNew subkey.

Q **I looked at a class definition associated with a particular file extension, but I don't see all the commands from the menu in the shell subkey. Where do they all come from?**

A Some, particularly those at the bottom of the menu, are hard coded by the operating system. Others come from the *, Unknown, and AllFilesystemObjects subkeys.

Workshop

The following quiz will enhance your understanding of the topics discussed in this hour.

Quiz

1. Which of the following items are the two types of subkeys you find under HKEY_CLASSES_ROOT?

    a. File associations

    b. Filename extension subkeys

    c. COM class identifier subkeys

    d. Class definition subkeys

2. True or false? Some programs legitimately store program settings in HKEY_CLASSES_ROOT.

3. True or false? The default value entry of a class definition subkey associates the class definition with a filename extension.

4. Which of the following subkeys control the items that appear at the bottom of each file's shortcut menu?

   a. ShellExt

   b. ShellFolder

   c. SysCommands

   d. Attributes

5. True or false? The default value entry of shell\open\command determines whether the command is the default item on the menu.

Answers to Quiz Questions

1. b and c

   Filename extension and class definition subkeys associate a filename extension with a program.

2. True

   Some programs store software settings in HKEY_CLASSES_ROOT when they're designed to run in both Windows 3.1 and Windows.

3. False

   The default value entry of a filename extension subkey associates a filename extension with a class definition.

4. b

   ShellFolder's attributes value determines what hard coded items Windows displays at the bottom of a file's shortcut menu.

5. False

   The default value entry of shell contains the name of the subkey that is the default item on the menu.

HOUR 11

HKEY_LOCAL_MACHINE

HKEY_LOCAL_MACHINE contains configuration data that describes the hardware and software that are installed on the computer, such as device drivers, security data, and computer-specific software settings such as uninstall information. This information is specific to the computer itself rather than to any one user who logs on to it. Thus, the operating system uses the settings stored in HKEY_LOCAL_MACHINE regardless of who logs on to the computer.

In this hour, you're going to learn about HKEY_LOCAL_MACHINE and its contents. Each of the sections describes a subkey of HKEY_LOCAL_MACHINE. Be sure to keep your eye on "Software," toward the end of the hour, which describes some of the most interesting settings in this part of the Registry.

Config

Within Config, look for one or more subkeys called 0001, 0002, and so on, each of which represents a single hardware profile. Remember that you create hardware profiles on the Hardware Profiles tab of the System Properties dialog box. Windows 95 and Windows 98 automatically manage hardware profiles in most cases, for example when a portable computer with docked and undocked configurations is detected. On such a configuration, `0001` might represent the docked configuration, whereas `0002` might represent the undocked configuration. Multiple profiles are highly unlikely on desktop computers and equally useless—unless you have situations in which a prominent device is available only part-time.

The subkeys under `Config`, `Display`, `Enum`, `Infrared`, `Software`, and `System` describe the hardware profile. Except for `Display`, these subkeys contain minimal amounts of information. If you're interested in learning more about this branch, though, take a look at Hour 13, "`HKEY_DYN_DATA`."

Enum

`Enum` contains configuration data for every device installed on the computer. Even if a device isn't present at the moment, you still see it listed in this branch. Needless to say, the contents of `Enum` are different from computer to computer because each computer's configuration is different. Not only that, but each hardware vendor has certain twists to how it stores configuration data in the Registry. If you want to get a glimpse of how a vendor configures the Registry for a certain device, take a look at the INF files that you used to install the device's drivers. You'll find them in \Windows\Inf.

`Enum` leads to a number of subkeys, one for each type of enumerator. (See the sidebar called "The Configuration Manager" for more information about enumerators.) Following each enumerator is a subkey—whose name represents a *device ID*—for each specific device that is installed on the computer. Thus, the Registry path `Enum\`*Enumerator*`\`*Device* represents a device that is—or was at one time—present. The name used for *Device* is different within different types of enumerators. Under `BIOS`, for example, *Device* looks like **PNPXXXX*. This is called the EISA format. It starts with an asterisk (*) and is followed by a three-letter manufacturer code, a three-digit identification number, and a one-digit revision number. If the device is generic, you'll typically see `PNP` used for the manufacturer code. In other enumerators, *Device* looks like *VENDOR&DEVICE&SUBSYS&REV*, which contains vendor and device codes as well a revision number.

`Enum\`*enumerator*`\`*Device*`\`*Instance* represents an actual instance of the device and is therefore called an *instance ID*. You might see two or more instances under a device ID if there are two or more devices of that type on the computer. For instance, if you have two communications ports, you'll see two instances under the device ID. The name used for *Instance* is typically one of three types: a sequence number, a device number as assigned on the bus, or a combination of the bus, device, and function numbers that looks like the following: *BUS&DEVICE&FUNCTION*. In cases where a device has a parent device (a serial mouse's parent device is the serial port), an instance ID might look like *BUS&DEVICE&INSTANCE*, enabling you to find the parent device by opening Enum*BUS**DEVICE**INSTANCE*. This gets a bit complicated when the parent device and instance IDs are *VENDOR&DEVICE&SUBSYS&REV* and *BUS&DEVICE&FUNCTION*, for example, because you end up with instance IDs that look like *BUS&VENDOR&DEVICE&SUBSYS&REV&BUS&DEVICE&FUNCTION*.

Enum*Enumerator* and Enum*Enumerator**Device* are usually devoid of any values. Windows 95 and Windows 98 frequently infer meaning from the name of *Device*, however, particularly in the case of devices listed under Enum\PCI or when a device has a parent listed elsewhere within Enum. The instance subkey, Enum*Enumerator**Device**Instance*, contains the actual configuration data for each device, and it usually contains all the following values and then some:

- Capabilities
- CompatibleIDs
- ClassGUID
- Class
- ConfigFlags
- Driver
- DeviceDesc
- FriendlyName
- HardwareID
- Mfg

Some of these values are interesting, but none of them are useful for configuring the Registry. Class contains a name that describes the device's hardware class. The string value in Class refers you to a branch under HKEY_LOCAL_MACHINE\System\CurrentControlSet\Services\Class for the class's plain-English description. The string value in Driver refers you to a branch under the same key that contains information about the device's driver, including its filename, date, INF file and section, provider, and so on. DeviceDesc is the device's description as you see it in the Device Manager. To make things a bit clearer, Figure 11.1 shows how these values relate to what you see in the Device Manager.

FIGURE 11.1

This diagram shows the relationship between the Device Manager and the settings in Enum *and* Class.

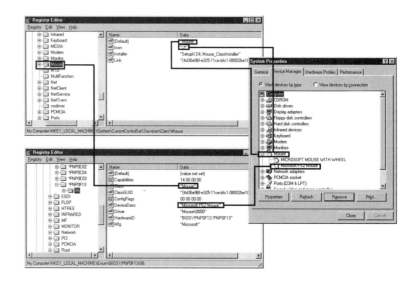

Within each device's subkey, you see a value called Driver. This string value indicates the path to the device's driver, starting from HKEY_LOCAL_MACHINE\System\CurrentControlSet\Services\Class. Thus, if you see MODEM\0001 in a device's Driver value, look up Class\MODEM\0001 to find more information about that device's driver and INF file.

Table 11.1 lists a variety of examples of how Windows 95 and Windows 98 store device information in Enum. I've divided this table into categories that are similar to those used by the Device Manager. The first column contains the device's description as you see it in the Device Manager. The second column indicates the branch under Enum in which the operating system stores the device's configuration.

TABLE 11.1 DEVICES UNDER HKEY_LOCAL_MACHINE\Enum

Device Description	Enumerator and Device
CD-ROM	
Sanyo CRD-S372B	SCSI\SANYO___CR
Disk Drives	
Generic NEC floppy disk	FLOP\GENERIC_NEC__FLOP...
Generic IDE disk type<7	ESDI\GENERIC_IDE__DISK...
Floppy Disk Controllers	
Standard Floppy Disk Controller	BIOS*PNP0700\08

Device Description	Enumerator and Device
Hard Disk Controllers	
Intel 82371AB/EB PCI Bus Mas...	PCI\VEN_8086&DEV_7111&...
Primary IDE controller (dual...	MF\CHILD0000\PCI&VEN_8...
Secondary IDE controller (du...	MF\CHILD0001\PCI&VEN_8...
Infrared Devices	
Infrared Communication Device	Root\Infrared\0000
Keyboard	
Standard 101/102-Key or Mi...	BIOS*PNP0303\05
Modem	
Standard PCMCIA Card Modem	PCMCIA\IBM-56K_PC_CARD...
Monitors	
Laptop Display Panel (800×600)	MONITOR\DEFAULT_MONITO...
Mouse	
PS/2 Compatible Mouse Port	BIOS*PNP0F13\06
Microsoft mouse with wheel	SERENUM\MSH0001\BIOS&*...
Network Adapters	
Dial-Up Adapter	Root\Net\0000
IBM ThinkPad Fast Infrared Port	BIOS*IBM0071\13
Xircom CreditCard Ethernet Adapter 10/100	PCMCIA\XIRCOM-...
PCMCIA Socket	
PCMCIA Card Services	PCMCIA\PCCARD\HTREE&ROOT&0
Texas Instruments PCI-1131...	PCI\VEN_104C&DEV_AC15&...
Texas Instruments PCI-1250...	PCI\VEN_104C&DEV_AC16&...
Texas Instruments PCI-1250...	PCI\VEN_104C&DEV_AC16&...
Ports (COM and LPT)	
Infrared Serial (COM) Port	INFRARED\COM\ROOT&INF...
Infrared Printing (LPT) Port	INFRARED\LPT\ROOT&INF...
Printer Port (LPT1)	BIOS*PNP0400\0B
Communications Port (COM1)	BIOS*PNP0501\0D

11

continues

TABLE 11.1 CONTINUED

Device Description	Enumerator and Device
Sound, Video, and Game Controllers	
Crystal PnP Audio System CODEC	BIOS*CSC0000\0E
Crystal PnP Audio System Con...	BIOS*CSC0010\0F
Gameport Joystick	BIOS*CSC0001\10
Crystal PnP Audio System MPU...	BIOS*CSC0003\11
System Devices	
Plug and Play Software Device...	Root\SwEnum\0000
Plug and Play BIOS	Root*PNP0C00\0000
System board	Root*PNP0C01\0000
Advanced Power Management support	Root*PNP0C05\0000
Programmable interrupt controller	BIOS*PNP0000\00
Direct memory access controller	BIOS*PNP0200\01
System timer	BIOS*PNP0100\02
System CMOS/real-time clock	BIOS*PNP0B00\03
System speaker	BIOS*PNP0800\04
Numeric data processor	BIOS*PNP0C04\07
PCI bus	BIOS*PNP0A03\09
Motherboard resources	BIOS*PNP0C02\0A
Motherboard resources	BIOS*PNP0C02\1B
IRQ Holder for PCI Steering	PCI\IRQHOLDER\60
IRQ Holder for PCI Steering	PCI\IRQHOLDER\61
IRQ Holder for PCI Steering	PCI\IRQHOLDER\63
Intel 82439TX Pentium Pro...	PCI\VEN_8086&DEV_7100&...
Intel 82371AB Power Manageme...	PCI\VEN_8086&DEV_7113&...
Composite Power Source	ACPI\COMPBATT\0
APM Battery Slot	VPOWERD\BATTERY\0
TapeDetection	TAPECONTROLLER\TAPEDET...
TapeDetection	TAPECONTROLLER\TAPEDET...
TapeDetection	TAPECONTROLLER\TAPEDET...

THE CONFIGURATION MANAGER

The Configuration Manager is at the heart of Plug and Play. It is responsible for managing the computer's configuration process. It identifies each bus on your computer (PCI, SCSI, ISA) and all the devices on each bus. It notes the configuration of each device, making sure that each device is using unique resources (IRQ, I/O address).

The Configuration Manager uses three key components to make all this happen: bus enumerators, arbitrators, and device drivers. Following is a summary of the purpose of each component:

- **Bus enumerators**—Bus enumerators are responsible for building the *hardware tree*. They query each device or device driver for configuration information.

- **Arbitrators**—Arbitrators assign resources to each device in the hardware tree. That is, they dole out IRQs, I/O addresses, and so on to each device, resolving conflicts as they arise.

- **Device drivers**—The Configuration Manager loads a device driver for each device in the hardware tree and communicates the device's configuration to the driver.

ACPI

ACPI stands for *Advanced Configuration and Power Interface*. Windows 98 stores power-management devices in this enumerator subkey. In my experience, the device ID is a plain-English name, and the instance number is just a sequence number.

BIOS

You see this enumerator subkey on computers that have a Plug and Play-compliant BIOS. It contains a variety of devices that are embedded in the computer's motherboard. The BIOS reports them to the operating system. Each device ID is in the EISA format (for example, `*PNP0001`), and each instance ID is a hexadecimal sequence number. Microsoft assigns certain ranges of device IDs to certain types of devices, as described in the following table:

Range	Description
PNP0000-PNP0004	Interrupt controllers
PNP0100-PNP0102	System timers
PNP0200-PNP0202	DMA controllers
PNP0300-PNP0313	Keyboard controllers

continues

Range	Description
PNP0400-PNP0401	Printer ports
PNP0500-PNP0501	Communication ports
PNP0600-PNP0602	Hard disk controllers
PNP0700	Standard floppy disk controller
PNP0800	System speaker
PNP0900-PNP0915	Display adapters
PNP0930-PNP0931	Expansion buses
PNP0940-PNP0941	Expansion buses
PNP0A00-PNP0A04	Expansion buses
PNP0B00	CMOS real-time clock
PNP0C01	System board extension
PNP0C02	Reserved
PNP0C04	Numeric data processor
PNP0E00-PNP0E02	PCMCIA controllers
PNP0F01	Microsoft Serial Mouse
PNP0F00-PNP0F13	Mouse ports
PNP8000-PNP8FFF	Network adapters
PNPA030	Mitsumi CD-ROM controller
PNPB000-PNPB0FF	Other adapters

EISA

You see this enumerator subkey on computers that have an *EISA* (*Extended Industry Standard Architecture*) bus. Each subkey represents a device that is installed on that bus. You see at least one subkey called *PNP0A00 under EISA that represents the ISA Plug and Play bus. Note that this subkey isn't common on newer computers that don't use this bus. Of course, the device IDs are in the EISA format.

ESDI

You see this enumerator subkey on computers that have an ESDI hard disks installed. The device IDs are plain-English names that usually indicate the type of disk, and the instance IDs look like *BUS&DEVICE&INSTANCE*, enabling you to find the parent device by following the path to Enum*BUS**DEVICE**INSTANCE*. Each instance's subkey contains additional values that are not found for other devices, such as CurrentDriveLetter, which indicates the drive letter assigned to the device. If you partitioned the drive, this string value entry contains a letter for each drive, such as "CD" for drives C and D.

> A good way to search the Registry for disk information is to search for value entries named CurrentDriveLetter.

FLOP

Most computers contain this enumerator subkey because it describes the floppy drives installed on the computer. Each device and instance ID is named similarly to those in ESDI. As with the subkeys of ESDI, you see additional values, such as CurrentDriveLetter, which indicates the drive letter assigned to the floppy drive.

HTREE

This subkey doesn't contain any devices. HTREE\RESERVED maintains a list of resources that you reserve via the Device Manager.

ISAPNP

You see this enumerator subkey on computers with ISA or EISA buses when the computer doesn't have a Plug and Play BIOS. Each subkey describes a device installed on that bus and uses the EISA name format without the asterisk (*).

INFRARED

Some computers, particularly newer portable computers, have infrared ports. You see a subkey under INFRARED for each virtual device that is attached to this port. In particular, you'll see COM and LPT.

LPTENUM

LPTENUM exists only if you install a Plug and Play printer on the parallel port.

MF

MF contains a subkey for each multifunction device installed on the computer. Because most modern computers have a primary and secondary IDE controller, you'll see two device IDs: CHILD0000 and CHILD0001. The devices in MF have parent devices that are

11

listed elsewhere in Enum. Like devices in ESDI, the instance IDs look like
BUS&DEVICE&INSTANCE, enabling you to find the parent device by opening
Enum*BUS**DEVICE**INSTANCE*.

> When you see an instance ID that begins with the name of an enumerator
> in Enum, it's a good indication that the ID refers to a parent device. Follow
> the path given in the instance ID, beginning with Enum. Therefore, if you see
> the instance ID BIOS&*PNP0700&0800, open BIOS under Enum, followed by
> *PNP0700 and 08.

MONITOR

MONITOR usually contains a single subkey: DEFAULT_MONITOR. If you're using two monitors, a new feature for Windows 98, you might see additional subkeys. Below the monitor's subkey, you see additional subkeys called 0001, 0002, and so on, one for each
hardware profile. The only time you'll see more than one key is in cases where you
might be using different monitors at different times, such as docked and undocked configurations. While a portable is docked, the computer might use a regular monitor, but
while it's undocked, the computer might use the LCD panel. To see which monitor
Windows 98 is using, you must look in HKEY_DYN_DATA\Config Manager\Enum.

Network

Unlike the other subkeys in Enum, this subkey doesn't describe hardware; it describes the
network protocols, clients, and services installed in Windows 95 or Windows 98. On a
Microsoft Network, you typically see the following subkeys:

- **FASTIR**—Fast Infrared Protocol
- **MSTCP**—TCP/IP
- **VREDIR**—Client for Microsoft Networks
- **VSERVER**—File and Printer Sharing

PCI

On computers that have a PCI bus, you see a subkey under PCI for each device on it.
Each device ID looks something like the following:
VEN_*XXXX*&DEV_*YYYY*&SUBSYS_*ZZZZZZZZ*&REV_*NN*. *XXXX* is a vendor code and *YYYY* is a
device code. Each instance looks like BUS_*XX*&DEV_*YY*&FUNC_*ZZ*, where *XX* is a bus code,
YY is a device code, and *ZZ* is a function code.

PCMCIA

PCMCIA contains a single subkey for each PC Card device installed in the computer. When you remove a PC Card from the computer, Windows 95 and Windows 98 retain its settings under PCMCIA. The device IDs used in PCMCIA seem to be plain-English values queried from each PC Card device. The instance ID can be a simple device number, or it can be in the form *BUS&DEVICE&INSTANCE*, which refers to the parent device within Enum.

Root

This enumerator subkey contains a subkey for each legacy ISA and VLB device that is installed on the computer. These devices include those that are detected via the Add New Hardware Wizard. You find a combination of names used for device IDs in this key. Device IDs that use the EISA format are actual legacy devices. Device IDs that have names such as SwEnum and Net are virtual Windows devices. For example, Net represents the Dial-Up Networking adapter.

SCSI

This enumerator subkey contains a single subkey for each SCSI device that is installed on the computer. Note that the host adapter is installed under the PCI key, not SCSI. SCSI uses naming conventions similar to those used by ESDI and FLOP.

SERENUM

SERENUM contains a single subkey for each device that is attached to a serial port. For example, if you plug a mouse into a serial port, you see a subkey for that mouse under SERENUM. The instance ID is *BUS&DEVICE&INSTANCE*; this enables you to find the serial port to which the device is attached by opening Enum*BUS**DEVICE**INSTANCE*.

USB

You see a single subkey for each device that is connected to the Universal Serial Bus. You also see a subkey that represents the USB hub called ROOT_HUB. The instance ID is *BUS&DEVICE&INSTANCE*; you can find the root hub by opening Enum*BUS**DEVICE**INSTANCE*.

VPOWERD

This enumerator subkey leads to additional subkeys that contain configuration data for the power management devices of Windows 95 and Windows 98. One such example includes the APM Battery Slot. The device IDs in this enumerator use plain-English names.

11

Hardware

Hardware is a tiny branch that contains dubious information about the computer's hardware configuration. The Description\System subkey leads to three additional subkeys called CentralProcessor, FloatingPointProcessor, and MultifunctionAdapter. Each subkey provides identification and configuration data for that particular component.

The Devicemap subkey is empty but leads to a key called SerialComm, which seems to map port names to actual communication ports. The *Microsoft Windows 98 Resource Kit*, published by Microsoft Press, states that this information is used by HyperTerminal—and apparently it has no other useful purpose.

Hardware seems to be borrowed from Windows NT, providing compatibility between the two operating systems' Registries. The same branch in Windows NT contains much more extensive information about the hardware that is installed in the computer, including information about keyboards, pointers, video adapters, SCSI adapters, and much more.

Network

Network\Logon is present on computers that are connected to a network. It contains information about the security provider and the current username. Logonvalidated indicates that the security provider validated the user's logon credentials. Note that if you install support for group policies using the Add/Remove Programs Properties dialog box, you see an additional value called PolicyHandler. This subkey indicates the name of the DLL file that handles group policies. Last, username always contains the username of the current user, assuming that the user logged on to the computer properly.

Security

Admin\Remote contains a value entry for each user or group that has administrative privileges on the user's computer. A computer using user-level security that's connected to a Microsoft Network usually has a single value entry called *DOMAIN*\Domain Admins, indicating that anyone in the Domain Admins group has administrative rights on the computer.

Provider describes the security provider on the network as indicated by the primary network logon. Container indicates the domain name on an NT network. Platform_Type indicates the type of server that is providing security: 00 00 00 00 for share-level, 01 00 00 00 for a domain, or 02 00 00 00 for a regular server.

Software

Software contains a variety of computer-specific software settings. That is, the settings that you find in this branch apply to every user who logs on to the computer. HKEY_CURRENT_USER has a similar key, which you'll learn about in Hour 12, "HKEY_USERS/HKEY_CURRENT_USER," but those settings apply to the individual user. Applications such as text editors and graphics programs tend to store settings in the Software subkey in HKEY_CURRENT_USER, whereas hardware and utility vendors tend to store settings in HKEY_LOCAL_MACHINE\Software. Seagate and Symantec are examples of vendors that store settings in HKEY_LOCAL_MACHINE.

> HKEY_LOCAL_MACHINE\Software\CLASSES is also known as HKEY_CLASSES_ROOT. Hour 10, "HKEY_CLASSES_ROOT," is dedicated to this branch, so you won't find it covered in this hour.

Within Software, applications use the following organization: Company\Product\Version. Company is the name of the company that produces the application, Product is the name of the application, and Version is the version of the application whose settings you find in that branch. Thus, Honeycutt\Power Tools\1.0 contains preferences for version 1.0 of a program called Power Tools developed by a company called Honeycutt. Some companies use the name CurrentVersion instead of an actual version number, as Microsoft does for Windows.

Microsoft, immediately under HKEY_LOCAL_MACHINE\Software, contains computer-specific settings for Microsoft products such as Office and, more importantly, Windows 95 and Windows 98. The settings in this portion of the Registry are very useful for troubleshooting and customizing the operating system. The following sections describe these in more detail.

Clients

Clients is an oddball; it doesn't conform to the same rules as the others. Within Clients, you find a single subkey for each type of client that you can configure on the Programs tab of Internet Explorer's Internet Options dialog box. In other words, you can associate mail, news, conferencing, calendar, and contact list clients with Internet Explorer. When you choose Go, Mail or Go, News from Internet Explorer, the browser opens the correct program.

11

Clients contains five subkeys: Calendar, Contacts, Internet Call, Mail, and News. The default value for each key names the application that is currently chosen and points to one of the subkeys one level below. Thus, the default value for Clients\Mail is Client, and Clients\Mail\Client describes that application. The organization of each client's subkey is virtually the same as it is for programs in HKEY_CLASSES_ROOT. For example, under Outlook, Express\shell\open\command contains the command line that starts the program. Outlook Express\Protocols\mailto\shell\open\command contains the command line that Internet Explorer launches when you click a mailto: link on a Web page. Other types of clients have the same two subkeys, shell and Protocols.

Microsoft\Active Setup

Microsoft first introduced Active Setup with Internet Explorer 4.0. Active Setup is different from other setup programs in that you download an installer from the Internet, which in turn downloads and installs the program to your computer.

Active Setup stores most of its settings in Active Setup. The most interesting thing you'll find in this subkey is a list of installed components. When you go to the Windows Update site, it takes an inventory of the components that you've installed and their version numbers. The information in Active Setup is how the setup program makes recommendations for components that you need to upgrade or install.

> Right after Active Setup, you'll see a key called ActiveSetup. This is an example of Microsoft getting sloppy with where it put configuration data. Thanks to a simple typo, the programmer left out a space, so there are two different keys for the same thing. Not only that, but Active Setup never looks in ActiveSetup, so the information stored there is just wasting space.

Microsoft\Internet Explorer

Internet Explorer contains browser settings that apply to every user who logs on to the computer. For example, AboutURLs has a number of values that point to HTML files for certain errors. Advanced Options contains templates that Internet Explorer uses to display the options on the Advanced tab of the Internet Options dialog box. Main is the most interesting subkey of Internet Explorer; it contains settings such as the default search URL, the amount of disk spaced used for the cache, and the size of placeholders used for images on a Web page.

Microsoft\Windows\CurrentVersion

Windows\CurrentVersion contains a plethora of values, most of which the Setup program created when you installed Windows 95 or Windows 98. Of interest are RegisteredOrganization and RegisteredOwner, which you can change if you don't like the values you supplied when you installed the operating system.

You find some of the most interesting configuration data under Microsoft\Windows\CurrentVersion. This is where the operating system stores its machine-specific settings, such as application paths and setup parameters. The following sections describe the most interesting of these subkeys and values.

Applets

Applets contains a single subkey for each Windows 95 or Windows 98 accessory that you've used. The actual data that each accessory stores is different, but in most cases you'll see things such as most recently used lists, paths, and anything else that is required for the applet to run.

App Paths

Immediately under CurrentVersion is a subkey called App Paths. This is how you can run a program from the Run dialog box or MS-DOS command prompt just by typing its name, even though the program isn't in the path.

The default value entry for App Paths*filename*, where *filename* is the name of the executable file including the EXE file extension, contains the command line that executes the program. An optional value called Path might contain a path that describes where to find other files, perhaps DLLs, that the program might require. Here's an example: If you want to run a program called Myprog.exe without putting the program in the path, add a subkey to App Paths called Myprog.exe and set the default value entry to the program's path and filename.

explorer

explorer contains settings that mostly affect Windows Explorer but sometimes affect the desktop. In reality, the similar key that you find in HKEY_CURRENT_USER is more customizable than this one, but there are still a few opportunities.

explorer\Desktop\Namespace contains subkeys whose names reflect class identifiers. For each subkey under Namespace, Explorer puts the corresponding object on the desktop. The default value entry for the key contains the name of the object, which you'll see under its desktop icon. Hour 14, "Files and Folders," contains more information about using Namespace to customize the desktop. MyComputer\Namespace, Internet\Namespace, RemoteComputer\Namespace, and NetworkNeighborhood\Namespace are

11

similar to `Desktop\Namespace`, but each subkey in these represents objects that Windows Explorer will add to the My Computer, Internet, Remote Computer, and Network Neighborhood folders, respectively.

When you choose Start, Find, you find that the submenu contains a number of commands that enable you to search in various places. Explorer gets these from `explorer\FindExtensions`. If you see an extension on the Find menu that you want to remove, remove its corresponding subkey from `FindExtensions`.

`explorer\Shell Folders` and `explorer\User Shell Folders` work in a way that is similar to the corresponding branches in `HKEY_CURRENT_USER`. The `HKEY_LOCAL_MACHINE` key's versions of these two subkeys are limited, though; they usually just contain values for two folders: `Common Desktop` and `Common Startup`.

`explorer\Shell Icons` enables you to redefine a variety of icons that Windows 95 and Windows 98 use in places such as the Start menu or Windows Explorer. Add the icon's value to this subkey and set its value to the icon's path and index. Hour 14 gives you explicit instructions for customizing this subkey, and even has a table that describes all the icons that are available in Shell32.dll.

FS Templates

`FS Templates` contains a subkey for each file system role that you can choose by clicking the File System button on the Performance tab of the System Properties dialog box. (You'll see this dialog box in Figure 11.2, later in this hour.) The default value entry in each subkey contains the name of the template. `NameCache` indicates the number of filenames that Windows 95 and Windows 98 store in the cache, and `PathCache` indicates the number of paths. After you choose a template, the operating system copies the values to `HKEY_LOCAL_MACHINE\System\CurrentControlSet\FileSystem`.

Run, RunOnce, RunOnceEx, and So On

A popular question on the Internet is "Why does such-and-such a program automatically start when I boot Windows 98?" If you don't see the program in the Start menu's Startup group, the answer must be one of the `Run` keys.

Each time you start the operating system—and possibly before the user closes the login dialog box—the operating system starts any application that it finds in `Run`. This subkey contains a value, whose name is arbitrary, for each application that the operating system runs at startup. The string data in each value is the command line that the operating system uses to launch the program. The operating system starts the program it finds in `Run Once` and then removes the value for it. That way, the program runs only once. An example of such a program, that you run only one time, is one that completes a program's installation after you restart the computer.

RunServices and RunServicesOnce are similar to Run and Run Once. The difference is that they are used for network and system services, as opposed to regular old programs, which load at a different point in the boot process. You'll frequently find programs in Run that really need to be in RunServices, given this distinction between the two.

> It's sometimes easier to edit the Run keys using the System Policy Editor than it is to use the Registry Editor.

Setup

Setup contains values that describe how you installed Windows 95 and Windows 98. In it, you find the following values (among many, many others):

- **BackupDir**—The folder that contains uninstall information. Used only if you're upgrading.
- **CommandLine**—The command line used to start the Setup program.
- **SourcePath**—The path from which you installed Windows 95 or Windows 98. Change this path if you've relocated the setup files.

Setup\OptionalComponents contains a subkey for each component that you see on the Windows Setup tab of the Add/Remove Programs Properties dialog box. Each subkey has three values: INF, Installed, and Section. INF and Section indicate the INF file and section that describe how to install the component. Installed indicates whether the component is installed on the computer.

SharedDLLs

Immediately under CurrentVersion is a subkey called SharedDLLs. This key contains a value for each DLL that is installed on the computer. The name of the value is the path and filename of the DLL. The value assigned to this DWORD is the number of applications that are using it. If you see a DLL in this subkey that's assigned the value of 2, two different applications are using it.

SharedDLLs is how uninstall programs know when it's safe to remove a DLL from the computer and when it's not. When a DLL's value under SharedDLLs is 0, removing the DLL is safe. That's the theory, but here's the rule: Because some programs don't use this subkey properly, you can't really rely on this method.

11

Uninstall

Uninstall is another interesting subkey of CurrentVersion. Each subkey, Uninstall*Application*, contains information about an application's uninstall program. The Add/Remove Program Properties dialog box uses the value of the string DisplayName to fill its list, and UninstallString contains the command line that starts the application's uninstall program.

If you manually remove a program from your computer as described in Hour 23, "Fixing Program Errors via the Registry," make sure that you remove the program's entry in Uninstall. That way, you won't see an entry for the program in the Add/Remove Programs Properties dialog box when the program no longer exists.

> Removing an application's uninstall program from Uninstall is a good way to prevent users from accidentally removing a program.

System\CurrentControlSet

System leads to two subkeys, Control and Services, that describe how Windows 95 and Windows 98 start. You'll learn about each of these subkeys in the following sections.

> If the name CurrentControlSet caught your attention, it's probably because unlike other similarly named keys—where Current*Something* implies an alias—CurrentControlSet isn't an alias for anything. This key represents the one and only control set in Windows 95 and Windows 98. Windows NT does allow multiple control sets, so the operating system uses CurrentControlSet as an alias for the one that is in use at the time.

Control

CurrentControlSet\Control contains a single value entry called Current User that indicates the name of the current user if he successfully logged on to Windows 95 and Windows 98.

ASD

The Automatic Skip Driver agent stores its settings in ASD. List contains a number of subkeys whose names resemble a GUID. List*Class* contains a single value called

Problem that contains a message. You'll find matching subkeys under Prob that are named after a device ID and whose values indicate whether there was a problem.

Change any of the values in Prob to 01, and then run the Automatic Skip Driver Agent by typing ASD in the Run dialog box and pressing Enter. You'll see the dialog box that is shown in Figure 11.2. The message to the left of => comes from List, and the device name on the right side comes from the device's name, as you see if you look up the device ID Prob within \HKEY_LOCAL_MACHINE\Enum.

FIGURE 11.2

ASD enables you to disable a device when it detects a problem related to that device.

ComputerName

ComputerName in ComputerName\ComputerName contains the name of the computer as provided on the Identification tab of the Network dialog box, which you open from the Control Panel. If you change its name here, you must also change it in Services\VxD\VNETSUP.

FileSystem

FileSystem contains a number of settings that control how the file system works. You can disable long filenames, for example, by changing Win31FileSystem from 00 to 01. You can change how Windows 95 and Windows 98 create 8.3 aliases for long filenames by adding a binary value called NameNumericTail and setting it to 00. This means that the operating system will try to create filenames that use eight full characters of the long filename (if doing so doesn't create a duplicate filename) instead of adding a tilde (~) followed by a number. The following table describes a variety of other settings that you can change in FileSystem, most of which you can gain access to by clicking the File System button on the Performance tab of the System Properties dialog box (see Figure 11.3):

11

Value	Description
AsyncFileCommit	00 = enable synchronous buffer commits 01 = enable asynchronous file commits
LastBootPMDrvs	Contains the number of the last boot driver
ReadAheadThreshold	Read-ahead optimization
DriveWriteBehind	00 00 00 00 = disable write-behind caching FF FF FF FF = enable write-behind caching
PreserveLongFilenames	00 00 00 00 = disable preservation FF FF FF FF = enable preservation
ForceRMIO	00 = use protected mode disk I/O 01 = force real mode disk I/O
VirtualHDIRQ	0 = disable protected mode HD interrupts 1 = enable protected mode HD interrupts
SoftCompatMode	00 = disable file-sharing semantics 01 = enable file-sharing semantics

FIGURE 11.3

Windows 98 describes each of these options in more detail.

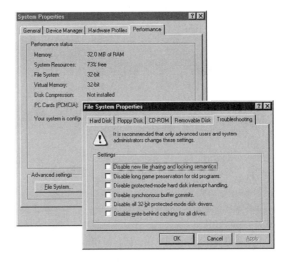

If you configured the computer as a desktop computer on the Hard Disk tab of the File System Properties dialog box, you won't see NameCache or PathCache in FileSystem. If you configured the computer for the remaining two roles, mobile or network server, you do see these values. NameCache specifies the number of filenames that Windows 95 and Windows 98 store in the cache. PathCache specifies how many paths to store in the cache. The larger these two caches are, the better the computer's performance, and the more risk there is that a sudden failure can cause data loss. That's why the mobile computer role has a smaller cache than the network server role.

Immediately under FileSystem, you see two subkeys. CDFS describes characteristics that control the CD-ROM file system's cache size. The operating system uses a combination of CacheSize, Prefetch, and PrefetchTail to calculate the total size of the cache. NoVolTrack disables volume tracking for certain disks. Normally, Windows 95 and Windows 98 write a volume ID to a disk in a region called the OEM field. This causes some disks to fail, however. The operating system looks at each value entry in NoVolTrack and notes the offset given in the first two bytes. Then it compares the value it finds on the disk at that offset to the remaining 8 bytes given in the value entry. If the values match, the operating system doesn't write a volume ID to the disk.

IDConfigDB

IDConfigDB indicates the current hardware profile. As you learned in Hour 13, HKEY_CURRENT_CONFIG is an alias for one of the hardware profiles in HKEY_LOCAL_MACHINE\Config, which are numbered 0001, 0002, and so on. CurrentConfig, under IDConfigDB, indicates which of those profiles is in HKEY_CURRENT_CONFIG. FriendlyName*XXXX* indicates the name of each configuration.

SessionManager

SessionManager leads to a series of subkeys that don't really relate to the name of this key. In fact, most of the subkeys in SessionManager help Windows 95 and Windows 98 keep track of various DLL files; or they help it determine if an application can run in Windows and what it takes in order for it to do so. Following is a description of each subkey:

- **AppPatches**—This subkey leads to additional subkeys, each of which leads to the name of a program. Windows 95 and Windows 98 can make these programs work by patching them after it loads them into memory. The subkeys under each application describe each patch.

- **CheckBadApps**—This subkey leads to additional subkeys, each of which describes a program that won't run in Windows 95 and Windows 98. The value entries in each subkey indicate a message that the operating system displays. The message explains why the application won't run properly.

- **CheckBadApps400**—This subkey fulfills the same purpose as CheckBadApps, but it's new to Windows 98.

- **CheckVerDLLs**—You find a value under this key for each DLL that is installed in Windows 95 and Windows 98. Each value contains version information that an installation program is to check to make sure it doesn't overwrite a newer version of the DLL.

11

- **HackIniFiles**—Each value entry under this subkey indicates a change that Windows 95 and Windows 98 will make to the INI file when it loads the file into memory.

- **Known16DLLs**—This subkey contains a value entry for each 16-bit DLL that Windows 95 and Windows 98 know about. When searching for DLLs in this list, The operating system changes the search order so that it looks in \Windows\System first instead of \Windows.

- **KnownDLLs**—This subkey contains a value entry for each 32-bit DLL that Windows 95 and Windows 98 know about.

Shutdown

Shutdown contains a single string value entry called FastReboot that indicates whether Windows 98 shuts down quickly. If you're having a problem with Windows 98 failing when you shut it down, change this value to 0.

Services

Services leads to a series of subkeys that define what happens when Windows 95 or Windows 98 loads. The most interesting of these include Arbitrators, Class, and VxD. You'll learn about all three in the following sections.

Arbitrators

AddrArb, DMAArb, IOArb, and IRQArb indicate the resources that Windows 95 or Windows 98 has allocated thus far. AddrArb keeps track of memory ranges, DMAArb keeps track of DMA channels, IOArb keeps track of I/O ports, and IRQArb keeps track of interrupt request numbers. The format of these values is irrelevant because changing them is senseless.

Class

There are two kinds of subkeys under Class: those that look similar to COM class identifiers ({4D36E964-E325-11CE-BFC1-08002BE10318}), and those that have regular names, such as Mouse. You find one of each for every device class. The IDs are new to Windows 98 and provide a method for accessing devices that's similar to how Windows 98 accesses other objects. Each ID has two value entries: Class and Link. In almost all cases, they both contain the same value, which is a reference to another subkey under Class that contains more information about the device class.

The subkeys with regular device class names such as Mouse and CDROM describe the device class. The default value contains the class's name as you see it in the Device Manager. You usually see the following three values and possibly more, depending on the device class:

- **Icon**—Indicates the icon that Windows 98 displays in the Device Manager. This is an index or resource ID. The icon comes from the DLL file given by `Installer`.

- **Installer**—Indicates the program file that's responsible for installing the device. This is also where the Device Manager gets the icon you see in the list.

- **Link**—Links the device class to its class definition, which is `Class\ClassName`.

Each instance ID under `HKEY_LOCAL_MACHINE\Enum` contains a value entry called `Driver` that points to one of the branches under `Class`. For example, `Enum\BIOS\*PNP0501\0D` contains a value called `Driver` whose string value is `Ports\0001`. Look up `Class\Ports\0001` to find more information about the device's driver, INF file, and so on. If you don't see any numbered subkeys under a device class, a device of that class is not installed on the computer. Otherwise, you see those familiar subkeys numbered `0000`, `0001`, and so on. Each subkey under a device class typically has the same types of values. You might find values and subkeys unique to a particular device, though, particularly in the case of more-complex devices such as modems and network adapters. Following is a description of the typical values you find for `\Class\ClassName\Device`:

- **DevLoader**—Describes the device driver that is responsible for the device. Drivers that begin with an asterisk (*) are part of the monolithic Vmm32.vxd or are loaded from \Windows\System\Vmm32.

- **DriverDate**—Contains the date that the device driver was released from the vendor.

- **DriverDesc**—Contains a brief description of the device driver. You see this description in the Device Manager.

- **InfPath**—Contains the filename of the INF file used to install the device. You find this INF file in \Windows\Inf.

- **InfSection**—Contains the section name within the INF file that was used to install the device.

- **MatchingDeviceId**—Contains the device ID of the device as you find it in `HKEY_LOCAL_MACHINE\Enum`.

- **ProviderName**—The name of the device driver vendor.

VxD

Within `VxD`, you find a subkey for each virtual device driver installed in Windows 95 or Windows 98. Many of these keys contain additional configuration data specific to each driver; thus, any subkeys you see under each subkey are unique to that driver.

Summary

HKEY_LOCAL_MACHINE, which you learned about in this hour, contains settings for the computer. The settings in this root key apply to all users who use the computer and are stored in \Windows\System.dat. Settings that you find here include hardware profiles, stored in Config, and hardware configuration, stored in Enum.

The most interesting subkey of HKEY_LOCAL_MACHINE is probably Software. This is the location in which the operating system stores software settings that apply to the computer and every person who uses the computer. You find settings here for Internet Explorer and Windows 95 or Windows 98, for example.

Q&A

Q Why do I need to learn how the operating system stores hardware configuration in the Registry?

A Understanding how Windows 98 stores hardware configuration data in the Registry is helpful—mostly because it enables you to separate fact from fiction when dealing with sticky configuration problems. Trying to configure hardware via the Registry is not a good idea. Stick with the Device Manager and Add New Hardware Wizard when configuring hardware.

Workshop

The following quiz will enhance your understanding of the topics discussed in this hour.

Quiz

1. True or false? After removing a device from the computer, Windows 95 and Windows 98 remove its configuration from HKEY_LOCAL_MACHINE\Enum.

2. Which of the following do not participate in the hardware configuration process?

    a. Bus enumerators

    b. Configuration nubs

    c. Arbitrators

3. True or false? HKEY_LOCAL_MACHINE\Software\CLASSES is the same thing as HKEY_CLASSES_ROOT.

4. Which of the following Registry keys contain most of Windows 95 and Windows 98's per-computer settings?

    a. `HKEY_LOCAL_MACHINE\Software\Microsoft\Windows`

    b. `HKEY_CURRENT_USER\Software\Microsoft\Windows`

    c. `HKEY_LOCAL_MACHINE\Software\Windows`

    d. Both a and c

5. Which of the following locations does not specify programs that start every time the operating system starts?

    a. `Run`

    b. `RunOnce`

    c. `Run=` in Win.ini

    d. StartUp folder under Programs on the Start menu

Answers to Quiz Questions

1. False

The operating system leaves a device's configuration information, even after removing the device from the computer. Thus, the Registry contains a history of the computer's configuration.

2. b

I've never heard of configuration nubs, have you?

3. True

`HKEY_CLASSES_ROOT` is an alias for `HKEY_LOCAL_MACHINE\Software\Classes`.

4. a

`HKEY_CURRENT_USER\Software\Microsoft\Windows` contains per-user settings.

5. b

`RunOnce` specifies programs that start one time, and then the operating system removes its entry from the Registry. And, yes, Windows 95 and Windows 98 still use the `Run=` line in Win.ini.

11

Hour **12**

HKEY_USERS / HKEY_CURRENT_USER

In this hour, you're going to learn about HKEY_USERS and
HKEY_CURRENT_USER. Windows 95 and Windows 98 store per-user settings in
these root keys. That is, the operating system stores software settings that
are different from user to user in HKEY_USERS, as opposed to per-computer
settings that the operating system stores in HKEY_LOCAL_MACHINE.

The most important thing that you learn in this hour is that
HKEY_CURRENT_USER is an alias for one of the subkeys under HKEY_USERS.
The exact subkey depends on the current user. For example, you learn that,
without user profiles, HKEY_USERS is always an alias for
HKEY_USERS\.DEFAULT—which is a great place to start this hour.

HKEY_USERS

HKEY_USERS contains subkeys that define user-specific preferences. What
you see under HKEY_USERS depends on whether or not you enable user profiles on your computer. If user profiles are not enabled on your computer,

you see a single subkey called `.DEFAULT`. This subkey contains settings that apply to all users, and it corresponds to the User.dat file in \Windows. Note that `.DEFAULT` is frequently called the *default profile* or the *default user* because all you see under `HKEY_USERS` is `.DEFAULT` if the user logs on to Windows 95 or Windows 98 without providing credentials by pressing Esc at the logon dialog box.

If user profiles are enabled and the user logs on to Windows 95 or Windows 98 properly, you see the same `.DEFAULT` subkey, as well as a subkey called *Username*, which is the name that the current user used to log on to the operating system. It still loads `.DEFAULT` from the User.dat file in \Windows, contrary to what other publications state. *Username* corresponds to the User.dat file that you find in \Windows\Profiles*Username*, though. If the administrator enables roving profiles, The operating system loads the user's profile, which includes User.dat, from the user's home folder on the network—as long as it's newer than the local profile.

Windows 95 and Windows 98 create new user profiles based on the existing default profile. That is, after creating a folder under \Windows\Profiles, the operating system copies User.dat from \Windows to \Windows\Profiles*Username*. The operating system also fixes any references to the default profile so that they now point to the user's profile. It replaces any reference to `.DEFAULT` with a reference to *Username* and replaces any reference to the profile folders in \Windows with references to the new profile folders in \Windows\Profiles*Username*.

> Windows 95 and Windows 98 enable anyone to gain access to a computer by bypassing the logon dialog box. Because this causes the operating system to use the default profile, you can protect the computer by enabling user profiles and using the System Policy Editor to set draconian restrictions as to what the default user can do on the computer.

HKEY_CURRENT_USER

`HKEY_CURRENT_USER` is an alias for `HKEY_USERS\`*Subkey*. *Subkey* depends on whether user profiles are enabled and whether the user logs on to the computer properly. It's an alias for `HKEY_USERS\`.DEFAULT if profiles aren't enabled or if the user bypasses the login dialog box by pressing Esc. Otherwise, it's an alias for `HKEY_USERS\`*Username*. To better understand which subkey `HKEY_CURRENT_USER` refers to, look at the whole matter from a different perspective:

- If the only subkey under `HKEY_USERS` is `.DEFAULT`, it means one of two things: profiles are not enabled on the computer or the user started Windows 95 or

Windows 98 without providing logon credentials. HKEY_CURRENT_USER is an alias for .DEFAULT in either case.

- If you see .DEFAULT and *Username* under HKEY_USERS, you know that profiles are enabled and that the user logged on to Windows 95 or Windows 98 properly. In either case, HKEY_CURRENT_USER is an alias for *Username*.

> Recall that an alias is a shortcut to another branch. When you change a value in the alias, the Registry reflects that change in the original branch. Thus, the Registry reflects any change you make to HKEY_CURRENT_USER in HKEY_USERS*Subkey*, and vice versa.

Below HKEY_CURRENT_USER, you normally see seven subkeys that define the user's preferences. You'll learn about each subkey in the following sections, starting with AppEvents.

AppEvents

In Windows 95 and Windows 98, an application event is any event to which you can assign a sound. The operating system plays the sound when that event occurs. For instance, maximizing a window is an event for which the operating system will play a sound, as is a critical error. You assign sounds to events using the Sounds Properties dialog box, which you open from the Control Panel.

Windows 95 and Windows 98—and each application you install—define the events that you can associate sounds with, so inventing events out of thin air does you little good. The operating system and applications only recognize events that they register. They register events by listing them in the following two subkeys of AppEvents, which is a subkey of HKEY_CURRENT_USER:

- **EventLabels**—Defines the label for each event.
- **Schemes**—Associates sounds with each event.

> Although you can certainly customize sound events in the Registry, doing so is senseless. First, trying to register new events for an application is useless because each application only looks for events that it registers. Second, the Sounds Properties dialog box makes choosing Sound Themes or associating sound files with particular events much easier than doing the same task in the Registry.

12

EventLabels

Figure 12.1 shows the relationship between the Sounds Properties dialog box and the two subkeys that you see under `AppEvents`: `EventLabels` and `Schemes`. `EventLabels` defines the name of each event. The name of each subkey under `EventLabels` is the internal name of the event, and the default value entry of each is the label for the event as you see it in the Sounds Properties dialog box. Thus, the subkey called `Close` describes an event whose label is `Close program`. Table 12.1 describes the event labels you typically find in `EventLabels`.

FIGURE 12.1

The Sounds Properties dialog box retrieves its information from the subkeys under `AppEvents`.

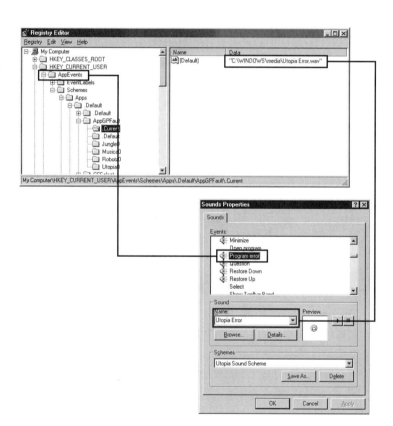

TABLE 12.1   SOUND EVENTS DEFINED IN WINDOWS 95 AND WINDOWS 98

Subkey	Event Label
Windows	
.Default	Default sound
AppGPFault	Program error

Subkey	Event Label
Windows	
CCSelect	Select
Close	Close program
InfraredBeginCommunication	Infrared: Begin Communication
InfraredBeginDeviceInRange	Infrared: Begin Device(s) In Range
InfraredEndCommunication	Infrared: End Communication
InfraredEndDeviceInRange	Infrared: End Device(s) In Range
InfraredInterrupted	Infrared: Interrupted
InfraredNewFiles	Infrared: New Files Notification
Maximize	Maximize
MenuCommand	Menu command
MenuPopup	Menu popup
Minimize	Minimize
Open	Open program
RestoreDown	Restore Down
RestoreUp	Restore Up
ShowBand	Show Toolbar Band
SystemAsterisk	Asterisk
SystemExclamation	Exclamation
SystemExit	Exit Windows
SystemHand	Critical Stop
SystemQuestion	Question
SystemStart	Start Windows
Windows Explorer	
ActivatingDocument	Complete Navigation
EmptyRecycleBin	Empty Recycle Bin
MoveMenuItem	Move Menu Item
Navigating	Start Navigation
Media Player	
Close	Close program
Open	Open program

12

continues

TABLE 12.1   CONTINUED

Subkey	Event Label
	Power Management
CriticalBatteryAlarm	Critical Battery Alarm
LowBatteryAlarm	Low Battery Alarm
	Sound Recorder
Close	Close program
Open	Open program
	Microsoft Office
Office97-AddItemtoView	Add Item to View
Office97-Alert	Alert
Office97-AutoCorrect	AutoCorrect
Office97-BestFit	Best Fit
Office97-Clear	Clear
Office97-Cut&Clear	Cut & Clear
Office97-Delete	Delete
Office97-DeleteRow	Delete Row
Office97-DialogCancel	Dialog Cancel
Office97-DialogOk	Dialog Ok
Office97-Drag	Drag
Office97-Drop	Drop
Office97-Expand/Collapse	Expand/Collapse
Office97-FolderSwitch	Folder Switch
Office97-GroupScopeSwitch	Group Scope Switch
Office97-GroupSwitch	Group Switch
Office97-InsertRow	Insert Row
Office97-ModeSwitch	Mode Switch
Office97-NewItem	New Item
Office97-PlyScroll	Ply Scroll
Office97-PlySelect	Ply Select
Office97-ProcessComplete	Process Complete
Office97-Redo	Redo
Office97-ScrollArrow	Scroll Arrow
Office97-ScrollBar	Scroll Bar

Subkey	Event Label
Office97-ScrollThumb	Scroll Thumb
Office97-Send	Send
Office97-Sort	Sort
Office97-ToolbarClick	Toolbar Click
Office97-ToolbarClose	Toolbar Close
Office97-ToolbarDock	Toolbar Dock
Office97-ToolbarDrop	Toolbar Drop
Office97-ToolbarFocus	Toolbar Focus
Office97-ToolbarUndock	Toolbar Undock
Office97-Undo	Undo
Office97-ViewSwitch	View Switch
Office97-ZoomIn	Zoom In
Office97-ZoomOut	Zoom Out

Schemes

Schemes\Apps associates sounds with the events that are registered by Windows 95 and Windows 98 and by each application. Underneath this key, you see a single subkey for each application. .Default contains events that the operating system registered, for example, and MPlayer contains the events that the Media Player registered. Look to the default value entry for each Schemes\Apps\AppName key to see the actual name of the application that registered the events. In a typical installation that includes Microsoft Office, AppName is the following subkeys:

AppName	Application Name
.Default	Windows
Explorer	Windows Explorer
MPlayer	Media Player
Office97	Microsoft Office
PowerCfg	Power Management
SndRec32	Sound Recorder

Each subkey under Schemes\Apps\AppName, which is called Event here, is one of the events you learned about in the preceding section. In other words, each is a registered event whose label can be found in EventLabels\AppName\Event. Underneath each event,

12

you see a subkey called `.Current` whose default value entry contains the path and file-name of the sound file associated with the event. You might see several other subkeys that associate sound files with sound themes, too, such as `Jungle0` and `Utopia0`. The default value entry of `Schemes` indicates the current sound theme, and Windows 95 or Windows 98 looks up that name in `Schemes\Names`. For instance, if the current sound theme is `Utopia0`, the operating system looks in `Schemes\Names\Utopia0` to find that the name of this sound theme is `Utopia Sound Theme`.

To help you sort through all this, take a look at what happens when an event occurs: The application looks up `HKEY_CURRENT_USER\AppEvents\Schemes\Apps\`*AppName*, where *AppName* is the name under which the application registered the event. Beneath that sub-key, the application looks up *Event*`\.Current`, where *Event* is the name of the registered event, and plays the sound file indicated by the default value entry of `.Current`. Also, look what happens when the Sounds Properties dialog box displays information about the events registered in `AppEvents`:

- In the Events list, you see one category for each subkey of `AppEvents\Schemes\Apps`. The label you see comes from the subkey's default value entry.

- In each category, you see an event for each subkey of `AppEvents\Schemes\Apps\`*AppName*. The label you see comes from `AppEvents\EventLabels\`*Event*, where *Event* is the same under both branches.

- The sound file you see in Name comes from the default value entry of `AppEvents\Schemes\Apps\`*AppName*`\`*Event*`\.Current`.

> Some applications don't register sound events in their own category. They add events to the Windows category, `Apps\.Default`.

Control Panel

Table 12.2 describes each subkey of `Control Panel` and indicates the Control Panel icon that sets the configuration data in it. The table is divided into sections, each of which describes a single Control Panel icon. The third column indicates the tab on which you configure the options found in each subkey. Keep in mind that only a handful of the icons in the Control Panel store configuration data in this branch of the Registry. Other Control Panel icons store configuration data in `HKEY_LOCAL_MACHINE`, especially machine-specific data, or in other branches within `HKEY_CURRENT_USER`.

Although Table 12.2 helps you determine which Control Panel icon sets configuration data in each subkey of `Control Panel`, the following sections help you make sense of the data you find in each of these subkeys. Some are completely uninteresting, so their descriptions are brief, but others contain very useful information.

TABLE 12.2 CONTROL PANEL SUBKEYS

Key	Subkey	Tab
Accessibility Options		
Accessibility		Keyboard
Accessibility	\HighContrast	Display
Accessibility	\KeyboardResponse	Keyboard
Accessibility	\MouseKeys	Mouse
Accessibility	\SerialKeys	General
Accessibility	\ShowSounds	Sound
Accessibility	\SoundSentry	Sound
Accessibility	\Stickykeys	Keyboard
Accessibility	\TimeOut	General
Accessibility	\ToggleKeys	Keyboard
Display		
Appearance		Appearance
Appearance	\Schemes	Appearance
Colors		Appearance
Desktop	\WindowMetrics	Appearance
Desktop		Screen Saver
Desktop		Background
Desktop		Effects
Mouse		
Cursor		Pointers
Cursor	\Schemes	Pointers
Infrared		
Infrared		Options
Infrared	\Monitor	Preferences

continues

12

TABLE 12.2   CONTINUED

Key	Subkey	Tab
Regional Settings		
International		Regional Settings
Power Management		
PowerCfg		Power Schemes
PowerCfg	\GlobalPowerPolicy	Power Schemes
PowerCfg	\PowerPolicies	Power Schemes

Accessibility

This subkey defines the accessibility settings you set in the Accessibility Options dialog box, which you open from the Control Panel. Table 12.2 showed you how each subkey matches up to each tab on this dialog box. Each value entry you find in these subkeys is self-explanatory. Although you can configure the accessibility options using the Registry Editor, stick with the Accessibility Options dialog box—it makes the task much easier.

The most interesting value entry in each of these subkeys is called HotKeyActive. Recall that a disabled user can activate accessibility options using one of the shortcuts. Pressing the Shift key five times turns on StickyKeys, for example. The problem is you must enable StickyKeys before using it, and some users can't use the computer without StickyKeys being turned on in advance. Get the paradox? If you support a user who is in this situation, you can enable the hot keys for him by opening his Registry in the Registry Editor and setting the appropriate value, as described in Table 12.3. Listing 12.1 is an INF file that you can distribute to users via their login script. Note that these changes don't take effect until the user logs on to the computer again.

TABLE 12.3   ACCESSIBILITY EMERGENCY HOT KEYS

Feature	Hot Key	Subkey of Accessibility
StickyKeys	Press Shift five times	StickyKeys
FilterKeys	Hold down Right Shift for eight seconds	KeyboardResponse
ToggleKeys	Hold down Num Lock for five seconds	ToggleKeys
High Contrast	Press Left Alt+Left Shift+Print Screen	HighContrast
MouseKeys	Press Left Alt+Left Shift+Num Lock	MouseKeys

LISTING 12.1   ENABLING ACCESSIBILITY EMERGENCY HOT KEYS

```
[Version]
signature="$CHICAGO$"

[DefaultInstall]
AddReg=Enable.Hotkeys

[Enable.Hotkeys]
HKCU,"Control Panel\Accessibility\Stickykeys",HotKeyActive,
➥0,"1"
HKCU,"Control Panel\Accessibility\KeyboardResponse",
➥HotKeyActive,0,"1"
HKCU,"Control Panel\Accessibility\ToggleKeys",HotKeyActive,
➥0,"1"
HKCU,"Control Panel\Accessibility\HighContrast",HotKeyActive,
➥0,"1"
HKCU,"Control Panel\Accessibility\MouseKeys",HotKeyActive,
➥0,"1"
```

Appearance

HKEY_CURRENT_USER\Control Panel\Appearance\Schemes contains a value entry for
each scheme you see in the Scheme list of the Display Properties dialog box's
Appearance tab. Each entry in this list corresponds to each value entry name under this
key. The format of each value's binary data is almost indecipherable, so you're better off
defining themes using the Display Properties dialog box.

Appearance does contain one interesting value, however. When you define custom colors
by clicking the Color button on the Appearance tab, you have to define those colors in
decimal notation or use the color wheel. Both are difficult to use because most people are
accustomed to defining RGB values in hexadecimal notation, as is common in HTML.
The binary value entry, CustomColors, defines these custom colors; they're in hexadecimal notation. The first four bytes define the first color in RGB notation followed by
0x00, the second four bytes define the second color, and so on. Therefore, if you want to
set the first color to the khaki that Microsoft uses on their Web pages, type CC CC 99 00
in the first four bytes of CustomColors. Figure 12.2 shows the relationship between these
values and the Color dialog box.

12

FIGURE **12.2**

*Defining custom colors
in the Registry is fre-
quently easier than
doing so via the Color
dialog box.*

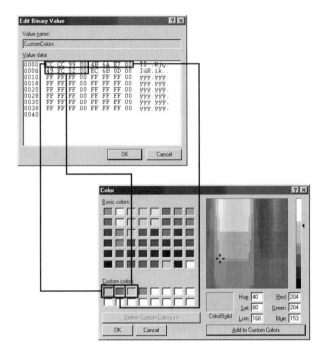

Colors

The values in `Colors` define the color for each element in the user interface.
`ActiveTitle` defines the color of each window's active title bar, for example, and `Window`
defines the background color for each window. Each value entry uses the RGB notation,
but it does so in decimal, not hexadecimal. This is one of those cases in which changing
these values on the Appearance tab of the Display Properties dialog box is easier than
changing them in the Registry. If you like to use the same odd colors every time you
install Windows 95 or Windows 98, you might consider saving this branch to a REG file
so that you can import your colors the next time you install the operating system.

Cursors

Each value under `Cursors` indicates the path and filename of a CUR file for that particular pointer. The value's name indicates the name of the pointer, which isn't necessarily
what you see in the Pointers tab of the Mouse Properties dialog box. Note that this key's
default value entry contains the name of the current scheme.

`Cursors\Schemes` defines the pointer schemes that you see in the Schemes list of the
Mouse Properties dialog box. Each value entry is named after a particular theme, and its

string contents contain a comma-separated list of CUR files for each pointer in the theme. The order of this comma-separated list is as follows:

- Arrow
- Help
- AppStarting
- Wait
- Crosshair
- IBeam
- NWPen
- No
- SizeNS
- SizeWE
- SizeNWSE
- SizeNESW
- SizeAll
- UpArrow

Desktop

Desktop is one of the most useful subkeys in Control Panel. It contains a variety of settings that control how Windows 95 and Windows 98 look and feel. You define most of these settings using the Display Properties dialog box; also note, however, that you can define any settings that you don't find in a traditional operating system dialog box via Tweak UI. With the exception of SmoothScroll and UserPreferenceMask, which are DWORDs represented as binary values, all the settings described here are string values. The following table describes the most useful settings for customizing the operating system:

Value	Description
DoubleClickHeight	Describes the maximum distance between two clicks for Windows 95 and Windows 98 to consider them a double-click. This value is in half-pixels (8 equals 4 pixels, for example).
DoubleClickWidth	See DoubleClickHeight.

continues

Value	Description
DragFullWindows	Determines whether you see the full window or its outline as you move it around the desktop: 0 = drag window outline 1 = drag full window contents
DragHeight	Describes the distance that the mouse pointer must move with the button held down before Windows 95 and Windows 98 recognize that you're dragging an object. This value is in pixels.
DragWidth	See DragHeight.
FontSmoothing	Determines whether Windows 95 and Windows 98 smooth fonts when they are displayed onscreen: 0 = don't smooth screen fonts 1 = smooth screen fonts
MenuShowDelay	Time in milliseconds that the user must hover the mouse pointer over a submenu's name before Windows 95 and Windows 98 open the menu (500ms equals [171] second).
PaintDesktopVersion	Determines whether Windows 95 and Windows 98 display the operating system version in the lower-right corner of the desktop: 0 = don't display version 1 = display version number
SmoothScroll	Determines whether windows scroll smoothly when you scroll them. This affects Windows Explorer and Internet Explorer. For example: 0 = don't scroll smoothly 1 = scroll window contents smoothly
UserPreferenceMask	See the following discussion.

Is the checkmark gray in Animate menus, windows, and lists on the Effects tab of the Display Properties dialog box? If so, SmoothScroll is set and animation is disabled in UserPreferenceMask—or vice versa. Animate menus, windows, and lists is linked to both values in the Registry.

UserPreferenceMask is the most interesting value in Desktop and is, in fact, one of the most useful values in the Registry for customizing the look and feel of Windows 98. UserPreferenceMask is a 32-bit DWORD represented in binary. You only care about the first two bytes of this value, though, which are a bit mask. Each bit is a flag that enables or disables an option. Table 12.5 describes what each bit represents. If you want to prevent menus, combo boxes, and list boxes from animating when you open them, turn off bits 1, 2, and 3 of the first word in UserPreferenceMask. Turn off bit 5 if you don't want Windows 98 to underline hot keys in menus. Bit 6 controls whether windows come to the foreground when you hover the mouse over them, and bit 7 controls whether you see those annoying tips in yellow boxes when you hover the mouse over the minimize, maximize, and close buttons in a program's title bar. The following table (Table 12.4) shows some examples.

TABLE 12.4   CHANGING SETTINGS IN UserPreferenceMask

Old Value	Old Binary	To Do This	New Binary	New Value
0x2e	00101110	Disable menu hot keys	00001110	0x0e
0x2e	00101110	Enable X-mouse effects	01101110	0x6e
0x20	00100000	Enable mouse tracking	10100000	0xa0
0x20	0010000	Enable animations	00101110	0x2e

TABLE 12.5   UserPreferenceMask

Bit	Mask	Hex	Description
0	00000001	0x01	Unused
1	00000010	0x02	Menu animation
2	00000100	0x04	Combo box animation
3	00001000	0x08	List box animation
4	00010000	0x10	Unused
5	00100000	0x20	Menu hot keys
6	01000000	0x40	X-mouse effects
7	10000000	0x80	Mouse tracking effects

The two subkeys of Desktop are ResourceLocale and WindowMetrics. The default value entry in ResourceLocale contains the locale for the version of Windows 98 that you purchased. This value is set when you install Windows 98, and you can't change it. You see a definition of this value in the Locale.inf file, which is found in \Windows\Inf. Note that the value that is used for the United States is 409, which is defined as English (United States). Versions of Windows 98 that are sold in other regions might have a different value. The remaining subkey, WindowMetrics, defines various characteristics of icons, menus, and so on. Most of these values are uninteresting, except for MinAnimate, which controls whether Windows 98 animates windows as they minimize to the taskbar and restore to the desktop. You'll learn more about this setting in Hour 15, "Menus and Windows."

BIT MASKS FOR THE BINARY-ILLITERATE

If you don't understand binary or hexadecimal notation, you'll have difficulty working with bit masks in the Registry. I won't teach you everything you need to know about these notations—I'll teach you just enough so that you can work with masks.

First, understand that each digit in a hexadecimal byte (there are two digits) has a 4-bit binary equivalent called a nibble. Therefore, the hexadecimal numbers 0xAC, 0x01, and 0xF3 are bytes that have two *nibbles* that are 4 bits each. To translate a hexadecimal byte into an 8-bit binary number, look up each nibble in the following table and combine (*concatenate*) them. If you were to translate 0xFA to binary, you'd find that F is 1111 and A is 1010, so 0xFA must be 11111010. Likewise, 0x93 is 10010011. Refer to Table 12.5 to translate bit numbers into masks.

Digit	Nibble	Digit	Nibble
0	0000	8	1000
1	0001	9	1001
2	0010	A	1010
3	0011	B	1011
4	0100	C	1100
5	0101	D	1101
6	0110	E	1110
7	0111	F	1111

Now that you know the binary representation for the byte, you need to figure out which bit you want to enable or disable. If you're working with bit 6, counting from 0, 1, 2, 3, 4, 5, 6 from the right, your mask is 01000000. Working with bit 3, your mask is 00001000. This mask helps you determine which bit you need to tweak in your 8-bit binary number. Line up your mask with the binary number so that you can identify the bit. Then turn that bit off in the number to disable the option, or turn that bit on to enable the option. After you've tweaked the bit in the mask, translate the number back to hexadecimal by reversing the procedure. For example, if you're left with 01111110, the first four digits represent a 7, and the second four represent an E. Thus, the hexadecimal number is 0x7E.

Following are some examples:

Hex	To Binary	Mask	Leaves Binary	To Hex
0x7E	01111110	Disable bit 3	01110110	0x76
0x2D	00101101	Enable bit 7	10101101	0xAD
0xFF	11111111	Disable bit 0	11111110	0xFE
0xB2	10110010	Enable bit 3	10111010	0xBA
0x25	00100101	Enable bit 4	00110101	0x35

Infrared

This subkey defines configuration data set by the Infrared Monitor dialog box in the Control Panel. Most of these settings are uninteresting because they're easier to configure in the dialog box than in the Registry.

International

In most cases, International contains a single value entry called Locale, which is similar to the ResourceLocale defined in the Desktop subkey. Locale.inf in \Windows\Inf defines each of the possible settings. You control this setting in the Regional Settings tab of the Regional Settings dialog box. If you further customize the computer's international settings, you'll see several other values. These define things such as the currency symbol, date format, list separator, and so on. It is not recommended that you change this value in the Registry because you'll miss a variety of related settings in the Registry that the Regional Settings dialog box changes.

PowerCfg

PowerCfg defines the schemes you see in the Power Schemes list in the Power Schemes tab of the Power Management Properties dialog box. CurrentPowerPolicy is a string value entry that contains the name of the current scheme. PowerCfg\PowerPolicies contains a subkey for each default scheme: 0, 1, or 3. Thus, if CurrentPowerPolicy is 1, PowerCfg\PowerPolicies\1 contains the current power management settings. Each subkey contains the following value entries to describe the power scheme:

- Description
- Name
- Policies

12

> So far in this hour, you've seen three different cases in which Windows 95 and Windows 98 store schemes in the Registry: colors, pointers, and power. You might have noticed that the operating system doesn't use the same organization for any of these. That's the usual case for data stored in the Registry: The same type of data is seldom stored using the same organization or data types.

Sound

The Sound subkey has a single value called Beep. This string value indicates whether Windows 95 and Windows 98 beep on errors. Yes means it will beep, and No means it won't.

InstallLocationsMRU

Control Panel\InstallLocationsMRU contains a value entry for each location from which you've installed components into Windows 95 and Windows 98. This includes times when you've added components using the Add/Remove Programs Properties dialog box or when you've clicked the Have Disk button in the Add New Hardware Wizard. The first value name is a, the second is b, and so on. Because the order of these values changes over time, the operating system stores the order in MRUList, which is a string value entry that indicates the order in which the operating system displays these paths in history lists. For instance, if MRUList contains ebcad, the value in e is first in the list, the value in b is the second, and so on.

> **MOST RECENTLY USED LISTS**
>
> Windows 95 and Windows 98 store MRU lists in a consistent manner throughout the Registry. The key with the MRU list contains a number of value entries, all named a through z. The data for each value depends on how the operating system uses the list.
>
> You also find a value called MRUList (or something similar). This value indicates the order of the items in the MRU list. It's a string value that contains a single character for each item a–z, and the order of the characters determines the order of the list. If MRUList contains feabcd, f is first, e is second, a is third, and so on. You'll also notice that MRUList contains as many characters as the key contains entries.

Keyboard layout

Keyboard layout\preload contains a numbered subkey for each keyboard language you install via the Language tab of the Keyboard Properties dialog box. The default value entry of each subkey contains the locale ID of the keyboard language as defined in Local.inf and Multilng.inf, which you find in \Windows\Inf.

Keyboard layout\substitutes contains a value entry that defines substitutes for many of the keyboard layouts defined in preload. The default value entry for a subkey called 00000809 might be 00010409, indicating that the keyboard language defined by 00010409 is a viable substitute for 00000809.

The last subkey, toggle, indicates whether the user can toggle between each keyboard layout using the shortcut keys Ctrl+Shift and Alt+Shift. You set this and the other options in the Languages tab of the Keyboard Properties dialog box.

> As with similar locale-type settings, changing Keyboard layout in the Registry is senseless. You're better off changing these values using the appropriate Control Panel icon because you're likely to miss related values or mess things up completely.

Network

Network contains two different subkeys: Persistent and Recent. You see these keys on networked computers when you map a network share to a drive letter using the Map Network Drive dialog box.

If you permanently map a drive by checking Reconnect at logon, you see a subkey under Persistent for the drive to which you mapped the network share. Persistent\Drive contains three value entries that define the network provider, path, and username that are used to connect to the share. If you disconnect from the mapped drive, Windows 95 and Windows 98 remove its subkey under Persistent.

Recent contains subkeys for recent network shares that the user has accessed but might or might not have permanently mapped, contrary to what other sources have to say on this topic. The name of each subkey is the path to the network share. Notice, however, that Windows 95 and Windows 98 store the path using ./ instead of a backslash because you can't use a backslash in a key's name (././SERVER./BOOKS). The value entries under each connection describe the type of connection, the network provider, and the username used to connect to the share.

12

RemoteAccess

RemoteAccess describes the Dial-Up Networking connections you've configured in the Dial-Up Networking folder. You see a binary value entry under RemoteAccess\Addresses for each connection you create. The content of this value is indecipherable.

RemoteAccess\Profile*Connection* contains additional information about each connection, if necessary. If you configure a connection to use a script, for example, you see information about that script in *Connection*. Likewise, if you configure a connection to use Multilink, you see information about the additional devices that you use for that connection. The format of the values in RemoteAccess is indecipherable, so don't try creating Dial-Up Networking connections using the Registry.

Dial-Up Networking connections aren't files. You can't copy them from computer to computer like you can files.... Or can you? You can export HKEY_CURRENT_USER\RemoteAccess to a REG file and then copy the file to another computer and import it into the Registry. This has the same effect as copying the connection between both computers. This is also a great way to back up your connections so that you can re-create them after reinstalling a fresh copy of Windows 95 or Windows 98.

Software

Most applications store user-specific configuration data in HKEY_CURRENT_USER\Software. They do so using organization similar to *Company**Product**Version*. *Company* is the name of the company that produces the application, *Product* is the name of the application, and *Version* is the version of the application whose settings you find in that branch. Thus, Honeycutt\Power Tools\1.0 contains preferences for version 1.0 of a program called Power Tools developed by a company called Honeycutt. Some companies use the name CurrentVersion instead of an actual version number, as Microsoft does for Windows.

Microsoft is generally the most interesting subkey of HKEY_CURRENT_USER. Aside from containing the user-specific settings for Windows 95 and Windows 98 in \Windows\CurrentVersion, it also contains a plethora of settings that govern Internet Explorer. This branch is so interesting that it is covered all by itself in the following sections.

Other sources of information about the Windows Registry make a distinction between the Software key under HKEY_CURRENT_USER and HKEY_LOCAL_MACHINE. You can't count on the case difference between the Software keys under each root because key names are not case-sensitive and because Windows 95 and Windows 98 capitalize both subkeys in the same way.

HKEY_CURRENT_USER\Software\Microsoft

This branch contains thousands of settings that control just about every user-specific aspect of Windows 95 and Windows 98 and Internet Explorer. Many of this key's subkeys are uninteresting; you can't really use them to troubleshoot, repair, or customize the operating system. For example, Internet Connection Wizard contains a value that indicates whether the user has completed the wizard. SystemCertificates contains information about the certificates installed in Internet Explorer. These aren't very useful.

Most of the immediate subkeys in this branch are new and are related to the Internet enhancements that Microsoft built into Windows 98. Conferencing, FrontPage Express, IEAK, and Internet Explorer are all examples of new Internet-related subkeys. Internet Explorer contains a number of settings that control aspects of the Web browser. Of particular interest is a subkey called Main, which contains values that reflect the settings in the Advanced tab of the Internet Options dialog box. The settings in this subkey are mostly self-explanatory, so this hour won't waste much space on them.

Windows\CurrentVersion contains settings that directly affect the operating system. Look and feel, shell folders, and menu settings are examples of what you find here. The remaining sections describe the various parts of this branch—at least those that are useful for customizing the operating system. In particular, you'll find discussions of Explorer and Policies.

12

Each accessory stores settings in the Windows\CurrentVersion\Applets branch of HKEY_CURRENT_USER\Software\Microsoft. Look for the following subkeys: Briefcase, Paint, PolEdit, Regedit, System File Checker, System Monitor, Volume Control, Wordpad, and more.

Windows\CurrentVersion\Explorer

HKEY_CURRENT_USER\Software\Microsoft\Windows\CurrentVersion\Explorer is one of the most important Registry branches for customizing Windows 95 and Windows 98. You can add objects to the desktop's name space via this branch. You can clear the MRU lists via this branch. You can relocate shell folders via this branch.

Advanced contains settings that you change in the Advanced tab of the Folder Options dialog box. In Windows Explorer, choose View, Folder Options and click the Advanced tab. Each setting in this tab reflects a value entry in Advanced. The names are—you guessed it—self-explanatory. AutoComplete, BrowseNewProcess, and SmallIcons come from the Advanced tab of the Internet Options dialog box, not Folder Options.

Some of the subkeys under Windows\CurrentVersion\Explorer are indecipherable, but you can make an educated guess as to their functions. CabinetState, DeskView, ExpView, StreamMRU, Streams, and StuckRects are among that elite group of subkeys. They mostly contain settings that reflect the current state of the desktop and Windows Explorer. These are mostly bit masks. Uncovering what each bit means is difficult, however.

MenuOrder

MenuOrder*Menu*, where *Menu* can be Favorites or Start Menu, indicates the sort order for the specified menu. Beneath *Menu*, you find a subkey for each submenu. Thus, under Start Menu, you'll find &Documents, &Programs, and so on. You'll also find a subkey called Menu, which contains a value called Order that indicates the sort order of each command on the menu. Go one level down, and you'll notice that this whole structure repeats itself. Look under the key for one of the submenus, and you'll notice more sub-keys, one for each command on the submenu. Again, you'll find another subkey called Menu with a value called Order.

The best way to sort all this out is to take a look at Figure 12.3. It shows the MenuOrder key with Favorites and Start Menu directly below it. Under Start Menu, you see sev-eral subkeys, one for each of the Start menu's submenus. Here, &Programs is expanded so that you can see the structure under it, which also has a subkey for each of the Program menu's submenus. This organization goes on until it arrives at a menu that doesn't have any more submenus. Also notice that each level has a Menu subkey with an Order value that indicates the menu's sort order.

FIGURE 12.3

MenuOrder *controls the sort order of the Start menu.*

Doc Find Spec MRU, Recent Docs, and RunMRU

The following three subkeys contain MRU lists:

- **Doc Find Spec MRU**—Contains the list of recent file specs used in the Find: All Files dialog box.

- **Recent Docs**—Contains the list of recently opened documents that you see on the Start menu's Documents submenu.

- **RunMRU**—Contains the list of recently run documents that you see in the Run dialog box.

Editing these MRU lists is senseless. For example, Recent Docs stores each entry as a binary value that contains the document's name and the filename of the shortcut in \Windows\Recent. The only reason you need to really care about these lists is if you want to clear them, in which case you can simply remove the entire subkey that contains the list that you want to delete. The earlier sidebar called "Most Recently Used Lists" described how Windows 95 and Windows 98 store MRU lists in the Registry. In this case, all three MRU lists use this format.

Shell Folders and User Shell Folders

These two subkeys contain paths for Windows 95 and Windows 98's shell folders. When the operating system or some other program wants to know the location of the Favorites folder, for instance, the operating system looks in these keys to find it.

12

`Shell Folders` contains string values for every shell folder that the operating system supports. Each value contains the fully qualified path to the folder. `User Shell Folders` contains similar values for each folder you customize. Note that in most cases, the operating system recognizes when you move a shell folder to a new location and updates these values automatically.

Windows\CurrentVersion\Policies

Many of the best customizations are actually policies that you can set with the System Policy Editor. If you don't want to install the System Policy Editor, or if you want to create an INF file that you can use to import the same policies repeatedly, you need to know how each policy translates to values in the Registry.

Table 12.6 describes the majority of user-specific policies you can set in Windows 95 and Windows 98 (many of these policies aren't available in Windows 95). The table is divided into sections. The title of each section indicates the subkey under `Windows\CurrentVersion\Policies` in which you create the DWORD value named in the first column. To enable a particular policy, set the DWORD value to `0x00000001`. To disable the policy, remove the value or set it to `0x00000000`. For example, if you want to remove the Network Neighborhood icon from the desktop, create a new DWORD value called `NoNetHood` under `HKEY_CURRENT_USER\Software\Microsoft\Windows\CurrentVersion\Policies\Explorer` and set its value to `0x00000001`. If you want to disable all items on the desktop, create a new DWORD value called `NoComponents` under `\ActiveDesktop` and set its value to `0x00000001`.

In general, setting policies is easier using the System Policy Editor. You can think of this program as another customization tool rather than an administrative tool.

TABLE 12.6 SYSTEM POLICIES AND VALUES

Value	Policy
\Explorer	
NoSaveSettings	Don't save settings at exit
NoActiveDesktop	Disable Active Desktop
NoActiveDesktopChanges	Do not allow changes to Active Desktop
NoInternetIcon	Hide Internet Explorer icon
NoNetHood	Hide Network Neighborhood icon

Value	Policy
	\Explorer
`NoDesktop`	Hide all desktop items
`NoFavoritesMenu`	Remove the Favorites submenu from the Start menu
`NoFind`	Remove the Find submenu from the Start menu
`NoRun`	Remove the Run submenu from the Start menu
`NoSetActiveDesktop`	Remove the Active Desktop item from the Settings submenu
`NoChangeStartMenu`	Disable drag-and-drop context menus on the Start menu
`NoFolderOptions`	Remove the Folder Options menu item from the Settings submenu
`NoRecentDocsMenu`	Remove the Documents submenu from the Start menu
`NoRecentDocsHistory`	Do not keep a history of recently opened documents
`ClearRecentDocsOnExit`	Clear history of recently opened documents
`NoLogoff`	Disable logoff
`NoClose`	Disable the Shut Down command
`NoSetFolders`	Disable changes to Printers and Control Panel Settings
`NoSetTaskbar`	Disable changes to the Taskbar and Start menu settings
`NoTrayContextMenu`	Disable the context menu for the Taskbar
`NoStartMenuSubFolders`	Hide custom Programs folders
`ClassicShell`	Enable the Classic Shell
`NoFileMenu`	Disable the File menu in Shell folders
`NoViewContextMenu`	Disable the context menu in Shell folders
`EnforceShellExtensionSecurity`	Only allow approved Shell extensions
`LinkResolveIgnoreLinkInfo`	Do not track Shell shortcuts during roaming
`NoDrives`	Hide Floppy Drives in My Computer
`NoNetConnectDisconnect`	Disable network connections and disconnections
`NoPrinterTabs`	Hide the General and Details tabs in Printer Properties
`NoDeletePrinter`	Disable Deletion of Printers
`NoAddPrinter`	Disable Addition of Printers
`RestrictRun`	Run only specified Windows applications
	\ActiveDesktop
`NoComponents`	Disable all desktop items
`NoAddingComponents`	Disable adding any desktop items

continues

12

TABLE 12.6 CONTINUED

Value	Policy
	\ActiveDesktop
NoDeletingComponents	Disable deleting any desktop items
NoEditingComponents	Disable editing any desktop items
NoClosingComponents	Disable closing any desktop items
NoHTMLWallPaper	No HTML wallpaper
NoChangingWallPaper	Disable changing wallpaper
NoCloseDragDropBands	Disable dragging, dropping, and closing all toolbars
NoMovingBands	Disable resizing all toolbars
	\WinOldApp
NoRealMode	Do not allow the computer to restart in MS-DOS mode
Disabled	Disable the MS-DOS prompt
	\System
DisableRegistryTools	Disable Registry editing tools
NoDispCPL	Disable the Display Control Panel
NoDispBackgroundPage	Hide the Background page
NoDispScrSavPage	Hide the Screen Saver page
NoDispAppearancePage	Hide the Appearance page
NoDispSettingsPage	Hide the Settings page
NoSecCPL	Disable the Passwords Control Panel
NoPwdPage	Hide the Change Passwords page
NoAdminPage	Hide the Remote Administration page
NoProfilePage	Hide the User Profiles page
NoDevMgrPage	Hide the Device Manager page
NoConfigPage	Hide the Hardware Profiles page
NoFileSysPage	Hide the File System button
NoVirtMemPage	Hide the Virtual Memory button
	\Network
NoNetSetup	Disable the Network Control Panel
NoNetSetupIDPage	Hide the Identification Page
NoNetSetupSecurityPage	Hide the Access Page
NoEntireNetwork	No "Entire Network" in Network Neighborhood
NoWorkgroupContents	No workgroup contents in Network Neighborhood

Summary

HKEY_USERS always contains a subkey called .DEFAULT, which comes from the User.dat file in \Windows. It might also contain a subkey named after the current user, if user profiles are enabled on the computer. In that case, HKEY_USERS\Username comes from \Windows\Profiles\Username. As you learned in this hour, Windows 95 and Windows 98 look for User.dat files in a variety of other places, depending on how the computer is configured. The operating system might look for a User.dat file on the network, for example, if roaming profiles are enabled.

You'll edit most per-user data using HKEY_CURRENT_USER, particularly because you're likely to be the current user and don't want to change the default user's configuration. A plethora of configuration data is in this branch. You find information about the sounds associated with different events, and you find software settings that are particular to Windows 95 or Windows 98. This hour provided an overview of the most interesting settings.

Q&A

Q **What's the most interesting branch of HKEY_CURRENT_USER\Control Panel?**

A Of all the subkeys in Control Panel, the most interesting is Desktop. This subkey contains a variety of settings that determine how Windows 95 and Windows 98 look and feel. You'll learn more about these settings in hours 14–16.

Q **I've noticed several values or keys that just seem out of place. Am I crazy, or do these belong where they are?**

A If you find a key or value that seems out of place, it probably is. Windows 98, more than any previous version of Windows, stores data in the Registry where it shouldn't be located. This problem is most likely due to human error—probably too many programmers with their hands in the cookie jar.

12

Workshop

The following quiz will enhance your understanding of the topics discussed in this hour.

Quiz

1. With user profiles enabled, where do you not find User.dat?

   a. \Windows

   b. \Windows\Profiles\Username

   c. \Windows\Username

2. True or false? An alias contains a second copy of a portion of the Registry.

3. True or false? Setting `MenuShowDelay` to some unusually large value prevents windows from automatically opening when users point to them.

4. Which of the following is the hexadecimal equivalent of `2503`?

    a. `0x2503`

    b. `0x09C7`

    c. `0xC709`

5. True or False? With user profiles enabled, `HKEY_USERS` won't have a subkey called `.Default`.

Answers to Quiz Questions

1. c

    Both Windows 95 and Windows 98 load the User.dat from `\Windows`, using it for the default user, and the User.dat from `\Windows\Profiles\`*`Username`*.

2. False

    An alias refers to the data in another portion of the Registry, but it doesn't duplicate the data.

3. False

    Setting `MenuShowDelay` to a large number prevents menus from opening too quickly when users point to them, but it doesn't disable this feature. It does, however, slow the feature down enough so as to not annoy users who hate menus that pop up when they are pointed to.

4. b

    `0x09C7` is the equivalent of `2503`.

5. False

    Windows always creates a subkey called `.Default` under `HKEY_USERS` and loads it with the User.dat file from the Windows folder.

HOUR 13

HKEY_DYN_DATA

This hour describes the contents of two different root keys:

- HKEY_CURRENT_CONFIG
- HKEY_DYN_DATA

In this hour you learn about the contents of both root keys. HKEY_CURRENT_CONFIG contains information about the computer's current configuration, and HKEY_DYN_DATA contains rapidly changing information, such as performance statistics. HKEY_DYN_DATA is a dynamic key. That is, Windows creates these keys when it starts and continues to maintain these keys throughout the session.

HKEY_CURRENT_CONFIG

Each subkey under HKEY_LOCAL_MACHINE\Config defines the settings for the hardware profiles that the user defines in the System Properties dialog box. The first hardware profile is called 0001, the second is 0002, and so on. If you have only one hardware profile, 0001 is the only subkey under Config.

To display the hardware profiles on your computer, open the System Properties dialog box and click the Hardware Profiles tab, shown in Figure 13.1.

FIGURE 13.1

*Hardware profiles are
common for portable
computers, where you
have separate docked
and undocked configu-
rations.*

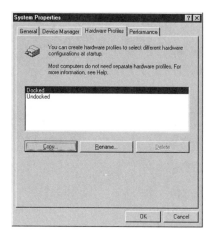

Windows stores the friendly name of each hardware profile in
`HKEY_LOCAL_MACHINE\System\CurrentControlSet\Control\IDConfigDB\` as value entries `FriendlyNameNumber`, where *Number* is the profile number under `Config`. The most important value entry in this key is called `CurrentConfig`, which tells you which hardware profile the operating system is using. This is also the hardware profile contained in `HKEY_CURRENT_CONFIG`.

`HKEY_CURRENT_CONFIG` is an alias for the current hardware profile under
`HKEY_LOCAL_MACHINE\Config`. If `IDConfigDB` indicates that `0002` is the current hardware profile, `HKEY_CURRENT_CONFIG` reflects the entire contents of
`HKEY_LOCAL_MACHINE\Config\0002`. `HKEY_CURRENT_CONFIG` contains three subkeys that are interesting and another that is erroneous. You see all of them in Figure 13.2. The following sections describe the first two. The `Software` subkey is an error on Microsoft's part. Instead of storing these few settings under `HKEY_LOCAL_MACHINE`, they store them here, under `HKEY_CURRENT_CONFIG`.

Most users don't need to worry about hardware profiles. If Windows detects that you need to use them, as in docked versus undocked configurations, it handles hardware profiles automatically.

FIGURE 13.2

HKEY CURRENT CONFIG *is an alias for the current hardware profile under* HKEY LOCAL MACHINE\Config.

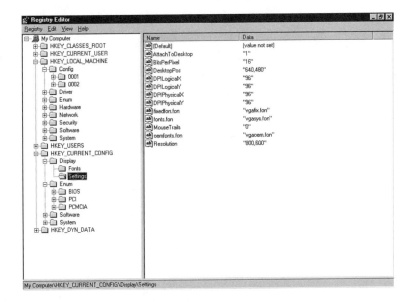

Display

Display contains two subkeys that contain different display settings. The first is Fonts, which maps screen fonts to font names. Windows 3.1 defined the same information in Win.ini. There just aren't many things you can do to this subkey to customize Windows.

The second subkey is Settings, which contains metric information for the current display adapter. The value entries in this subkey define the color depth of the display, the logical and physical dot pitch of the display, and the system fonts that were originally set in the [boot] section of System.ini. Because this subkey just reflects the computer's current configuration, changing them has no effect. It is an interesting place to check up on your display adapter's settings, however.

Enum

This subkey contains additional subkeys that indicate the devices that are included in the current hardware profile. Subkeys to look for include BIOS, PCMCIA, and SCSI. Each of these subkeys is typically empty, but each branch just below HKEY_CURRENT_CONFIG\Enum reflects the same organization as HKEY_LOCAL_MACHINE\Enum, enabling you to look up each device in HKEY_LOCAL_MACHINE so that you can identify it. Figure 13.3 illustrates this relationship.

13

FIGURE 13.3

The organization of
Enum *is the same under*
HKEY_LOCAL_MACHINE
and
HKEY_CURRENT_CONFIG.

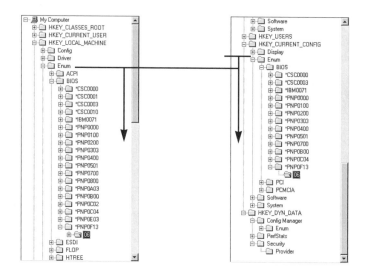

System

HKEY_CURRENT_CONFIG\System leads to a number of subkeys that indicate which printers are available. Similar to Enum, this subkey reflects the organization of another portion of the Registry, HKEY_LOCAL_MACHINE\System, so that you can easily find additional information about the printer in the hardware profile. Therefore, if you see System\CurrentControlSet\Control\Print\Printers\HP LaserJet 5 under HKEY_CURRENT_CONFIG, look up the same branch under HKEY_LOCAL_MACHINE to see more configuration data for the printer, such as port, name, printer driver, and so on.

HKEY_DYN_DATA

HKEY_DYN_DATA is a dynamic root key that Windows rebuilds and stores in memory each time it starts. It never writes this key to disk as it does with HKEY_LOCAL_MACHINE and HKEY_USERS*Name*.

You see two subkeys under HKEY_DYN_DATA: Config Manager and PerfStatus. They contain data that has the following two characteristics:

- The data is dynamically updated during the session.
- Quick access to the data is necessary due to the data's purpose (performance data, for example).

Config Manager

The Configuration Manager is the component responsible for making Plug and Play work. It recognizes and configures the devices that it finds on the computer. The Configuration Manager stores the hardware tree in `Config Manager`.

In turn, `Config Manager` contains a single subkey called `Enum`, which leads to a large number of subkeys that define the configuration of each device that the Configuration Manager recognizes. Each of these subkeys has an eight-digit hexadecimal name such as `C29A2530`, `C29A4070`, and so on. The `HardwareKey` value entry in each subkey defines the device's corresponding branch under `HKEY_LOCAL_MACHINE\Enum`. Therefore, if a `HardwareKey` value entry contains `BIOS\*PNP0501\0D`, look up `HKEY_LOCAL_MACHINE\Enum\BIOS\*PNP0501\0D` to discover that this device is COM1. Figure 13.4 shows this relationship.

FIGURE 13.4

`HardwareKey` *indicates the relationship between similar information in* `Config Manager` *and* `HKEY_LOCAL_MACHINE\Enum`.

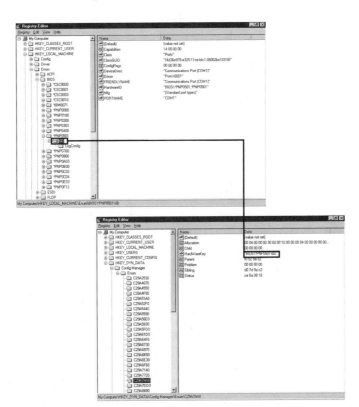

13

The `Allocation` value entry under each subkey indicates which computer resources are allocated to the device, including IRQs, I/O ports, and DMA channels. The format of this binary value entry isn't decipherable, but if you compare what you see in it to the resources that the Device Manager indicates are allocated to the device, you can easily pick out the appropriate portions of the value. An interesting relationship to note is that each entry under `HKEY_LOCAL_MACHINE\Enum` has a subkey further down called `LogConfig`. This subkey contains a binary value entry for each *basic configuration* you see in on the Resources tab of the device's property sheet: `0000`, `0001`, `0002`, and so on. `Allocation` contains one of these values.

`HKEY_DYN_DATA` is dynamic and updated continuously throughout the session. As such, it's always up-to-date, and it always reflects the hardware that is currently recognized by the Configuration Manager. Because they are dynamic, however, the names of each subkey under `Config Manager` are different from machine to machine, and the hardware that each subkey refers to in `HKEY_LOCAL_MACHINE\Enum` is different depending on which hardware Windows finds in the computer. Still, Table 13.1 gives you a sample of what I found in `Config Manager` on my computer. The first column contains the subkey under `Config Manager`. The second column lists the contents of `HardwareKey`, which identifies a branch under `HKEY_LOCAL_MACHINE\Enum`. The third column lists the name of the device as indicated by the `DeviceDesc` value entry.

TABLE 13.1   SUBKEYS IN `HKEY_DYN_DATA\Config Manager`

Subkey	Branch	Device Description
C29A2530	HTREE\ROOT\0	N/A
C29A4070	BIOS*PNP0700\08	Standard floppy disk controller
C29A4550	BIOS*PNP0F13\06	Standard PS/2 port mouse
C29A4F90	HTREE\RESERVED\0	N/A
C29A51A0	ROOT\SWENUM\0000	Plug and Play software device enumerator
C29A52F0	ROOT*PNP0C00\0000	Plug and Play BIOS
C29A5440	ROOT*PNP0C01\0000	System board
C29A5590	ROOT*PNP0C05\0000	Advanced power management support
C29A56E0	ROOT\INFRARED\0000	Infrared communication device
C29A5830	ROOT\PRINTER\0000	HP LaserJet 5
C29A5FD0	BIOS*PNP0000\00	Programmable interrupt controller
C29A61D0	BIOS*PNP0200\01	Direct memory access controller
C29A64F0	BIOS*PNP0100\02	System timer
C29A6730	BIOS*PNP0B00\03	System CMOS/real-time clock

Subkey	Branch	Device Description
C29A6970	BIOS*PNP0800\04	System speaker
C29A6B50	BIOS*PNP0303\05	Standard 101/102-key or Microsoft Natural Keyboard
C29A6E30	BIOS*PNP0C04\07	Numeric data processor
C29A6F60	BIOS*PNP0A03\09	PCI bus
C29A7140	BIOS*PNP0C02\0A	Motherboard resources
C29A7720	BIOS*PNP0400\0B	Printer port (LPT1)
C29A7AA0	BIOS*PNP0501\0D	Communications port (COM1)
C29A7DD0	BIOS*CSC0000\0E	Crystal PnP audio system CODEC
C29A8680	BIOS*CSC0010\0F	Crystal PnP audio system control registers
C29A8920	BIOS*CSC0001\10	Gameport joystick
C29A8AD0	BIOS*CSC0003\11	Crystal PnP audio system MPU-401 compatible
C29A8CB0	BIOS*IBM0071\13	IBM ThinkPad fast infrared port
C29A92E0	BIOS*PNP0C02\1B	Motherboard resources
C29AE7D0	PCI\IRQHOLDER\60	IRQ holder for PCI steering
C29AE960	PCI\IRQHOLDER\61	IRQ holder for PCI steering
C29AEB20	PCI\IRQHOLDER\63	IRQ holder for PCI steering
C29B31D0	ACPI\COMPBATT\0	Composite power source
C29B32F0	VPOWERD\BATTERY\0	APM battery slot
C29B6BB0	PCMCIA\PCCARD\...	PCMCIA card services
C29B6E30	PCMCIA\IBM-56K...	Standard PCMCIA card modem
C29B80D0	MONITOR\DEFAUL...	Laptop display panel (800×600)
C29B8330	MF\CHILD0000\P...	Primary IDE controller (dual fifo)
C29B84E0	MF\CHILD0001\P...	Secondary IDE controller (dual fifo)
C29B8B70	NETWORK\FASTIR...	Fast infrared protocol
C29BFA00	USB\ROOT_HUB\P...	USB root hub
C29C0EB0	FLOP\GENERIC_N...	Generic NEC floppy disk
C29C1140	ESDI\GENERIC_I...	Generic IDE disk type <7
C29C1510	SCSI\SANYO___CR	Sanyo CRD-S372B

13

The Parent, Child, and Sibling value entries indicate the relationships between each device in the hardware tree. However, deciphering these values to graph the hardware tree is next to impossible.

PerfStats

Windows stores dynamic performance data in PerfStats, which you can view using the System Monitor. You see the five subkeys described here:

- StartSrv
- StartStat
- StatData
- StopSrv
- StopStat

The best way to see the relationship between the data in PerfStats and System Monitor is to start with the program itself. Open System Monitor and add the Threads item. You see a window similar to the one shown in Figure 13.5. It shows the Processor Usage (%) and Threads items for the Kernel category. Notice the last value shown for the Threads graph in the status bar: 48. Now, look in PerfStats\StatData for the value entry called Kernel\Threads, which corresponds to this graph. This is a 4-byte binary value that contains the last value for this performance measurement. Because this is a DWORD value represented as a 4-byte binary value, you must reverse the order of the bytes before converting to decimal. The hexadecimal value 30 corresponds to the decimal value 48, reported by System Monitor.

System Monitor gets the descriptions of each performance measurement from a source other than HKEY_DYN_DATA. Look in HKEY_LOCAL_MACHINE\System\CurrentControlSet\ Control\PerfStats\Enum\, as shown in Figure 13.6. You see a subkey for each category; the default value entry of each subkey provides the name of the category. Each subkey under the category represents a performance measurement, and it contains the item's name and description. Therefore, under the Enum key, you see branches such as KERNEL\CPUUsage and KERNEL\Threads. Look familiar? The structure beneath the Enum key corresponds to the value entry names you learned about earlier. The Kernel\Threads value that indicates the number of running threads has a matching subkey at HKEY_LOCAL_MACHINE\System\CurrentControlSet\Control\PerfStatus\Enum\ KERNEL\Threads. Here, you find the name of the performance measurement and a brief description of it. System Monitor displays the item's name in a variety of places, including at the top of the graph. It displays the description when you click the Explain button in the Add Item dialog box.

FIGURE 13.5

System Monitor is a useful tool for checking the health of Windows and your computer.

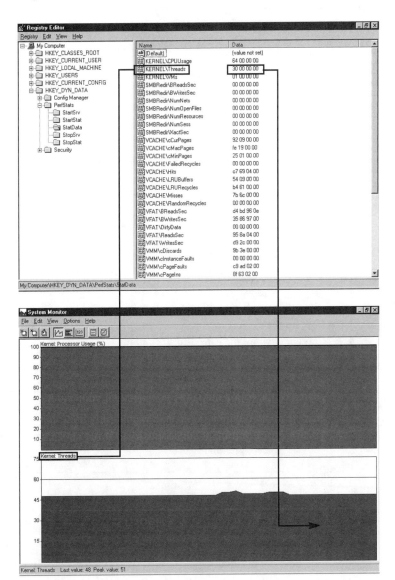

13

FIGURE 13.6

Each branch under
`PerfStats\Enum`
*matches a value entry
name under*
`HKEY_DYN_DATA\PerfSt
ats\StatData.`

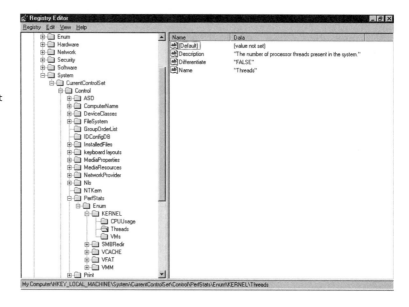

Taking the opposite approach, which is what System Monitor actually does, you'd start with `HKEY_LOCAL_MACHINE` and end up in `HKEY_DYN_DATA`. Look up the performance measurement in `HKEY_LOCAL_MACHINE\System\CurrentControlSet\Control\PerfStats\Enum`. Note its branch, perhaps `VMM\cPageFaults`, as well as its name and description. Then look up the corresponding value entry under `HKEY_DYN_DATA\PerfStats\StatData` to see the latest value measured for this item.

> If the values you see in `PerfStats` don't agree with the information that System Monitor reports, try refreshing the Registry by pressing F5 in the Registry Editor. Also keep in mind that performance statistics can change in milliseconds due to simple actions such as switching between windows or moving the mouse.

Security

`HKEY_DYN_DATA\Security` is an alias for `HKEY_LOCAL_MACHINE\Security`. It contains a single subkey called `Provider` that describes the primary security provider as you configured it in the Network dialog box. You'll typically see the following four value entries in this subkey, assuming that you're logging on to a network:

Value Entry	Example	Description
Address_Book	Msab32.dll	The network address book
Address_Server	MyServer	The server providing security
Container	MyDomain	The domain providing security
Platform_Type	02 00 00 00	The authenticator platform

Platform_Type deserves special mention. This value indicates the type of authenticator you chose in the Network dialog box, as shown in Figure 13.7. If you choose share-level security, Platform_Type is 00 00 00 00 and you don't see the Security subkey under HKEY_DYN_DATA. You do see it under HKEY_LOCAL_MACHINE\Security. You also see Security under HKEY_DYN_DATA with the remaining two choices, which correspond to the following options in the list of authenticators:

01 00 00 00	Windows NT Server
02 00 00 00	Windows NT Domain

FIGURE 13.7

The Authenticator Type determines whether credentials are validated by a standalone server or an NT domain.

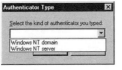

CHANGING VALUES IN HKEY_DYN_DATA

If you try to change a value in HKEY_DYN_DATA, you'll see an error that says Error writing the value's new contents. Remember that you can't change dynamic values in the Registry, so there is little value in this branch for configuration or customization.

13

Summary

HKEY_CURRENT_CONFIG is an alias for one of the subkeys under HKEY_LOCAL_MACHINE\Config. It defines the current hardware profile, which devices are enabled and which are not.

In addition to describing the computer's current configuration, HKEY_DYN_DATA also contains quick access to data that changes rapidly. You find performance data in this branch, for example, which you can view using System Monitor.

Q&A

Q Other than technical interest, is there any good reason to worry with the values in `HKEY_CURRENT_CONFIG` or `HKEY_DYN_DATA`?

A Not really. Understanding these two branches is interesting for those who want to master the Registry, but their usefulness as a customization or administrative tool is limited.

Workshop

The following quiz will enhance your understanding of the topics discussed in this hour.

Quiz

1. `HKEY_LOCAL_MACHINE\Config` contains a single subkey for each hardware profile. Which subkey of `HKEY_LOCAL_MACHINE\System\CurrentControlSet\Control` indicates the current hardware profile?

    a. `IDConfig`

    b. `CurrentProfile`

    c. `CurrentConfig`

    d. `IDConfigDB`

2. True or false? A dynamic root key is stored in System.dat or User.dat.

3. Which of the following applications can you use to see the contents of `HKEY_DYN_DATA\PerStatus`?

    a. Network Monitor

    b. Performance Monitor

    c. System Monitor

Answers to Quiz Questions

1. d

    `IDConfigDB` contains a value called `CurrentConfig`, which indicates the current hardware profile.

2. False

    The operating system builds a dynamic root key when it first starts, and continues updating the data throughout the session.

3. c

    System Monitor displays the statistics from this branch of the Registry.

PART V
Customizing Windows

Hour

Hour **14**

Files and Folders

When many people learn about the customizations that are discussed in this hour, they're floored—they had no idea that they were capable of these types of things. You can do the following:

- Relocate the Windows shell folders.
- Customize shell folders in a variety of ways.
- Change a file, folder, or object's icon.

This hour shows you how to move Windows shell folders and how to display different icons for different folders or drives. This hour focuses entirely on files and folders, however. If you want to learn how to customize the Windows shortcut menus, take a look at the next hour, "Menus and Windows."

Relocating Shell Folders

Folders that Windows uses for special purposes are called *shell folders*. For example, the Favorites folder is a shell folder, as are the Start Menu and My Documents folders. Table 14.1 describes the shell folders that Windows 98 defines. Furthermore, the table includes the default path for each (the default path is different if you've enabled profiles). Windows 95 has similar folders. The actual location of each folder isn't important, though, because Windows uses the internal name of the folder to look up its path in the Registry. You're free to change a shell folder's location by pointing the operating system to the new location.

You might want to change a shell folder's location for a variety of reasons. You can share a single Favorites folder among several users, for example, by pointing Windows to a folder on a network share. Or maybe you prefer to put the My Documents folder on your desktop or move the Startup folder to a different location.

TABLE 14.1 WINDOWS 98 SHELL FOLDERS

Name	Default Location
AppData	\Windows\Application Data
Cache	\Windows\Temporary Internet Files
Cookies	\Windows\Cookies
Desktop	\Windows\Desktop
Fonts	\Windows\Fonts
Favorites	\Windows\Favorites
History	\Windows\History
NetHood	\Windows\NetHood
Programs	\Windows\Start Menu\Programs
Personal	\My Documents
PrintHood	\Windows\PrintHood
Recent	\Windows\Recent
Start menu	\Windows\Start Menu
Startup	\Windows\Start Menu\Programs\StartUp
SendTo	\Windows\SendTo
Templates	\Windows\ShellNew

The actual location of each shell folder is different if user profiles are enabled on the computer. In that case, look in \Windows\Profiles\username for the folders you see in Table 14.1.

Windows retrieves the location of each shell folder from HKEY_CURRENT_USER\Software\
Microsoft\Windows\CurrentVersion\Explorer\Shell Folders. Within this key, you
find a value entry for each shell folder, each of which has one of the names shown in
Table 14.1. The string value of the value entry is the fully qualified path of the folder's
location. You'll notice another subkey at the same level called User Shell Folder,
which contains value entries for any shell folders that you've customized. Get this
straight—Shell Folders contains value entries for all the shell folders, including the
ones you've customized, and User Shell Folders contains only value entries for the
ones you've customized. Armed with this information, here's how to change the location
of a shell folder:

1. Add a string value entry for the shell folder to
   HKEY_CURRENT_USER\SOFTWARE\Microsoft\Windows\CurrentVersion\explorer\
   User Shell Folder. Get the name for the new value from Table 14.1. Set its value
   to the fully qualified path of the folder, starting from the root of the drive.

2. Change the value of the corresponding value entry in HKEY_CURRENT_USER\
   SOFTWARE\Microsoft\Windows\CurrentVersion\explorer\Shell Folder. The
   path in this value matches the path you specified in step 1.

3. Restart the computer because this change won't take effect until you do so.
   Alternatively, you can log off and back on again.

Changing Machine-Specific Shell Folders

You find similar branches under HKEY_LOCAL_MACHINE. However, the shell folders in
HKEY_CURRENT_USER are user-specific, whereas the shell folders in HKEY_LOCAL_MACHINE
apply to every user who logs on to the computer. The values have different names, too,
including Common Desktop and Common Startup. By default, these are the only two common shell folders that Windows defines. You can customize the location of each common
shell folder using the same steps you learned for customizing user-specific shell folders.

SHARING THE FAVORITES FOLDER

There are two reasons for sharing a common Favorites folder. First, you can share a single
Favorites folder among all the users on a network. Second, you can share a Favorites
folder between your portable and desktop computers so that you can take your favorite
Internet shortcuts with you on the road.

In either case, the instructions for sharing a Favorites folder are roughly the same:

1. Determine where you want to put the Favorites folder. If you're sharing it on the
   network, create a share for it by clicking Share on the folder's shortcut menu. If
   you're sharing it between networked portable and desktop computers, create a
   share on the portable computer.

14

2. Copy the contents of the original folder to the new Favorites folder that you shared in step 1. Be sure to copy all the hidden files you find in the original Favorites folder so that you'll pick up the various Desktop.ini files in it.

3. Change the location of the Favorites folder on each user's computer. You might want to use an INF or REG file to distribute this customization to multiple users. Or you can use the System Policy Editor, as described in Hour 21, "Controlling the Desktop via System Policies."

Working with Shell Folders

Some of the folders that you see in My Computer or on the desktop don't actually exist on the hard disk. They look just like folders in Windows Explorer, but they're actually objects that display the contents of the folder in a window. Table 14.2 shows you the unique class identifier for many of these objects, which Windows 98 defines in the Registry under `HKEY_CLASSES_ROOT\CLSID`. Windows 95 defines the same folders if you've installed Internet Explorer 4.0. Therefore, you find the Control Panel at `{21EC2020-3AEA-1069-A2DD-08002B30309D}` and the Recycle Bin at `{645FF040-5081-101B-9F08-00AA002F954E}` under `HKEY_CLASSES_ROOT\CLSID`.

As you've learned, these folders don't exist on the hard disk; they exist in Windows Explorer's or the desktop's name space. *Name space* is an abstract term that describes all the objects within that folder, real or imaginary. Notice that Windows Explorer's name space is consistently referred to separately from the desktop's name space; this is because Windows defines two different name spaces, one for each of these objects, as shown in Figure 14.1. Windows defines each in the Registry at `HKEY_LOCAL_MACHINE\Software\Microsoft\Windows\CurrentVersion\explorer`. The subkey `Desktop\NameSpace` contains the name space for the desktop, and `MyComputer\NameSpace` contains the name space for My Computer.

Windows adds each subkey it finds in `Desktop\NameSpace` to the desktop's name space and each subkey it finds in `MyComputer\NameSpace` to the name space of My Computer. You usually see the class identifiers for the Recycle Bin and My Documents folders in the desktop's name space and the class identifiers for the Dial-Up Networking and Scheduled Tasks folders in My Computer's name space. What you don't see in either `NameSpace` key are subkeys for the Control Panel, Printers, Network Neighborhood, and Internet Explorer folders. These are built into the operating system. You can't remove the Control Panel or Printers folders from My Computer, but you can remove the Internet Explorer and Network Neighborhood icons from the desktop, as you will learn in the next section.

FIGURE 14.1

*The desktop and
Windows Explorer use
separate name spaces.*

Desktop
Name
Space

My Computer
Name Space

After removing the Network Neighborhood icon from the desktop, you can't use UNC paths, which look like \\Server\Resource, to access resources on the network. You'll have to map directly to those resources instead. Removing this icon also prevents Direct Cable Connection from properly displaying the contents of the host computer.

TABLE 14.2 CLASS IDENTIFIERS FOR WINDOWS 98 SHELL FOLDERS

Folder	Class Identifiers
Control Panel	{21EC2020-3AEA-1069-A2DD-08002B30309D}
Dial-Up Networking	{992CFFA0-F557-101A-88EC-00DD010CCC48}
Internet Explorer	{FBF23B42-E3F0-101B-8488-00AA003E56F8}
My Computer	{20D04FE0-3AEA-1069-A2D8-08002B30309D}
Network Neighborhood	{208D2C60-3AEA-1069-A2D7-08002B30309D}
Printers	{2227A280-3AEA-1069-A2DE-08002B30309D}
Recycle Bin	{645FF040-5081-101B-9F08-00AA002F954E}
Scheduled Tasks	{D6277990-4C6A-11CF-8D87-00AA0060F5BF}

14

Table 14.2 lists the folders that you can put on the desktop or on the Start menu after installing Windows, but other applications might provide special folders you can use as well. How do you find them? Search the Registry for any class identifiers that have a `ShellFolder` subkey with an `attributes` value entry. The default value entry of the class identifier describes the folder.

Removing a Shell Folder from the Desktop

How you remove a shell folder from the desktop depends on the folder. If you're removing the Recycle Bin or My Documents folders, for example, delete the folder's class identifier subkey from `HKEY_LOCAL_MACHINE\Software\Microsoft\Windows\CurrentVersion\explorer\Desktop\NameSpace`. Easy enough. You don't see a subkey for Internet Explorer or Network Neighborhood in the desktop's name space, but you can remove them from the desktop by setting the values shown in Table 14.3 under `HKEY_CURRENT_USER\Software\Microsoft\Windows\CurrentVersion\Policies\Explorer`:

TABLE 14.3 REMOVING ITEMS FROM THE DESKTOP'S NAME SPACE

Icon	Value Entry	Enabled	Disabled
Internet Explorer	`NoInternetIcon`	00 00 00 00	01 00 00 00
Network Neighborhood	`NoNetHood`	00 00 00 00	01 00 00 00

Renaming Desktop Folders Such as Recycle Bin

You can rename the My Computer, Network Neighborhood, and Internet Explorer icons on the desktop. Right-click any of them, choose Rename, type the new name of the icon, and press Enter. Renaming the Recycle Bin and some other icons is a bit harder, however, because they don't have a similar command on their shortcut menu. Note that none of the icons in `Desktop\NameSpace` or `MyComputer\NameSpace` have Rename on their shortcut menus.

Regardless, you can rename the icons you see in Table 14.2 by changing the default value entry of the icon's class identifier in `HKEY_CLASSES_ROOT\CLSID`. To rename the Recycle Bin, change the default value entry of `HKEY_CLASSES_ROOT\CLSID\{645FF040-5081-101B-9F08-00AA002F954E}` to the name that you want Windows to display on the desktop and in Windows Explorer. To rename the Control Panel icon, change the default value entry of `HKEY_CLASSES_ROOT\CLSID\{21EC2020-3AEA-1069-A2DD-08002B30309D}`.

The default value entry of each class identifier under Desktop\NameSpace and MyComputer\NameSpace also contains the name of the icon. Changing it doesn't change the name of the icon on the desktop or in My Computer, however.

Customizing Icons for Files and Other Objects

Icons come from EXE, DLL, RES, and ICO files. ICO, BMP, and similar files contain a single icon, and you specify them by giving the path and filename of the ICO file. EXE, DLL, and RES files can contain any number of icons, however. You reference a particular icon in such files using the icon's index, starting from 0. The first icon is 0, the second is 1, and so on. You specify an icon in an EXE, DLL, or RES file by giving the path and filename of the file, followed by the index of the icon, as follows: *path\filename,index.*

There is one more convention of which you need to be aware. Windows enables a programmer to assign a fixed identifier to each icon. This identifier is usually called a *resource ID*. The resource ID is any arbitrary integer value, such as 1037, that provides an easier way for the programmer to reference an exact icon without having to figure out the icon's index. The programmer can assign the integer value to a symbol and then use that symbol in the code. You can also specify an icon using its resource ID, assuming that you know it, by writing a line similar to the following: `path\filename,-resource`. The following list shows you an example of both methods for specifying the location of an icon:

- **Index**—C:\Windows\System\Shell32.dll,9
- **Resource ID**—C:\Windows\System\Shell32.dll,-37

Shell Folders

Windows retrieves the icon that is to be used for shell folders from the DefaultIcon subkey of the class identifier in HKEY_CLASSES_ROOT\CLSID. The default value entry of this subkey contains the icon specification you just learned about. To change the icon that Windows uses for a shell folder, follow these steps:

1. Remove a file called ShellIconCache from \Windows.
2. Change the default value entry of HKEY_CLASSES_ROOT\CLSID*clsid*\DefaultIcon to the location of the icon. *clsid* is the class identifier of the object you're changing. See Table 14.2 for a list of possibilities.

14

3. Refresh the desktop and Windows Explorer so that you can see your changes. To refresh the desktop, right-click it and choose Refresh. To refresh Windows Explorer, choose View, Refresh.

> Windows caches icons in a file called ShellIconCache, which is found in \Windows. This way, it can display icons on the desktop and in Windows Explorer much faster because it doesn't have to reload the icons from their original locations. You can adjust the size of this cache by changing the value entry called Max Cached Icons in HKEY_LOCAL_MACHINE\Software\Microsoft\Windows\CurrentVersion\ explorer to any number greater than 512, which is the default value. Create this DWORD value if it doesn't exist.

Files

Changing the icons for files is similar to changing the icon for a shell folder. Instead of changing the default value entry of HKEY_CLASSES_ROOT\CLSID\clsid\DefaultIcon to the location of the icon, change the default value entry of HKEY_CLASSES_ROOT\progid\DefaultIcon. The trick is to find the program identifier that is associated with a file extension. Look up the file extension in the Registry under HKEY_CLASSES_ROOT. For example, the subkey for the DOC file extension is HKEY_CLASSES_ROOT\.doc. The default value entry of each file extension's subkey is the name of the program identifier with which it is associated. To change the icon that is displayed for a file using a particular extension, follow these steps:

1. Note the default value entry of HKEY_CLASSES_ROOT\.ext, where ext is the file extension. The default value entry is the program identifier with which the extension is associated.

2. Open HKEY_CLASSES_ROOT\progid\DefaultIcon, where progid is the program identifier you looked up in step 1.

3. Change the default value entry of DefaultIcon to indicate the location of the icon that you want to use for files associated with that program.

If you don't notice any change after changing the icon for a program identifier and refreshing the display, you'll have to do a bit of tracking to find any overriding DefaultIcon keys. Check to see if a class identifier is associated with the program identifier (look in the program identifier's CLSID subkey), and look up that class under HKEY_CLASSES_ROOT\CLSID. If you see a DefaultIcon subkey under the class identifier's subkey, it might be overriding the icon that is specified in the program identifier. Note also that some icons are specified via the ShellIcons key, as you'll learn in the next section.

Shell Icons

Unlike the icons for shell folders and files, the icons you see on the Start menu don't come from HKEY_CLASSES_ROOT. They come from Shell32.dll, as do the icons that Windows displays for different types of disk drives.

You can replace any shell icon by adding a string value entry to HKEY_LOCAL_MACHINE\Software\Microsoft\Windows\CurrentVersion\explorer\ Shell Icons. If you don't see this subkey, add it. The name of the value entry is the index of the icon in Shell32. Refer to Table 14.4 to determine the index of each icon. The value is the location of the icon: a path if you're using an ICO file, or a path and index if you're using a DLL, EXE, or RES file. Windows substitutes your icon for each entry it finds in Shell Icons. Therefore, to use icon 28 in Cool.dll instead of the default icon for My Computer, create a new value entry called 15 in Shell Icons and set its value to C:\Windows\System\Cool.dll,28. If you don't see the change you made after refreshing the desktop, follow these steps to force Windows to notice the new icon:

1. Restart the Computer in Safe Mode. To do so, hold down the Ctrl key while you start the computer, and then choose Safe Mode from the boot menu.

2. Delete the ShellIconCache file from \Windows. You might have to show hidden files in Windows Explorer in order to see this file.

3. Change the icon in Shell Icons as described in the preceding paragraph.

4. Restart the computer normally.

Specifying certain icons in Shell Icons has no effect. Windows uses the icon that is specified in the DefaultIcon subkey of a class identifier instead of the icon listed in Shell Icons. Therefore, adding entries for the Recycle Bin, Dial-Up Networking, Control Panel, and Printers icons to Shell Icons doesn't do anything. To change these icons, change their DefaultIcon subkey as described in the earlier section, "Shell Folders." Windows defines the icons for various DefaultIcon keys, too, so changing that icon in Shell Icons doesn't change what you see in Windows Explorer.

Shell32.dll contains more icons than are shown in Table 14.4. Windows contains other files that have icons, too. The easiest way to view the icons in a file is to download an icon viewer from your favorite shareware site. My personal favorite is IconRipper, which can be downloaded from http://www.hotfiles.com.

14

Individual Disks and Network Volumes

Adding value entries 5–12 to Shell Icons affects every drive of that type (see Table 14.5 to determine which value entries correspond to which drive types). For example, specifying a new icon for removable drives by adding a value entry of 7 to Shell Icons changes the icon for every removable drive on the computer.

You can use a different icon for each disk individually, however, including individual hard disks, floppy disks, and network volumes. Have you ever noticed that when you insert a certain CD-ROM into the drive, Windows automatically starts it and changes the icon that it displays in Windows Explorer? This works because the disk has an Autorun.inf file in its root folder. This file contains a line that looks like the following: icon=*location*. This line causes Windows to display the icon specified by *location* in Windows Explorer as long as that disk is mounted. *location* can be the path to an ICO file or it can be the path to a DLL, EXE, or RES file and an index.

The first trick to displaying a different icon for devices other than CD-ROMs is to enable Autorun.inf for those devices. Open HKEY_USERS\.DEFAULT\Software\Microsoft\ Windows\CurrentVersion\Policies\Explorer. You see a value entry called NoDriveTypeAutoRun. This value entry indicates the drives for which Autorun.inf is disabled. It's a four-byte binary value entry, and each bit corresponds to a different type of drive, as described in Table 14.5. Setting the bit that corresponds to a drive type to 1 disables Autorun.inf for that type. Setting the bit to 0 enables Autorun.inf. The default value for this entry is 95 00 00 00 (or 1001 0101 binary), which means that hard drives, CD-ROMs, and RAM drives are enabled, whereas other drive types are not. Change this value to 91 00 00 00 (or 1001 0001 binary) if you want to include removable disks such as floppies and Zip disks in the list of drives for which Autorun.inf is enabled.

TABLE 14.5 NoDriveTypeAutoRun

Bit	Drive Type
0	Unknown Drives
2	Removable Drives
3	Hard Drives
4	Remote Drives
5	CD-ROM Drives
6	RAM Drives

Now that you've enabled Autorun.inf for the appropriate devices, you're ready to change the icon that Windows Explorer displays for each disk. Create an Autorun.inf and place it in the root folder of each disk. The Autorun.inf file looks similar to Listing 14.1. Replace everything to the right of `icon=` with the location of the icon, whether it's an ICO file or an indexed icon within an EXE, DLL, or RES file. Remember that you can create a unique Autorun.inf file for each disk. Every one of your floppies can use a distinct icon, for example, and you can store the icon file on the disk itself.

LISTING 14.1   A SAMPLE AUTORUN.INF FILE

```
[autorun]
icon=c:\windows\system32\cool.dll,8
```

> Changing a drive's icon by creating a Autorun.inf file does not work in all drives in all computers. It depends largely on the hardware and the device driver provided by the manufacturer. Experiment with this file to see what you can customize. Note that you might have to press F5 in Windows Explorer in order to see the disk's new icon.

Specific Drive Letters

Windows Explorer examines an undocumented and seldom-used branch of `HKEY_LOCAL_MACHINE` called `Software\Microsoft\Windows\CurrentVersion\explorer\DriveIcons` to find drive icons. It looks for a subkey that matches each possible drive letter, as well as a subkey under `DefaultIcon`. The default value entry of `DefaultIcon` is the specification of an icon. As you learned a moment ago, you can specify the path and filename of an ICO or other image file. You can also use the path and filename of a DLL, EXE, or RES file in combination with an index number, or you can use the path and filename of a DLL, EXE, or RES file in combination with a resource ID.

If you want to display a custom icon for drive D, for example, add `D\DefaultIcon` to `DriveIcons` and change the default value entry of `DefaultIcon` to the location of the icon. If you want to display a custom icon for drive X, add `X\DefaultIcon` to `DriveIcons`, and change the default value entry of `DefaultIcon`.

Specific Folders in Explorer

The capability to display unique icons for specific folders is a feature that Internet Explorer 4.0 added to Windows 95. Windows 98 includes it by default. Windows Explorer takes special notice any time it finds a hidden file called Desktop.ini within a system folder. The attribute of the folder in conjunction with this file indicates that the folder is special, and usually points to an object that handles the folder's contents.

14

You can use this file, as well as a ScreenTip that Windows Explorer displays when you hover over the folder with the mouse pointer, to indicate an icon for any folder. Create a Desktop.ini file, as in Listing 14.2. Place it in the folder, setting the hidden attribute using the MS-DOS Attrib command or the General tab of the file's property sheet by choosing Properties from the file's shortcut menu.

You need to also turn on the folder's system attribute, which you can only do by typing attrib +s *foldername* at the command prompt. Set *IconFile* to the path of the ICO file or to the path of an EXE, DLL, or RES file, and the icon's index. You can also set *InfoTip* to any text that you want Windows Explorer to display in a ScreenTip when you hover the mouse pointer over the folder.

LISTING 14.2 A SAMPLE DESKTOP.INI

```
[.ShellClassInfo]
IconFile=C:\Windows\Winupd.ico
InfoTip=This is the tip Windows displays when you hover over
➥the folder.
```

> ### DOCUMENTING CHANGES TO THE REGISTRY
>
> Keeping track of each change you make is difficult. You can keep a separate log file, but you're not likely to keep it updated, and the information isn't handy when you really need it.
>
> The best way to document each change you make to the Registry is to add a bogus value entry containing a description of the change you made. You might include the date on which you made the change, too, so that you can relate changes you make to changes in the operating system's behavior. The best name to use for this bogus value entry is a combination of the changed value entry's name and the word "Note." Thus, if you change a value entry called maxMTU, add a new string value entry called maxMTUNote and set its value to a brief description of the change you made and the date you made it.
>
> When you name the notes this way and put them within the subkey containing the changed value entry, they appear next to the original value. For instance, to continue the example, the two value entries maxMTU and maxMTUNote appear next to each other in the Registry key that contains them both.

Summary

Windows provides a variety of ways in which you can customize files and folders in Windows Explorer. For example, you can change the location of each shell folder. Recall that shell folders are folders that Windows uses for special purposes, such as the Start Menu and Favorites folders.

More popular customizations include those that enable users to change how shell folders look or whether they appear at all. Some customizations enable users to rename or remove shell folders from the desktop. Removing the Network Neighborhood icon is easily done, for instance. Other customizations enable users to change the icon that Windows displays for a file or object.

Q&A

Q Why would I ever want to relocate a shell folder in Windows?

A In most cases, you don't. The biggest value in understanding how Windows handles shell folders is that you can repair problems when they occur. If you don't like where Windows is storing a certain type of file, you can still use this information to put it in a different location.

Q I want to locate my Favorites and My Documents folders in the same location. Is that OK?

A No. Be careful about overlapping shell folders. For instance, don't use the same path for the Favorites and My Documents folders. Windows 98 writes special information to Desktop.ini, which is a hidden file in these folders, and the information for one shell folder wipes out information for the other. Note that Windows 95 doesn't create a Desktop.ini file unless you've installed Internet Explorer 4.0. For these same reasons, you can't create a use a briefcase folder as a Favorites folder.

Workshop

The following quiz will enhance your understanding of the topics discussed in this hour.

Quiz

1. Which of the following keys contain user shell folders?
    a. `HKEY_CURRENT_USER`
    b. `HKEY_LOCAL_MACHINE`

2. True or false? All shell folders you see in Windows Explorer occupy space on the computer's disk.

3. Which of the following methods can you use to remove the Network Neighborhood icon from the desktop?
    a. Remove its subkey from `namespace`
    b. Set the `NoNetHood` policy to 0x01
    c. Both a and b

14

4. True or false? Program.exe,-2 specifies the second icon in a file called Program.exe.

5. Within `shell icons`, which value entry do you change or add in order to redefine the icon used for open folders?

Answers to Quiz Questions

1. a

   `HKEY_CURRENT_USER` contains user shell folders, whereas `HKEY_LOCAL_MACHINE` contains shell folders that apply to all users.

2. False

   Some shell folders only appear in Windows Explorer's name space; they don't actually have a folder on the hard disk.

3. b

   The only way to remove Network Neighborhood from the desktop is to set the `NoNetHood` policy.

4. False

   Program.exe,-2 represents an icon in Program.exe whose resource ID is 2.

5. 4

   The index of the open folder icon is 4.

Hour 15

Menus and Windows

No one should be happy with the default Windows user interface—it's too customizable. Why not take advantage of this fact to create a work environment that suits you better? For example, you can

- Customize shortcut menus for files and folders.
- Customize the contents of the Start menu.
- Fix a number of annoying menu and window behaviors.
- Remove the overlay from shortcut icons.

This hour packs a lot of power. You can change virtually any part of any shortcut menu, for example. You can restore the Start menu to its original sort order and determine which Windows commands appear on it. You can fix a variety of behavior problems, as well. For instance, if you don't like those zooming windows in Windows 98, you can disable them. If menus flop around on the screen because you're a bit clumsy with the mouse, you can change the time delay before a menu opens by simply pointing at its name. The handful of customization tips in this hour present an endless number of ways in which you can bend Windows to your will.

Mastering Shortcut Menus for Objects and Files

Figure 15.1 shows a typical shortcut menu, which you open by right-clicking a file or folder. Windows Explorer builds a shortcut menu from a variety of sources, all of which are under `HKEY_CLASSES_ROOT`, in the following order:

- `\class\shell`—You see these at the top of the shortcut menu, as shown in the figure.

- `\class\shellex\ContextMenuHandlers`—Each subkey under this key defines an object that adds commands to the shortcut menu. The name of the subkey is the class identifier of the object, and its default value entry is its name; or the subkey is the name of the object, and the default value entry contains its class identifier.

- `\*\shell`—This key adds commands that are common to all types of files. You see these just below the class' own commands and just above the first divider.

- `\*\shellex\ContextMenuHandlers`—Each subkey under this key defines an object that adds commands to every file's shortcut menu. See `\class\shellex\ContextMenuHandlers`, earlier in this list.

- `\AllFilesystemObjects\shellex\ContextMenuHandlers` —Each subkey under this key defines an object that adds commands to every file system object's shortcut menu. In most cases, this just adds the Send To submenu.

- **Shell32.dll**—Windows adds a number of commands that are built into the operating system. These are also known as *canonical verbs*, which means that they're officially supported commands that are defined by the operating system. Windows Explorer places these at the bottom of each file's shortcut menu, including commands such as Cut, Copy, and so on.

FIGURE 15.1

Windows defines menu items, such as Properties, that you see below the first divider.

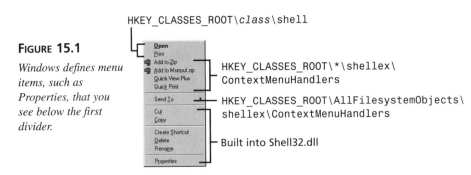

HKEY_CLASSES_ROOT*class*\\shell

HKEY_CLASSES_ROOT*\shellex\ContextMenuHandlers

HKEY_CLASSES_ROOT\AllFilesystemObjects\shellex\ContextMenuHandlers

Built into Shell32.dll

When you right-click a file for which Windows Explorer doesn't find an associated program, you see the Open With command, which opens the Open With dialog box so that you can choose the program in which you want to open the file. This is also the default command, so if you double-click a file with no association, you also see the Open With dialog box. The commands for files with no associations come from HKEY_CLASSES_ROOT\unknown\shell. unknown\shell typically contains a single subkey, a verb, for the Open With command; however, you can add additional commands to it, just as you can for any other file or class. You can add a command to unknown\shell that opens an unassociated file in Notepad, for instance.

> The easiest way to find a subkey for a file type or object is to search the Registry for its name. To find the class identifier for the Recycle Bin in the Registry, for instance, search the Registry for the string Recycle Bin. To quickly find a file type in the Registry, note the description that Windows Explorer displays for it in a file's property sheet, and search for that string in the Registry.

Windows Explorer handles the shortcut menu for objects in a similar manner, except that it looks in HKEY_CLASSES_ROOT\CLSID*clsid*\shell for commands, as well as in HKEY_CLASSES_ROOT\CLSID*clsid*\shellex\ContextMenuHandlers, which you learned about earlier in this section. One addition, however, is that it looks in HKEY_CLASSES_ROOT\CLSID*clsid*\shellfolder for an attributes value entry that enables or disables build-in or canonical verbs defined in Shell32.dll. You'll learn more about attributes a bit later in this hour.

The organization of each shell subkey is the same. The default value entry of the shell subkey contains the name of the verb that defines the default command on the shortcut menu. You see a subkey for each verb, each of which has a command subkey whose default value entry contains the command line that is to be executed. The default value entry for the verb optionally contains the text that Windows Explorer will display on the shortcut menu for the command. For example, the Open command on a text file's shortcut menu is due to the Registry entries shown in Figure 15.2. What you don't see in the figure is that the default value entry of shell can contain the name of the default verb, and the default value entry of open can contain the text that Windows Explorer displays on the shortcut menu.

Command Line for the Command

FIGURE 15.2

This figure shows two commands: Open and Print.

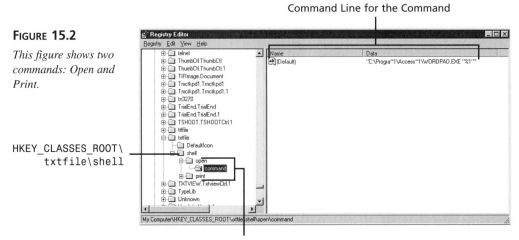

HKEY_CLASSES_ROOT\
txtfile\shell

Commands for the `txtfile`

Adding Commands

Adding commands to a shortcut menu requires that you duplicate the structure under the class's `shell` key, which you learned about in the preceding section. This structure looks like *verb*\command. *verb* is the name of the verb, and the default value entry of `command` contains the command line that you want to execute when the user chooses that verb. Thus, to add a command to a TXT file's shortcut menu that opens it in WordPad, use the following steps (see Listing 15.1 for an outline of the subkeys and value entries that are added using these steps):

1. Look up the program identifier associated with a TXT file by looking at the default value entry of `.txt` under `HKEY_CLASSES_ROOT`.

2. Open `HKEY_CLASSES_ROOT\`*progid*`\shell`, where *progid* is the program identifier that you looked up in step 1. If you don't see the `shell` subkey, add it.

3. Add a subkey under `shell` called `wordpad`. Change the default value entry of `wordpad` to `Open in Wordpad` so that you'll see this text on the shortcut menu.

4. Add a subkey under `shell\wordpad` called `command`, and set its default value entry to `C:\Program Files\Accessories\Wordpad.exe "%1"`, which causes Windows to open the target file in WordPad when you choose this command from the shortcut menu.

15

LISTING 15.1   ADDING A COMMAND TO A TEXT FILE'S SHORTCUT MENU

```
HKEY_CLASSES_ROOT
    txtfile
        shell
            wordpad
                default = "Open in Wordpad"
                command
                    default = "C:\Program Files\Accessories\
                ➥Wordpad.exe "%1"
```

The command line for commands varies. In cases in which you want to open the file in a specific program, you can sometimes get away with providing just the path and filename of the program. You can use long or 8.3 filenames. Windows automatically passes the name of the target file as a command line argument to the program. In other cases, you must explicitly specify the location of the filename by using the %1 placeholder, which Windows substitutes with the target filename when it launches the command line. This becomes particularly important when the command line contains switches and you must include the filename in a specific place within it: myprog /p /k "%1" /s, for example. If you think that the program might have trouble with long filenames that include spaces, be sure to put %1 in quotes, as shown in Listing 15.1. This ensures that the program won't assume that everything up to the first space is the filename and that everything after the first space is additional filenames or garbage.

> Put "%1" in the command line at the exact location at which you want Windows to expand the path and name of the target file when it launches the command line.

USEFUL THINGS TO ADD TO A CONTEXT MENU

Following are some useful commands to add to a folder or file's shortcut menu:

- To open a command prompt with a particular folder as the current working directory, add a new verb to the Directory and Drive classes, whose command line is c:\windows\command.com /k cd "%1". Then, right-click any folder or disk, and choose the new command that you added to the shortcut menu.

- To open Windows Explorer with a particular folder at the root, add the following command to the Folder class: explorer.exe /e,/root,/idlist,%I. Then, right-click any folder and choose the new command that you added to the shortcut menu.

- To open a Control Panel icon by typing its filename in the Run dialog box, rename the `cplopenkey` subkey of the `cplfile` file type that is to open. Then, type the filename, perhaps Powercfg.cpl, of the Control Panel icon in the Run dialog box and press Enter.
- To open Tweak UI from My Computer, add the following command line to `{20D04FE0-3AEA-1069-A2D8-08002B30309D}`: `C:\WINDOWS\rundll32.exe shell32.dll,Control_RunDLL Tweakui.cpl`. Then, right-click My Computer, and choose the new command that you added to the shortcut menu. You can add any other Control Panel application to My Computer's shortcut menu by replacing `Tweakui.cpl` with the application's filename.

Changing the Default Command

The default command of any shortcut menu is the command that Windows Explorer executes whenever you double-click the file. You'll also notice that the default command is bolded in the shortcut menu. Here's how to change the default for any shortcut menu:

1. Locate the class's `shell` subkey under `HKEY_CLASSES_ROOT` in the Registry. For instance, text files are in `HKEY_CLASSES_ROOT\txtfile\shell`.

2. Note the names of the verbs under `shell`, `open`, and `print` for text files, choosing the one that you want as the default command on the shortcut menu.

3. Change the default value entry of the `shell` key so that it contains the name of the verb that represents the default command. Set it to `print` if you want the default command for text files to print them.

Here's a real-world example for changing the default command of a shortcut menu: When you open a folder on the desktop, Windows opens it in a single-pane window instead of a double-pane Explorer window. If you change the default command of `HKEY_CLASSES_ROOT\folder` from `open` to `explore`, Windows opens it in a double-pane Explorer window instead of a single-pane window.

Changing the default value entry of `folder\shell` to `explore` also changes the default command for the My Computer icon's shortcut menu. After making this change, double-click the My Computer icon on the desktop to open it in the double-pane Explorer window rather than the single-pane window.

Changing the Menu's Appearance

You can change the text that Windows Explorer displays on any shortcut menu command that comes from a shell key. It doesn't matter whether the key comes from a program identifier, defined as HKEY_CLASSES_ROOT*progid*, or from an object, defined as HKEY_CLASSES_ROOT\CLSID*clsid*. However, you can't change the text that a context menu handler, defined in a ContextMenuHandler subkey of a class, puts on a shortcut menu. Nor can you change the text that Windows displays for the built-in commands that you see at the bottom of a shortcut menu.

To change the text that you see on a shortcut menu, find the class's shell key in the Registry. As you'll recall, each command is a verb in shell. Change the default value entry of each verb to the text that you want to see on the shortcut menu. To change the text that you see for the Open command of a text file's shortcut menu to Edit, for instance, change the default value entry of \txtfile\shell\open to &Edit under HKEY_CLASSES_ROOT. Windows Explorer maintains the capitalization that you use in the default entry, and you can indicate a hot key by putting an ampersand (&) in front of the letter. Following are a few examples of how various default value entries look on a shortcut menu:

In the Registry	On the Shortcut Menu
open	open
&Open	Open
open in Wordpad	open in Wordpad
open in &Wordpad	open in Wordpad

Things get a bit more complicated if the default value entry for a verb is empty. Windows Explorer gets the name from one of two places if a name is not explicitly defined in the Registry:

- **Shell32.dll**—Windows retrieves the string that is to be displayed on the shortcut menu from Shell32.dll. It does this for the canonical verbs Find, Open, Open With, and Print.

- **Subkey name**—Windows uses the name of the verb as the text it displays on the shortcut menu. For instance, if HKEY_CLASSES_ROOT\txtfile\shell\edit's default value entry is empty, Windows puts edit on the shortcut menu.

Removing Commands

To remove a command from a shortcut menu, identify where in the Registry the command is defined. Then remove the command as described in the following list:

- **shell**—If the command comes from a `shell` key, remove the command's verb. This is true for *, unknown, and any other place where you see a `shell` subkey.

- **shellex\ContextMenuHandler**—If the command comes from a `ContextMenuHandler` subkey of a file type or object, remove the handler's subkey. This might remove multiple commands from the shortcut menu, however, depending on how many commands it adds.

- **Shell32.dll**—If the command is on an object's shortcut menu and is one of the canonical verbs that is defined by Shell32.dll, change the object's `attributes` value. You'll learn more about this value in the paragraphs following this list.

Many objects have an `attributes` value in `HKEY_CLASSES_ROOT\CLSID\`*clsid*`\ShellFolder`, where *clsid* is the class identifier of the object. This value indicates the canonical verbs, or built-in commands, that Windows displays on the object's shortcut menu. `attributes` is a 4-byte binary value, with each bit representing a flag that enables or disables a specific command. Table 15.1 describes the bits that are currently used by Windows. Setting a particular bit to 0 disables the command, whereas setting it to 1 enables the command. Remember that you count bits right-to-left in a binary value, so bit 0 is the first bit on the right, bit 1 is the second bit on the right, and so on. Because the Registry shows `attributes` as a hexadecimal value, you must convert it to binary to figure out which commands are enabled. Work with this value in binary until you're ready to change `attributes`, and then convert it to hexadecimal.

Here's a real-world example: The `attributes` value for the Internet Explorer icon is `72000000` in hexadecimal, which is `1110010000000000000000000000000` in binary. Counting from right to left, bits 25, 28, 29, and 30 are 1s. Thus, Windows displays the Cut, Rename, Delete, and Properties commands on Internet Explorer's shortcut menu. You can remove the Cut command from the shortcut menu by turning off bit 25, which leaves you with a hexadecimal value of `70000000`.

TABLE 15.1   BITS IN THE `attributes` VALUE

Bit Number	Command
30	Properties
29	Delete
28	Rename

Bit Number	Command
25	Cut
24	Copy
16	Paste
5	Open and Explore for the Recycle Bin

 Many times, you'll need to convert hexadecimal to binary and vice versa as you edit the Registry. Use the Windows Calculator in Scientific mode to do so quickly.

Adding Templates to the New Menu

Right-click any folder and choose New to display a menu of new documents that you can create in the folder, as shown in Figure 15.3. This is a quick way to create a new document. Then open the document to edit its contents.

FIGURE 15.3

The Folder and Shortcut items are hard-coded by the operating system; you can't change or remove them.

HKEY_CLASSES_ROOT\.*ext*\ShellNew, where .*ext* is a file extension such as .doc or .txt, defines a template for the New menu. You can put only one template on the New menu for each file extension. You add one of three value entries to this subkey to add the extension to the New menu:

- **NullFile**—Make sure that this string value entry is empty, causing Windows to create an empty file in the folder when the user chooses this file type.

- **FileName**—Copy a template file with the same file extension to \Windows\ShellNew, and then set this value entry to the name of the file, excluding the path. When the user chooses this file type from the New menu, Windows creates a new file using the template in \Windows\ShellNew.

- **Data**—This is a binary value whose contents Windows uses to create the new file when the user chooses it from the New menu. Windows just copies the bytes from this value entry directly into the file.

Customizing the Start Menu and Its Contents

The following sections describe various ways in which you can customize the Start menu:

- How to restore a sorted Start menu
- How to disable any submenu on the Start menu
- How to customize a submenu's icon
- How to add shell folders as cascading menus
- How to point Find to a better location

Restoring a Sorted Start Menu

With the introduction of Internet Explorer 4.0 into Windows 95, and subsequently into Windows 98, the Start and Favorites menus became customizable. The user can sort the menu using drag and drop, or even edit both menus in place by right-clicking the objects on it.

Windows stores the sort order of the Start menu in `HKEY_CURRENT_USER\Software\Microsoft\Windows\CurrentVersion\Explorer\MenuOrder`. You find two subkeys here: `Favorites` and `Start Menu`. Within each, you find a subkey for each submenu as well as a subkey called `Menu` that indicates the sort order of all the items on the menu. Each of the subkeys for submenus contains a `Menu` subkey as well. Take a look at Figure 15.4 if this description confuses you. You can't really change the sort order by editing the `Menu` subkey because editing it is almost impossible. You can use the following two tricks to make working with the Start menu's sort order easier, however:

- Export the entire `MenuOrder` branch to a REG file that you can later import to restore the sort order of the Start menu if it goes awry.

- Remove the `Favorites` and `Start Menu` subkeys of `MenuOrder` to restore the sort order for both menus to their Windows defaults.

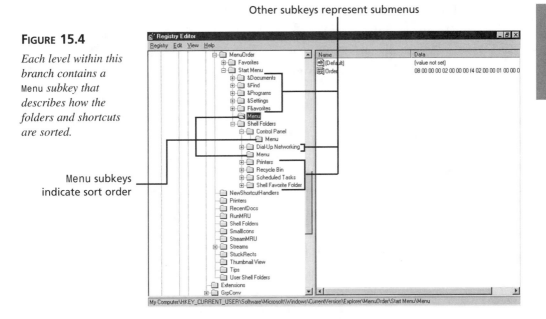

FIGURE 15.4

Each level within this branch contains a Menu *subkey that describes how the folders and shortcuts are sorted.*

Other subkeys represent submenus

Menu subkeys indicate sort order

15

Disabling Commands: Documents, Run, and So On

One of the biggest questions I hear from administrators is how to remove commands such as Run and Find from the Start menu. Prior to Internet Explorer 4.0, it was impossible to accomplish such a task in Windows 95.

Each of the policies that you see in Table 15.2 is under `HKEY_CURRENT_USER\Software\Microsoft\Windows\CurrentVersion\Policies\ Explorer`. If you don't find this branch in the Registry, create it. Then add the DWORD value entry that corresponds to the submenu or command you want to disable, as shown in the table. To disable the menu command, set the policy value to 1; to enable the menu command, set the policy value to 0. Note that Windows doesn't provide policies for removing Programs, Settings, or Shut Down from the Start menu.

TABLE 15.2 POLICIES FOR DISABLING ICONS ON THE START MENU

Value Entry	Description
NoFavoritesMenu	Enables or disables the Favorites menu
NoFind	Enables or disables the Find menu
NoRecentDocsMenu	Enables or disables the Documents menu
NoRun	Enables or disables the Run command
NoLogOff	Enables or disables the Log Off command

Customizing Each Command's Icon

Hour 14, "Files and Folders," showed you how to customize the icons that Windows displays in various locations. These icons include the images you see on the Start menu. Specifically, you add a string value entry to `HKEY_LOCAL_MACHINE\Software\Microsoft\Windows\CurrentVersion\explorer\Shell Icons` that corresponds to the command you want to change, as described in Table 15.3. If you want to change the icon that the Start menu displays for the Settings command, for example, create a string value entry called `21` in this key. Assign to the default value entry of the new key the location of the icon you want to use. The location can be the path and filename of an ICO file, or it can be the path and filename of an EXE, DLL, or RES file combined with the index of the icon. Here are more specific instructions for changing an icon on the Start menu to make sure that Windows updates your changes:

1. Restart the Computer in Safe Mode.
2. Delete the ShellIconCache file from \Windows. You might have to show hidden files in Windows Explorer in order to see this file.
3. Add the value entry that corresponds to one of the value entries in Table 15.3, and set its default value entry to the location of the icon.
4. Restart the computer normally.

TABLE 15.3 CUSTOMIZING ICONS ON THE START MENU

Value Name	Command
19	Programs
20	Documents
21	Settings
22	Find
23	Help
24	Run
25	Suspend
26	Eject PC
27	Shut Down

Adding Shell Folders as Cascading Menus

Some shell folders make great additions to the Start menu. In particular, the Control Panel, Dial-Up Networking, Printers, Recycle Bin, and Scheduled Tasks folders work well on the Start menu (but the other shell folders don't). When you add them, Windows displays their contents as cascading menus instead of opening a separate folder to display their contents. Figure 15.5 shows you how the Control Panel looks when you add it to the Start menu as a cascading menu.

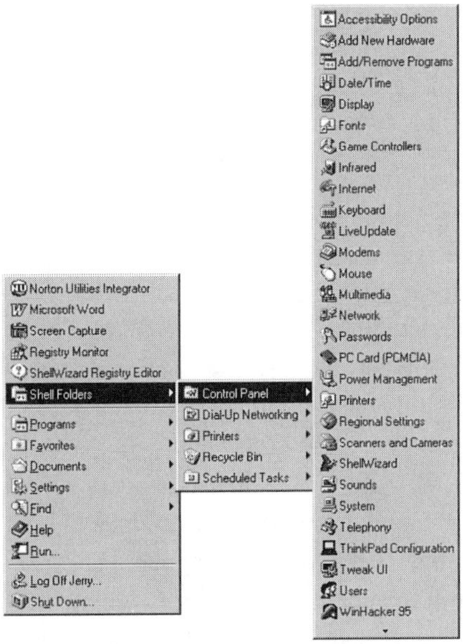

FIGURE 15.5

The Control Panel is much easier to access if you add it to the Start menu as a cascading menu.

To add one of the objects to the Start menu, create a new folder anywhere within the Start Menu folder and name it *name.clsid*. *name* is the name of the folder as shown in the table, and *clsid* is the class identifier of the folder as shown in the table. By the way, make sure that you include the brackets in the class identifier. For example, to add the Control Panel to the Start menu, create a new folder in the Start Menu folder called `Control Panel. {21EC2020-3AEA-1069-A2DD-08002B30309D}`. The following list shows you the names to use for the five folders mentioned and shown in Figure 15.5:

Control Panel	`{21EC2020-3AEA-1069-A2DD-08002B30309D}`
Dial-Up Networking	`{992CFFA0-F557-101A-88EC-00DD010CCC48}`
Printers	`{2227A280-3AEA-1069-A2DE-08002B30309D}`
Recycle Bin	`{645FF040-5081-101B-9F08-00AA002F954E}`
Scheduled Tasks	`{D6277990-4C6A-11CF-8D87-00AA0060F5BF}`

Fixing Menu and Window Behavior Problems

Windows have a habit of zooming when you minimize or restore them. That is, you see the outline of the window grow as a minimized window restores onto the desktop. You also see the outline of a window shrink as a normal window minimizes to the taskbar. Microsoft designed this behavior so that users can more easily see where the window lands. However, this feature isn't necessary for most users and actually robs the user of that crisp feeling when a window pops open on the desktop or instantly minimizes to the taskbar. You can prevent windows from zooming by setting `MinAnimate` to `0` in `HKEY_CURRENT_USER\Control Panel\Desktop\WindowMetrics`. If this string value entry doesn't exist, add it.

Another annoying behavior is that menus tend to follow the mouse like a stray dog looking for kibble. This behavior is noticable on the Start menu. Hover the mouse pointer over any submenu, and Windows automatically opens the submenu after half a second (500ms). Hover the mouse pointer over any other submenu, and Windows automatically closes the previous menu and opens the submenu. Some people like the delay to be a bit shorter so that the menus follow the mouse more quickly, and others like the delay to be longer so that menus work more like they did in Windows 95, prior to this feature. To adjust this setting, change the `MenuShowDelay` value entry that you find under `HKEY_CURRENT_USER\Control Panel\Desktop`. `MenuShowDelay` is a string value entry that you can add if you don't see it in the key. It represents the delay in milliseconds before a menu follows the mouse. The default value is `500`. Set it to a lower number to make the menus snappier, or set it to an extremely large number, such as 65,535, to keep menus from following the mouse.

You can cause Windows to align menu commands to the left or the right. Set the `MenuDropAlignment` value entry under `HKEY_CURRENT_USER\Control Panel\Desktop` to `1` if you want to align menus to the right, or set it to `0` to align menus to the left.

Each time you shut down Windows, it remembers the position of all the desktop icons, taskbar, and any open Explorer windows. If you put Explorer in your StartUp program folder and forget to close Explorer before shutting down Windows, for example, you'll have two copies of Explorer on your desktop when you restart Windows. These are the copies you loaded in the StartUp program menu and the copy that you left on your desktop when you shut down Windows. If you want Windows's memory to be a bit less permanent, set the binary value entry `NoSaveSettings` under `HKEY_CURRENT_USER\Software\Microsoft\Windows\CurrentVersion\Policies\Explorer\` to `1`. If you don't see this value entry, add it.

Removing the Overlay from Shortcut Icons

Windows displays a small arrow in the bottom-left corner of shortcut icons. Microsoft calls this an *overlay*. Remove this arrow by removing the IsShortcut value entry from HKEY_CLASSES_ROOT\lnkfile. Remove the same value entry from HKEY_CLASSES_ROOT\piffile so that you don't see arrows on the bottom-left corner of PIF files.

Removing the overlay from shortcuts by removing the IsShortcut value entry might cause Windows to behave erratically.

Summary

Windows defines each command on the top of a file's shortcut menu in the class definition's shell subkey. You find more commands in the subkey called shellex\ContextMenuHandlers, as well as the *\shell, *\shellex\ContextMenuHandlres, and AllFilesystemObjects\shellex\ ContextMenuHandlers keys. The items that you see at the bottom of a shortcut menu are hard-coded by the operating system. The text comes from Shell32.dll, and a subkey called shellfolder contains a value called attributes that defines which of these appear on the menu. You can use all these facts to customize just about every shortcut menu that Windows displays.

The Start menu is almost as customizable as are shortcut menus. You can use policies to choose whether the Favorites, Find, Documents, Run, and Log Off items are on the menu. You can also change each and every icon on the Start menu by changing the appropriate value in Shell Icons. Furthermore, you can add some of the shell folders to the Start menu so that they appear as cascading menus, revealing the shell folder's contents as a submenu.

Q&A

Q Is there any easier way to add actions to a file's shortcut menu than to edit the Registry?

A Yes, and use it whenever possible. Click Folder Options on Windows Explorer's View menu; then, click the File types tab. This tab enables you to add actions for a file type using a series of simple dialog boxes.

Q Can I change the New menu so that it shows two different files for a single program?

A Not unless both files use different file extensions. The ShellNew subkey is underneath each filename extension subkey, and, therefore, there can be only one per file extension.

Workshop

The following quiz will enhance your understanding of the topics discussed in this hour.

Quiz

1. True or false? You can associate more than one class definition with a single file extension.

2. Which of the following characters do you put before the hotkey in a menu command?

    a. @

    b. $

    c. &

    d. *

3. From which of the following files do the hard-coded commands come?

    a. System.dll

    b. Win32.dll

    c. Kernel.dll

    d. Shell32.dll

4. Which of the following policies removes the Documents menu from the Start menu?

    a. NoDocsMenu

    b. NoRecentMenu

    c. NoRecentDocsMenu

Answers to Quiz Questions

1. False

   A filename extension can only be associated with a single class definition, but a class definition can be associated with multiple filename extensions.

2. c

   & is indicates that the next character is a hotkey.

3. d

   Shell32.dll defines the hard coded items you see on the bottom of most shortcut menus.

4. c

   NoRecentDocsMenu is the policy that controls whether the Start menu displays the Documents submenu.

15

Hour 16

Other Customizations

The previous two hours showed you how to customize files and folders as well as menus and windows. Well, this hour isn't so neatly categorized. In it, you learn about the following:

- Personalizing Internet Explorer 4.0
- Disabling Internet Explorer 4.0's integration
- Clearing the Windows MRU lists
- Running programs when Windows starts
- Logging on to Windows automatically
- Changing installation information
- Removing Registry editing restrictions

This hour contains a mixed bag of customizations. Some of them show you how to personalize Internet Explorer 4.0 or even disable the browser's integration in Windows 98. Other tips in this hour show you how to clear the ubiquitous MRU (most recently used) lists and how to customize the Run subkey so that you can specify a command line that Windows executes every time the operating system starts. This hour is packed, so the best way to get a feel for what it contains is to take a brief look at the headings.

You don't have to read this hour from beginning to end to take advantage of it, by the way. If you see something that looks interesting, but it's right in the middle of the hour, go for it.

Personalizing Internet Explorer 4.0

There are a number of ways to customize Internet Explorer 4.0. The *Internet Explorer Administration Kit* (*IEAK*) enables you to completely customize Internet Explorer. You can even change the text that appears on the browser's title bar. You can't change most of the settings via the Registry; you can only change them by creating INS files via the administration kit. The *Microsoft Windows 98 Resource Kit,* published by Microsoft Press, includes a copy of the Internet Explorer Administration Kit.

The remainder of this section describes three ways in which you can customize Internet Explorer 4.0 via the Registry. You can extend its shortcut menus, for one. You can also change the bitmap that is displayed on the background of toolbars, and you can change the default protocol that the browser uses when you type a URL with the protocol.

Extending the Shortcut Menus

Internet Explorer 4.0 displays a shortcut menu when you right-click anywhere within a Web page. You can add items to this shortcut menu, each of which are linked to scripts that you create and place in an HTML file. You can customize the shortcut menu to open a frame in a new window, for example, or you can customize it to resize the font in a block of text.

To add a command to Internet Explorer 4.0's shortcut menu, create a new subkey under `HKEY_CURRENT_USER\Software\Microsoft\Internet Explorer\MenuExt`. If you don't see `MenuExt`, add it. Internet Explorer uses this name for the command's text on the shortcut menu. You can put an ampersand (&) in front of any character to indicate that it is a hotkey. Then, set the default value to the path and filename of the HTML file containing the script that executes the command. If you want to add a command called Test, which launches an HTML file called Test.htm in C:\Windows, to the shortcut menu, you add a subkey called `&Test` to `MenuExt` and set its default value entry to `C:\Windows\Test.htm`.

When you click the command in the shortcut menu, Internet Explorer opens the HTML file and executes any inline scripts that it finds there. The scripting property external.menuArguments contains the window object on which you executed the command. Thus, if you right-click a Web page and choose Test, external.menuArguments contains the window object on which you right-clicked. With access to the window object, you can pretty much do anything you want to the current Web page, including changing its contents, format, and so on. With all that said, Listing 16.1 is an example of an HTML file that changes the font size of a text selection so that you can read it more easily. To try it out, type the listing in an HTML file and add a subkey to MenuExt and set its default value entry to the path and filename of the HTML file. Then, open a Web page in Internet Explorer, select some text, right-click the selected text, and choose the new command that you added.

LISTING 16.1 SCRIPTING INTERNET EXPLORER SHORTCUT MENUS

```
<HTML>
<SCRIPT LANGUAGE="JavaScript" defer>
var objWin = external.menuArguments;
var objDoc = objWin.document;
var objSel = objDoc.selection;
var objRange = objSel.createRange();
objRange.execCommand( "FontSize", 0, "+2" );
</SCRIPT>
</HTML>
```

There is an additional value that you can add to the command's subkey that controls which context menus display the command. It's called Contexts. Add this one byte binary value to the command's subkey and set its value according to the masks described in the following table. If you want to limit the previous example so that it only appears on the shortcut menu that is displayed for text selections, add the binary value called Contexts to the new subkey under MenuExt and set its value to 0×10. Note that you might have to restart Internet Explorer 4.0 in order to see your changes to this subkey.

Value	Menu
0×01	Default Menu
0×02	Image Menu
0×04	Control Menu
0×08	Table Menu
0×10	Text Selection Menu
0×11	Anchor Menu
0×12	Unknown Menu

16

This section assumes some familiarity with how to write scripts for Web pages, whether they are in VBScript or JavaScript. If you don't know how to write scripts, check out Macmillan Publishing's *Special Edition Using HTML* or one of Macmillan's other books on the topic. You can also find more information about extending Internet Explorer 4.0's shortcut menus at Microsoft's Web site:

`http://www.microsoft.com/ie/ie40/powertoys/Contextm.htm.`

Changing the Toolbar's Background

The background that you see on Internet Explorer's toolbar is nothing more than a bitmap. To change the background, create a new string value entry called `BackBitmap` under `HKEY_CURRENT_USER\Software\Microsoft\Internet Explorer\Toolbar`. Change the value to the path of the bitmap that you want to display on the background of Internet Explorer's toolbar. If the bitmap doesn't fill the entire toolbar, Internet Explorer tiles it horizontally and vertically.

Changing the Default Protocol

If you type a URL in Internet Explorer's toolbar or in the Run dialog box, Internet Explorer automatically prefixes it with the appropriate protocol. If you type `www.microsoft.com`, for example, Internet Explorer changes it to `http://www.microsoft.com`. If you type `ftp.microsoft.com`, Internet Explorer changes it to `ftp://ftp.microsoft.com`. Notice that it chooses the protocol based on how the URL begins. But what happens when you type `rampages.onramp.net/~jerry`? By default, Internet Explorer is going to assume it's a Web page and add `http://` to the beginning of it. If this isn't the behavior you want, you can specify a different prefix by changing the default value entry of `HKEY_LOCAL_MACHINE\Software\Microsoft\Windows\CurrentVersion\URL\DefaultPrefix` to the protocol that you want Internet Explorer to use by default (for example, `ftp://`).

Disabling Internet Explorer 4.0 Integration

Many people, myself included, think that Internet Explorer's integration into Windows 98 is a good thing. Although it doesn't quite blend the Internet into my desktop, as

Microsoft claims (because the separation between the two realms is still very distinguishable), it *does* add new features—terrific features. It brings Web-style navigation to the desktop, for instance. It provides powerful scripting capabilities. It enables me to customize the look and feel of the desktop and individual folders. Thus, there are two simple reasons that Internet Explorer integration is good: It makes Windows more customizable and easier to use.

That's just one side of the story, however; here's the other side. Microsoft has forced end-users to accept and use software that they don't necessarily want; for example, maybe they'd rather use a different browser, or perhaps they don't want to be forced to use Internet Explorer to view the contents of their computers or to browse the Internet. The don't like the new features. (Animated menus and flying-paper animations, I'll concede, are very annoying.) Most importantly, they're afraid that Internet Explorer's integration into the Windows operating system gives Microsoft a shot at monopolizing the Internet.

If you're in the first camp, you can skip the rest of this section. If you're in the second camp, you'll be interested to note that you can minimize the integration of Internet Explorer into the operating system. You can't remove Internet Explorer because Microsoft makes Windows 98 almost totally dependent on its code. However, you can return Windows 98 to a look and feel that's closer to Windows 95 sans Internet Explorer 4.0. Doing so is quite easy; you change only a few Registry settings. You can pick and choose which of the settings in Table 16.1 you want to change. All the values you see in the table are in
`HKEY_CURRENT_USER\Software\Microsoft\Windows\CurrentVersion\Policies\`
`Explorer` and are therefore policies. The first column indicates the name of the DWORD value entry that is to be added to this key, and the second column describes what it does. In each case, set the value to 1 to enable that policy, or set it to 0 to disable it. Alternatively, you can use Microsoft Tweak UI, the Registry Power Tools program that you find on my Web site (`http://www.honeycutt.com`), or the INF file in Listing 16.2 to change these settings. The INF file in Listing 16.3 reverses them, enabling you to switch back and forth. Also, you can change many of the settings in Table 16.1 using the Folder Options dialog box (click Folder Option on Windows Explorer's View menu) or by using the System Policy Editor as described in Hour 21, "Controlling the Desktop via System Policies."

TABLE 16.1 DISABLING INTERNET EXPLORER 4.0 INTEGRATION

Value	Description
ClassicShell	Enables the classic shell, which has the old double-click user interface.
NoActiveDesktop	Disables the Active Desktop, reverting to the classic desktop.
NoActiveDesktopChanges	Removes the Web tab from the Display Properties dialog box.
NoChangeStartMenu	Disables drag and drop on the Start menu, reverting to the old version.
NoFavoritesMenu	Removes the Favorites command from the Start menu.
NoInternetIcon	Removes the Internet icon from the desktop.
NoSetActiveDesktop	Removes the Active Desktop command from the Start menu's Settings submenu.

You can change the settings listed in Table 16.1 using the System Policy Editor—almost. The policy template uses the wrong Registry key for some of the values, including NoChangeStartMenu. Therefore, you're better off relying on the INF files that are shown in this section or the Registry Power Tools.

The ClassicShell value has side effects. Setting ClassicShell disables the taskbar's toolbar features and removes the as Web Page command from Windows Explorer's View menu. It also disables the Windows Desktop Update section of Explorer's Folder Options dialog box so that the user can't re-enable the new shell. Likewise, NoActiveDesktop prevents the user from using the Active Desktop by removing the Active Desktop command from the desktop's shortcut menu.

Even though you disable the Active Desktop, you might still see Internet Explorer's channel bar on the classic desktop. You can easily remove it by closing it. When Windows 98 asks if you want to open it again when you restart the operating system, click No. Alternatively, you can disable it in the Registry. Set the string value entry Show_ChannelBand to No in HKEY_CURRENT_USER\Software\Microsoft\Internet Explorer\Main.

LISTING 16.2   DISABLING INTERNET EXPLORER 4.0 INTEGRATION

```
[version]
signature="$CHICAGO$"

[DefaultInstall]
AddReg=Integration

[Integration]
HKCU,Software\Microsoft\Windows\CurrentVersion\Policies\
➥Explorer, ClassicShell,0x10001,01,00,00,00
HKCU,Software\Microsoft\Windows\CurrentVersion\Policies\
➥Explorer, NoActiveDesktop,0x10001,01,00,00,00
HKCU,Software\Microsoft\Windows\CurrentVersion\Policies\
➥Explorer, NoActiveDesktopChanges,0x10001,01,00,00,00
HKCU,Software\Microsoft\Windows\CurrentVersion\Policies\
➥Explorer, NoChangeStartMenu,0x10001,01,00,00,00
HKCU,Software\Microsoft\Windows\CurrentVersion\Policies\
➥Explorer, NoFavoritesMenu,0x10001,01,00,00,00
HKCU,Software\Microsoft\Windows\CurrentVersion\Policies\
➥Explorer, NoInternetIcon,0x10001,01,00,00,00
HKCU,Software\Microsoft\Windows\CurrentVersion\Policies\
➥Explorer, NoSetActiveDesktop,0x10001,01,00,00,00
HKCU, "Software\Microsoft\Internet Explorer\Main",
➥Show_ChannelBand,0,"No"
```

16

LISTING 16.3   ENABLING INTERNET EXPLORER 4.0 INTEGRATION

```
[version]
signature="$CHICAGO$"

[DefaultInstall]
DelReg=Integration
AddReg=ChannelBand

[Integration]
HKCU,Software\Microsoft\Windows\CurrentVersion\Policies\
➥Explorer, ClassicShell
HKCU,Software\Microsoft\Windows\CurrentVersion\Policies\
➥Explorer, NoActiveDesktop
HKCU,Software\Microsoft\Windows\CurrentVersion\Policies\
➥Explorer, NoActiveDesktopChanges
HKCU,Software\Microsoft\Windows\CurrentVersion\Policies\
➥Explorer, NoChangeStartMenu
```

continues

LISTING 16.3 CONTINUED

```
HKCU,Software\Microsoft\Windows\CurrentVersion\Policies\
➥Explorer, NoFavoritesMenu
HKCU,Software\Microsoft\Windows\CurrentVersion\Policies\
➥Explorer, NoInternetIcon
HKCU,Software\Microsoft\Windows\CurrentVersion\Policies\
➥Explorer, NoSetActiveDesktop

[ChannelBand]
HKCU,"Software\Microsoft\Internet Explorer\Main",
➥Show_ChannelBand,0,"Yes"
```

Clearing the Most Recently Used Lists

Windows keeps various history lists, also called *MRU* or *most recently used* lists. It keeps histories of the documents you've opened recently, programs you've run, file specifications you've searched for, and computers you've searched for on the network. You might consider this a personal security risk if you're concerned about other people knowing what you've been up to recently. You can clear all these history lists by removing the keys listed in Table 16.2 from HKEY_CURRENT_USER\Software\Microsoft\Windows\ CurrentVersion\explorer.

TABLE 16.2 HISTORY LISTS

Location	Location in Registry
Documents menu	RecentDocs
Run dialog	RunMru
Find Files dialog	Doc Find Spec MRU
Find Computer dialog	FindComputerMRU

After removing these keys from the Registry, you have to erase the contents of \Windows\Recent to finish clearing the contents of the Documents menu. If user profiles are enabled on the computer, erase the contents of \Windows\Profiles*username*\Recent, where *username* is your logon name.

Clearing Automatically

Microsoft Tweak UI, which you learned about in Hour 8, "Using Microsoft's Tweak UI," can automatically clear the MRU lists. You can also clear these history lists automatically by creating an INF file to remove them. Right-click the INF file and choose Install.

Listing 16.4 shows the INF file, which you might want to call Cleanup.inf (or something similar). To automatically launch the INF file and simultaneously erase the contents of \Windows\Recent, create a BAT file that looks similar to Listing 16.5, and call it Cleanup.bat.

LISTING 16.4   AN INF FILE TO CLEAR THE MRU LISTS

```
[version]
signature=$Chicago$

[DefaultInstall]
DelReg=DelRegKey

[DelRegKey]
HKCU,"Software\Microsoft\Windows\CurrentVersion\Explorer\
➥Doc Find Spec MRU",
HKCU,Software\Microsoft\Windows\CurrentVersion\Explorer\
➥FindComputerMRU,
HKCU,Software\Microsoft\Windows\CurrentVersion\Explorer\
➥RecentDocs,
HKCU,Software\Microsoft\Windows\CurrentVersion\Explorer\RunMRU
```

LISTING 16.5   CLEANING OUT THE MRU LISTS AND \WINDOWS\RECENT

```
@Echo Off
C:\Windows\rundll.exe setupx.dll,InstallHinfSection
➥DefaultInstall 132 Cleanup.inf
Echo Y ¦ Erase C:\Windows\Recent
```

 The quotation marks around the first key in Listing 16.5 are a must because the key name contains spaces, which confuse Windows if you don't use the quotes.

Clearing When Windows Starts

Launching the BAT file every time you want to clean up the MRU lists isn't convenient, particularly if you want to do it every time you start Windows. You can add the BAT file to your StartUp folder. Alternatively, you can add the BAT file to `HKEY_LOCAL_MACHINE\Software\Microsoft\Windows\CurrentVersion\Run\`. You'll learn more about this key in the following section.

16

Locating Programs that Open When Windows Starts

Windows launches any shortcuts it finds in the StartUp folder after the user logs on to the computer. These are obvious. What's not obvious is why certain programs run automatically even though they don't appear in the StartUp group. Programs that start automatically *before* a user logs on to the computer do so because of entries in the Run and RunOnce subkeys under HKEY_LOCAL_MACHINE\Software\Microsoft\Windows\CurrentVersion. Windows launches the command line specified in every value entry it finds there, and it does so every time the operating system starts. RunOnce is a special case that contains value entries for commands that Windows launches once and then removes. The name of each value entry isn't important, but each name needs to be descriptive.

HKEY_CURRENT_USER\Software\Microsoft\Windows\CurrentVersion also contains Run and RunOnce subkeys. Windows launches the commands in these subkeys after the user logs on to the computer. Again, the name of each value entry doesn't matter, but its value contains the command line that is to be executed. Windows executes commands in Run every time the operating system starts, and it executes commands in RunOnce a single time before removing them from the Registry.

Logging on to the Network Automatically

Windows requires a username and password if you configure it to connect to the network. It also asks for a username and password even if you don't connect to a network. Change the following value entries under HKEY_LOCAL_MACHINE\Software\Microsoft\Windows\CurrentVersion\Winlogon so that you can log on to Windows automatically without retyping your credentials:

Value	Description
DefaultUserName	Set this string value entry to the username that you use to log on to Windows.
DefaultPassword	Set this string value entry to the password you use to log on to Windows.
AutoAdminLogon	Set this string value entry to 1 to enable automatic logon, or set it to 0 to disable automatic logon.

Don't use this customization if you're logging on to a network on which security is a concern. This enables anyone to walk up to your computer and access the network without providing credentials.

Changing Installation Information

Windows stores the path of its installation folder in the Registry at HKEY_LOCAL_MACHINE\Software\Microsoft\Windows\CurrentVersion\Setup. If you change the location of the source files, you might want to change the SourcePath value entry in this key so that the next time you add components to Windows it automatically finds the files without having to prompt you for their location.

Windows prompts you for a username and organization when you install it. Windows doesn't provide a means to change this information after installation, but you can change it in the Registry. It stores the organization, owner, and product ID in the following value entries found in HKEY_LOCAL_MACHINE\SOFTWARE\Microsoft\Windows\CurrentVersion:

- RegisteredOrganization
- RegisteredOwner
- ProductID

FINDING MORE REGISTRY HINTS AND TIPS

Many of the customization tips in Hours 14–16 were found on the Internet. Several Web pages on the Internet are dedicated to Windows hints and tips. My Web site, http://www.honeycutt.com, contains links to some of the best. If you're not content with the list in my Web site, you can use one of the search tools in the following table to find your own:

Search Tool	Web Address
AltaVista	http://www.altavista.digital.com
Deja News	http://www.dejanews.com
Excite	http://www.excite.com
Lycos	http://www.lycos.com
WebCrawler	http://www.webcrawler.com
Yahoo	http://www.yahoo.com

If you type the word `registry` in these search tools, you'll find everything from bridal registries to a registry that documents speed traps across the nation (`http://www.nashville.net/speedtrap`). Limit your search a bit more by including the word `Windows`. Also, I suggest that you not limit your search to Windows NT if you're a Windows NT user. Most of the Windows hints-and-tips-type of Web pages contain information that's equally useful to Windows NT. The following list shows you some of the keyword phrases that I've found to be useful for finding Windows Registry tips:

```
windows registry

windows registry tip

windows hint

windows custom

windows q&a

windows registry faq

windows secret
```

If you're using a search tool that supports advanced searches with Boolean logic (Alta Vista), you'll have even better luck by combining search terms. Try the following:

```
(windows and registry) and (hint or tip or secret)
```

This searches for all Web pages that contain the words *windows* and *registry* (it must find both) and that contain at least one of *hint*, *tip*, or *secret*. So, a Web page that contains *windows*, *registry*, and *tip* will match your search. A Web page that contains *windows* and *tip*, without the word *registry*, won't match your search.

Many Web pages containing Registry tips also provide REG files that you can use to automatically make the changes for you. Before merging the REG file with your Registry, open it in Notepad. Make sure that you fully understand and agree to the changes that it will make. Well-meaning authors sometimes provide REG files that might break Windows.

Removing Restrictions That Prevent Registry Editing

If you've been playing with the System Policy Editor, shown in Figure 16.1, you might have set a policy that locked you out of the Registry Editor: Disable Registry editing tools. Or the system administrator might have intentionally locked you out of the Registry Editor. The problem is that you must have access to the Registry in order to remove this restriction, but you don't have access to the Registry because of it.

Microsoft's documentation indicates that there isn't an alternative to this problem other than reinstalling Windows or restoring a backup copy of the Registry.

Not so fast.

Windows enables you to change the Registry even though this restriction is in place. You can import REG files even when this policy is active. Therefore, you can add or change any value in the Registry by creating a REG file and importing it, even though you can't use the Registry Editor to change the Registry. This behavior is by design, in case you're wondering. Many applications use REG files to import their settings into the Registry, and locking out REG files prevents you from installing those programs. Note that you'll find listing 16.6 on my Web site at http://www.honeycutt.com.

16

FIGURE 16.1

Some rather draconian policies in the System Policy Editor can prevent you from doing anything but a single task.

Listing 16.6 shows the REG file that you must create in order to remove the restrictions that prevent you from editing the Registry with Registry Editor. Type it in exactly as shown, and save it to a file called Unlock.reg. Then double-click Unlock.reg, or right-click it and choose Merge.

LISTING 16.6   REMOVING RESTRICTIONS FROM THE REGISTRY

```
REGEDIT4

[HKEY_CURRENT_USER]\Software\Microsoft\Windows\
➥CurrentVersion\Policies\Explorer]
"RestrictRun"=dword:00000000

[HKEY_CURRENT_USER]\Software\Microsoft\Windows\
➥CurrentVersion\Policies\System]
"DisableRegistryTools"=dword:00000000
```

Summary

Internet Explorer 4.0 can be customized in a variety of ways. You can add items to its shortcut menu, for example, which you can then display by right-clicking on a Web page. You can personalize the image that appears behind the toolbar or change the default protocol that the browser uses. The customization that most users are interested in is the capability to display the browser's desktop integration, however, a feat that can be accomplished using system policies as easily as editing the Registry.

Other customizations are a bit less glamorous, but they are useful nonetheless. Users can clear the most recently used lists, for example, which appear in places such as the Run dialog box or Documents menu on the Start menu. Users can also add commands to the Run subkey of HKEY_CURRENT_USER to cause programs to load automatically after they log on to the computer, or commands can be added to the Run subkey of HKEY_LOCAL_MACHINE to cause programs to load automatically after the operating system starts, but before a user logs on.

Q&A

Q Are the value entries that disable Internet Explorer 4.0's desktop integration available in the System Policy Editor?

A Yes. Hour 21 shows you how to use the System Policy Editor. It also tells you which policy templates you have to load in order to set these policies.

Q Why does a particular program always start when I load Windows? I've checked the Run subkeys and the StartUp group, but I don't see the program at all.

A Have you checked the Load= and Run= items in Win.ini? Believe it or not, Windows still uses these lines.

Workshop

The following quiz will enhance your understanding of the topics discussed in this hour.

Quiz

1. True or false? Users can completely remove Internet Explorer 4.0 from Windows 98.

2. Which of the following keys contain a Run key that launches programs each time the computer starts?

   a. HKEY_LOCAL_MACHINE

   b. HKEY_CURRENT_USER

   c. Both a and c

3. Which of the following subkeys restores the desktop to the state to which users were accustomed before Internet Explorer 4.0?

   a. NoActiveDesktop

   b. OldDesktop

   c. ClassicShell

   d. RestoreShell

4. True or false? Registry editing restrictions can be easily removed by importing a REG file or installing an INF file.

Answers to Quiz Questions

1. False

   The best a user can do is to disable much of Internet Explorer 4.0's desktop features. Removing it entirely is out of the question.

2. c

   This was a trick question. The Run subkey of both keys contains command that the operating system executes after it starts. The commands in the Run subkey in HKEY_CURRENT_USER don't execute until after the user logs on to the computer, though.

3. c

   ClassicShell causes Windows 98 to use the shell that most users are familiar with in Windows 95.

4. True

   Listing 16.6 shows you an INF file that you can use to easily remove any Registry editing restrictions.

HOUR 17

Tracking Registry Changes

Tracking changes to the Registry isn't a fun thing to do just for the sake of doing it. Tracking changes to the Registry helps you isolate keys and values that you can use to customize Windows. It also helps you fix problems, undo changes a program makes, and more. In this hour, you learn about

- Comparing two different REG files
- Comparing backup copies of the Registry
- Monitoring the Registry in real-time
- Comparing two Registries across the network
- Tracking the Registry with ConfigSafe

No easier method exists for locating changes in the Registry than to compare two REG files that you export from the Registry Editor. Export the Registry to a REG file before and after performing an action that changes the Registry, and then compare both REG files using a text-comparison utility. The comparison utility highlights the differences between each file, enabling you to determine which keys were added and removed, as well as which values were added, removed, and changed. This method is quicker than the tracking tools you'll learn about later in this hour, and the results are often easier to read.

Hours 14–16 offer dozens of ways in which you can customize the operating system— don't stop there. You can find your own customizations by tracking down the settings that the operating system or any other program uses in the Registry. I found many of the customizations that are discussed in Hours 14–16 using the same techniques you'll learn about in this hour.

Comparing REG File Snapshots

You can export the Registry to a REG file using the Windows-based or real mode Registry Editor. Recall that REG files are nothing more than text files, which makes them ideally suitable for comparison. Each fully qualified key name is bracketed on a line by itself and is followed by each of its value entries. Each value looks like *name=value*, except for the key's default value entry, which looks like *@=value*. To export the Registry using the Windows-based Registry Editor, choose Registry, Export Registry File. Select All to make sure that you're exporting the entire Registry, and specify the path and filename of the REG file in the spaces provided. Click Save to export the Registry to the REG file, a process that takes a few minutes. To export the Registry using the real mode Registry Editor, type the following command line at an MS-DOS command prompt or in the Run dialog box:

```
regedit /e filename.reg
```

The following sections describe a few text-comparison utilities that you can use to compare REG files. All of them do a good job, but aren't equally suitable. My preference is Norton File Compare because it's more intuitive in that it recognizes that you're comparing REG files and formats its output accordingly. Norton File Compare sometimes chokes on extremely large REG files, however, and is a bit slower than WinDiff. Regardless, both programs do the same thing, so the choice is yours. If neither of these programs is available to you, you can use your word processor's comparison feature, but expect to wait a long, long time while the word processor crunches the thousands of lines that are found in a typical REG file. Regardless of which utility you choose, the process is the same:

1. Export the complete Registry, including both HKEY_LOCAL_MACHINE and HKEY_USERS, to a REG file. Name this file Before.reg (or something similar).

2. Perform the actions that you believe change the Registry. If you want to see how a program stores options in the Registry, for example, set those options. If you want to see what values a setup program changes, install the application.

3. Export the complete Registry to another REG file. Name this file After.reg (or something similar).

4. Compare both REG files, Before.reg and After.reg, using a text-comparison utility. The utility indicates the differences between the two files.

> Breaking news! Just before this book went to the printer, I learned about a new product called RegSnap. This product completely automates the process that is described in this section. It takes snapshots of the Registry, compares them, and reports the changes. This program offers numerous advanced features and, best of all, compares two snapshots so fast it'll make your head spin. You can download RegSnap from the Web at `http://www.webdon.com`.

17

TIPS FOR CREATING SNAPSHOTS

If the change you're seeking is in a specific part of the Registry, don't export the entire thing; just export that specific branch. Be sure to export the exact same branch in both the before and after REG files. To export a specific branch, select the key at the top of the branch before choosing Registry, Export Registry File from Registry Editor. Select Selected branch instead of All.

If you enable user profiles and export the entire Registry, you might worry about whether the REG file contains all your settings as well as the default user's settings; don't. The Registry Editor exports HKEY_USERS, which means that it exports .DEFAULT and *Username*. .DEFAULT corresponds to the User.dat file in \Windows, and *Username* corresponds to the User.dat in your profile folder. Just be sure to log on to the computer properly, and don't export the Registry in MS-DOS mode. In both cases, the Registry Editor only exports the settings from User.dat in \Windows.

WinDiff

WinDiff is a classic text-comparison tool that programmers are familiar with. It comes with the software development kit that they use to write Windows programs. WinDiff comes with Windows 98; you find it on the CD-ROM under \Tools\Reskit\File. Copy Windiff.exe and Windiff.hlp to any folder on your computer. To make accessing WinDiff easier, add a shortcut to the Start menu. If you installed the Microsoft Windows 98 Resource Kit Sampler by running Setup.exe from \Tools\Reskit, you already have WinDiff on your computer under \Program Files\Win98RK; run WinDiff from the command prompt or the Run dialog box.

If you installed the Microsoft Windows 98 Resource Kit Sampler from \Tools\Reskit on the CD-ROM, you have the *Microsoft Management Console* (*MMC*). MMC provides easy access to a plethora of Windows 98 utilities, including WinDiff. Start MMC by choosing Start, Programs, Windows 98 Resource Kit, Tools Management Console. WinDiff is under the File Tools category.

When you start WinDiff, it displays an empty window. Specify the files that you want to compare by choosing File, Compare Files. Pick the first file and click Open, and then pick the second file and click Open. WinDiff displays a single line at the top of the window that indicates whether the two files are the same or different. Double-click that line to compare the files and display the comparison results. Alternatively, click the Expand button on the toolbar or choose View, Expand. Figure 17.1 shows how WinDiff looks after the comparison of two REG files.

FIGURE 17.1

You can't see the colors in this figure, but the darker band is red, and the lighter band is yellow.

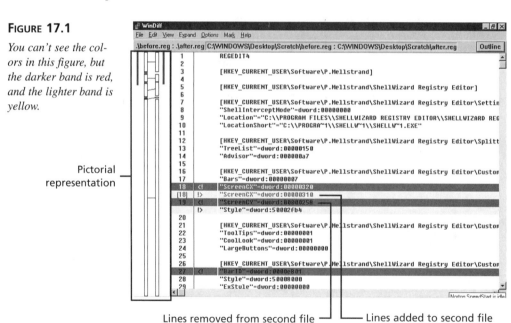

Pictorial representation

Lines removed from second file ———⌐   ⌐——— Lines added to second file

WinDiff combines both files, highlighting the differences between them. Press F8 to view the next difference between the files, or press F7 to view the previous difference. Lines with a white background are common to both files; WinDiff indicates differences with a red or yellow background. A red background means that the line is present in the first file but not in the second. A yellow background means that the line is in the second file but not in the first. Therefore, a red background indicates lines that were removed from the second file, and a yellow background indicates lines that were added to the second file. You also see arrows beside each changed line that point left or right. They are easier to remember than the colors. An arrow pointing to the left means that the line was removed from the second file, and an arrow pointing to the right means that the line was added to the second file. When using WinDiff, refer to the following table to jog your memory about what each color and arrow means:

Color	Arrow	Meaning
Red	<!	Line present in first file, not in second
Yellow	!>	Line present in second file, not in first

The bars you see along the left edge of WinDiff's window are a pictorial representation of the two files' differences. You see two columns; the first represents the first file, and the second represents the second file. You also see red and yellow bands within each column. These bands indicate differences between the two files. The two blue vertical lines on either side of the columns show what portion of the files WinDiff is displaying in the window. Click anywhere in the picture to display that portion of the files in WinDiff. Click one of the red or yellow bands in the picture to display that particular difference in the window. This is a great way to move directly to differences between the files.

WinDiff represents changed lines by showing them deleted from the first file and added to the second. Thus, alternating red and yellow bands indicate changes rather than additions or deletions. Also note the line numbers. When WinDiff detects a changed line, it shows the line as it appears in the first file with a line number such as 18. It shows the line as it appears in the second file with a line number such as (18).

Norton File Compare

Hour 1, "Understanding the Registry," describes where to purchase Norton Utilities and where to get an evaluation copy. After you've installed Norton Utilities, you start File Compare by choosing Start, Programs, Norton Utilities, Norton File Compare.

After you start Norton File Compare, it prompts you for the left and right files; these correspond to the first and second files. Select new files by choosing File, Open Left Pane and File, Open Right Pane. After scanning both files for changes, File Compare them, one in each pane, as shown in Figure 17.2. When you scroll up and down, File Compare synchronizes the files in the two panes. This makes it possible to compare them side-by-side as you move up and down. Note that File Compare recognizes that you're comparing REG files and formats the output accordingly. It shows Registry keys and subkeys using the appropriate hierarchy and displays the correct icons for each value's type. It doesn't change the format of each text line, however; rather, it leaves each as it appears in the REG file.

FIGURE 17.2

Norton File Compare shows you the path and filename above each pane. It also indicates which file is newer.

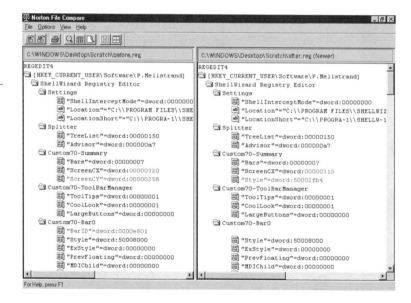

Norton File Compare indicates unchanged text with black characters and changed text with red characters. If these colors are difficult for you to see, change them by choosing Options, Settings, and then clicking the Display tab. You can scroll up and down to look for individual differences, or you can use File Compare's search feature to locate each difference. Choose Options, Search, or press F3. Select Non Matching Block, and click Search Down or Search Up. File Compare brings each block of differences to the top of the window. If you only want to see the changes, choose View, Show Differences Only. This feature collapses the display so that you only see the lines that are different between each file. You won't see the changed lines in their original context, but this is the best means by which to locate changes in the Registry.

Norton File Compare is designed to work hand-in-hand with Registry Tracker. Registry Tracker uses File Compare to compare the differences between two versions of the Registry. Registry Tracker is painfully slow, however, so you're better off comparing REG files that you create yourself.

Most Word Processors

Instead of using WinDiff or Norton File Compare, you can use your word processor's compare feature to find changes between two REG files. Most popular word processors, such as Microsoft Word, have this feature, but it's not the best choice. Using a word processor to compare two REG files is much slower than using a program that is designed for that purpose. Still, using your word processor might be your only choice if you don't have access to either WinDiff or Norton File Compare.

Revision tracking, as it's called in most word processors, works differently in different programs. In most cases, you open the second REG file first and compare it to the first. Opening the files in this order ensures that the word processor correctly interprets whether lines are added to, changed in, or removed from the older file.

In Microsoft Word, choose File, Open to open the second REG file. Make sure that you choose All files from Files of type so that you can see REG files, not just DOC files. Select the REG file and click Open. Be patient because opening a large REG file can take a long time. After Word opens the REG file, choose Tools, Track Changes, Compare Documents. Then select the first REG file, and click Open. Word doesn't actually open the file. It highlights the differences between the open REG file and the REG file that you chose to compare it to. By default, Word formats deleted lines using strikethrough and new lines using underline, as shown in Figure 17.3.

17

SOME CHANGES JUST DON'T MATTER

You'll see some of the same changes repeatedly after comparing a handful of REG files. They don't mean anything. They're just normal changes that occur over time and have little to do with the changes for which you're searching. If you compare two REG files that were created before and after restarting the computer, for instance, you'll find several changes to HKEY_LOCAL_MACHINE\System. These changes just reflect the results of Plug and Play's configuring the hardware as you start the operating system. In the course of normal operation, various values change in the Registry. A variety of MRU lists change as you run programs, open documents, or search for files. Windows Explorer saves different settings that indicate the position, size, and appearance of each Explorer window. Ignore all these incidental changes and focus on finding the important ones.

FIGURE 17.3

*Differences between
REG files aren't as
easy to discern in
Microsoft Word as they
are in Norton File
Compare.*

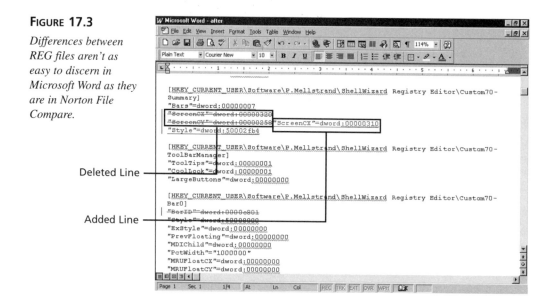

Comparing Registry Checker Backups

You've used your computer for weeks with no problems. Without warning, it starts acting up, and you don't know why. You suspect that the problem is with the data in the Registry, but you haven't taken any snapshots using ConfigSafe, and you didn't export the contents of the Registry to a REG file prior to the problem's occurring. You're out of luck, eh?

Not so fast.

Recall that Registry Checker backs up the Registry to CAB files once each day. It stores these CAB files in \Windows\Sysbckup. At the very least, you have five days of backups, but if you followed the advice given in Hour 3, "Backing Up/Restoring the Registry," you have ten days. Compare the Registry files in these CAB files to find the change in your configuration that's causing the problems. You can extract System.dat and User.dat using Windows Explorer or Extract.exe. Note that you must start the computer in MS-DOS mode to export the extracted System.dat and User.dat to a REG file. The Registry Editor won't properly recognize the /l and /r command line options when you're running Windows 98. Follow these instructions closely, and refer to Hour 3 for more specific instructions about how to extract System.dat and User.dat from a CAB file:

1. In \Windows\Sysbckup, a hidden folder, locate the two CAB files that contain the Registry backups that you want to compare. Remember that a higher-numbered CAB file is newer than a lower-numbered CAB file; thus, RB004.cab is newer than RB003.cab.

2. Extract System.dat and User.dat from each CAB into two separate folders. Right-click the CAB file and choose View. Drag the file from the Explorer window to the folder that you created for the file. After finishing this step, you have two folders, possibly C:\Before and C:\After, each of which contains different versions of System.dat and User.dat.

3. Restart the computer in MS-DOS mode. Step 4 won't work properly unless you do so because it relies on the capability to redirect the real mode Registry Editor to a different set of Registry files.

4. Export the Registry files in each folder to a REG file. Assuming that you saved both sets of Registry files in C:\Before and C:\After, the following command lines get the job done:

```
regedit /l:c:\before\system.dat
/r:c:\before\user.dat /e c:\before\before.reg

regedit /l:c:\after\system.dat
/r:c:\after\user.dat /e c:\after\after.reg
```

5. Restart Windows 98 and compare both REG files using the techniques that you learned earlier in this hour.

Listing 17.1 is a batch file that automates the preceding steps, through step 4. You can find it on my Web site, http://www.honeycutt.com. Start the computer in MS-DOS mode and run Listing 17.1. The command line is cabreg *reg1* *reg2*, where *reg1* is the older CAB file and *reg2* is the newer CAB file. An example is cabreg rb003.cab rb004.cab. The batch file extracts System.dat and User.dat from each CAB file. It puts the first in C:\Before and the second in C:\After. Then it exports the System.dat and User.dat files in each folder to a REG file. Exporting both DAT files in MS-DOS mode takes a long time, so be patient. After restarting Windows 98, compare the REG files that this batch file generates to locate any differences between each backup. Note that this batch file depends on Extract.exe, a program that extracts files from CAB files. To learn more about using this program, type extract /? at the MS-DOS command prompt.

17

LISTING 17.1 CABREG.BAT

```
Echo Off
if "%2" == "" goto Error

extract /y /l c:\before c:\windows\sysbckup\%1 system.dat
➥user.dat
extract /y /l c:\after  c:\windows\sysbckup\%2 system.dat
➥user.dat

regedit /l:c:\before\system.dat /r:c:\before\user.dat /e
c:\before\before.reg
regedit /l:c:\after\system.dat /r:c:\after\user.dat /e
➥c:\after\after.reg

Goto Finished

:Error

Echo You must specify the CAB files containing the Registry
Echo that you want to export. The command line looks like
➥this:
Echo .
Echo cabreg cab1 cab2
Echo .
Echo cab1 - Older CAB file (ex. rb003.cab)
Echo cab2 - Newer CAB file (ex. rb004.cat)

:Finished
```

Exporting alternative System.dat and User.dat files to a REG file in MS-DOS mode is painfully slow. On my computer, the batch file in Listing 17.1 completed after two hours. However, you don't have any choice if you want to compare two backups of the Registry made by Registry Checker. Be patient and wait out the process.

Monitoring Access to the Registry

Up to this point, you've learned how to compare snapshots that you take at different times. Watching how a program uses the Registry in real-time might be a better means to discover how it uses the Registry, though. Registry Monitor is a program that does just that. You learn how to download and install this program in Hour 8, "Using Microsoft's Tweak UI." In short, you can get a free copy of Registry Monitor from http://www.sysinternals.com. It's a very small program that takes just a few minutes to retrieve.

Figure 17.4 shows Registry Monitor. The window contains six columns. The first contains line numbers. The second and third contain the name of the process that is accessing the Registry and the type of request the process is making. Table 17.1 describes each of the different requests you'll see in this column. These types correspond to the different API functions that are available to programs accessing the Registry. The remaining columns contain the Registry path, the result (success or failure), and any other data, as described in Table 17.1. Registry Monitor also divides its window into rows and adds a new line to the end of the list every time a program accesses the Registry.

FIGURE 17.4

Although Registry Monitor tracks every access to the Registry, it doesn't affect your computer's performance.

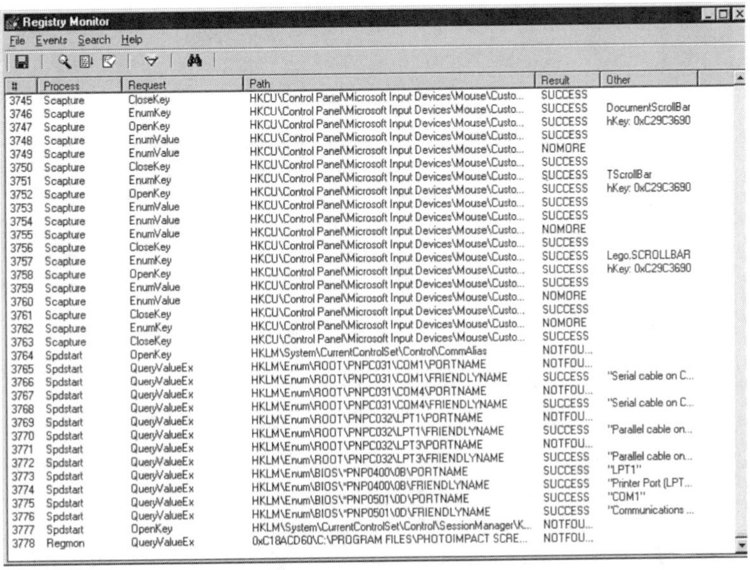

17

TABLE 17.1 REQUEST TYPES IN REGISTRY MONITOR

Type	Data in the Other Column
CloseKey	Unused
CreateKey	Handle to the newly created key
CreateKeyEx	Handle to the newly created key
DeleteKey	Unused
DeleteValue	Unused
EnumKey	Name of the next enumerated subkey
EnumKeyEx	Name of the next enumerated subkey
EnumValue	Unused

continues

TABLE 17.1 CONTINUED

Type	Data in the Other Column
FlushKey	Unused
OpenKey	Handle to the opened key
OpenKeyEx	Handle to the opened key
QueryValue	Data queried from the value entry
QueryValueEx	Data queried from the value entry
SetValue	Data stored in the value entry
SetValueEx	Data stored in the value entry

> Most of the time, Registry Monitor displays the correct Registry path for each line in the window. If a program opened a key before you started Registry Monitor, however, Registry Monitor can't look up the key's path and therefore can't display the path in the window. In such cases, Registry Monitor displays the key's handle instead of its path. The best you can do is take an educated guess at which path the handle represents.

Without a filtering capability, Registry Monitor wouldn't be suitable for tracking down specific Registry changes. In the several minutes that I had Registry Monitor open, it recorded more than 12,000 accesses to the Registry. Pinpointing small changes is almost impossible in this case. The program does enable you to filter the lines it displays, though, so that you can focus on access by a particular process or on specific types of access by any program. Choose Events, Filter; you'll see the Regmon Filter dialog box. Type the name of the process that you want to watch in Process. You can also choose the types of access you want to observe: Log Reads, Log Writes, Log Success, and Log Errors. Note that an asterisk (*) is a wildcard. Click Apply to start filtering using the criteria you chose.

Make sure that you use the application's process name when filtering in Registry Monitor, and not the application's proper name or EXE filename. The best way to discover the application's process name is to observe the names that Registry Monitor displays in the second column. Note that some processes are named Run32dll, indicating that the process was a DLL file that was launched via Run32dll.exe. In this case, you won't see the name of the DLL file, and many processes might share this name.

You can watch for hits to a specific Registry branch by filtering on it. Type the path to the branch you want to watch in Path Include, which is in the Regmon Filter dialog box. Be sure to format the path just as you'd see it in Registry Monitor's window. That is, use the abbreviated root keys, such as HKLM and HKCU.

Comparing Registries Across the Network

CompReg is on the *Microsoft Windows 98 Resource Kit* CD-ROM. Look in \Reskit\Registry. This program is not on the Windows 98 CD-ROM's Resource Kit Sampler, so you must own the full version of the Resource Kit in order to use it.

CompReg, an MS-DOS program, compares two branches of a Registry or compares the Registries from a local computer and a remote computer. The program's output looks like Listing 17.2. You can run CompReg from the Resource Kit's CD-ROM, or you can copy its EXE file to your computer. The Resource Kit's setup program copies Compreg.exe to your computer, so you might already have it. Look in \Program Files\Win98RK.

LISTING 17.2 SAMPLE OUTPUT FROM COMPREG

```
1 \ShellNew
1 \ShellEx
2 \Wordpad.Document.1
2 \Word.Document.6
2 \WordDocument
2 \ShellEx
2 \Word.Document.8
1 ! REG_SZ,[Paint.Picture]
2 ! REG_SZ,[Word.Document.8]
1 !Content Type REG_SZ,[image/bmp]
2 !Content Type REG_SZ,[application/msword]
End of search : 9 differences found.
```

The following list describes CompReg's command line:

compreg <1> <2> [-v] [-r] [-e] [-d] [-q] [-n] [-h] [-?]

1	Path of the first key
2	Path of the second key
-v	Shows differences and matches

-r	Visits subkeys that exist only in *1* or *2*
-e	Sets errorlevel to the previous error code
-d	Limits output to just key names, not values
-q	Limits output to the number of differences
-n	Disables the use of color in the output
-h	Displays help
-?	Displays command-line options

Some aspects of CompReg's command line bear more explanation. In particular, *1* and *2* specify the Registry paths you're comparing. The notation is *Name**Path*. *Name*, if provided, can be the name of any computer on the network. *Path* is a Registry path within that computer's Registry. If you don't provide a computer name, CompReg assumes that the path is within the local Registry. *Path* is usually a fully qualified path starting from one of the root keys. You must use one of the abbreviations shown in Table 17.2, though, rather than the conventional abbreviations you learned about in Hour 2, "Looking Inside the Registry." If you specify just a computer name for *2*, CompReg compares the path specified by *1* to the same path on the machine specified by *2*. The following list shows several examples to speed you on your way:

```
compreg lm\software cu\software

compreg us\.default us\jerry

compreg lm\software \\Other

compreg \\Workstation\lm \\Other\lm

compreg \\Workstation\lm\software \\Server
```

If the paths that you specify to CompReg contain spaces, be sure to enclose the entire path in quotation marks.

TABLE 17.2   ROOT KEY ABBREVIATIONS FOR COMPREG

Abbreviation	Root Key
lm	HKEY_LOCAL_MACHINE
cu	HKEY_CURRENT_USER
cr	HKEY_CLASSES_ROOT
us	HKEY_USERS

Using Norton Registry Tracker—Not!

Norton Registry Tracker, shown in Figure 17.5, is my only disappointment with Symantec's otherwise fine suite of utilities. It seriously affects the performance of any computer on which it is used to track the Registry. The reason is that Registry Tracker continuously monitors the Registry for changes, creating a new snapshot every time it detects one. If you monitor too much of the Registry's content, Registry Tracker takes snapshots all the time, sapping the computer's resources.

FIGURE 17.5

Norton Registry Tracker relies on File Compare to show the differences between two snapshots.

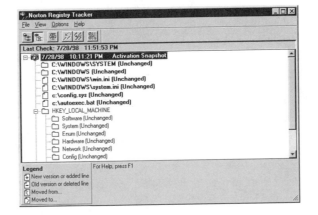

17

If you allow Norton Registry Tracker to monitor the Registry in the background, you'll suffer for it. Using Registry Tracker to take occasional snapshots of the entire Registry isn't practical either. On my computer, a 233Mhz Pentium with 32MB of memory, I closed Registry Tracker via the Task Manager after giving Registry Tracker more than 40 minutes to take a full snapshot of the Registry. This is not acceptable performance, given that you can export the Registry to a REG file in a matter of minutes, or that you can use ConfigSafe, which is covered next, to fulfill the same purpose in a fraction of the time. The only practical use for Registry Tracker is to take occasional snapshots of very specific portions of the Registry.

If you want an excellent alternative to Registry Tracker, one that offers most of the same features, try ConfigSafe. You'll learn about this product in the following section.

Tracking the Registry with ConfigSafe

ConfigSafe was originally designed to help hardware manufacturers better support their customers. It records the configuration of a computer when the manufacturer ships it. Then, when a customer calls in with a problem, the support person uses ConfigSafe to determine what the user has changed on his or her computer.

ConfigSafe is just as valuable to you. Use it to take occasional *snapshots* of your computer's configuration; then, you can see what changed on your computer from time to time, from snapshot to snapshot. For example, if you installed a program that changed your Autoexec.bat without asking, you can see exactly what the program changed. If a program messed up the Registry, you can use ConfigSafe to see exactly how. ConfigSafe is also a good program to use for tracking down changes in the Registry when you're hunting down that next great customization.

The easiest—and fastest—way to start using ConfigSafe is to download an evaluation copy. Open `http://www.imagine-lan.com`, click the Download button, and follow the instructions that you see on the Web page. You can also order ConfigSafe directly from imagine LAN:

> imagine LAN, Inc.
>
> 76 Northeastern Blvd., Suite 34B
>
> Nashua, NH 03062-3174
>
> (603) 889-3883

When you first install ConfigSafe, it takes an initial snapshot of the computer's configuration. After the first snapshot, you don't really have to do much. Just sit back and allow ConfigSafe to do its job. By default, ConfigSafe takes a new snapshot once a week. This is more than enough to protect your computer against most problems. The following list shows the items that it records in each snapshot; you can see that ConfigSafe covers all the bases:

- **Configuration files**—Protocol.ini, System.ini, Win.ini, Autoexec.bat, Config.sys, and Msdos.sys

- **System information**—Processor, coprocessor, memory, and Windows version

- **Drive information**—Free space on each drive

- **Directory information**—Files in C:\Dos and in C:\Windows and all its subdirectories

- **Registry information**—All value entries for all keys in the Registry

Even though ConfigSafe tracks a variety of configuration data, this discussion is limited to how you use the program to track Registry changes. ConfigSafe's help describes the program's remaining features.

Viewing Changes

To run ConfigSafe, choose Start, Programs, ConfigSafe, ConfigSafe. It monitors HKEY_LOCAL_MACHINE and HKEY_USERS, which includes every key and value in System.dat and User.dat. You don't need to add any other keys to the list because these two cover all the bases. Click the Registry Information button on the toolbar to see both the Registry keys that ConfigSafe is tracking and the changes to each value entry. You'll see a view similar to Figure 17.6. My only beef with this program is that it doesn't use a tabbed interface as similar programs do.

17

FIGURE 17.6

See the section "Sniffing Out Customizations" to learn how to use this view to track down changes in the Registry.

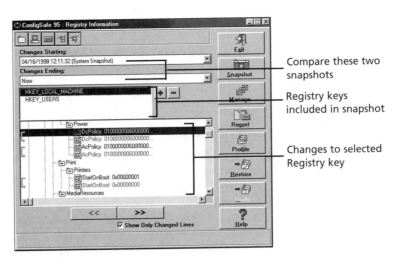

Compare these two snapshots

Registry keys included in snapshot

Changes to selected Registry key

You have to tell ConfigSafe which snapshots you want to compare when it is building the list of changes. You can compare any two snapshots, as well as any snapshot and the current configuration. For example, you can compare a snapshot you took two weeks ago to the current configuration, represented by the word *Now* instead of a date and time. You can also compare a snapshot that you took four weeks ago to a snapshot that you took two weeks ago. Choose the beginning snapshot from Changes Starting. Choose the ending snapshot from Changes Ending.

To see changes to a particular Registry key and all its subkeys, select a key from the list. ConfigSafe goes away again, possibly for a very long time, so keep your fingers off Ctrl+Alt+Delete. Look under the list of Registry keys to see the actual value entries that have changed. You see a plus sign by each new Registry key and a minus sign beside each deleted Registry key. ConfigSafe displays before and after versions of changed keys with a green arrow pointing from the older value data to the newer value data. The following table describes the conventions:

Type	Color	Icon
Add	Blue	+
Delete	Red	−
Change	Green	

Most of the time, you'll want to compare the most recent snapshot to your current configuration. This enables you to determine recent changes to your configuration. Other times, you'll want to compare two different snapshots that occur before and after a specific configuration change, such as installing a new program. This enables you to figure out what changes the program made.

Taking New Snapshots

Create a new snapshot at any time by clicking the Snapshot button. Type a name in the Create Configuration Snapshot dialog box, and click OK.

Maybe changing ConfigSafe's snapshot schedule is what you really wanted to do. ConfigSafe takes a configuration snapshot once every week by default. If you find yourself taking a snapshot every morning, change ConfigSafe's schedule so that it does so automatically. A monthly snapshot might be more suitable for users who don't use their computers much. A daily snapshot is more appropriate for someone who toys with his configuration regularly. Follow these steps to change the schedule:

1. Click Manage to display the Manage Configuration Snapshots dialog box.
2. Make sure that Enable Scheduled Snapshot is checked.
3. Select Daily, Weekly, Monthly, or At Windows Startup.
4. Click OK to save your changes.

MISSED A SNAPSHOT

If ConfigSafe misses a snapshot, either because you didn't start the computer that day or because you temporarily disabled the program, it takes the snapshot immediately at the next available opportunity.

Sniffing Out Customizations

ConfigSafe can track down Registry settings that a program changes. Use the following steps to compare a snapshot that is taken after the program makes its changes to a snapshot that you take beforehand:

1. Create a new *profile* so that you can easily clean up your mess when you're finished. Profiles are individually named collections of snapshots. Click the Profile button, name the profile, and click OK.

2. Take a snapshot of the configuration by clicking Snapshot, typing a name, and clicking OK. This saves your current configuration. Close ConfigSafe.

3. Run the program, and cause it to make the changes to the Registry that you want to uncover. You might have to set various options, move the window, and so on. The steps depend on what you're trying to discover.

4. After you're sure that the program has changed the Registry, close it. Then run ConfigSafe again and compare the previous snapshot to the current configuration.

This hour has shown you how to track Registry changes using ConfigSafe, but you must understand that ConfigSafe is more than that. As its name implies, it's a good way to stash your configuration for safekeeping. You can restore any portion of your configuration if needed. Few problems can sneak by ConfigSafe, meaning that as long as it's protecting your computer, you can fix any problem.

Summary

The easiest way to track down changes to the Registry is to export the Registry to a REG file, before and after something changes it, and then compare both REG files using a text comparison utility. You learned about some of the best text comparison utilities in this hour, including WinDiff and Norton File Compare. If all else fails, you can rely on most word processors to do the comparison.

This hour also described a few specialized utilities. Registry Monitor is good for watching changes to the Registry as they occur, for example. ConfigSafe is a good utility to keep track of the Registry over a long period of time. It takes regularly scheduled snapshots of the Registry that you can compare to see what changes occurred.

17

Q&A

Q Which is the best method for comparing two REG files?

A My favorite is Windiff—it has a simple user interface and is quicker than the alternatives.

Q I tried using my word processor to compare two REG files, but the process is so slow. How can I make it work faster?

A If you must use your word processor to compare two REG files, be sure to disable its spell and grammar checkers. If they are enabled, your computer grinds to a halt because the word processor will find spelling and grammar errors on every line of each file. Consult your word processor's documentation to learn how to disable spell and grammar checking.

Workshop

The following quiz will enhance your understanding of the topics discussed in this hour.

Quiz

1. Which of the following command lines exports the contents of the entire Registry to a REG file?

   a. `regedit /export registry.reg`

   b. `regedit /x registry.reg`

   c. `regedit /e registry.reg`

2. True or false? Microsoft Word is better suited to comparing REG files than WinDiff.

3. Which of the following methods are more appropriate for determining what changes a setup program makes to the Registry?

   a. Comparing before and after snapshots in WinDiff

   b. Monitoring the setup program in Registry Monitor

   c. Either a or b

4. Which of the following programs do you use in order to compare your Registry to a remote computer's Registry?

   a. WinDiff

   b. Registry Monitor

   c. CompReg

5. Which of the following is the best program for monitoring the Registry on a regular basis?

    a. ConfigSafe

    b. Registry Tracker

    c. Either a or b

Answers to Quiz Questions

1. c

   /e exports all or portions of the Registry.

2. False

   WinDiff is designed specifically for comparing source files, whereas Microsoft Word was never intended for this purpose.

3. a

   Changes to the Registry occur very quickly. Monitoring them in Registry Monitor isn't feasible.

4. c

   CompReg, included with the Windows 98 Resource Kit, can compare two Registries over the network.

5. a

   Registry Tracker is just too slow to be used on a regular basis.

17

Hour 18

Scripting Changes to the Registry

In this hour, you learn three different methods that you can use to make automatic changes to the Registry:

- REG Files
- INF Files
- Scripts

REG files are the easiest by far because you can create a REG file by exporting a portion of the Registry. INF files are a bit more powerful, enabling you to delete keys and values, but they have a special language that you have to learn. Lastly, scripts are a great way to programmatically control the Registry. Scripts can be quite difficult to write for those of you who don't have programming experience, however, and you need to limit their usage to times when you're doing more than just reading and writing Registry values.

Updating the Registry with REG Files

REG files are the classic method for updating values in the Registry. The main reason is that they are so easy to create using a text editor or the Registry Editor's export feature. Importing REG files is easy, too: Just double-click the file, or right-click it and choose Merge.

Listing 18.1 shows a typical REG file. It makes several changes to the Registry, most of which you learned about in Hours 14—16. The first line always contains REGEDIT4, indicating that the file is a valid Registry Editor file, and the second line must always be blank. The Registry Editor won't import the file if it doesn't begin with REGEDIT4 and a blank line.

The remainder of Listing 18.1 changes various value entries, adding them if they don't already exist. The file is split into three sections, with each Registry key in its own section. The fully qualified name of the key is given between brackets, as follows: [*Keyname*]. A fully qualified key name includes the entire path to a key (such as HKEY_CLASSES_ROOT\txtfile\shell) rather than just a portion of the path (such as txtfile\shell). In this case, the three sections are for the following Registry keys:

    HKEY_CURRENT_USER\MyKey

    HKEY_LOCAL_MACHINE\Software\Microsoft\Windows\CurrentVersion\Winlogon

    HKEY_CURRENT_USER\Control Panel\Desktop

LISTING 18.1   A SAMPLE REG FILE

```
REGEDIT4

[HKEY_CURRENT_USER\MyKey]
@="Default Value"

[HKEY_LOCAL_MACHINE\Software\Microsoft\Windows\
➥CurrentVersion\Winlogon]
"DefaultUserName"="Jerry"
"DefaultPassword"="Password"
"AutoAdminLogon"="1"

[HKEY_CURRENT_USER\Control Panel\Desktop]
"ScreenSaveUsePassword"=dword:00000000
"SmoothScroll"=hex:01,00,00,00
```

You must begin every REG file with the keyword REGEDIT4 on the first line, and the second line must be blank. Thereafter, divide the file into sections, with each section containing a Registry key followed by value entries.

Under each key in Listing 18.1, you see a list of value entries that belong to that key. Except for default value entries, the name appears in quotation marks. Use an at sign (@) for the default value entry within a key. Obviously, you need to include only one default value entry within a single section. The name goes on the left side of the equal sign, as shown, and the value you're assigning to it goes on the right side. The listing shows how to write string, DWORD, and binary values, each of which looks a bit different:

- **String**—"This is a string value"
- **DWORD**—DWORD:00000001
- **Binary**—HEX:FF,00,FF,00,FF,00,FF,00,FF,00,FF,00

String value entries sometimes contain special characters. It's common to include quotes within a command line, such as Wordpad.exe "%1", for example, so that WordPad can open long filenames that contain spaces. I've also seen string value entries that contain linefeeds and carriage returns. The format for REG files makes special provisions for these characters; it's called *escaping*. When you prefix a special character with a backslash, the Registry Editor knows to replace the combination with the actual character that is represented. \n represents the newline character, for example, which is an ASCII 10. Table 18.1 describes the special characters that the Registry Editor supports, and gives examples.

TABLE 18.1 ESCAPE CHARACTERS

Esc	Expanded	Escaped in the REG File	Expanded in the Registry
\\	\	"\\\\Server\\Drive"	\\Server\Drive
\"	"	"This is \"quoted\""	This is "quoted"
\n	Newline	"First\nSecond"	First newline Second
\r	Return	"First\nSecond"	First return Second

REG files don't have separate syntaxes for adding new entries and changing them. If you specify a key or value entry that doesn't exist, the Registry Editor creates it. If you specify a value entry that doesn't exist, the Registry Editor creates and changes its value. If you specify a value that does exist, the Registry Editor merely changes the existing value.

Creating REG Files by Hand

Creating a REG file by hand is easy enough. Create a new text file with a REG extension and follow these steps:

1. Put `REGEDIT4` at the top of the file. This must be the first line in the file. Also, be sure to insert one blank line between `REGEDIT4` and the first section of the REG file, as shown in Listing 18.1.

2. Add a section for each key to which you want to add or that you want to change in the Registry. Put each key name in square brackets, as follows: `[Keyname]`. Make sure that you use the fully qualified path to the key, beginning with the root key.

3. Put an entry under each key for each value entry that you want to add or change. Each entry has the form `"Name"=Value`, where `Name` is the name of the value entry that you're adding or changing. If you're changing the default value entry, use the at sign (@) for `Name`, without the quotes. `Value` is the value to which you want to set the value entry. Make sure that it follows one of the forms shown in Table 18.1.

4. Save your changes to the REG file.

 You can't use a REG file to remove a key from the Registry. If you require this capability, use an INF file or a Windows Scripting Host script. You'll learn how to do both later in this hour.

Creating REG Files Using REGEDIT

Creating REG files by hand seems easy enough, but it is not recommended. There are entirely too many chances for errors—especially if you're a poor typist. Therefore, you need to use the Registry Editor, if possible. Hour 5, "Importing/Exporting the Registry," showed you how to export a branch of the Registry to a REG file. For your convenience, however, those instructions are repeated here:

1. In the left pane of the Registry Editor, highlight the key that represents the branch that you want to export.

2. Choose Registry, Export Registry File. The Registry Editor displays the dialog box that is shown in Figure 18.1.

FIGURE 18.1

If you don't type a file extension, REGEDIT uses the default file extension (REG).

3. Select Selected branch. REGEDIT automatically fills in the key that you selected in step 1.

4. Type the filename into which you want the Registry exported in the File name box, and click Save.

There are a couple of issues that you need to be aware of when using this technique:

- **Trimming**—When you export a key using the Registry Editor, you're exporting all that key's subkeys and value entries as well. Thus, you'll need to open the file (right-click it and choose Edit) and remove any keys and value entries that you don't want to distribute in the REG file.

- **Editing**—You can change any of the values in the REG file. That is, if you're not satisfied with the settings that you exported from the Registry, you can alter those settings in the REG file before you distribute it. Be sure to stick to the formats that you learned earlier in this hour.

18

Editing the Registry with INF Files

Windows describes INF files as "setup information" files. This is a much more generic description than Microsoft usually uses for INF files, which is that INF files contain device driver information. In fact, you can put much more in an INF file than device driver information. You can put software setup information in it. More importantly, you can put statements in an INF file that add, change, and remove Registry entries when the user installs the INF file. In that manner, INF files are similar to scripts, which you'll learn about in the section "Writing Scripts to Update the Registry," but they're much simpler.

Listing 18.2 shows a complete sample INF file that adds and removes values from the Registry. It also shows you how to remove an entire key from the Registry. You'll learn how to build INF files such as this in the following sections. For now, try out this INF file using the following steps:

1. Create a new text file and type in the contents as shown in Listing 18.1. Save the file to your disk with an INF file extension.

2. Create a new subkey, under HKEY_CURRENT_USER, called MyKey. Add a few subkeys under this one. This helps demonstrate the line that removes this key.

3. Right-click the INF file, and choose Install. Open the Registry Editor to observe the changes.

LISTING 18.2   EDITING THE REGISTRY WITH INF FILES

```
[Version]
signature=$CHICAGO$

[DefaultInstall]
AddReg=My.Add.Reg
DelReg=My.Del.Reg

[My.Add.Reg]
HKLM,Software\Microsoft\Windows\CurrentVersion\Winlogon,
➥AutoAdminLogon,0,"0"
HKCU,Control Panel\Desktop,SmoothScroll,1,01,00,00,00
HKCU,Control Panel\Desktop,ScreenSaveUsePassword,1,00,00,
➥00,00

[My.Del.Reg]
HKCU,MyKey
HKLM,Software\Microsoft\Windows\CurrentVersion\Winlogon,
➥DefaultUserName
HKLM,Software\Microsoft\Windows\CurrentVersion\Winlogon,
➥DefaultPassword
```

INF files are complex. Microsoft has created a whole language for INF files, defining intricate rules that link various sections. Most of the statements and sections that programmers use in INF files are irrelevant to the topic at hand. The *Microsoft Windows 98 Resource Kit,* published by Microsoft Press, contains complete documentation for INF files. You'll also find an online version of the resource kit on your Windows 98 CD-ROM in \Tools\Reskit\Help.

Creating an INF File

The first section in all INF files is the [Version] section. It's also called a header. For the purpose of editing the Registry, this section always starts with the following two lines. Note that the Class item, which you normally see in INF files, isn't required in order to create a file to edit the Registry. $CHICAGO$ indicates that the INF file is for Windows (Chicago was the code name for Windows 95):

```
[Version]
signature=$CHICAGO$
```

The remaining sections specify the Registry entries that you're working with and what you want to do to them. The [DefaultInstall] section points to other sections within the INF file—the AddReg and DelReg sections. Each AddReg and DelReg section contains a list of Registry entries that you want to add, change, or remove. You can think of the INF file as a tree with [DefaultInstall] as the trunk, branching out to the AddReg and DelReg sections, which in turn branch out to a list of Registry entries.

[DefaultInstall]

The [DefaultInstall] section has two entries: AddReg and DelReg. AddReg indicates the name of the section that contains the Registry entries that you want to add or change. DelReg indicates the name of the section that contains the Registry entries that you want to remove. In most cases, the [DefaultInstall] section of your INF file looks just like the following:

```
[DefaultInstall]
AddReg=My.Add.Reg
DelReg=My.Del.Reg
```

You must type the name of each item (on the left side of each equal sign) exactly as shown. Remember that the keywords AddReg and DelReg have special significance, indicating sections that include Registry entries to add or remove. You can name the section (on the right side) anything you want, however, and you can use periods in the name, as shown in the example. You can also list multiple sections for AddReg and DelReg, as shown here:

AddReg=*Name1*[,*Name2*[,*Name3*[,...]]]

DelReg=*Name1*[,*Name2*[,*Name3*[,...]]]

> The order in which you list the AddReg and DelReg items within [DefaultInstall] has no bearing on how Windows processes the INF file. The operating system processes the DelReg sections first, followed by the AddReg sections. You can use this to your advantage to completely remove a Registry key, clearing out all its contents and then replacing the key with new contents.

The AddReg and DelReg Sections

For each item that you put in the [DefaultInstall] section, you have to create another section. The name of the section is the value on the right side of each item's equal sign. Continuing the example from the preceding section, create two sections, called [My.Add.Reg] and [My.Del.Reg]. Windows adds the items listed in [My.Add.Reg] to the Registry. It removes the items listed in [My.Del.Reg] from the Registry.

Each line within these sections has a similar format, as shown in the following list. You use all the parameters that are shown if you're adding a value entry. If you're removing a value entry, you use the first three. If you're adding or removing a key, you use the first two.

HKEY, *Subkey*, *ValueName*, *Type*, *Value*

HKEY	One of the abbreviations listed in Table 18.2 for the root key.
Subkey	The subkey under the root key, not including the name of the root key.
ValueName	The name of the value entry that you're adding. Leaving this item blank implies that you're working with the default value entry.
Type	The type of value entry. Use 0 for a string. Use 1 for binary. Use 0x10001 for DWORD.
Value	The data for the value entry. Use the appropriate format for the type you specified. That is, strings need to be in quotation marks. DWORD and binary values need to be in hexadecimal notation with each byte separated by a comma.

TABLE 18.2   ABBREVIATIONS FOR ROOT KEYS

Abbreviation	Root Key
HKCR	HKEY_CLASSES_ROOT
HKCU	HKEY_CURRENT_USER
HKLM	HKEY_LOCAL_MACHINE
HKU	HKEY_USERS
HKCC	HKEY_CURRENT_CONFIG
HKDD	HKEY_DYN_DATA

To make things a bit clearer, Table 18.3 shows several examples. Notice that in a number of the examples one of the parameters has been completely omitted; you see two commas side by side, with no value between them. This has special significance in both the AddReg and DelReg sections. If you leave out the type, for example, it defaults to string. Omitting the value entry name within an AddReg section means that you're changing a key's default value entry. Omitting the value entry name within a DelReg section means that you're removing a key and its subkeys.

TABLE 18.3   EXAMPLES FOR THE AddReg AND DelReg SECTIONS

Example	Description
[My.Add.Reg]	
HKCU,MyKey,MyValue,0,"String"	Adds a string value called MyValue to MyKey, if it doesn't exist, and sets its value to String.
HKCU,MyKey,MyValue,,"String"	Adds a string value called MyValue to MyKey, if it doesn't exist, and sets its value to String.
HKCU,MyKey,MyValue,1,77,34,05,20	Adds a binary value called MyValue to MyKey, if it doesn't exist, and sets its value to the binary string 77 34 05 20.
HKCU,MyKey,,0,"Default Value"	Sets the default value entry of MyKey to the string Default Value.
HKCU,MyKey,,,"Default Value"	Sets the default value entry of MyKey to the string Default Value.
HKCU,MyKey	Adds the Registry key called MyKey without setting any values.
[My.Del.Reg]	
HKCU,MyKey,MyValue	Removes the value entry called MyValue from the key MyKey.
HKCU,MyKey	Removes MyKey and all its subkeys, deleting the entire branch.

18

> **USING SETUP SCRIPTS AND MSBATCH.INF**
>
> The Windows 98 CD-ROM includes a utility called Microsoft Batch 98 (Windows 95's CD-ROM has a similar utility), which you can use to create setup scripts. Setup scripts enable a user to install or upgrade to Windows 98 with little user intervention because you specify most, if not all, of the installation options within the setup script. You can specify options that go far beyond installation, too, such as network configuration, user profiles, and so on.
>
> You'll find Batch 98 in \Tools\Reskit on the Windows 98 CD-ROM.
>
> Batch 98 creates a file called Msbatch.inf that contains all the settings that you specify. You start the setup program with this INF file by typing *path*\setup.exe *path*\msbatch.inf, including the paths to Setup.exe and Msbatch.inf, if necessary.
>
> Msbatch.inf includes a section called [Install] that is similar to the [DefaultInstall] section that you'll learn about in this hour. It enables you to add or remove Registry entries when the user installs Windows 98. One typical case in which you might want to do this is if you're enabling user profiles as the user installs the operating system. You can add the AddReg and DelReg items to this section if they don't already exist. Then add the appropriate AddReg and DelReg sections to the remainder of the file.

Understanding How INF Files Work

In the previous sections, you learned how to create INF files. You'll do better by understanding how they work, however. HKEY_CLASSES_ROOT\inffile\shell\install\ command contains the command line that Windows executes when you right-click an INF file and choose Install. It looks similar to the command line that is described in the following list:

```
C:\WINDOWS\rundll.exe setupx.dll,InstallHinfSection
➥DefaultInstall 132 %1
```

rundll.exe	A small program that invokes a particular routine within a DLL. You can't normally execute a DLL file, but some DLL files have special functions in them that you can execute using Rundll.exe.
setupx.exe,...	Setupx.dll contains a function called InstallHinfSection that knows how to install INF files.
DefaultInstall	Remember [DefaultInstall]? This is the name of the section that contains the AddReg and DelReg sections within the INF file.

132   Who knows what this means.

%1   Windows executes this command line, substituting the
                                 name of the INF file for %1.

The following steps describe the process from beginning to end:

1. The user right-clicks an INF file and chooses Install. As a result, Windows executes
   the command line that was just described.

2. Rundll.exe loads Setupx.dll, calling the function that's called
   InstallHinfSection. Setupx.dll passes the remainder of the command line to this
   function as follows: DefaultInstall 132 %1.

3. InstallHinfSection loads the INF file specified by %1 and looks for the section
   named on the command line. It processes each item within that section, which happens to be [DefaultInstall] in this case.

4. InstallHinfSection processes the DelReg item first, which leads it to the
   [My.Del.Reg] section of the INF file, removing each specified key or value.

5. InstallHinfSection processes the AddReg item second, which leads it to the
   [My.Add.Reg] section of the INF file, adding and changing each Registry entry as
   specified.

> The process that you read about in this section describes what happens with
> an INF file that contains only the AddReg and DelReg sections of an INF file.
> INF files can contain many more sections, however, including Copyfiles,
> LogConfig, Renfiles, Delfiles, UpdateInis, UpdateIniFields, Ini2Reg,
> UpdateCfgSys, and UpdateAutoBat.

Using INF Files to Set DWORD Values

Many people believe that INF files can't write DWORD values to the Registry—they're
wrong. INF files can indeed write DWORD values to the Registry, but you get there via
a twisted path through binary and little-endian values.

Remember that a DWORD value is a four-byte, or 32-bit, integer number. Take 52,059,
for example, which is 0x0000CB5B in hexadecimal. Within memory, the computer stores
DWORD values in reverse byte order (also called *little-endian*), so it stores 0x0000CB5B
as 5B CB 00 00. The computer turns the bytes back around when a program loads the
four-byte number from memory. The same goes for values that a program stores in the

Registry. You see DWORD values represented normally in the Registry Editor only because it reads the value as a DWORD, automatically flipping the bytes around as they are supposed to be.

Therefore, the first solution to writing DWORD values to the Registry is to write them as binary strings using reverse byte order. For instance, if you want to store 21,465 in a value entry, store it as a four-byte binary value with the bytes reversed. Thus, 21,465 is 0x000053D9, so you store the binary string D9 53 00 00 in the value entry. You must be sure to use a four-byte value, however, not three-byte and not five-byte. Note that if you're trying to change an existing DWORD value entry, you might have to remove the original value and replace it with a new binary value. If you're using a script, REG, or INF file, however, Windows automatically changes the type for you.

Just to make sure you understand, Table 18.4 contains a number of examples. The first two columns show a value that you might try to write to the Registry, and the third column shows the little-endian binary string that you'd actually write to represent that value.

TABLE 18.4 EXAMPLES OF WRITING DWORD VALUES TO THE REGISTRY

DWORD (Decimal)	DWORD (Hexadecimal)	Binary (Little-Endian)
01	0x00000001	01 00 00 00
331	0x0000014B	4B 01 00 00
4096	0x00001000	00 10 00 00
5001	0x00001389	89 13 00 00
7779863	0x0076B617	17 B6 76 00
53896313	0x03366479	79 64 36 03
2147483649	0x80000001	01 00 00 80

Little-endian is an addressing scheme in which the bytes with lowest significance are stored first in memory (little end first). Big-endian (big end first) is an addressing scheme in which the bytes with the most significance are stored first in memory. For the most part, Intel computers use little-endian addressing. (By the way, the names "big-endian" and "little-endian" come from a story in Gulliver's Travels.)

The second solution is to use 0x10001 as the type. This is a relatively unknown type that indicates the DWORD data type, and that you can use in the AddReg section of your INF file. Even when using 0x10001, you must still write the value as a four-byte little-endian binary string. Thus, to write the value 2147483649 to the Registry as a DWORD value, convert it to hex, which is 0x80000001, and then to a little-endian binary string, which is 01 00 00 80. As a result, you add a line similar to this to your INF file:

```
HKLM, MyKey, MyValue, 0x10001, 01,00,00,80
```

Writing Scripts to Update the Registry

The Windows Scripting Host is new to Windows 98. It includes two Active Scripting engines, JScript and VBScript—and more scripting engines are coming down the pike. You're probably familiar with Active Scripting because Internet Explorer 3.0 and greater support it already. The Windows Scripting Host brings that same technology to the Windows desktop. Think of it this way: The Windows Scripting Host is to Windows 98 what batch files were supposed to be to MS-DOS.

Scripts are ideal for administrators and power users alike. Administrators can use scripts to automate complex administrative tasks such as advanced login scripts or updates to the user's Registry. Power users can use scripts to automate repetitive tasks. You might use a script to arrange your Windows 98 desktop, for example, or to perform a series of tasks that you do every day.

18

 Following are some real-world examples of things that you can do automatically with scripts: Back up important configuration files, control the programs running on your desktop, collect system information and post it on the server, and connect to the Internet and download files. You can, of course, use scripts to update the Registry with the customization tips you learned in Hours 14—16.

Teaching you how to write scripts is beyond the scope of this book. Additional information is available from a variety of sources, however, all of which are close at hand. \Tools\Reskit\Scrpting on the Windows 98 CD-ROM contains more information about WSH files, which you use to set the properties that control how scripts run. If you need more information about writing scripts, visit Microsoft at http://www.microsoft.com/management/WSH.htm. Similarly, Microsoft's Developer Network provides documentation for the object model (the operating system objects, such as network connections or the shell, that you control from scripts) at http://www.microsoft.com/msdn/sdk/inetsdk/help/wsh/wobj.htm.

The following sections show you how to write scripts that work with the Registry, however. You'll learn how to create and run scripts; how to write scripts that add, remove, and change Registry entries; and how to check for errors and report them to the user.

Creating New Script Files

Scripts are text files that use the extensions that are listed in Table 18.5. JS stands for JScript scripts, Microsoft's incarnation of JavaScript, and VBS stands for VBScript scripts. Note that Windows 98 associates both types of files with Notepad, but I prefer to edit scripts in WordPad. If you do, too, change the Edit command of the JScript Script File and VBScript Script File types. Don't try associating WordPad with either file type's Open command, however, because this prevents you from running scripts by double-clicking them in Windows Explorer. Use Windows Explorer's Folder Options dialog box, or change the default values of the following keys to `"C:\Program Files\Accessories\Wordpad.exe" "%1"`:

    HKEY_CLASSES_ROOT\JSFile\Shell\Edit\Command

    HKEY_CLASSES_ROOT\VBSFile\Shell\Edit\Command

TABLE 18.5   VBSCRIPT AND JSCRIPT SCRIPTS

File Extension	Language	Sample Statement
JS	JScript	`WSHShell.RegDelete ("HKCU\\MyKey\\");`
VBS	VBScript	`WSHShell.RegDelete "HKCU\MyKey\"`

> WordPad makes a better editor for scripts than does Notepad. For one thing, its search and replace feature is far better than Notepad's. More importantly, however, it handles tabs and indentations better than Notepad, so you can format your scripts properly. Associate the JScript Script File and VBScript Script File types with WordPad using the File Types tab in Explorer's Folder Options dialog box. Make sure to save REG, INF, and script files as text, though.

A script starts its life as an empty file. The first line you need to add to this file is always the same, depending on the language you're using. The first of the following two examples shows you that first line for a JScript script. The second example shows you the same line in VBScript. Both of these statements create a shell object, which provides access to the Registry methods and assigns that object to WSHShell. You can, of course, add a few comments to the top of the file, as shown in Listing 18.3, so that the script is easier to read and understand. Note that JScript comments begin with two forward slashes (//) and VBScript comments begin with a single apostrophe (').

```
var WSHShell=WScript.CreateObject("WScript.Shell");

Set WSHShell=WScript.CreateObject("WScript.Shell")
```

The second statement in Listing 18.3 shows you how to display a message on the screen. It uses the shell object's Popup method to display whatever you pass it as a parameter. Remember that you created a shell object in the first statement and assigned it to WSHShell, so you use the syntax WSHShell.Popup to invoke the Popup method. You'll use this same approach when invoking the shell object's Registry methods, as you'll learn in the following sections.

LISTING 18.3   A BASIC JSCRIPT SCRIPT

```
// A Basic Script
//
// This example shows you how to start your script files.
// Begin each file with a brief description of what the
// script does. You might even include your name and a brief
// history of all the changes you make in order to better
// document it. Note that JScript uses two forward slashes
// to start a comment, whereas VBScript uses an
// apostrophe (').

var WSHShell = WScript.CreateObject( "WScript.Shell");
WSHShell.Popup( "This is a basic JScript script!" );
```

18

Running Scripts in Windows and MS-DOS

Double-click a VBS or JS script file to run it. Windows 98 associates the Open command of both file extensions with the Windows Scripting Host and makes that the default command. You can also launch a script from the Run dialog box. Select Start, Run; then type the path and filename of the script in the space provided, and click OK.

Windows 98 includes two different script interpreters—one DOS-based and one Windows-based. The DOS-based interpreter is Cscript.exe, and it enables you to run scripts from the MS-DOS command line. The Windows-based interpreter is Wscript.exe. As you learned, you don't have to do anything special to start scripts using Wscript.exe; just double-click the script file in Windows Explorer or launch it from the Run dialog box. To launch scripts using the DOS-based interpreter, you must run Cscript.exe and pass it the path and filename of the script, as follows:

```
cscript.exe myscript.vbs
```

Both the DOS-based and Windows-based interpreters enable you to specify options that change their behaviors. The DOS-based interpreter accepts a number of command-line options. Note that each of these options begins with two forward slashes, not one. That's because you can pass options to the script itself; you specify these options using a single forward slash. In general, the command line for Cscript.exe looks like this:

```
cscript filename [host options] [script options]
```

//?	Displays help for command line options.
//i	Allows the interpreter to display prompts and script errors.
//b	Prevents the interpreter from displaying prompts and script errors.
//T:n	Kills the script if it runs for longer than *n* seconds. This is good for debugging.
//logo	Displays an execution banner.
//nologo	Prevents the execution banner from being displayed.
//H:Cscript	Registers Cscript.exe as the default script interpreter in the Registry.
//H:Wscript	Registers Wscript.exe as the default script interpreter in the Registry.
//S	Saves the current options as the default.

You can specify options for the Windows-based interpreter, too. These are similar to the command-line options for Cscript.exe. Right-click a script file, choose Properties, and click the Script tab. You see the dialog box shown in Figure 18.2. You'll recognize the options in this dialog box because they're similar to the command-line options for Cscript.exe. Click OK to save your changes. Windows 98 creates a WSH file, which looks similar to an INI file, in the same folder as the script file. Think of WSH files as you do PIF files, each of which contains options for running a particular MS-DOS program: They point to a particular script file, and they contain options for running that script. Listing 18.4 shows you what a typical WSH file looks like.

FIGURE 18.2

The property sheet for a script file enables you to set options that are similar to Cscript.exe's command line.

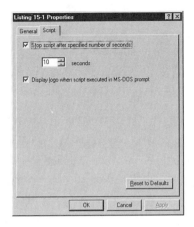

LISTING 18.4 A SAMPLE WSH FILE

```
[ScriptFile]
Path=C:\Windows\Desktop\Scratch\Listing 18-3.js

[Options]
Timeout=10
DisplayLogo=1
BatchMode=0
```

18

Right-click a script, choose Properties, and click the Script tab to create a WSH file for that script. The WSH file, which has the same root filename as the script, contains all the options that you specified in the script file's Property sheet. You can launch the script by double-clicking the script or WSH files.

Writing Statements to Change the Registry

Before learning how to change the Registry using a script, there are a few things that you need to know about specifying key and value names. First, you must use a double backslash (\\) in Jscript, instead of a single backslash, because the backslash character has special meaning in that language. Second, a backslash at the end of a name has special significance. Ending a name with a backslash, such as HKLM\MyKey\, means that you're specifying a key, whereas ending a name without a backslash, such as HKLM\MyKey\MyValue, means that you're specifying a value entry. The last thing to note is that you can use the short or long root key names. Table 18.2 describes the abbreviations you can use for each of the root keys. In general, the short names are more manageable than the long names. Following is a summary of what you have just learned:

- Use double backslashes with JScript, not VBScript.
- End key names with a backslash, values without.
- Use the abbreviations in Table 18.2, shown earlier in this hour, for root keys.

The following sections show you how to perform the tasks that you normally perform, with a script, in the Registry Editor. You'll learn how to add a new key or value entry, how to set a key's default value entry, how to change a value entry, and how to remove keys and value entries. You do all this with only three of the shell object's methods: `RegWrite`, `RegRead`, and `RegDelete`.

> The result of omitting the double backslash (\\) in a key when using JScript is interesting. Windows 98 removes all the backslashes, leaving you with a long name that Windows 98 assumes is a value entry. Thus, `HKLM\My\Value` becomes `HKLMMyValue`. In this case, Windows 98 reports an error that says `The System cannot find the path specified`. If you typed `HKLM\\My\Value`, you'd end up with `HKLM\MyValue`.

Adding a New Key

Use the `RegWrite` method of the shell object to write new keys to the Registry. The following examples show you how the syntax looks in both JScript and VBScript:

- **JScript**—`WSHShell.RegWrite( KeyName\\ );`
- **VBScript**—`WSHShell.RegWrite KeyName\`

The only argument to `RegWrite` is the name of the key you're adding. Don't forget to use double backslashes in the key name if you're using JScript, and end the name with a backslash to specify that you're writing a Registry key. Following is an example that creates a key called `Test` under `HKEY_CURRENT_USER`:

```
WSHShell.RegWrite( "HKCU\\Test\\" );
```

Setting the Default Value of a Key

Setting the default value entry for a key isn't much different than creating a new key. You use the `RegWrite` method as well, but you specify an additional parameter: a value. The following examples show you the syntax for setting a key's default value entry in JScript and VBScript:

- **JScript**—WSHShell.RegWrite(*KeyName*\\, *Value*);
- **VBScript**—WSHShell.RegWrite *KeyName*\, *Value*

The difference between creating a new key and changing the default value entry is that you add the value to the parameter list. Note that this assumes that the default value entry is a string, which is usually the case. Listing 18.5 shows you a complete example that automatically changes the default command for folders to Explorer so that you can open My Computer in a two-pane Explorer window by double-clicking it.

LISTING 18.5   CHANGING THE DEFAULT COMMAND FOR FOLDERS

```
// Changing the Default Action for Folders
//
// This script changes the default action of folders so
// that you can open My Computer in a two-pane Explorer
// window by double-clicking it on the desktop.

var WSHShell = WScript.CreateObject( "WScript.Shell");
WSHShell.RegWrite( "HKCR\\Folder\\shell\\", "explore" );
WSHShell.Popup( "Double-click My Computer to open Windows
➥Explorer" );
```

> The RegWrite method enables you to change the type of a key's default value entry. You can do so by specifying an additional parameter to RegWrite that indicates the type, as described in the next section. Note that you need to leave default value entries as string values because you can't predict the outcome.

Adding or Changing a Value Entry

RegWrite strikes again: You also use it to add or change a value entry. There are a couple of differences between using RegWrite for keys and using it for value entries, however. First, you omit the backslash from the end of the name, indicating that you're working with a value entry. Second, you specify an additional parameter to tell Windows 98 the

18

value entry's data type. Following is the syntax for this form of `RegWrite` in both languages:

- **JScript**—WSHShell.RegWrite(*Key**Name*, *Value*, *Type*);
- **VBScript**—WSHShell.RegWrite *Key**Name*, *Value*, *Type*

If the value entry given by *Key**Name* doesn't exist, Windows 98 adds the value entry, changes its type to *Type*, and sets it to *Value*. If the value entry already exists, Windows 98 changes it and its value. Note that if you don't specify a type, Windows 98 assumes that you meant to specify REG_SZ, which is a string value entry. Table 18.6 describes the values that you can assign to *Type*. REG_SZ works about as you'd expect it to; you must specify *Value* as a quoted string. Both REG_DWORD and REG_BINARY types enable you to use an integer for *Value*. You can optionally put the integer number in quotes if you specify REG_DWORD.

TABLE 18.6 VALUE TYPES FOR RegWrite

Type	*Description*
REG_SZ	Quoted string: "This is a string"
REG_DWORD	Integer between 0 and 2147483647
REG_BINARY	Integer between 0 and 2147483647

Listing 18.6 shows an example that adds a new value entry and changes an existing one. First, it adds an additional command to the program identifier for text files: txtfile. Note what's going on in the second RegWrite statement. The value that is being assigned looks something like "\"C:\ ... \" \"%1\"". If you use quotes to specify the beginning and end of strings in JScript, you must have some method of writing quotes into the middle of a string; otherwise, you cannot properly change commands in the Registry. \" is that method. In the second RegWrite method, JScript replaces each occurrence of \" with a single quote when it writes the string to the Registry.

LISTING 18.6 ADDING A NEW COMMAND FOR A FILE TYPE

```
// Adding a New Action for a File Type
// Turning Off Windows Animation
//
// This script does two things to demonstrate changing
// a value entry. First, it adds a action to the txtfile
```

```
// type for opening a TXT file in WordPad. Second, it turns
// off window animation, just in case it annoys you.

var WSHShell = WScript.CreateObject( "WScript.Shell");

// Add the "Open in Wordpad" action to the txtfile type

WSHShell.RegWrite( "HKCR\\txtfile\\shell\\wordpad\\",
➡"Open in &Wordpad", "REG_SZ" );
WSHShell.RegWrite( "HKCR\\txtfile\\shell\\wordpad\\
➡command\\", "\"C:\Program Files\Accessories\
➡Wordpad.exe\" \"%1\"", "REG_SZ" );

// Change MinAnimate to 0

WSHShell.RegWrite( "HKCU\\Control
Panel\\Desktop\\WindowMetrics\\MinAnimate",
➡"0", "REG_SZ" );

WSHShell.Popup( "Right-click a file in Explorer and choose
➡Open in Wordpad" );
```

Even though RegWrite supports the REG_BINARY data type, it doesn't handle binary strings very well. First, it only supports four-byte binary values, not the binary strings that you're accustomed to seeing in the Registry. You can get around this problem by creating a small REG file, however, and importing that REG file by launching it using the Run method: WSHShell.Run("import.reg");

Removing a Key or Value Entry

Enough of RegWrite. It's time to move on to the RegDelete method, which you use to remove a key or value entry from the Registry. The following examples show you how the syntax of RegDelete looks in both JScript and VBScript. The first example for each language shows the syntax for removing a key. The second shows the syntax for removing a value entry.

JScript	WSHShell.RegDelete(*KeyName*\\ );
	WSHShell.RegDelete(*KeyName**Value*);
VBScript	WSHShell.RegDelete *KeyName*\
	WSHShell.RegDelete *KeyName**Value*

The only argument to RegDelete is the name of the key or value entry that you're removing. Remember to end the name with the backslash (a double backslash for

JScript) if you're removing a Registry key. If you remove a Registry key, Windows 98 deletes the entire branch, beginning with that key, so be careful. Listing 18.7 shows you a real-world example. It clears out the MRU history lists from the Registry as described in Hour 16, "Other Customizations." This is written in VBScript for two reasons: to demonstrate a complete VBScript script, and to take advantage of VBScript's On Error statement for easy error handling. Because there is a good chance that one or more of the keys you're removing in this script might not exist in the Registry, you must use the error handling illustrated here to avoid seeing error messages.

LISTING 18.7   REMOVING THE HISTORY LISTS FROM THE REGISTRY

```
' Removing the History List from the Registry
'
' This script cleans out the history lists by removing
' the following subkeys of HKEY_CURRENT_USER\Software\
' Microsoft\Windows\CurrentVersion\explorer:
'
' RecentDocs
' RunMru
' Doc Find Spec MRU
' FindComputerMRU
'
' Because the user will likely run this script at
' startup, it doesn't display a message.

Dim WSHShell
Set WSHShell = WScript.CreateObject( "WScript.Shell" )

On Error Resume Next

WSHShell.RegDelete "HKCU\Software\Microsoft\Windows\
➥CurrentVersion\explorer\RecentDocs\"
WSHShell.RegDelete "HKCU\Software\Microsoft\Windows\
➥CurrentVersion\explorer\RunMru\"
WSHShell.RegDelete "HKCU\Software\Microsoft\Windows\
➥CurrentVersion\explorer\Doc Find Spec MRU\"
WSHShell.RegDelete "HKCU\Software\Microsoft\Windows\
➥CurrentVersion\explorer\FindComputerMRU\"
```

In the process of experimenting with these methods, I have made more than a few typos, leaving out the second backslash, typing the key's name wrong, or forgetting to provide the value entry name. The results were costly, particularly in the latter case. Windows 98 removed the entire branch instead of simply removing the value that I wanted to nuke. So back up the Registry first.

Reading a Value from the Registry

The shell object's `RegRead` method enables you to read any value from the Registry and assign it to a variable in your script. Then you can do a variety of things with the value, such as writing it to a new location in the Registry or displaying it to the user. The following examples show the syntax for both JScript and VBScript. The first example for each language shows the syntax for reading a key's default value entry. The second shows the syntax for reading any other value entry.

JScript	`WSHShell.RegRead( KeyName\\ );`
	`WSHShell.RegRead( KeyName\\Name`
VBScript	`WSHShell.RegRead KeyName\`
	`WSHShell.RegRead KeyName\Name`

The only argument to `RegRead` is the name of the value entry that you're reading. If you want to read a key's default value entry, be sure to end the name with a backslash. Don't end the name with a backslash if you're reading a normal value entry. Listing 18.8 shows you how to read both a default value entry and a normal value entry. Also notice that this script assigns the result to a variable and displays that variable so that the user can see it.

18

LISTING 18.8 READING VALUE ENTRIES FROM THE REGISTRY

```
' Reading Value Entries from the Registry

Dim WSHShell
Set WSHShell = WScript.CreateObject( "WScript.Shell" )

CRLF = Chr(13) + Chr(10)

Dim Name, Org, Wordpad

Name = WSHShell.RegRead( "HKLM\Software\Microsoft\Windows\
➥CurrentVersion\RegisteredOwner" )
Org = WSHShell.RegRead( "HKLM\Software\Microsoft\Windows\
➥CurrentVersion\RegisteredOrganization" )
Wordpad = WSHShell.RegRead( "HKLM\Software\Microsoft\Windows\
➥CurrentVersion\App Paths\WORDPAD.EXE\\" )

WSHShell.Popup Name + CRLF + Org + CRLF + wordpad
```

In Listing 18.8, you might have noticed parentheses around the parameters to RegRead. For normal *procedure calls,* which don't return a value, you don't need to include parentheses. However, you must enclose the parameters in parentheses when calling a method that returns a value (also called a *function*), such as RegRead.

CHOOSING SCRIPTS, REG, OR INF FILES

Scripts are complex. Aside from access to the Registry, scripts provide access to the rest of the user's computer, including the file system. Thus, they're more appropriate if changing the Registry is part of a larger task, such as editing files on the user's computer.

If your needs are simpler, however, and you only need to change a value or add a value to the Registry, use REG files. They're quite easy to create by hand or by using the Registry Editor's export feature. The one drawback of REG files is that you can't use them to remove keys or value entries from the Registry. If that's your requirement, move on to INF files.

INF files are the ultimate method for editing the Registry, especially if you need to remove keys or value entries. They are easier to read than REG files, in my opinion, but they are harder to create. One other benefit of using INF files is that the default command for an INF file is not to install, so Windows 98 doesn't load the INF file when you double-click it, as the operating system does when you double-click a REG file.

The table that follows this sidebar summarizes these details for your convenience.

Feature	Script	REG	INF
Accesses OS features	Yes	No	No
Adds keys and values	Yes	Yes	Yes
Changes value entries	Yes	Yes	Yes
Deletes keys and values	Yes	No	Yes
Easy to learn and use	No	Yes	Yes
Easy to read/understand	No	No	Yes
Installs on a double-click	Yes	Yes	No

Distributing Scripts, REG, and INF Files

A good way to impress the users that you support is to distribute fixes to them without their asking. Better yet, make it as simple as possible, and they'll adore you.

If you have an intranet in your organization, you can make REG and INF files available on a Web page. If you do not have an intranet, you can distribute REG files in mail messages or in the user's login script. You'll learn about each in the remaining sections.

Remember that the default Windows 98 command for a REG file is to import it. The default command for an INF file is not to install it, however, so you can't distribute an INF file on a Web page. (You can use email or other methods, as shown later.)

On a Web Page

You can put a link to a REG file on a Web page. Then, when a user clicks that link, the browser downloads the file to the user's computer and automatically applies the change that it contains. This works fine for Internet Explorer users, but Netscape users have to register a helper application for REG files. Figure 18.3 shows an example of a Web page that contains a few REG files. When you build such a Web page, it's recommended that you follow these suggestions:

- Provide clear information about who needs to apply each particular REG file. For example, if you post a REG file that affects only Microsoft Mail users, say so on the Web page.

- Provide clear information about what the REG file does to the user's computer. Some people are a bit nervous about doing something like this when they don't know exactly what's going to happen.

- Provide instructions that the user can use to download the REG file to his own computer without applying it. That way, if the user wants to, he can inspect the file before applying it.

- Provide contact information for yourself—your office number, phone number, pager number, and so on. If a user is about to panic, he'll feel better knowing that he can quickly contact you.

18

FIGURE 18.3

Some Web pages are simple, containing only a few REG files. Make sure that yours fits in with the overall Web site.

Contact information ─

Description of who the REG file is for

Instructions for saving the REG file to disk ─

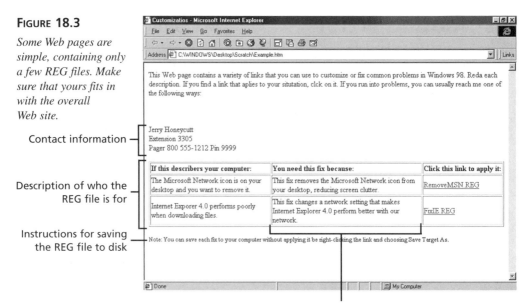

Description of what the REG file does

In an Email Message

If you don't have an intranet in your organization, the next best thing to do is distribute a REG or INF file in an email message. Attach the file to the message and instruct the user on how to apply the file. In most email programs, users either have to double-click an attachment to apply a REG file or right-click an INF file and choose Install.

> You can also distribute REG and INF files via Lotus Notes or similar group-ware packages. Consult the documentation for your groupware package for more information.

The same recommendations apply as for Web pages. Tell the recipients whether or not they need to apply the REG file, tell them what it will do to their computer, tell them how to view the file, and make sure they know how to contact you. Figure 18.4 shows an example of such an email message.

FIGURE 18.4

You can post a REG file on a Web page and then email a notice containing its description and URL.

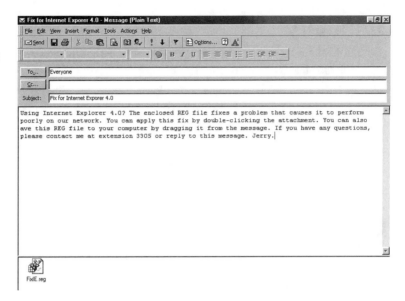

In a Login Script

It takes a bit of work, but you can also put a command in each user's login script that automatically applies the REG or INF file when the user logs on to the network. If you've set up a login script for multiple users, you can slip the command into that script instead. All you have to do is put the following command in the script (*filename* is the name of the REG file):

```
start filename.reg
```

The one problem with this method is that every time the user logs on to the network, the login script applies the REG file. You can avoid this problem by putting the command in a batch file. Then, the login script can check for the existence of this batch file on the user's computer. If it doesn't exist, the login script copies the batch file to the user's computer and executes it. Otherwise, it just ignores it.

The command line for INF files is a bit more convoluted. That's because the default command for an INF file is to not install it. Thus, you'll actually specify the command line that Windows uses for INF files' Install command (see the earlier section "Understanding How INF Files Work"). *Filename* is the name of the INF file:

```
C:\WINDOWS\rundll.exe setupx.dll,InstallHinfSection
➡DefaultInstall 132 Filename.inf
```

18

Summary

In this hour, you learned about the format of a REG file and how to create one by hand. You also learned that creating REG files by hand isn't as easy as just exporting a key to a REG file and then whittling it down to the values you want to keep.

Two alternatives to REG files are INF files and scripts. Both have their special purposes. INF files are the best choice if you're creating a complex customization or if you want to remove keys or values from the Registry. Scripts are the best choice if you need to do more than just read and write values in the Registry because scripts give you access to other parts of the operating system, and you can write complex algorithms using a script.

Q&A

Q **Is there any significance to the order of items in a REG file that I create by exporting the Registry?**

A An interesting aspect of REG files is the order in which the Registry Editor writes values under each key. Although you might expect it to write values in alphabetical order by name, it doesn't. The Registry Editor writes values in the order in which they were created in the Registry. This is a great way to see the order in which values were created under a key. For instance, export `HKEY_CURRENT_USER\Control Panel\Desktop` to a REG file, and you can see the order in which the values in this key were created.

Q **Of all the methods that this hour describes, what's the best way to update the Registry?**

A The best method to use depends on the situation. Rarely are scripts the best method, unless you must do something more complex than just add, change, or remove values. Use an INF file if you must remove a value from the Registry; otherwise, use a REG file.

Workshop

The following quiz will enhance your understanding of the topics discussed in this hour.

Quiz

1. Which of the following lines sets the default value in a Registry key?

    a. `Default="My Value"`

    b. `(Default)="My value"`

    c. `@="My Value"`

    d. `#="My Value"`

2. True or false? `"This is how \"Quote\""` expands to `This is how you "Quote"` in the Registry.

3. True or false? You can use a REG file to remove a value from the Registry.

4. Which of the following sections of an INF can't specify values to add values to the Registry?

    a. [My.Add.Reg]

    b. [Doozledorf]

    c. None of the above

Answers to Quiz Questions

1. c

    In a REG file, @ represents the default value.

2. True

    `\"` expands to a quotation mark in the Registry.

3. False

    You must use an INF file or script to remove values from the Registry; REG files can't perform this task.

4. c

    The name of the section is arbitrary; all that matters is that you refer to that section within the `[DefaultInstall]` section.

18

PART VI

Administering the Registry

Hour

HOUR 19

Enabling Remote Administration

If you don't have to administer computers, you can probably skip this hour. Otherwise, here's what you're going to learn:

- How to enable remote administration
- How to enable remote administration using scripts
- How to remotely administer other computers

Remote administration enables the administrator to inspect and change settings on one computer, the *target* or *remote* computer, from another computer on the network, the *administrative* computer. You can browse another computer's file system, for example, or set policies that control what the user can and can't do on the computer. Given that this book is about the Registry, this hour focuses on the tools that enable you to inspect or change values in a remote computer's Registry.

This hour only touches on the topic of remote administration, however. You learn more about that in the next couple of hours. If you want to learn even more, Macmillan Computer Publishing publishes a variety of Windows books that include information about remote administration tools, such as *Platinum Edition Using Windows 95* and *Platinum Edition Using Windows 98*.

Enabling Remote Administration

You must configure Windows correctly in order to use remote administration. In particular, the administrative and target workstations must meet the following requirements in order for you to administer the target computer remotely:

- **Network Protocol**—Both the target and administrative computer must use at least one common network protocol. Both computers can use TCP/IP, for example, or both can use IPX/SPX. However, this requirement doesn't prevent you from installing additional protocols that might not be common. You install network protocols using the Network dialog box, which you open from the Control Panel. Click the Add button to display the Select Network Component Type dialog box, choose Protocol from the list, and click Add. Choose the manufacturer from the list on the left and the protocol from the list on the right. Click OK to install the protocol.

- **User-Level Security**—Even though some tools don't require user-level security, most do. In particular, you can't use the Registry Editor or System Policy Editor to edit a remote computer's Registry without it. You'll learn how to configure user-level security later in this hour.

- **Remote Administration**—You enable remote administration in the Passwords Properties dialog box, which you open in the Control Panel. By enabling remote administration, you can specify which users or groups have the right to administer the workstation. You'll learn more about enabling remote administration later in this hour.

- **Microsoft Remote Registry Service**—This service provides RPC support for the Registry, which allows the Registry Editor on the administrative computer to make calls to the Registry API on the remote computer. You'll learn how to install this service, which is at the heart of remote administration when it involves the Registry, later in this hour.

- **File and Printer Sharing Service**—This is not an absolute requirement for remote administration, but some tools won't work without it. Note that you must install the File and Printer Sharing Service for Microsoft Networks or the File and Printer Sharing Service for NetWare Networks—depending on which is appropriate.

Installing the File and Printer Sharing service is easier than installing a protocol. Open the Network dialog box from the Control Panel and click the File and Printer Sharing button. Select whether you want to share files and whether you want to share printers. Click OK to save your changes.

Remote Administration

To enable remote administration on a computer, follow these steps on that computer:

1. Open the Passwords Properties dialog box from the Control Panel, and click the Remote Administration tab. You see the dialog box shown in Figure 19.1.

FIGURE 19.1

You'll see a different dialog box if this computer is using share-level security.

2. Select Enable remote administration of this server to enable remote administration. This enables the remaining controls in the dialog box, which are different depending on whether the computer uses user-level or share-level security:

   - **User-Level**—Windows gives the Domain Admins group on a Windows NT network, or the Admin account on a NetWare network, initial rights to administer the computer. To add a new group or users to the list, click Add.
   - **Share-Level**—In the space provided, type a password that an administrator must know before Windows enables him to administer the computer remotely.

3. Close the Passwords Properties dialog box to save your changes. Windows doesn't require you to restart the computer.

19

When you enable user-level security, Windows automatically enables remote administration and adds the Domain Admins group to the list of administrators on a Windows NT network or the Admin account on a NetWare 4.0 network. Thus, computers that are using user-level security probably already have remote administration enabled for the network's administrators. Note that user-level security requires either an NT or NetWare server to validate credentials.

After setting up remote administration on a computer, you'll notice a few special, hidden network shares. You can access any of the following network shares by launching the UNC path to the network share from the Run dialog box:

- **C$, D$, and so on**—Provides network shares for each non-removable drive on the workstation's computer. You can browse these with Explorer.

- **ADMIN$**—Gives full access to the folder in which Windows is installed.

- **IPC$**—Provides a channel for inter-process communication between two computers. IPC$ remains hidden, and you can't browse it.

Network shares whose names end with a dollar sign ($) are invisible. That is, they don't show up in Network Neighborhood. You can create hidden network shares, which other users can connect to only if they know the exact name, by appending a dollar sign to the end of any network share when you name it using the Share dialog box.

Microsoft Remote Registry Service

Enabling the Microsoft Remote Registry service is different from enabling remote administration. Remote administration is useful for inspecting the files and network shares on a remote computer, but it doesn't give you access to the other computer's Registry. Access to the Registry is required if you want to use tools such as the Registry Editor, System Monitor, or System Policy Editor. You must enable Remote Administration before you can use the Microsoft Remote Registry service, though, so I hope you didn't skip the preceding section. The Microsoft Remote Registry service has a few requirements before you can enable it:

- The network must have a security provider: NT domains and NetWare servers are equally suitable.
- Both your computer and the computer you're administering must have remote administration enabled. The preceding section describes how to enable it on each workstation.
- Both computers must use user-level security.

You have to install the Microsoft Remote Registry service on both the target and administrative computers. The following steps describe how to do so:

1. Open the Network dialog from the Control Panel.
2. Click Add to display the list of network components. Select Service from this list, and click Add. Windows might pause a bit while it builds the driver information database. Then you'll see the Select Network Service dialog box.
3. Click Have Disk to locate the Microsoft Remote Registry service on your Windows CD-ROM. The Remote Registry service isn't a part of the Windows source files; therefore, you'll point Windows to a different folder on the CD-ROM.
4. In the space provided in the Copy Manufacturer's Files From dialog box, type `d:\tools\reskit\netadmin\remotreg` to install the Remote Microsoft Registry service from the Windows 98 CD-ROM, where *d* is the drive letter representing the CD-ROM; or type `d:\admin\nettools\remotreg` to install it from the Windows 95 CD-ROM. Click OK to continue. You see the Select Network Service dialog box, shown in Figure 19.2.

FIGURE 19.2

The contents of this dialog box come from the INF file that is contained in the folder to which you pointed Windows in the preceding step.

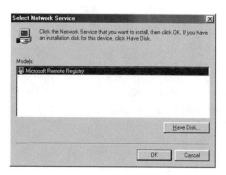

5. Select Microsoft Remote Registry from the list, and click OK.
6. Close the Network dialog box. Windows copies the appropriate files to your computer. Restart your computer when you are prompted.

Enabling Remote Administration Via Setup Scripts

Remote administration isn't practical if you're physically enabling it on each computer. A better alternative is to plan well ahead and enable remote administration as you roll out Windows. You do so with custom setup scripts.

The Windows 98 CD-ROM comes with a program called Microsoft Batch 98, which you use to build a script. A *script* is an INF file that specifies the settings that Setup uses when installing the operating system. You can specify as few or as many settings as you want. After creating the script, you can push it to the user via his logon script, or you can have the user launch the setup program with the script as its only command-line argument. You'll find Batch 98, and documentation about this program, in \Tools\Reskit\Deploy on the CD-ROM. You find an equivalent program on the Windows 95 CD-ROM in \Admin\Nettools\Bsetup.

> Batch 98 is one part of the automated installation process for Windows 98. First you use Batch 98 to create a file called Msbatch.inf. Then you copy Msbatch.inf and the Windows 98 source files to a network share that is accessible by everyone installing Windows 98. You can allow users to start the installation on their own, or you can push the installation to the user in his login script or via an email message. The *Microsoft Windows 98 Resource Kit*, published by Microsoft Press, contains more information about automated installations. The *Microsoft Windows 95 Resource Kit*, also published by Microsoft Press, contains information about the Windows 95 batch editor.

To enable remote administration using a setup script, add the lines shown in Listing 19.1 to the Msbatch.inf file that the Batch Editor creates. If the sections that you see in this listing already exist within the Msbatch.inf file, merely add the settings you see in this file to those sections. Set Security to either domain or server, enabling user-level security, and set PassThroughAgent to the name of the domain or server that is providing validation for user-level security. Server_Domain_Username indicates the group or account that has administrative rights on the computer.

LISTING 19.1 ENABLING REMOTE ADMINISTRATION IN A SETUP SCRIPT

```
[Install]
AddReg=Remote.Admin

[Remote.Admin]
HKLM,"Security\Access\Admin\Remote",
➥%Server_Domain_Username%,1,ff,00

[Network]
Security=domain ¦ server
PassThroughAgent=provider
services=remotereg

[strings]
Server_Domain_Username="server\account"
```

Connecting to a Remote Computer's Registry

Having met the requirements for the target and administrative computers, remote administration is straightforward. You use tools you're already familiar with, but you must first
connect to the remote computer. The following list describes the tools that you'll learn
about in this section:

- **Registry Editor**—Use this tool to make changes to the remote computer's
  Registry directly.

- **System Policy Editor**—Use this tool to make changes to the remote computer's
  Registry using policy templates.

- **Performance Monitor**—Use this tool to monitor performance measurements that
  are stored in the remote computer's Registry.

- **Net Watcher**—Use this tool to monitor user and administrative network shares on
  a remote computer.

19

> You can access most of these tools via Network Neighborhood. Right-click
> any computer in the Network Neighborhood folder, choose Properties, and
> click the Tools tab. Click Net Watcher to open the computer in Net Watcher.
> Click System Monitor to monitor the remote computer's performance. Click
> Administer to access the remote computer's file system in Windows Explorer.

CHANGING MULTIPLE REGISTRIES AT ONCE

To administer a Windows workstation remotely, you must log on to the administrative computer using an account name that has administrative privileges on the remote computer. Your account name can be explicitly listed in the remote computer's Passwords Properties dialog box, or it can be implicitly implied by one of the groups that is given administrative privileges in this dialog box. In other words, the name that you use to log on to your computer must jibe with a name explicitly or implicitly implied on the Remote Administration tab of the Passwords Properties dialog box on the user's computer.

Using the Registry Editor to change values on multiple computers at one time is not very convenient, particularly if you're changing values on a large number of computers at one time. Multi-Remote Registry Change is a useful program that enables you to change a value on any number of computers at one time.

Here's how it works: You select the computers that you want to change from the left pane of the program's window. The program gets this list from the network's browse list. On the right side of the program's window, you specify the value that you want to change. Then you turn Multi-Remote Registry Change loose as it changes that value on each networked computer you chose.

Note that this is different from using the System Policy Editor with a group of computers on the network. You use the System Policy Editor to create a Config.pol file that Windows downloads from the network and loads into the user's Registry each time the user logs on to his computer—it doesn't permanently change the Registry. Also, the System Policy Editor limits you to a predefined set of Registry values that you can change unless you create custom policy templates. Multi-Remote Registry Change makes permanent changes to every computer you specify, and it enables you change any Registry setting.

Does this utility sound like it's right up your alley? If so, see Hour 9, "Trying Other Registry Programs," which describes how to download, install, and use this program.

Registry Editor

Browsing and making changes to a remote computer's Registry requires that you install the Microsoft Remote Registry service on both the target and administrative computers. Doing so also requires that you set up user-level security and enable remote administration on the remote computer.

To connect to a remote computer's Registry, choose Registry, Connect Network Registry. Then type the name of the remote computer or click Browse to select a computer on the network. You see your computer and the remote computer in the Registry Editor, as shown in Figure 19.3.

Local computer

FIGURE 19.3

You can connect to more than one Registry at a time.

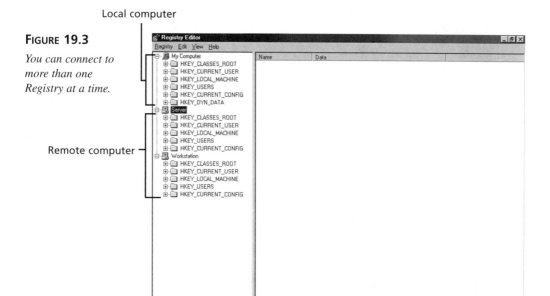

Remote computer

After you've connected to the remote computer's Registry, everything works as usual. For example, you can add and remove Registry keys, and you can add, remove, and change value entries. Just make sure that you're selecting keys and value entries on the proper computer. Otherwise, you might change a Registry key on your own computer when you really intended to change a key on the remote computer.

19

> Changing settings in a remote computer's Registry is no less dangerous than changing settings in your own Registry. Windows implements no Registry security whatsoever. Thus, the remote user's entire Registry is at your disposal. Review the precautions that are discussed in Hour 7, "Taking the Necessary Precautions," before making any changes to another user's Registry.

System Policy Editor

Because the System Policy Editor changes the Registry just as the Registry Editor does, it has the same requirements. You must install the Microsoft Remote Registry service on both the target and administrative computers. Doing so also requires that you set up user-level security and enable remote administration on the remote computer.

To launch System Policy Editor, choose Start, Programs, Accessories, System Tools, System Policy Editor. If you don't see the System Policy Editor on the Start menu, type `poledit` in the Run dialog box and click OK. Figure 19.4 shows you what the Policy Editor looks like. The background window is the Policy Editor itself. The foreground window, which pops up when you double-click one of the icons in the Policy Editor, contains the actual policies for the selected user or computer. To connect to a remote computer, choose File, Connect. Type the name of the computer to which you want to connect, and click OK.

The System Policy Editor isn't part of the Windows source files; thus, the setup program doesn't install it by default. You can find it on the Windows 98 CD-ROM, however, in \Tools\Reskit\Netadmin\Poledit. On the Windows 95 CD-ROM, look in \Admin\Apptools\Poledit.

FIGURE 19.4

If the remote computer uses user profiles, you'll see an icon for each user who logs on to that computer.

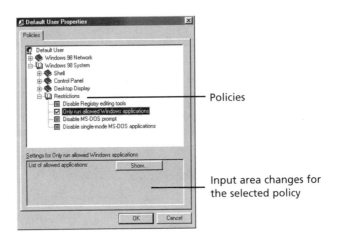

Policies

Input area changes for the selected policy

The System Policy Editor works in two modes. You can create a policy file called Config.pol that Windows automatically downloads from the network. Windows merges the Registry settings found in the policy file with the user's existing Registry, overriding the user's settings with the settings contained in the policy file. Alternatively, you can use the System Policy Editor in Registry mode, which enables you to connect to a remote computer's Registry and make immediate changes. For more information about applying system policies to groups of users, individual users, or individual computers on the network, see Hour 21, "Controlling the Desktop via System Policies."

System Monitor

You launch System Monitor in Windows 98 by selecting Start, Programs, Accessories, System Tools, System Monitor. To monitor a remote computer's performance, choose File, Connect from System Monitor. Type the name of the computer that you want to monitor, and click OK.

You use System Monitor to monitor the target computer's performance. You can monitor dozens of variables, including file system, CPU, memory, and network-performance variables. You can also watch as many variables as you want at one time. Click the Add button on the toolbar to watch additional variables for this computer. Figure 19.5 shows System Monitor while it's monitoring a remote computer.

FIGURE 19.5

You can open multiple instances of System Monitor so that you can monitor more than one computer at a time.

Add button

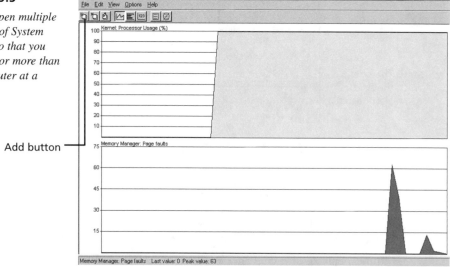

 Other Registry programs support remote administration, too. The Norton Registry Editor enables you to connect to a remote computer's Registry, for example, by choosing Registry, Connect Network Registry.

Net Watcher

Net Watcher has requirements that are similar to those of the other administration tools. You must be using user-level security, and you must have enabled remote administration. You must also use File and Printer Sharing, but you don't have to install the Microsoft Remote Registry service.

Launch Net Watcher in Windows 98, shown in Figure 19.6, by selecting Start, Programs, Accessories, System Tools, Net Watcher. The left pane shows you each user who is using a resource on this computer. The right pane shows you the network shares to which the selected user is connected and the files he has open. Besides inspecting the network shares on a remote computer, you can also add or remove network shares.

FIGURE 19.6

Net Watcher is the only tool in which you can see the hidden network shares IPC$ and ADMIN$.

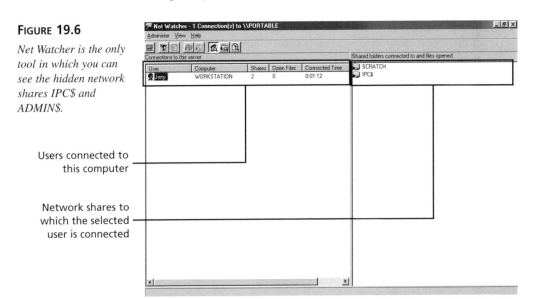

Users connected to this computer

Network shares to which the selected user is connected

Note the following restrictions on using Net Watcher:

- If the administrative computer is using share-level security, it can only monitor other computers that are also using share-level security.
- If the administrative computer is using user-level security, it can monitor other computers regardless of the type of security they're using.
- If the administrative computer is using File and Printer Sharing for NetWare Networks, it can only monitor other computers that are also using the same service.
- You can't close files on a remote computer that is participating on a NetWare network.

If, after enabling remote administration and the Microsoft Remote Registry service, you can't connect to the other computer using System Monitor, make sure that you enabled remote administration and the Microsoft Remote Registry service on both computers. That is, you must enable the Microsoft Remote Registry service on the computer from which you're administering, as well as the computer you are administering. If you've successfully administered a particular computer many times, but recently have been unable to connect to it, realize that Remote administration works only if someone is logged on to the remote computer. Thus, make sure someone is logged on before you administer the computer.

How Remote administration Works

Remote Procedure Calls (RPC) is the technology behind remote administration. It enables developers to build distributed applications. An application on one computer can invoke code running on another computer on the network, for example.

The Microsoft Remote Registry service uses RPC. The Registry Editor on the administrative computer calls the Registry *API (application programming interface)* on the remote computer. If you use the Registry Editor to remove a key from another computer's Registry, for example, the Registry Editor that is running on your computer invokes code on the remote computer that carries out the task. RPC access to a remote computer's Registry is secure and gives the administrator full access to the remote computer's Registry.

Each workstation that is running the Microsoft Remote Registry service has an RPC client and server. In this case, the administrative computer acts as the RPC client, and each remote computer acts as an RPC server. The client invokes code on the server, and the server returns the result to the client.

19

Summary

In order to enable remote administration on a computer, it must meet certain requirements. It should be using user-level security, but this isn't a total requirement. Remote administration must be enabled in the Passwords Properties dialog box. File and printer sharing services need to be installed for some of the remote administration tools, but some tools don't require it. Furthermore, the administrator's computer must be using the same network protocol as the computer to which the administrator is trying to connect. The minimum requirements for connecting to a remote computer's Registry is that the computer have the Remote Registry service installed and running and that Remote Administration be enabled.

Windows 98 automatically enables remote administration when you enable user-level security. If, for some reason, you're using share-level security or remote administration is not enabled, you can enable remote administration in the Passwords Properties dialog box, which you open from the Control Panel. The second step is to install the Remote Registry service. You install this from the Windows 98 CD-ROM in \tools\reskit\ netadmin\remotreg or from the Windows 95 CD-ROM in \admin\nettools\remotreg.

Q&A

Q What is the result of enabling remote administration with share-level security?

A Some of the remote administration tools will still work. Registry Editor and System Policy Editor still work, for example. Other tools that require user-level security, such as Net Watcher, won't work.

Q Can I administer a Windows computer from a Windows NT server?

A Yes. The Registry Editor works when connecting to a Windows computer. Don't try using Windows NT's policy templates to edit a Windows Registry, however; they're not compatible.

Q Do I have to enable remote administration to use features such as user profiles and policies?

A No. User profiles enhance remote administration by separating each user's settings, but user profiles aren't a requirement to use the remote administration tools. Likewise for policies—Windows downloads policies from the network as the operating system starts. Effective use of policies does require you to enable user profiles, though.

Workshop

The following quiz will enhance your understanding of the topics discussed in this hour.

Quiz

1. True or false? If the administrator's computer uses TCP/IP and IPX/SPX while a user's computer uses NetBEUI and IPX/SPX, remote administration will work properly.

2. Which of the following features represent(s) the minimum requirements for remotely editing another user's Registry?

    a. User-level security

    b. Remote administration enabled

    c. Microsoft Remote Registry service

    d. File and Printer Sharing Service

    e. Both a and c

    f. Both b and c

3. True or false? Network shares whose name end with a pound sign (#) are invisible.

4. Of the following programs, which is not useful as a remote administration tool?

    a. Registry Editor

    b. System Policy Editor

    c. Performance Monitor

    d. Remote Registry Checker

    e. Net Watcher

Answers to Quiz Questions

1. True

Remote administration requires that the administrator and target computer have at least one protocol in common. Other protocols that each computer is using don't matter.

2. f

Remotely editing another computer's Registry requires that both computers have remote administration enabled and that the Remote Registry service be installed.

3. False

Network shares whose names end with a dollar sign ($) are invisible in Network Neighborhood.

4. d

I've never heard of the Remote Registry Checker, have you?

19

Hour **20**

Administering Multiple Users with Profiles

In this hour, you're going to learn about one of the best administrative tools in Windows, user profiles:

- Enabling user profiles
- Enforcing mandatory user profiles
- Disabling user profiles

Most users don't share their computer. It sits neatly on their desktop and they take a certain amount of ownership of it. Still, some users have no choice. Either they work in shifts, and each shift gets a crack at the computer, or they don't have dedicated computers and they have to log on to whatever is available.

Without user profiles, administering multiple users on each machine is a giant headache. How do you keep each user's files separate? How do you give some users permission to customize their desktops, while preventing other users from doing the same? For that matter, how can each user keep their settings separate from all other users without having the desktop look totally different every time they log on to the computer?

User profiles—that's how.

User profiles is the technology that Windows uses to keep each user's settings and documents separate from every other user. The operating system doesn't enable user profiles by default, however; that's the topic of this hour. Upcoming hours show you how to do even more with user profiles, such as setting policies that control how much each user can do on the computer.

Understanding User Profiles

A user profile is the user-specific portion of the Registry, User.dat, as well as a number of folders such as Start Menu, Desktop, and Favorites. Storing configuration data separately for each user enables multiple users to log on to Windows with their own individual settings. Enabling user profiles in Windows doesn't change how it stores machine-specific settings—all that still goes in System.dat. Windows provides a few twists on user profiles, too, such as roving profiles and mandatory profiles. *Roving* profiles make a user's configuration available no matter which machine he uses. *Mandatory* user profiles create a configuration for the user that he can't change. You'll learn about both capabilities in this hour.

Windows supports two types of user profiles, local and network, which differ only by their locations:

- **Local**—Windows stores local profiles on the workstation. You find a folder for each user in \Windows\Profiles*Name,* where *Name* is the username.
- **Network**—Network profiles are also known as roving profiles. Windows stores a network profile in the user's home or mail folder, depending on the type of network (Microsoft or NetWare).

Folders in a Profile

As I mentioned, a user profile is more than just a copy of User.dat. It includes a number of folders, too. Note that Windows 98 keeps more folders in each profile than Windows 95 does (unless you have installed Internet Explorer 4.0 on Windows 95).

For local profiles, you find these in \Windows\Profiles*Username*. For network profiles, you find these in the user's home or mail folder on the network:

- **Application Data**—Applications such as the Windows Address Book, QuickLaunch toolbar, and Outlook Express Mail and News store user-specific data in this folder. It doesn't contain documents; it contains configuration files.

- **Desktop**—This folder contains the contents of the user's desktop. It includes shortcuts, folders, or other files that the user puts on the desktop.

- **Cookies**—Internet Explorer 4.0 stores cookies in this folder. Web sites use cookies to store the data that they need between sessions.

- **History**—In this folder, Internet Explorer 4.0 stores information about each Web site the user visits so that the user can see a list of recent sites.

- **NetHood**—This folder contains shortcuts that the user adds to the Network Neighborhood folder.

- **Recent**—Some applications store a shortcut for each document you open in this folder. You see these shortcuts on the Start menu's Documents submenu.

- **Start Menu**—This folder is where Windows gets the contents of the Start menu. Anything in \Start Menu is at the top of the Start menu, whereas anything under \Start Menu\Programs is in the Programs submenu.

> When Windows copies the user's profile to the network, it doesn't copy any folders or documents in the Desktop folder, but it does copy shortcuts. Documents and folders are, therefore, only part of the local profile, and not of the network profile.

How Windows Chooses Profiles

The best way to understand how user profiles work is to take a look at the process that Windows uses to locate the profile each time a user logs on to the operating system. Windows looks in the Registry at `HKEY_LOCAL_MACHINE\Software\Microsoft\Windows\CurrentVersion\Profile List` to determine if the user has a local profile. Then it looks for a user profile in the user's home or mail folder on the network. Which profile Windows chooses depends on a number of criteria:

- **Newer Network Profile**—If the network profile is more current than the local profile, or if the user doesn't have a local profile, Windows copies the user profile from the network to the local profile and loads User.dat into the Registry.

20

- **Newer Local Profile**—If the local profile is more current than the network profile, Windows uses the local profile and updates the network profile when the user logs off the operating system. This means that the user can still log on to an undocked portable computer and use the local profile, and Windows updates the network profile the next time the user connects to the network.
- **Unavailable Network Server**—If the server isn't available to validate the user's credentials, Windows uses the local profile, if it's available, and updates the network profile the next time the user logs on to the network.
- **No Profile Available**—If the user doesn't have a local or network profile, Windows creates a new profile using the default configuration.

Windows enables a user to log on to multiple workstations. With regard to user profiles, this creates some confusion. Windows updates the network profile each time the user logs off. If the user logs on to two different workstations, the network profile reflects the machine from which he last logged off. In other words, Windows doesn't merge changes to a user profile when the user is working on two different computers.

> If you're using network profiles, make sure that Windows can accurately determine whether the network or local profile is more current by keeping the clock current. The easiest way to do so is to add the command net time \\server /set /y (where \\server is the name of a server on the network) to the user's login script. This command causes Windows to synchronize the clock with the server.

Enabling Local User Profiles

You can enable user profiles individually on each Windows workstation, you can enable them using a custom setup script, or you can use the System Policy Editor, which you'll learn about in Hour 21, "Controlling the Desktop via System Policies." You can enable user profiles locally using the Passwords Properties dialog box. Open it from the Control Panel. As well as enabling user profiles, the Passwords Properties dialog box enables you to determine how much information to include in the profile. You can choose whether to include the contents of the Desktop and Network Neighborhood folders, for example. Here's how to enable user profiles in Windows:

1. Open the Password Properties dialog box from the Control Panel, and click the User Profiles tab. You see the dialog box that is shown in Figure 20.1.

FIGURE 20.1

The User Profiles tab of the Passwords Properties dialog box.

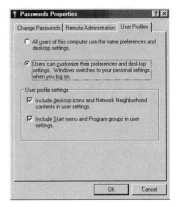

2. Select Users can customize their preferences and desktop settings.

3. Choose how much content you want to include in each user profile under User profile settings. You can choose to include the Desktop, Network Neighborhood, and Start Menu folders.

4. Close the Passwords Properties dialog box and restart the computer. Windows uses the configuration data that existed before you enabled profiles to create the profile when a new user logs on to the operating system.

> When Windows enables user profiles, it creates a value entry called
> UserProfiles under HKEY_LOCAL_MACHINE\Network\Logon and sets its
> value to 1.

Windows 98 provides an alternative means to enable user profiles—the Enable Multi-user Settings Wizard, which acts as a portal to Windows 98 user administration. Open the Enable Multi-user Settings dialog box by double-clicking the Users icon from the Control Panel. This wizard walks you through the process step by step. You provide the user's credentials, which are the username and password, and then you set options that indicate what the user profile contains:

- Desktop folder and Documents menu
- Start menu
- Favorites folder
- Downloaded Web pages
- My Documents folder

20

The primary differences between the Enable Multi-user Settings Wizard and the Passwords Properties dialog box are that you can use the wizard to create a new user profile during a work session, and you can customize the contents of each user profile individually. Note that you don't have to have any sort of *administrative* privileges to create profiles using this wizard. Any user can use it to create profiles as long as that capability isn't disabled via system policies.

> A good way to tighten security in Windows is to prevent new users from logging on to the operating system. Then, you use the Enable Multi-user Settings Wizard to add users individually. You must require validation from a security provider, as described in Hour 21, so that users can't circumvent the Logon dialog box.

Enabling Profiles on a Network

Enabling user profiles on a network enables users to log on to different computers with their own settings. This is called roving profiles, and it enables the user to log on to different computers with familiar settings. To support network profiles, Windows and the network must meet certain requirements:

- **32-bit networking client**—You must use 32-bit networking clients on each Windows workstation.

- **Support for long filenames**—The network must support long filenames. If it doesn't, Windows copies only User.dat to the server, not the remaining folders in the profile.

- **Home folders on the network**—Each user must have a home folder on a Microsoft network or a MAIL*user*_ID folder on a Novell NetWare network.

- **Primary network logon**—You must specify a primary network logon in the Network dialog box. Windows stores the network version of the profile on that server.

- **Hard disk organization**—Each workstation must have a similar organization if you want the user to be able to log on to multiple workstations with the same configuration. In particular, be sure to install Windows in the same folder on every machine.

The following sections provide more specific information about enabling network profiles on each type of server.

Windows NT Networks

To use profiles with a Windows NT network, you must complete the following tasks on each Windows workstation:

- Install the Client for Microsoft Networks.
- Enable user profiles.
- Set the primary network logon to Client for Microsoft Networks.
- Assign a home folder for each user on the server.

> You can put each user's home folder in \Winnt\Profiles, but you must explicitly configure the location of each profile in the User Manager for Domains. I recommend that you store each user's home folder on a separate volume so that you don't have to worry about running short of disk space on the boot disk.

NetWare Networks

To use profiles with a NetWare network, you must complete the following tasks on each Windows workstation:

- Install the Client for NetWare Networks.
- Enable user profiles, as you just learned how to do.
- Set the primary network logon to Client for NetWare Networks.
- Make sure that each user has a home folder if the user is logging on to the network with Novell Directory Services (NDS). Otherwise, if the user logs on in bindery mode, Windows stores the profile in the user's mail folder.

> If you want to prevent a user from logging on to a computer with the network version of his user profile, you can prevent Windows from using it by adding the DWORD value entry called UserHomeDirectory to HKEY_LOCAL_MACHINE\Network\Logon, leaving the value empty.

20

Other Networks

Windows supports network profiles on other types of networks, even peer-to-peer networks. Because the network client probably won't support network profiles, however, you must use an alternative configuration to accomplish the same thing. The following steps show you how to force Windows to support network profiles even though the networking client doesn't:

1. Create a folder on the network using an arbitrary name, such as Users, and share it, giving all users read-only access to it. Below that, create a home folder for each user and give each person full access to his home folder. You can use the user's logon name for each folder, or you can use any arbitrary folder name, such as User0001.

2. Create a text file named Profiles.ini that looks similar to the file shown in Listing 20.1. Each line under [Profiles] is named after the user's logon name, and the value you assign to it is the UNC path to the user's home folder. Copy this file to the folder you created in step 1. If you called the top-level folder Users, copy Profiles.ini to Users on the server.

3. Disable network profiles on each workstation (see the following section, "Disabling User Profiles"). That is, add the DWORD value entry called UserHomeDirectory to HKEY_LOCAL_MACHINE\Network\Logon, leaving the value empty.

4. Add a new string value entry called SharedProfileList to HKEY_LOCAL_MACHINE\Network\Logon. Assign the UNC path of Profiles.ini to this value. The path needs to be the root folder that you created in step 1. If you created a folder called Users and shared it using the same name, for instance, assign *Server*\Users\Profiles.ini to SharedProfileList, where *Server* is the name of the server that contains the folder.

When the user logs on to Windows, Windows looks in Profiles.ini for an entry that matches the user's logon name. If it finds one, it uses the profile that is indicated in the file. Otherwise, it uses the user's local profile or creates a new profile for the user.

LISTING 20.1 PROFILES.INI

```
[Profiles]
Jerry=\\server\users\jerry
Bones=\\server\users\bones
Turbo=\\server\users\turbo
Corky=\\server\users\corky
```

Enabling Mandatory User Profiles

A mandatory user profile is a configuration that Windows uses every time the user logs on to the operating system. The user can change the configuration during the session, but Windows doesn't save any changes to it; thus, the user starts with the same configuration every time. You can create mandatory profiles for use on Microsoft or Novell networks using the following steps:

1. Enable user profiles on the workstation.

2. Create a profile on a Windows computer, customizing the user preferences as required.

3. Copy the folders and files that you want to include in the profile to the appropriate folder, as described in the earlier section "Enabling Profiles on a Network." Be sure to copy User.dat, too.

4. Rename User.dat to User.man, indicating that this is a mandatory user profile.

When Windows copies the profile from the network, it takes notice of User.man, copying it to the user's profile as User.dat. Windows saves changes to the local User.dat, but it doesn't copy this file back to the server when the user logs off the computer. This ensures that the user starts with the same configuration every time he logs on to the computer.

MANDATORY PROFILES VERSUS SYSTEM POLICIES

Mandatory profiles and system policies both enable you to control the user's preferences. Mandatory profiles work only with the user-specific settings that you find in User.dat, and they require that you control every setting in it. System policies work with both con-figurations, machine-specific and user-specific, and they enable you specify exactly which settings you want to control.

In most cases, using system policies to lightly enforce certain settings is the most appro-priate choice. Mandatory profiles require the user to pay a performance penalty when he logs on to the computer, and they don't enable the user to permanently change any user-specific setting, even if it's not one you particularly care about.

20

Disabling User Profiles

User profiles aren't without problems. First, they affect the computer's performance ever so slightly. Second, user profiles add more complexity to the Windows configuration.

Not only does the user have to keep track of the profile folder in which he'll find his stuff, but Windows and other applications have to do this as well. Some applications don't even recognize user profiles, behaving as though user profiles aren't enabled at all.

If user profiles prove not to be the boon that you had hoped for, you can remove them, restoring your configuration to its original state. Windows doesn't provide an easy way to do this, however, so you must follow these steps:

1. Restart Windows without logging on. In other words, press Esc when you see the Logon dialog box.

2. Disable user profiles on the User Profiles tab of the Passwords Properties dialog box by choosing All users of this computer use the same preferences and desktop settings.

3. Remove `HKEY_LOCAL_MACHINE\Software\Microsoft\` `Windows\CurrentVersion\ProfileList` from the Registry.

4. Remove \Windows\Profiles.

Windows restores the original settings that it was using before you enabled user profiles. You can try copying one of the profiles to \Windows, but chances are it won't work properly because paths to the profile are stored in User.dat.

Summary

Enabling user profiles in Windows is simple when you use the Passwords Properties dialog box. You open this dialog box from the Control Panel. Windows 98 provides an alternative method for enabling profiles, which is the Users dialog box. Again, you open this dialog box from the Control Panel. The Users dialog box isn't any easier than the Passwords Properties dialog box, but it offers more options for determining what is included in a user profile.

Windows supports two different types of user profiles: local and roving. The operating system stores locale profiles in \Windows\Profiles. It puts roving profiles on the network in the user's home folder, on Microsoft networks, or in the mail folder, on NetWare networks.

To use user profiles on the network, thereby enabling roving profiles, the computer must meet certain requirements. First, the computer must be using a 32-bit networking client. The primary network logon must be properly configured so that it points to the network that contains the user's home or mail folder. Furthermore, the network must support long filenames, and each user must have a home folder on a Microsoft network or a MAIL*user*_ID folder on a NetWare network.

Q&A

Q I use Windows at home. Can I benefit from user profiles?

A Maybe. If you share the computer with other family members, you can definitely benefit from user profiles. You can even use policies in conjunction with user profiles to keep children from wrecking the computer by experimenting with it. Profiles also prevent other family members from messing up the desktop that you worked so hard to organize just the way you want it.

Q Can I add additional folders to a user profile?

A You certainly can. Adding a folder directly underneath \Windows\Profiles*Username* makes accessing the folder in Windows Explorer inconvenient, though. Therefore, you're better off adding folders underneath the My Documents or Desktop folders.

Q What happens if I'm using roving profiles on a portable computer and make changes while I'm not connected to the network?

A Windows updates the network copy of the profile the next time that you log on to the network. Be careful that you don't log on to another computer that is connected to the network and make changes that affect your profile. Windows 98 has to choose which profile to use, the one on the portable or the one on the server; this leaves you with a loss, no matter which way you cut it.

Q Can I log on to both Windows 95 and Windows 98 computers using a single roving profile?

A No! Windows 98 uses the Registry in sufficiently different ways as to make the two incompatible. Windows 98 can't start with a Windows 95 Registry, and vice versa.

Workshop

The following quiz will enhance your understanding of the topics discussed in this hour.

Quiz

1. True or false? A user profile includes Registry settings from `HKEY_USERS` and `HKEY_LOCAL_MACHINE`.

2. User profiles are enabled and a user named Jerry logs on to the computer. Under which folder does Windows store the user's profile?

   a. \Windows\Users\Jerry

   b. \Windows\All Users\Jerry

20

    c. \Windows\Profiles\Jerry

    d. \Windows\Home\Jerry

3. True or false? Windows copies each document that it finds in a profile's Desktop folder to the network, assuming that roving profiles are enabled.

4. In the Control Panel, which icon do you use to enable user profiles in both Windows 95 and Windows 98?

    a. Users

    b. Profiles

    c. Profiles and Policies

    d. Passwords

Answers to Quiz Questions

1. False

Each user profile contains the user's user-specific settings found in HKEY_CURRENT_USER.

2. c

Each user's profile is stored in \Windows\Profiles*Username*, where *Username* is the name that the user used to log on to the computer.

3. False

Windows does not copy documents from the Desktop folder to the network; it only copies shortcuts.

4. d

Both versions of Windows have the Passwords icon in the Control Panel. Windows 98 provides an alternative means by which you can enable profiles, and that's the Users icon.

Hour **21**

Controlling the Desktop via System Policies

System policies enable you to override certain machine- and user-specific settings. In this hour, you learn about the following:

- How policies work on and off the network
- How to enable policies on various networks
- How to install and use the System Policy Editor
- How to create custom policy templates
- How to secure Windows using system policies

If you put policies in a file called Config.pol and place it on the network server that is specified in the user's primary network logon, Windows updates the Registry with the contents of this file. System policies are the most underused—but most powerful—administration tool that Windows provides. Even though administrators can ease their burden considerably, most continue to ignore this valuable resource. You, as administrator, can restrict the user in countless ways, for example preventing him from modifying the

Active Desktop or from running certain programs. You can apply policies to individual users or to groups of users as defined on a Microsoft or Novell network. You can use the policy templates that Windows provides, or you can create your own, for any application that uses the Windows Registry. The possibilities for administrators are endless.

How Policies Work

To understand how to implement system policies, you must understand how policies work. Three different components are responsible for making them work the way they do:

- **Templates**—Templates are text files that have an ADM file extension and that describe the Registry values that you want to set. Think of templates as scripts that define forms and relate each field on that form to a value in the Registry.

- **Policy Files**—These are binary files that have a POL file extension. You create policy files with the System Policy Editor: Open a template in the System Policy Editor, define values for one or more policies defined in the templates, and save the result as a POL file. Each item in the POL file is an ordered entry with a name and a value, just like the Registry.

- **Registry**—Each time Windows starts and loads a policy file, it overwrites values in the Registry with values it finds in the policy file. The values in the policy file always supercede the values in the Registry.

> You can prevent users from accessing the Registry by enabling the Disable Registry editing tools policy. Doing so helps ensure that the policies you define stay the way you defined them.

As with user profiles, understanding how Windows loads system policies helps you understand how to configure them. Following is a description of that process:

- **User policies**—Windows looks for a policy that has the same name as the user's. If Windows finds a user policy, it loads the settings from that policy. Windows always loads the default user policy.

- **Group policies**—Windows creates a list of any groups to which the user belongs and looks for policies that have the same name as each group. Windows downloads groups that have the lowest priority first and the highest priority last, ensuring that higher-priority groups always overwrite lower-priority groups. Windows doesn't copy group policies if it finds a user policy for the user.

- **Machine policies**—Windows looks for a policy that matches the computer's name and downloads the settings it finds in that policy. It always loads the default computer policies, whether or not it finds a policy for that computer.

Enabling System Policies on the Network

You must configure each workstation in order to use system policies. You can complete these tasks manually, or you can perform them as part of a setup script:

1. Install the System Policy Editor on the administrator's Windows workstation.
2. Enable user profiles on each Windows workstation with which you want to use policies. If you fail to enable user profiles, system policies work only with machine-specific configuration data.
3. Install group policy support on every Windows workstation that you're configuring for policies.
4. Create policy files, as discussed later in this hour. The policy file can include default user and default machine, user- and machine-specific, and group policies.
5. Copy the policy file, Config.pol, into the Netlogon folder of a Windows NT server or the SYS:PUBLIC directory of a NetWare server. The Netlogon share is typically \Winnt\System32\Repl\Import\Scripts, which is the same folder in which you stash login scripts.

Hour 18, "Scripting Changes to the Registry," contains more information about building custom setup scripts. You can do so in Windows 98 using the Batch 98 utility that you find on the Windows 98 CD-ROM. Install it from \Tools\Reskit\Batch. In Windows 95, use a similar editor, which you install from \Admin\Nettools\Bsetup.

The average user can get around system policies because they have weaknesses. Following are a few examples. (I'm sure a clever user can come up with more ways to circumvent policies.) The user can prevent Windows from loading the policy file by booting to Safe Mode or by not logging on to the network. Here's another one: Even though you enabled the Disable Registry editing tools policy, users can still edit the Registry because this policy requires the cooperation of each Registry program. A variety of shareware Registry editors are available that do not honor this restriction. Not only that, but a user can still change the Registry using INF and REG files, as described in Hour 18.

21

Automatic Downloading

Windows automatically downloads the policy file from the Netlogon folder of a Windows NT server or the SYS:PUBLIC directory of a NetWare server. Be sure to put the policy file on the server that is chosen as the primary network logon in the Network dialog box. The following instructions show you how to configure Windows so that it automatically downloads system policies from the network:

1. Set the primary network logon to Client for Microsoft Networks or Client for NetWare Networks, depending on your network.

2. Copy the policy file Config.pol to the Netlogon folder of a Windows NT server or the SYS:PUBLIC directory of a NetWare server. Be sure to copy Config.pol to the user's preferred server if you're using a NetWare network.

Manual Downloading

If you want to control the location of the policy file, or if the networking client you're using doesn't support policies—as is the case with most 16-bit clients—you must configure Windows to manually download policies. You must also configure Windows to manually download policies if you're using a policy file that is stored locally instead of on the network. Here's how to configure Windows to manually download a policy file:

1. Start the System Policy Editor and choose File, Open Registry. Alternatively, choose File, Connect to configure a remote computer; then type the name of the computer in the space provided, and close the Connect dialog box.

2. Click the Local Computer icon, or the icon that represents the remote computer; expand the Network item, followed by the Update item.

3. Select Remote update and type the UNC path and filename of the policy file in Path for manual update.

4. Save your changes to the Registry and close the System Policy Editor.

Alternatively, you can use the following steps to configure a computer that is automatically downloading policies to manually download policies:

1. Open the network copy of Config.pol in the System Policy Editor.

2. Open the Default Computer icon and expand the Network item, followed by Update.

3. Select the Remote update checkbox, select Manual in Update Mode, and type the UNC path and filename of the system policy file in Path for manual update.

4. Save your changes to Config.pol and close the System Policy Editor.

Installing the System Policy Editor

As I've hinted, you use the System Policy Editor to read template files (ADM), to specify settings, and to create policy files (POL). The System Policy Editor isn't part of the Windows source files. You have to install it from \Tools\Reskit\Netadmin\Poledit on the Windows 98 CD-ROM or from \Admin\Apptools\Poledit on the Windows 95 CD-ROM. Microsoft suggests that you copy these files to your computer, but I recommend that you follow these steps instead:

1. Open the Add/Remove Programs Properties dialog box, and click the Windows Setup tab.

2. Click Have Disk, and type the path to the \Tools\Reskit\Netadmin\Poledit folder on the Windows 98 CD-ROM or \Admin\Apptools\Poledit on the Windows 95 CD-ROM. Close the Install from Disk dialog box, and you see the Have Disk dialog box (shown in Figure 21.1). This dialog box contains an entry for the System Policy Editor.

FIGURE 21.1

This dialog box shows the components it finds in all the INF files that are contained in the folder you specified.

3. Select System Policy Editor from the list. Click Install. Windows 98 copies the files to the computer. Insert the Windows CD-ROM if you are asked to.

Start the System Policy Editor by choosing Start, Programs, Accessories, System Tools, System Policy Editor. If you don't see System Policy Editor on the Start menu, type poledit in the Run dialog box and click OK.

If you intend to use group policies, you must also install support for group policies on each Windows workstation, including the administrator's. In Windows 98, use the Add/Remove Programs Properties dialog box to install group policies. Windows 98 copies Grouppol.dll to \Windows\System and updates the Registry accordingly. Note that

21

you can also install support for group policies, using the preceding instructions, by choosing Group Policies from the list. In Windows 95, install support for group policies by right-clicking Grouppol.inf in \Admin\Apptools\Poledit on the Windows 95 CD-ROM and choosing Install.

Using the System Policy Editor

You can use the System Policy Editor in two different modes:

- **Registry mode**—In this mode, you can edit a local or remote computer's Registry directly. You don't create a policy file. This is similar to using the Registry Editor, except that you're editing the Registry using a template; this causes much less concern about human error. Choose File, Open Registry to open the local computer's Registry, or choose File, Connect to open a remote computer's Registry. Figure 21.2 shows how the System Policy Editor looks in Registry mode.

- **Policy File mode**—In this mode, you create a policy file from a template. You copy the policy file (POL) to the network, as you learned earlier in this hour. Windows automatically downloads the POL file to the user's computer when he logs on to the network. Choose File, New Policy to create a new policy file, or choose File, Open Policy to open an existing policy file.

 Use Registry mode when you're using the System Policy Editor on a single computer. This is good as a customization tool, for instance. Use policy mode if you're using the System Policy Editor on a network and you're configuring settings for one or more users on the network. You can use policy mode on an individual computer, but doing so adds needless complexity to the startup process.

Each option you see in the System Policy Editor has three states: selected, cleared, and not defined. Each time you click an option, it toggles between these three states.

- **Selected**—Indicated with a checkmark, this means that the selected policy appears in the file and is enabled.

- **Cleared**—Indicated with a clear checkbox, this means that the selected policy appears in the file and is disabled.

- **Not Defined**—Indicated with a >grayed checkbox, this means that the selected policy does not appear in the file.

FIGURE 21.2

Local represents the local computer. When you are editing a remote computer, you see the name of the computer and user.

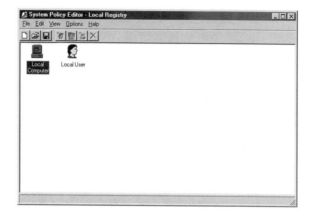

Be careful that you don't clear an option that you really intend to leave out of the policy. Clearing an option means that you want to include it in the policy file but disable it on the user's computer. If you clear the Enable User Profiles policy, for instance, Windows doesn't allow the user to enable user profiles on that computer. To enable the user to choose, you must gray out this policy.

Policies for Default Users and Computers

Policies for the default user and default computer apply to every user and every computer. To define default policies, follow these steps:

1. Open the policy file, perhaps Config.pol, in the System Policy Editor. Create a new policy file if necessary.

2. Click the Default User icon to display the Default User Properties dialog box (shown in Figure 21.3). Select the policies that you want to include in the policy file, and then close the dialog box.

3. Open the Default Computer icon. You see the Default Computer Properties dialog box, which is similar to the Default User Properties dialog box. Select the policies that you want to include in the policy file, and then close the dialog box.

Make your life easier by defining as much as you can for the default user and computer. Then, define user- and group-specific policies to handle specific needs. That way, default policies define the rules, whereas user and group policies define the exceptions.

21

FIGURE 21.3

Remember that the System Policy Editor stores cleared options in the policy file as disabled. If you want to omit a policy, gray it out.

Policies for Users, Computers, or Groups

Before defining policies for groups, make sure that you're ready. You define policies for groups that are defined on a Windows NT or NetWare server. You can't create new groups in the System Policy Editor; you must rely on the groups that are reported by the server, so plan and define your groups ahead of time. Also note that you must install support for group policies on every Windows workstation, as described in the earlier section "Installing the System Policy Editor." To keep things simple, consider installing this as part of your setup script when you roll out Windows.

You learned how to edit policies in previous sections. Editing policies for specific users, computers, or groups is no different, except that you open a different icon. Here's how to do each:

- **User**—To add a user to a policy file, choose Edit, Add User. Type the name of the user in the space provided, and click OK. You can browse a list of names on the network by clicking Browse.

- **Computer**—To add a computer to a policy file, choose Edit, Add Computer. Type the name of the computer in the space provided, and click OK. You can browse a list of computers by clicking Browse.

- **Group**—To add a group to the policy file, choose Edit, Add Group. Type the name of the group in the space provided, and click OK. You can browse a list of groups by clicking Browse.

Defining policies for a particular user prevents Windows from applying any group policies to that user. This might be a nasty surprise if you think that Windows still applies your group policies to a user after you define user policies.

Windows can handle the situation in which a user might belong to more than one group. You prioritize groups so that the policies in a higher-priority group always overwrite policies in a lower-priority group. Choose Options, Group Priority to display the Group Priority dialog box (shown in Figure 21.4). Move groups up and down in the list to change their priority, and then close the Group Priority dialog box to save your changes.

FIGURE 21.4

The top of the list is a higher priority than the bottom is.

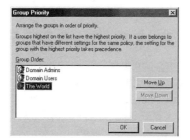

Using Custom Policy Templates

Policy templates define the input forms and relationships between each input field and a particular field in the Registry. Most of the Windows 98 policies that you need are in Windows.adm and Common.adm, which Windows 98 installs in the System Policy Editor by default. (Common.adm is actually void of any policies, but Windows 98 installs it anyway.) You find these files and more in \Windows\Inf. Table 21.1 describes the remaining template files that you can use in Windows 98 with the System Policy Editor. Windows 95 provides a single policy template called Admin.adm.

TABLE 21.1   POLICY TEMPLATES IN \WINDOWS\INF

File	Description
Chat.adm	Microsoft Comic Chat
Conf.adm	NetMeeting
Inetres.adm	Internet Explorer
Inetset.adm	Internet Explorer

continues

21

TABLE 21.1 CONTINUED

File	Description
Oem.adm	Outlook Express
Pws.adm	Personal Web Server
Shellm.adm	Additional shell policies
Subsm.adm	Internet Explorer Channels

> Shellm.adm is one of the most useful policy templates for Windows 98. This policy file contains settings that control Internet Explorer, the Active Desktop, and even the Start menu. Windows 98 copies it to \Windows\Inf but doesn't install it in the System Policy Editor; therefore, you must add it to the System Policy Editor if you want to use it.

You can also create your own policy templates if the ADM files that Windows provides don't do the job for you. For example, if you have a custom-built application that you want to control, create a template for that program. The program must rely on the Registry for its customization data, but most programs do these days. Here's how to add a custom policy template—or one of the templates you learned about in Table 21.1—to the System Policy Editor:

1. Close the open policy file.
2. Choose Options, Policy Template. You see the Policy Template Options dialog box, which lists all the policy templates that you've added to the editor.
3. Click Add, specify the template's path and filename, and close the Open Template File dialog box to add a template.
4. Close the Policy Template Options dialog box to start working with the additional template. This file doesn't replace your existing templates; it merely adds to the list of available options.

> The *Microsoft Windows 98 Resource Kit* and *Microsoft Windows 95 Resource Kit*, both published by Microsoft Press, describe how to create policy templates using the appropriate keywords. You can find an online version of the resource kit on the Windows 98 CD-ROM in \Tools\Reskit\Help or on the Windows 95 CD-ROM in \Admin\Reskit\Helpfile.

MUST-SEE POLICIES

The best way to find out which policies Windows 98 makes available is to open the System Policy Editor and browse. Some policies deserve special mention because they serve very useful purposes in most organizations. The following table is divided into sections, with each section representing a policy template. The first column indicates whether the policies in the second column are machine or user policies. The second column contains the actual policy name, whose purpose is self-evident. Windows 95 supports very few of the policies that are described in the following table:

Shellm.adm Template	Policy Name
User	Desktop Restrictions
	Active Desktop Items
	Start Menu Shell

Windows.adm Template	Policy Name
Machine	Disable Windows Update
	Minimum Windows password length
	Require validation from network for Windows access
	Require alphanumeric Windows password
User	Hide Start Menu subfolders
	Disable Shut Down command
	Hide Drives in My Computer
	Hide Network Neighborhood
	Hide all items on Desktop
	Remove Run command
	Remove folders from Settings on Start Menu
	Remove Taskbar from Settings on Start Menu
	Remove Find command
	Restrict Display Control Panel
	Restrict Network Control Panel
	Restrict Passwords Control Panel
	Restrict Printer Settings
	Restrict System Control Panel
	Disable Registry editing tools
	Only run allowed Windows applications
	Disable MS-DOS prompt

continues

21

> *continued*
>
> Note that of all the policies in Shellm.adm, Start Menu is the most useful because it fulfills the needs that I frequently hear about from administrators. In particular, this policy allows you to enable or disable individual commands on the Start menu. You can remove the Find and Run commands from the Start menu, for instance, as well as other commands. The Shell policy is useful, too, because it enables you to disable shortcut menus in Windows Explorer or to restrict the user the classic Windows shell.

Securing Windows

Windows is not a secure operating system. If you require serious workstation security, consider installing Windows NT Workstation instead of Windows. Windows NT Workstation has security features that you don't find in Windows, such as file system security and control over user rights.

One example is that a user can log on to any Windows workstation without providing credentials; all he has to do is press Esc at the logon prompt to bypass the validation process. As a result, Windows uses the default profile for that user (a fact that you can use to your advantage). Likewise, Windows doesn't secure the Registry against tampering. The user can move or delete the Registry's files, for example, or make changes in the Registry Editor—Windows won't prevent him from doing so. As an administrator, you can take definitive steps to improve security in Windows and, more specifically, in the Registry.

Use the System Policy Editor to restrict what the default user can do in Windows. The only requirement is that you enable user profiles on the computer so that each user has a profile that is separate from the default profile. When a user bypasses the logon prompt by pressing Esc, Windows uses the default profile for that user. This enables you to control what a guest user can do on the computer. The settings that you apply to this default user don't apply to other users who log on to the computer—as long as you enable user profiles.

Most of the techniques that you'll learn about in this section involve policies, but some are outside that realm. A simple method for protecting the Registry is to keep backups, as you learned in Hour 3, "Backing Up/Restoring the Registry," because doing so enables you to restore the Registry if the user tampers with it. Also make sure that you disable AutoAdminLogon in Winlogon so that Windows won't automatically log the user on to the workstation without his credentials. You learned about this setting in Hour 16, "Other Customizations." If you've configured a Windows workstation for remote administration, make sure that you know who has permission to administer the computer's Registry. Hour 19, "Enabling Remote Administration," shows you how to specify which users have the right to administer a Windows computer.

> Other security methods, despite being a bit draconian, provide even more protection—particularly from a user who wants to abscond with data from your computer. Consider disabling the floppy drives in the BIOS, for instance, so that a user can't copy files to a disk and take off with them. Be sure to password-protect your BIOS settings, though. Disable the user's capability to display the boot menu or use the boot keys so that he can't start the computer in MS-DOS mode or Safe mode, thus circumventing all the policies that you establish. You can change these settings easily using Tweak UI, as you learned in Hour 8, "Using Microsoft's Tweak UI."

The following sections describe a variety of polices that you can use to tighten up security in Windows. These sections don't cover all the available policies, just the ones that I think are most appropriate for protecting a workstation and the network. Note that Windows 95 does not support most of the policies that you read about in these sections. Furthermore, Windows 95 only provides the single Admin.adm policy template, as opposed to the variety of policy templates that Windows 98 provides.

Securing the User Interface

Windows 95 never gave the administrator much control over the shell. It was tough to remove commands from the Start menu, for example, or to disable shortcut menus in Windows Explorer. Windows 98 remedies this situation with a handful of policies, which are found in the Shellm.adm policy template. You must specifically load this template in the System Policy Editor because it isn't loaded by default.

All the following user policies are within the Start Menu, Shell, and System categories for a default or specific user (The first item, Remove *Name* menu from the Start Menu, isn't actually a single policy because you see a policy for each command on the Start menu. Just replace *Name* with the submenu's name):

- Remove *Name* menu from Start Menu
- Disable File menu in Shell folders
- Disable context menu in Shell folders
- Hide Floppy Drives in My Computer

21

- Disable net connections/disconnections
- Do not allow computer to restart in MS-DOS mode

Windows 98 allows the administrator to remove specific shortcuts from the Start menu, and to totally disable shortcut menus in Windows Explorer. You see one policy for each submenu on the Start menu called Remove Name menu from the Start menu, where Name is the name of the submenu. You can disable shortcut menus in Windows Explorer by enabling the Disable context menu in Shell folders policy. This doesn't do you much good unless you also disable the File menu using the Disable File menu in Shell folders policy.

Controlling Access to the Network

Policies that control network access are in the Windows.adm template file, which the System Policy Editor loads by default. You find all these policies under the Access Control, Logon, Password, and Dial-Up Networking subcategories of the Network category, and under the Programs to Run and Windows Update subcategories of the System category:

- User-level access control
- Require validation from network for Windows access
- Don't show last user at logon
- Disable password caching
- Require alphanumeric password
- Minimum Windows password length
- Disable dial-in
- Disable Windows Update

The Require validation from network for Windows access policy ensures that the user can't access the workstation unless a security provider validates the user's credentials. It tightens up security considerably by preventing guest users from accessing the Windows workstation unless they have an account on the network server.

Preventing Access to the Control Panel

In some situations, you don't want the user changing system settings without your knowledge. The following policies are in the Control Panel subcategory of the System category for a default or specific user:

- Restrict Display Control Panel
- Restrict Network Control Panel
- Restrict Passwords Control Panel
- Restrict Printers Control Panel
- Restrict System Control Panel

> Restrict Passwords Control Panel is an effective way to keep the user from changing his remote administration settings, as you'll learn later in this hour. Set the Hide Remote Administration Page option so that the user can't add or remove users from this list.

Restricting the User's Activities

The following policies, which are all self-explanatory, are under the Restrictions subcategory of the System category:

- Disable Registry editing tools
- Only run allowed Windows applications
- Disable MS-DOS prompt
- Disable single-mode MS-DOS applications

> Disable Registry editing tools is an effective policy for preventing the user from editing the Registry with Registry Editor. Other Registry-editing tools don't honor this policy, however, so it's not a sure thing. In reality, there is no way to keep a determined user from editing the Registry unless you also use the Only run allowed Windows applications policy to specify a list of programs that the user is allowed to run. Note that a user with access to the System Policy Editor can remove this restriction.

21

> **MICROSOFT MANAGEMENT CONSOLE**
>
> The Windows 98 CD-ROM includes the Microsoft Management Console, which you install by running the Microsoft Windows 98 Resource Kit Sampler's setup program: *d*:\tools\reskit\setup.exe, where *d* is the drive letter of the CD-ROM.
>
> The Microsoft Management Console (MMC) provides a convenient location for accessing all the utilities in the resource kit. Microsoft calls each program in MMC a *snap-in*. You can easily add programs that are built as snap-ins or otherwise to MMC. Just remember that MMC doesn't actually provide any maintenance—it just provides a convenient location from which you can access all the administrative programs that you use.

Troubleshooting System Policies

Before you assume the worst, double-check the following three items, which are the most common reasons that policies fail to work properly:

- Make sure that Config.pol is in the Netlogon folder on a Microsoft network or in the PUBLIC directory on the SYS: volume of a NetWare server.
- On a Microsoft network, make sure that the primary network logon points to the server on which you've put the policy file. On a NetWare network, make sure that Preferred Server is set to the NetWare server on which you've placed the policy file.
- Make sure that the user can log on to the network properly and that he has access to the network directory that contains the policy file.

If group policies don't work for an individual user or group, check the following:

- Make sure that the user is really a member of the group for which you've defined the policies.
- Make sure that you haven't defined a user-specific policy for the user that overrides default and group policies.
- Make sure that you've installed support for group policies, as described in the section "Installing the System Policy Editor."
- Make sure that you've enabled user profiles on the user's computer. See Hour 20, "Administering Multiple Users with Profiles," for more information.

Summary

Using the System Policy Editor is quite simple. You install it from \Tools\Reskit \Netadmin\Poledit on the Windows 98 CD-ROM or \Admin\Apptools\Poledit on the Windows 95 CD-ROM. You can use it in Registry mode, which enables you to make direct changes to a user's Registry, or you can use it in policy file mode, which enables you to create policy files.

Policies have several different components. Templates (ADM files) relate a policy to a registry setting, defining how the System Policy Editor collects the setting from the administrator. Policy files (POL files) contain the policies that are defined by the administrator, including the name of the value entry and its value as defined by the policy.

In order for policies to work properly, user profiles must be enabled on each Windows workstation. Then, you must create a policy file called Config.pol in the Netlogon folder of a Windows NT Server or in the SYS:PUBLIC directory of a NetWare server. When Windows starts, it downloads a policy file called Config.pol from the network and changes each Registry to reflect what it finds in the policy file. You must also make sure that the primary network logon on each workstation represents the server that contains the policy file. For instance, if the policy file is on a Microsoft network, set the primary network logon to Client for Microsoft Networks.

Q&A

Q I have Windows 95 with Internet Explorer 4.0 or greater installed. If I want to use some of the Windows 98 policies I learned about in this hour, can I copy the ADM files from a Windows 98 CD-ROM and use them on a Windows 95 computer?

A Sure, give it a try. Although many of the Windows 98 policies don't work properly in Windows 95, a good number of them do because Internet Explorer 4.0 supports them. In the majority of cases, you can't do any harm to the computer because policies are usually stored in the Policies branch of the registry (see Hours 11, "HKEY_LOCAL_MACHINE," and 12, "HKEY_USERS/HKEY_CURRENT_USER"). Be careful, though, and always backup the Registry before experimenting in this way.

Q Which is the better method to edit the Registry: System Policy Editor or Registry Editor?

A The System Policy Editor, used in Registry mode, is always the best way to edit the Registry. If the settings that you want to change are available in the policy templates that the operating system provides, by all means use the System Policy Editor. Otherwise, use the Registry Editor and be careful.

21

Q What are the differences between the Windows 95 and Windows 98 policy editors?

A There is little or no difference. The biggest difference between the two versions of Windows is in the policy templates that come with each. The actual program that you use to edit policies hasn't changed much since the first release of Windows 95.

Workshop

The following quiz will enhance your understanding of the topics discussed in this hour.

Quiz

1. True or False? You can create a policy file with a policy template.

2. True or False? Setting the Disable Registry editing tools policy is a sure-fire way to keep users from tampering with the Registry

3. Which of the following items are required in order to use policies?

    a. User profiles

    b. PTP (policy transmission protocol)

    c. Primary network logon

    d. Policy registry

    e. Both a and c

    f. Both a and d

4. Which of the following modes does the System Policy Editor support?

    a. User mode

    b. Group mode

    c. Registry mode

    d. Machine mode

    e. Policy mode

    f. Both a and b

    g. Both c and e

5. True or False? Windows 95 supports the same policies that Windows 98 supports.

Answers to Quiz Questions

1. False

   Policy templates describe to the System Policy Editor how to collect input from the administrator and how to save the values he provides to a POL file.

2. False

   Users can still gain access to the Registry. They can import a REG file or install an INF file that disables this policy, for example. Hour 16 describes this process.

3. e

   Policies require that user profiles be enabled on each computer, as long as you want to set policies on a per-user basis. They also require that the primary network logon be correctly configured on each workstation. The primary network logon is how Windows determines where to look for a policy file.

4. g

   The System Policy Editor supports Registry mode and policy mode. Registry mode enables the administrator to directly edit the Registry. Policy mode enables the administrator to create POL files. User, Group, and Machine better describe the different types of policies that an administrator can set.

5. False

   Windows 95, on its own, supports far fewer policies than does Windows 98. With Internet Explorer, Windows 95 does support many of the same policies, but still not the plethora that Windows 98 provides.

21

Part VII
Repairing Registry Errors

Hour

HOUR **22**

Fixing Errors in the Registry

In this hour, you learn how to repair errors in the Registry using a variety of tools:

- Registry Checker
- REGCLEAN
- Safe Mode

Microsoft produced a number of utilities for the Windows 95 Registry, none of which were built into the operating system; rather, they were provided separately. CFGBACK made backup copies of the Registry, for example. REGCLEAN fixed a variety of common problems, most of which related to HKEY_CLASSES_ROOT. ERU made backup copies of the most important configuration files, including the Registry. You could even kludge other tasks using the Registry Editor. For instance, it was common practice to compress the Registry by removing the Registry files and importing a REG file that you previously exported. You could back up the Registry, too, by exporting all or portions of it to a REG file.

With the exception of REGCLEAN, these utilities aren't necessary in Windows 98—nor are they even desirable—because Windows 98 provides the Registry Checker instead. This utility handles a variety of the tasks that you had to look elsewhere to perform in Windows 95. It automatically makes multiple backup copies of the Registry, providing a sort of version control for your configuration. It can also compress the Registry on demand, or you can let it compress the Registry automatically whenever it includes more than 500KB of unused space. Last, and most importantly, Registry Checker scans the Registry for errors and can fix most of the errors that prevent Windows 98 from starting properly.

Registry Checker does have its limitations, however. It's not as robust as Norton WinDoctor, nor does it go as far as Norton Optimization Wizard does when optimizing the Registry for performance. For example, WinDoctor scans the Registry for *orphaned* values, which are values that refer to nonexistent files and Registry keys. Other programs that complement or replace the features of the Registry Checker include Tweak UI, which you learned about in Hour 8, "Using Microsoft's Tweak UI," and the other shareware programs that you learned about in Hour 9, "Trying Other Registry Programs."

Using Registry Checker to Scan the Registry for Errors

As you might remember from Hour 3, "Backing Up/Restoring the Registry," Windows 98 provides two different versions of Registry Checker: a Windows version and a DOS-based version. Windows 95 doesn't have Registry Checker. The Windows version, whose filename is Scanregw.exe, scans the Registry for errors but doesn't fix them. It also determines whether the Registry requires optimization but, again, doesn't perform the optimization itself. Last, it backs up the Registry files, System.dat, User.dat, System.ini and Win.ini, to CAB files that you can find in \Windows\Sysbckup. The first backup is named Rb000.cab, the second is Rb001.cab, and so on. The file with the highest number is the most recent backup file; thus, Rb004.cab is a more recent backup than Rb002.cab.

If SCANREGW detects an error or detects that the Registry must be optimized, it prompts you to restart the computer. The DOS-based version, whose filename is Scanreg.exe (without the *w*), attempts to fix the Registry. It tries to restore the previous backup first, repairing the Registry only if it can't find a good backup. If SCANREGW determines that the Registry requires optimization, SCANREG optimizes the Registry the next time you start Windows 98. This is a bit much to remember, so look at Table 22.1. It summarizes all this information so that you can remember the differences between SCANREGW and SCANREG.

TABLE 22.1 SCANREGW VERSUS SCANREG

Feature	SCANREGW	SCANREG
Runs automatically	Yes	Yes, if a problem is detected
Backs up the Registry	Yes	Yes
Compresses backups	Yes	No
Operating environment	Windows	MS-DOS
Repairs the Registry	No	Yes
Restores the Registry	No	Yes
Runs in Safe Mode	Yes	No
Scans the Registry	Yes	Yes

Each time you start Windows 98, it automatically launches Registry Checker to back up the Registry. This happens because `HKEY_LOCAL_MACHINE\Software\Microsoft\Windows\CurrentVersion\Run` contains `C:\WINDOWS\scanregw.exe /autorun`.

Both SCANREGW and SCANREG support similar command-line options, all of which are listed in Table 22.2. `/backup` and `/comment` work in both versions of Registry Checker. `/opt`, `/restore`, and `/fix` are available only with SCANREG, and `/autorun` and `/scanonly` are available only with SCANREGW.

TABLE 22.2 SCANREGW AND SCANREG COMMAND LINES

Switch	Description
/autorun	Automatically scans the Registry, but backs it up only once a day. You see this switch used in the Run key of HKEY_LOCAL_MACHINE.
/backup	Backs up the Registry without prompting the user. Backups are stored in CAB files that are found in \Windows\Sysbckup.
"/comment=x"	Associates a comment with the backup. Use this switch with /backup, and be sure to enclose the entire switch in quotation marks.
/fix	Repairs the Registry.
/opt	Stands for *optimize*. Compresses unused space.
/restore	Enables you to choose from a list of backup configurations that you can restore.
/scanonly	Scans the Registry and returns an error code. It doesn't back up or repair the Registry.

22

For more information about using Registry Checker to make backup copies of the Registry, see Hour 3.

> The *Microsoft Windows 98 Resource Kit* includes additional Registry tools that you might find useful when troubleshooting. These utilities enable you to edit the Registry from the MS-DOS command line.

Scanning the Registry for Errors

The Windows-based Registry Checker scans for errors but doesn't fix them. You can launch it anytime by running Scanregw.exe. After scanning the Registry for errors, it asks you if you want to make an additional backup copy of the Registry. Click Yes if you want to. Otherwise, click No.

The DOS-based Registry Checker scans for and fixes errors. It reports its progress as it goes along. First, it tells you that it's looking for valid system Registry keys. Then it reports that it's checking the system Registry structure. Last, it reports that it's rebuilding the system Registry. To use SCANREG to fix errors in the Registry, follow these steps:

1. Start the computer in MS-DOS mode.
2. Type `scanreg /fix` at the command prompt. SCANREG runs, reporting its progress as was just described.
3. Press Enter when SCANREG reports that `Windows successfully fixed your Registry`.

If SCANREG finishes without indicating that it successfully fixed the Registry, your problems are more serious than you thought. The only solution is to restore a backup copy of the Registry as described in Hour 9.

> SCANREG is the best utility that you can use for fixing physical problems in the Registry. It's also the best utility that you can use for backing up and restoring the Registry. It doesn't, however, fix organizational problems—such as orphans—in the Registry. The best solution for this problem is a utility such as Norton WinDoctor.

Refining Registry Checker's Configuration

Both versions of Registry Checker, SCANREGW and SCANREG, load settings from Scanreg.ini. Table 22.3 describes the settings that you can change in this file. The most interesting settings include `MaxBackupCopies` and `Files`. The first controls the number of backups that the Registry keeps. The first backup is the first one to be deleted. The default value for this setting is 5, which is a bit small if you want to make sure that you can always recover from configuration problems. Sometimes you can go several days before noticing that Windows 98 has a problem, and by then, Registry Checker has already replaced the last good backup copy of your configuration with a broken copy.

TABLE 22.3 SETTINGS IN SCANREG.INI

Setting	Description
`Backup=[0¦1]`	Specifies whether to run SCANREGW each time Windows 98 starts, backing up the Registry. The default value is 1, meaning that the Registry Checker backs up the Registry once each day.
	0 = Don't run SCANREGW at startup
	1 = Run SCANREGW at startup
`Optimize=[0¦1]`	Specifies whether to automatically optimize the Registry. The default value is 1, meaning that Registry Checker optimizes the Registry as required.
	0 = Don't automatically optimize
	1 = Automatically optimize
`MaxBackupCopes=x`	Specifies the maximum number of backup copies of the Registry to make each time Windows 98 starts. The default value is 5, meaning that Registry Checker keeps only five backup copies. Possible values are 0[nd]99.
`BackupDirectory=x`	Specifies the location in which to store the CAB files that contain the configuration backup. The default value is \Windows\Sysbckup. If you use this setting, you must provide a full path, starting from the root folder.
`Files=[code,]f1,f2`	Specifies additional files to include in the configuration backup. You can include this setting as many times as required. Table 22.4 describes the directory codes that you can use for *code*.

`Files` enables you to specify additional configuration files that you want to include in each backup. By default, Registry Checker backs up System.ini and Win.ini, but what if you want to include Protocol.ini or your Autoexec.bat file? The syntax looks similar to the following:

```
Files=[dir code,]file1,file2,file3
```

dir code is one of the codes listed in Table 22.4. These codes indicate the location of the configuration file. Note that code 31 is useful only if you're using Registry Checker on a computer with compressed volumes. To back up Protocol.ini from \Windows, for example, you'd write a line such as the following:

```
Files=10,protocol.ini
```

You can include more than one file in each statement, with each separated by a comma.

TABLE 22.4   VALUES FOR dir code

Code	Directory	Example
10	Windows installation folder	\Windows
11	Windows system folder	\Windows\System
30	Boot drive	C:\
31	Boot host folder	H:\

Cleaning Up the Registry with REGCLEAN

Microsoft provides a free utility called REGCLEAN that you can use to clean up the contents of the Registry. Although Microsoft provided this utility for Windows 95, it works equally well with Windows 98. You can download REGCLEAN from Microsoft's Web site or from any of the shareware software sites that are described in Hour 9. After you've downloaded the file, sometimes called Regcln41.exe, launch it to extract its contents into C:\Program Files\RegClean. You can copy a shortcut for Regclean.exe to the Start button.

REGCLEAN works only with Registry keys about which it has previous knowledge. This includes keys common to all versions of Windows and Microsoft Office. It looks for orphans, for example, which you'll learn about later in this hour. Most of the work that REGCLEAN does is in HKEY_CLASSES_ROOT, HKEY_CLASSES_ROOT\Classes, and HKEY_CLASSES_ROOT\Classes\TypeLib. REGCLEAN has some very important limitations that might cause you to use a different utility for this purpose:

22

- It doesn't fix orphans. It just removes any Registry keys or values that contain orphans.
- REGCLEAN works only on Registry keys that belong to Windows 95, Windows 98, or Microsoft Office. It doesn't help with Registry keys that belong to other products.

With those caveats out of the way, here's how to use REGCLEAN to clean up the Registry:

1. Start REGCLEAN. REGCLEAN scans the disk for errors, which can take quite a long time. You see the window that is shown in Figure 22.1.

FIGURE 22.1

REGCLEAN was written for Windows 95, but it works equally well in Windows 98 because the Registry's organization hasn't changed much.

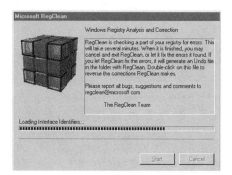

2. Click Fix Errors to make the changes that REGCLEAN recommends. If you aren't sure, click Cancel.

3. Open the REG file that REGCLEAN created in the same folder in which it's installed. The filename begins with the word *Undo*. This REG file indicates any Registry keys that REGCLEAN removed from the Registry. If the file is empty, you're finished. If the file contains keys, start again with step 1. Microsoft states that you might have to run REGCLEAN numerous times before it completely cleans the Registry.

If you find that you want to undo the changes that REGCLEAN makes, you can merge the REG files that it created back into the Registry. Each filename has the format Undo *computername date time*.reg, and is in the same folder that contains Regclean.exe. Double-click each file, or right-click each file and choose Merge.

> Don't use REGCLEAN if the Registry is corrupted. Use Registry Checker to fix the Registry first because REGCLEAN only cleans up the Registry's contents, and it relies on a working Registry.

CHECK OUT THE AUTHOR'S REGISTRY

My Web site, `http://www.honeycutt.com`, contains the Registry from one of my computers. After installing a fresh copy of Windows 98, I exported the entire Registry to a file called Registry.reg.

Borrow what you need from these files. You can use them in cases where the tools described in this hour aren't helping you fix the Registry and you need a reference to see what a particular branch of the Registry contains. In some cases, you can copy a key or value from the Registry.reg file on my Web site, build a new REG file that contains it, and import the file into your Registry. Use a bit of common sense when doing this, however. You don't want to import the hardware settings from Registry.reg unless you know for sure that those settings match your own configuration.

Starting in Safe Mode

If you can't start Windows, and you suspect that the culprit is configuration data in the Registry, start the operating system in Safe Mode. This is a special mode that forces the operating system to load without most of its device driver support. It loads the standard VGA, mouse, and keyboard drivers only. It skips everything in the Registry, Config.sys, Autoexec.bat, and the [Boot] and [386Enh] sections of System.ini. Note that most of your other devices won't work properly in Safe Mode because the operating system loaded their device drivers or configuration from the Registry. The following steps explain how to start in Safe Mode:

1. Hold down the left Ctrl key or press F8 as Windows starts to display the boot menu.

2. Choose Safe Mode from the boot menu. The boot menu contains other useful options, such as Safe Mode Command Prompt Only, which is guaranteed to work even when regular Safe Mode doesn't, and Command Prompt Only, which starts directly to the MS-DOS command prompt. Here's how a typical boot menu looks:

   1.Normal

   2.Logged (\BOOTLOG.TXT)

   3.Safe mode

   4.Step-by-step confirmation

   5.Command prompt only

   6.Safe mode command prompt only

22

Windows 98 introduces a new way to display the boot menu. After restarting the computer, hold down the Ctrl key until you see the boot menu. The Ctrl key makes more sense than F8 because the Ctrl key doesn't automatically repeat like F8 does.

Safe Mode is useful for recovering from serious problems. Your video configuration might cause Windows to crash as it starts, for instance, but you can change the configuration in Safe Mode and boot normally into a working operating system.

There are a few caveats with Safe Mode, however. The CD-ROM is unavailable, for example—even if you load the real mode driver in Config.sys. To avoid this problem, add the real mode driver to Config.sys and Mscdex.exe to Autoexec.bat, and then start the computer to the command prompt by choosing Command Prompt Only from the boot menu. After you've recovered your configuration and started Windows normally, you'll notice that your desktop might be messed up. Safe Mode operates at a video resolution of 640×480, so the operating system moves things around on the desktop to make sure that everything fits. The last issue I have with Safe Mode is that it changes the Start menu to large icons, even though you might have configured it to use small icons.

You might be surprised when Windows occasionally starts the computer in Safe Mode without your consent. It does so in the following situations:

- The previous attempt at starting failed.
- The signature file Wnbbotng.sts exists in \Windows.
- An application requested Safe Mode.
- The Registry file is corrupted.

Before problems strike, create one or more emergency disks that contain all the files you think you'll need if things go awry. You can also copy the most important bits of the Windows CD-ROM to your computer's hard disk, assuming that you have enough space. Copying the \Tools and \Win98 folders requires approximately 200MB of free disk space.

Summary

A number of repair utilities are available for the Registry. REGCLEAN can fix problems that are specific to Microsoft Office. Utilities such as CFGBACK and ERU can make backup copies of the Registry. This book also describes a handful of shareware programs that you can use to repair the Registry.

There are really only two programs that you need to know about, however. Registry Checker can optimize the Registry as well as repair common errors in its structure, and Norton WinDoctor fixes most other errors, including orphans.

Q&A

Q Why can't the Windows Registry Checker, SCANREGW, restore the Registry?

A SCANREGW only runs in the graphical user interface. While running the GUI, many portions of the Registry are in use and can't be changed. Because restoring the Registry requires the program to replace the contents of the entire Registry, SCANREGW can't do it.

Q If, for some reason, I'm unable to start the computer from the hard disk, what do I do?

A Use your emergency repair disk to start the computer. You make this disk using the Add/Remove Programs dialog box. This disk includes drivers that work with most CD-ROM drives, so you'll have access to your CD-ROM drive.

Q Where does Registry Checker store comments that are specified using the /comment **switch?**

A Registry Checker stores each comment in the CAB file, which is the cabinet file that contains System.dat, User.dat, and so on.

Workshop

The following quiz will enhance your understanding of the topics discussed in this hour.

22

Quiz

1. Of the following tasks, which one can the Registry Checker not perform?

   a. Backup the Registry

   b. Optimize the Registry's clusters

   c. Repair Registry errors

   d. Scan the Registry for errors

2. True or False? When SCANREGW detects an error, it fixes the error.

3. Which of the following options causes SCANREG to scan the Registry for errors?

   a. /opt

   b. /scanonly

   c. /fix

Answers to Quiz Questions

1. b

   Registry Checker can't optimize the Registry files' disk clusters. For that, you must use Norton Speed Disk.

2. False

   SCANREGW, after finding an error, restarts the computer to MS-DOS mode and uses SCANREG to repair the error.

3. c

   /scanonly just scans the Registry for errors, returning an error code. /opt optimizes the size of the Registry, freeing unused space in the Registry.

Hour 23

Fixing Program Errors via the Registry

This hour teaches you how to repair the Registry. In particular, you learn the following:

- How to redetect the computer's hardware
- How to reinstall a broken application
- How to reassociate a filename extension with a program
- How to manually remove a program from the computer
- How to extract files from CAB files
- How to fix a variety of specific Registry errors

Avoid editing the Registry whenever possible; it's a good rule to live by because human error doesn't affect the result nearly as much as when you're editing the Registry. Simple changes that you make via the Windows user interface ripple throughout the Registry. The simple act of enabling the Active Desktop by right-clicking the desktop and choosing Active Desktop,

View as Web Page causes Windows 98 to write data to more than 30 value entries that are scattered across three areas of the Registry. Which way do you prefer to perform the task?

Windows fixes some errors before you even know they exist, and you can fix the remaining problems using the variety of tools that the operating system provides. Let the Device Manager and Add/Remove Hardware Wizard deal with hardware problems, and let the Folder Options dialog box in Explorer handle problems with file associations. Instead of trying to fix an application's corrupted Registry entries, run the application's setup program to restore its Registry entries. You'll learn about these solutions in the remainder of this hour.

Redetect Your Hardware

If your hardware configuration is behaving strangely, you can't fix it using the Registry Editor. Figure 23.1 shows a portion of the Registry that contains configuration data for the display adapter. This branch isn't the only portion of the Registry that is connected to the display, and sorting it all out is a real nightmare. The bottom line is that the hardware entries in the Registry are far too complicated to do anything other than delete hardware profiles.

FIGURE 23.1

Entries for a single device are scattered throughout the Registry.

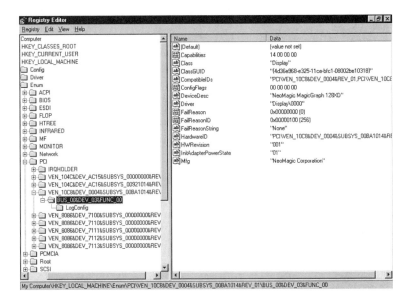

It is recommended that you rely on the Add New Hardware wizard or the Device Manager tab of the System Properties dialog box to work with your hardware configuration. If you're changing the resources that are allocated to a device, use the Device Manager. If you're trying to fix a configuration problem, use a combination of both. The following list describes a few different approaches:

- **Reconfiguring a device**—Use the Device Manager tab of the System Properties dialog box to change a device's resources. Double-click the device to open its property sheet, and then click the Resources tab (shown in Figure 23.2). The Device Manager warns you when you're setting up a device conflict and automatically programs Plug and Play devices to use the resources that you assign.

- **Troubleshooting a device**—Run the Add New Hardware Wizard from the Control Panel. It presents a list of devices that aren't working properly. If you see the device that you're troubleshooting, select it so that the Add New Hardware wizard can help you figure out what's wrong with it.

- **Reloading a device**—Open the Device Manager and remove the device with which you're having trouble. Restart the computer to see if Windows automatically detects the device. If it doesn't, run the Add New Hardware wizard. When it asks you if you want to automatically detect the hardware in your computer, click Yes.

FIGURE 23.2

Deselect Use automatic settings if you want to override the default settings.

Don't assume that the Device Manager represents the extent to which you can configure the hardware on your computer. The Device Manager enables you to shuffle resources and set some very low-level settings, but it doesn't enable you to specify preferences or higher-level settings. For that, turn to the variety of icons in the Control Panel. Allocate memory regions to a display adapter in the Device Manager, for example, but set its scan rate and resolution using the Display Properties dialog box. Bind your network adapter to particular protocols using the Network dialog box. The same goes for multimedia devices, input devices, power management, and so on.

> The Windows 98 online help provides a number of troubleshooters that help you diagnose and fix common hardware problems. These troubleshooters aren't just for novices, however. They include help for modems, display adapters, hardware conflicts, and more.

Reinstall an Offending Program

If a program's settings are messed up, it's often easier to reinstall the program. You don't have to remove the program first—just install right over it. You'll replace the program's files on the hard drive and the program's settings in the Registry. This is a particularly good way to fix problems with property sheet handlers and other shell extensions that an application installs. Be sure to install over the same folder, or you'll end up with two copies of the application on your computer—and only one will be usable.

Smarter programs know enough to leave your preferences alone while they correctly fix other Registry settings. If you reinstall Netscape Navigator, for example, it preserves all your server settings while it resets all the program's settings in HKEY_CLASSES_ROOT. Internet Explorer 4.0 isn't as smart because it trashes many of your personal preferences each time you install the latest service pack.

There are other ways to restore a program's Registry settings. Many setup programs use one or more REG files to create their initial settings in the Registry. You can possibly use the REG file again to restore damaged settings without reinstalling the program. Look in the program's installation folder and carefully inspect the REG file. If it looks like the REG file can fix the problem, merge it into the Registry. If you want to merge only a portion of the REG file, make a copy of it, remove the extraneous content, and merge it into the Registry. REG files aren't nearly as common as INF files, though. They're a bit harder to understand, but they contain similar information for adding, removing, and changing values in the Registry. Again, look in the program's installation folder for its INF file (see Hour 18, "Scripting Changes to the Registry") and examine it carefully to determine which portions you want to merge with your configuration.

Reassociate a Filename Extension

The portion of the Registry that loses its wits most often is HKEY_CLASSES_ROOT. Not surprisingly, this is also the single largest branch in the Registry. The order in which you install programs affects file associations. Shockingly, some programs disregard your preferences altogether and change associations that have extremely loose ties. Internet Explorer is one of the worst culprits, taking associations for most image files for itself. There is one other scenario, in which a particular filename extension remains unassociated with any program; you'll notice one of the following two symptoms:

- You double-click a document, and Windows opens it in the wrong program.
- You double-click a document, and Windows opens the Open With dialog box, which prompts you for the name of the program in which you want to open the document.

Some programs, such as Internet Explorer and WinZip, are good about detecting the fact that they're no longer associated with a particular filename extension. In such cases, you can allow the program to fix the problem automatically. In other cases, you'll have to manually associate the program with a particular program:

1. Open Windows Explorer, and then select a file that has the extension that you want to associate with a program.

2. Hold down the Shift key, right-click the file, and choose Open With. You see the Open With dialog box (shown in Figure 23.3).

FIGURE 23.3

This list shows the programs with which you can open files.

3. Choose the program that you want to associate with the filename extension, select Always use this program to open this type of file, and click OK. Alternatively, click Other to locate an unregistered program.

Remember that program identifiers and filename extensions are separate entities. Program identifiers include information about a program, such as actions that you can perform on a file. In the Registry, filename extensions subkeys associate a file's extension with a program's identifier. Windows can associate more than one filename extension with each program.

Borrow a Key from Another Computer

If you've tried everything you can think of and nothing fixes your configuration, try borrowing the offending Registry key from another computer. Take some precautions before doing so, however. First, make sure that you're not overreaching your capabilities and that you're comfortable doing this. Also, don't try borrowing hardware information from another computer, even if it's the same make and model. This technique is fine for repairing file associations, but not for repairing your hardware configuration. Finally, be sure to back up your own Registry before importing a portion of another computer's Registry into your own.

Here's how to borrow a key from another computer, importing it into your computer's Registry:

1. On the source computer, export the key that you're borrowing to a REG file.

2. Trim the REG file so that it contains only the information that you need—and no more. Remember that the Registry Editor exports the entire branch below the key. If that's your intention, fine, but inspect the contents of the REG file to make sure that you know what you're getting.

3. Back up your Registry using Registry Checker or a comparable utility. Don't skip this step, no matter how unnecessary you think it is.

4. Copy the REG file to your computer and merge it into the Registry by double-clicking it.

If you don't have a computer from which you can borrow a key, use the Registry.reg file on my Web site: http://www.honeycutt.com. This REG file contains an exported copy of my Registry, which I created after a fresh installation of Windows 98 using a somewhat typical setup. I removed the ProductKey subkey so as not to upset Microsoft, and I have removed any other keys that I don't want the public to see. Other than that, the REG file is complete.

You can change most of the configuration data in the Registry via the Settings submenu on the Start menu, which provides access to the Control Panel.

Removing a Program from the Registry Manually

Most programs are rather predictable, storing the same types of information in the same types of places. They store program files in C:\Program Files and file associations in HKEY_CLASSES_ROOT. They put user-specific and machine-specific configuration data in HKEY_CURRENT_USER\SOFTWARE and HKEY_LOCAL_MACHINE\SOFTWARE, respectively. Furthermore, they sprinkle some settings in places such as the uninstall list and the installed components list.

Take advantage of this information to remove an application that doesn't provide an uninstall program. Back up your computer, including the Registry. Then make a list of the DLL and EXE files that you find in the program's installation folder, and delete the folder. (You'll probably find them in a folder under C:\Program Files.) After removing the program's folder, open the Registry Editor to search for any entries that belong to the program, and then remove them. Following are some suggestions for the types of things to search for:

- Search the Registry for each of the program's installation paths. If the program has two paths, C:\Program Files*Company* and C:\Program Files*Company\Program,* search for both paths in the Registry. Delete any keys or value entries that contain this path. Use a bit of common sense here, and don't remove a key that another application obviously uses.

- Search the Registry for the program's name. If you're removing a program called "Elvis Lives for Windows 98," search the Registry for any key or value entry that contains Elvis or Elvis Lives. Search for the program's executables, too. Within reason, delete any keys or value entries that contain the name of the program or the filename of the executable.

- Search the Registry for the EXE and DLL files that you recorded earlier. Delete the key or value entry that contains the reference to the file. Again, use common sense and don't remove keys that other programs obviously use.

- Use a utility such as REGCLEAN or Norton WinDoctor to scan the Registry for errors and to remove orphaned value entries from the Registry. After removing a program by hand, you're likely to leave several value entries in the Registry; these programs can help fix them.

> If you can't start Windows after installing a new program, the program is most likely loading shell extensions, device drivers, or other files when the operating system tries to start; these files are preventing the operating system from starting properly. You have two choices. You can start the operating system in Safe Mode, and then remove the program using the Add/Remove Programs Properties dialog box from the Control Panel. Or you can remove the program using more drastic measures. Restart the computer to the command prompt, and completely remove the program's installation folder from C:\Program Files. Restart the computer. The operating system starts, complaining all the while about missing files. Using the steps in this section, remove the program's Registry entries. After doing so, restart the computer. The operating system no longer complains about the missing files.

Extracting Files from CAB Files

At some point, you'll have to restore system files from the Windows 98 CD-ROM. The problem is that Microsoft stores these files in CAB files that you find in \Win98, making finding the exact location of the system file a challenge. Use the Find dialog box to locate the CAB file. Choose Start, Find, Files or Folders and fill in the Find dialog box so that it searches the \Win98 folder of the Windows 98 CD-ROM for all CAB files that contain the filename. Figure 23.4 shows you an example.

FIGURE 23.4

Each CAB file contains a list of its contents, so Find can locate the CAB file that has the system file that you need.

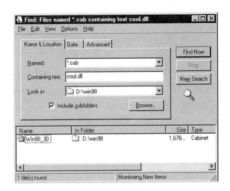

After locating the CAB file in the Find dialog box, right-click it and choose View. Windows 98 opens the CAB file in an Explorer window so that you can view its contents. Locate the file in the list, and then extract it by dragging it from the list to another folder on your computer, such as the desktop. In most cases, you can replace the system file by copying the new file over the old one and confirming that you want to replace it when Windows 98 asks. If the file that you're trying to replace is in use, however, you can't replace it. If that's the case, restart the computer in MS-DOS mode, copy the new file over the old, and restart the computer.

23

Fixing Other Common Problems

The following sections show you how to fix a variety of common problems in Windows. Some of these problems occur when an errant program messes up your system. Other problems are peculiar to the operating system:

- Restrictions are too restrictive.
- The wrong program runs when you open a file.
- Fonts don't work properly.
- Property sheets don't work properly.
- Special folders won't open.
- Duplicate or bad options on shortcut menus.
- Shortcuts don't work properly.
- Your password doesn't work after you upgrade.
- The Logitech mouse doesn't work properly.
- Internet security settings aren't accessible.
- Program won't install because of Windows version.

Restrictions Are Too Restrictive

Here's the rub: You can't edit the Registry because of policy restrictions, but you can't change the policy restrictions because you can't edit the Registry. There are a couple of different solutions to this problem that your administrator probably doesn't want you to know about. First, create the INF file that is shown in Listing 23.1. Then right-click the INF file and choose Install. This works because Windows allows an application to change the Registry via an INF file even though policies prevent the user from editing the Registry. Note also that you can use the System Policy Editor to remove this restriction as long as you have access to the program.

LISTING 23.1 THE INF FILE TO REMOVE RESTRICTIONS

```
[version]
signature="$CHICAGO$"

[DefaultInstall]
DelReg=Restrictions

[Restrictions]
HKCU,SOFTWARE\Microsoft\Windows\CurrentVersion\Policies
```

The second solution is even more straightforward. Start the computer in MS-DOS mode by choosing Command Prompt Only from the boot menu. Then type the following command line at the prompt, and press Enter:

```
regedit /d HKEY_CURRENT_USER\SOFTWARE\Microsoft\Windows\
➥CurrentVersion\Policies
```

This command removes the entire `Policies` branch from the Registry, and the operating system doesn't balk a bit.

The steps that you learn in this section work when policies are defined in the Registry. If restrictions are coming from a Config.pol on your computer, disable the POL file by renaming or removing it to remove the restrictions. If the restrictions are coming from a Config.pol that Windows automatically downloads from the network, you're out of luck as long as you log on to the network. For more information, see Hour 21, "Controlling the Desktop via System Policies."

The Wrong Program Runs When You Open a File

This problem is self-explanatory. You double-click a document's filename and Windows doesn't open it in the program you expect. The solution is to reassociate the filename extension with the program in which you want to open the file. You learned how to do this in the earlier section "Reassociate a Filename Extension."

Fonts Don't Work Properly

The most common cause of fonts not working correctly is that `HKLM\SOFTWARE\Microsoft\Windows\CurrentVersion\Fonts` is either corrupted or missing from the Registry. Windows 98 provides a small utility, called Fontreg.exe, to fix these Registry settings. Execute this program to fix the font information in the Registry.

Note that this program doesn't open a window, display progress information, or tell you if it succeeds or fails.

If you run Fontreg.exe but the Fonts folder still doesn't work properly, rebuild \Windows\Fonts:

1. Move the contents of \Windows\Fonts to a scratch folder on your desktop.
2. Delete the contents of \Windows\Fonts and remove HKLM\SOFTWARE\Microsoft\Windows\CurrentVersion\Fonts from the Registry.
3. Drag each font file from the scratch folder to \Windows\Fonts. This task might be easier if you use file cut-and-paste or if you open two different Explorer windows.

Property Sheets Don't Work Properly

Property sheets don't get messed up very often, but when they do, they wreak havoc. A Registry entry that refers to a missing property sheet handler causes Windows to not open the property sheet at all. A corrupted property sheet handler might cause Explorer to crash when it tries to display the property sheet.

Your first step in fixing this problem is to identify the program or class identifier that is causing it. If you know that the Recycle Bin's property sheet causes Explorer to crash, for example, locate the Recycle Bin's key in HKEY_CLASSES_ROOT\CLSID. If Explorer won't open the property sheet for a particular file, locate the extension for that file in HKEY_CLASSES_ROOT. Then use that key's default value entry to locate the program identifier with which it's associated, and open the program identifier in HKEY_CLASSES_ROOT. Then again, if the problem affects virtually every document in Windows Explorer, start with HKEY_CLASSES_ROOT*, which adds features to every file's shortcut menu and property sheet.

If you can pinpoint an application that is causing problems with a property sheet, reinstall it. The application's setup program restores health to the property sheet while maintaining most of your preferences.

After locating the problem key, which is either a program or class identifier, examine the shellex\PropertySheetHandlers subkey beneath it. This key contains an additional subkey for each handler that adds tabs to the object's property sheet. Take a look at Figure 23.5 to better understand this organization. Identify the application that owns each subkey in PropertySheetHandlers by looking up each class identifier in

HKEY_CLASSES_ROOT\CLSID. In Figure 23.5, HKEY_CLASSES_ROOT\CLSID\{ABBE31D0-6DAE-11D0-BECA-00C04FD940BE} is opened; you can see that Internet Explorer's subscription manager owns this property sheet and that it's implemented via a DLL called Webcheck.dll. You also learn that {FBF23B40-E3F0-101B-8488-00AA003E56F8} is implemented via Shdocvw.dll, implementing the Internet shortcut tab. After gathering this information, the action you take depends on the problem you're having:

- **The property sheet displays tabs it shouldn't**—The property sheet displays duplicate tabs or includes a tab that just doesn't make sense. Either way, the solution is the same. You've already made the connection between each subkey and the application that owns it. Using that information, remove the subkey that belongs to that subkey.

- **A tab is missing from the property sheet**—This is a bit more difficult to fix because the problem is probably that the subkey for that tab is missing from the PropertySheetHandlers key. You must somehow identify the class identifier of the property sheet handler, which you can do by looking at another computer's Registry or by looking through the application's REG and INF files to see what value was used when you installed the program.

- **Explorer crashes when opening the property sheet**—First, try removing the subkey for each property sheet handler from PropertySheetHandlers and test the change in Windows Explorer. If it works, one of the DLL files might be corrupted. Restore each DLL file from the Windows CD-ROM as described in the section "Extracting Files from CAB Files," earlier in this hour. If you're still out of luck, try reinstalling the application.

Special Folders Won't Open

This problem isn't very common, but it's frustrating nonetheless. You double-click the Control Panel icon and nothing happens. You can't access the Recycle Bin to recover files you deleted. This is easily fixed.

Make sure that each shell folder's class identifier's subkey is correctly configured in the Registry. Table 23.1 shows the class identifiers for the Windows shell folders, as well as the name of the DLL files that implement them. You can find a subkey under HKEY_CLASSES_ROOT\CLSID for each class identifier. Each class identifier's subkey also contains an InprocServer32 subkey whose default value entry indicates the correct DLL file, as described in Table 23.1. Remember to type the complete path of the DLL file in InprocServer32 so that Windows can find the file.

Figure 23.5

Property sheet handlers are much more common for program identifiers than for class identifiers.

Program identifier

Class identifiers for property sheets

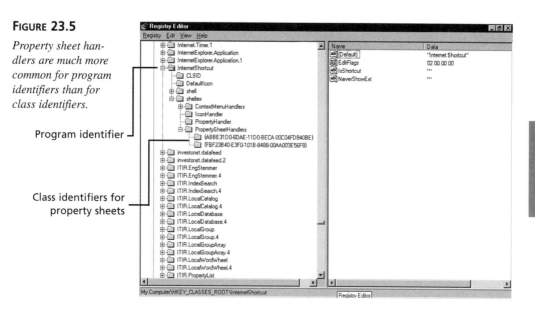

If fixing the shell folder's subkey in the Registry doesn't help, restore the DLL file from the CD-ROM. You can also run the System File Checker to verify that the system has been corrupted. Choose Start, Programs, Accessories, System Tools, System File Checker. Follow the instructions that you see onscreen.

TABLE 23.1 REPLACING A SHELL FOLDER'S CLASS IDENTIFIER

Name	Class Identifier/DLL File
Control Panel	{21EC2020-3AEA-1069-A2DD-08002B30309D} C:\Windows\System\Shell32.dll
Dial-Up Networking	{992CFFA0-F557-101A-88EC-00DD010CCC48} C:\Windows\System\Rnaui.dll
Printers	{2227A280-3AEA-1069-A2DE-08002B30309D} C:\Windows\System\Shell32.dll
Recycle Bin	{645FF040-5081-101B-9F08-00AA002F954E} C:\Winodw\System\Shell32.dll
Scheduled Tasks	{D6277990-4C6A-11CF-8D87-00AA0060F5BF} C:\Windows\Shell\Mstask.dll
Briefcase	{85BBD920-42A0-1069-A2E4-08002B3039D} C:\Windows\System\Syncui.dll

continues

TABLE 23.1 CONTINUED

Name	Class Identifier/DLL File
My Computer	{20D04FE0-3AEA-1069-A2D8-08002B30309D} C:\Windows\System\Shell32.dll
The Internet	{3DC7A020-OACD-11CF-A9BB-00AA004AE837} C:\Windows\System\Shdocvw.dll
Network Neighborhood	{208D2C60-3AEA-1069-A2D7-08002B30309D} C:\Windows\System\Shell32.dll

Duplicate or Bad Commands on Shortcut Menus

Hours 14–16 describe how to customize a shortcut menu in two different ways. First, you can add or remove built-in menu commands, such as Cut and Properties, to or from a shortcut menu using the Attributes subkey. Second, you can add additional commands to a file's shortcut menu by adding them to the appropriate shell subkey. Use the information that you learned in those hours to help you remove bogus commands on the shortcut menu, add missing commands, or change how the menu works.

Shortcuts Don't Work Properly

When shortcuts stop working, the problem is usually with HKEY_CLASSES_ROOT\piffile or HKEY_CLASSES_ROOT\lnkfile. If DOS shortcuts no longer work, import the REG file that is shown in Listing 23.2, or repair the Registry so that it matches the listing. If shortcuts don't work, import the REG file shown in Listing 23.3.

LISTING 23.2 THE REG FILE FOR DOS LINKS

```
REGEDIT4

[HKEY_CLASSES_ROOT\piffile]
@="Shortcut to MS-DOS Program"
"EditFlags"=hex:01,00,00,00
"IsShortcut"=" "
"NeverShowExt"=""

[HKEY_CLASSES_ROOT\piffile\shell]

[HKEY_CLASSES_ROOT\piffile\shell\open]
@=""

[HKEY_CLASSES_ROOT\piffile\shell\open\command]
@="\"%1\" %*"
```

```
[HKEY_CLASSES_ROOT\piffile\shellex]

[HKEY_CLASSES_ROOT\piffile\shellex\PropertySheetHandlers]

[HKEY_CLASSES_ROOT\piffile\shellex\PropertySheetHandlers\
➥{86F19A00-42A0-1069-A2E9-08002B30309D}]
@=""

[HKEY_CLASSES_ROOT\piffile\shellex\IconHandler]
@="{00021401-0000-0000-C000-000000000046}"
```

23

LISTING 23.3   THE REG FILE FOR WINDOWS LINKS

```
REGEDIT4

[HKEY_CLASSES_ROOT\CLSID\
➥{00021401-0000-0000-C000-000000000046}]
@="Shortcut"

[HKEY_CLASSES_ROOT\CLSID\
➥{00021401-0000-0000-C000-000000000046}\InProcServer32]
@="shell32.dll"
"ThreadingModel"="Apartment"

[HKEY_CLASSES_ROOT\CLSID\
➥{00021401-0000-0000-C000-000000000046}\shellex]

[HKEY_CLASSES_ROOT\CLSID\
➥{00021401-0000-0000-C000-000000000046}\shellex\
➥MayChangeDefaultMenu]
@=""

[HKEY_CLASSES_ROOT\CLSID\
➥{00021401-0000-0000-C000-000000000046}\ProgID]
@="lnkfile"

[HKEY_CLASSES_ROOT\lnkfile]
@="Shortcut"
"EditFlags"=hex:01,00,00,00
"IsShortcut"=" "
"NeverShowExt"=""

[HKEY_CLASSES_ROOT\lnkfile\CLSID]
@="{00021401-0000-0000-C000-000000000046}"

[HKEY_CLASSES_ROOT\lnkfile\shellex]
```

continues

LISTING 23.3 CONTINUED

```
[HKEY_CLASSES_ROOT\lnkfile\shellex\IconHandler]
@="{00021401-0000-0000-C000-000000000046}"

[HKEY_CLASSES_ROOT\lnkfile\shellex\DropHandler]
@="{00021401-0000-0000-C000-000000000046}"

[HKEY_CLASSES_ROOT\lnkfile\shellex\ContextMenuHandlers]

[HKEY_CLASSES_ROOT\lnkfile\shellex\ContextMenuHandlers\
➥{00021401-0000-0000-C000-000000000046}]
@=""
```

Your Password Doesn't Work After You Upgrade

Upgrading to Windows 98 isn't always as seamless as Microsoft might have wanted it to be. In some cases, for example, after you upgrade to Windows 98, you see an error message that says Invalid Password—even though you're absolutely sure you typed the correct password, and even though it worked properly before you upgraded. This is true if you're connecting to an older server that doesn't support encrypted passwords and you enabled the use of plain-text passwords. The upgrade process disables this feature. To fix this problem, re-enable plain-text passwords by creating a DWORD value called EnablePlainTextPassword under HKEY_LOCAL_MACHINE\System\CurrentControlSet \Services\Vxd\Vnetsup.

The Logitech Mouse Doesn't Work Properly

It doesn't happen all the time, but sometimes Windows 98 doesn't recognize Logitech mice correctly. I don't want to speculate on the reason for this, but I can offer you a solution if you're stuck without a working mouse. By default, Windows 98 uses the standard mouse drivers when it detects a Logitech mouse, and these don't always work properly. To fix the problem, install Logitech's version 8.0 or greater mouse drivers, which come with Windows 98. Use the Device Manager:

1. Open the System Properties dialog box from the Control Panel and choose Device Manager.
2. Open the property sheet for the mouse and choose the Driver tab.
3. Choose Update Driver, and use the Update Device Driver Wizard to choose the appropriate driver. The manufacturer is Logitech, and the actual device depends on the model you purchased. Look on the bottom of the device if you're not sure.

If you're using a C-series Logitech mouse, which you can verify by checking the model number on the bottom of the mouse, you also need to change a value in the Registry in order for it to work properly. Change the `SearchCSeries` value entry under the `HKEY_LOCAL_MACHINE\Software\Logitech\MouseWare\CurrentVersion\Technical` Registry key so that it says `Off`.

> You can learn about other mouse features that you can enable via the Registry by visiting Logitech's Web site at `http://www.logitech.com`. Examples include enabling DragLock and Double-click.

23

> You can force Windows 98 to redetect your mouse by removing a handful of subkeys from `HKEY_LOCAL_MACHINE`. Remove `0000` and so on from `System\CurrentControlSet\Services\Class\Mouse`. Remove the same subkeys from `Enum\Root\Mouse`. Then, if they exist, remove `Enum\Serenum` and `Software\Logitech\Mouseware`. After removing these keys, use the Add New Hardware Wizard to redetect your mouse.

Internet Security Settings Aren't Accessible

`HKEY_CURRENT_USER\Software\Microsoft\Windows\CurrentVersion\Internet Settings\Zones` contains Internet Explorer's security settings. If it becomes damaged, Windows 98 can't display the Security tab in the Internet Properties dialog box. The solution to this problem is to completely remove the key from the Registry and allow Internet Explorer to rebuild it.

A Program Won't Install Because of Windows Version

Some programs look for a specific version of Windows and won't install if they don't find what they expect. However, you can use the following steps to fool this kind of setup program into thinking that you're installing it in Windows 95 (by changing the version in the Registry):

1. Record the value you find for `VersionNumber` in `HKEY_LOCAL_MACHINE\Software\Microsoft\Windows\Current_Version`. Do the same for `Version`. `VersionNumber` is normally something such as `4.10.1998`, and `Version` is normally `Windows 98`.

2. Change `VersionNumber` to `4.00.1111`, and change `Version` to `Windows 95`. Both values are string value entries.

3. Install the program as normal. It doesn't complain about the version of Windows you're using anymore.

4. Change `VersionNumber` and `Version` back to their original values.

 Don't try to fool disk utility programs into running under Windows 98 when they only support Windows 95. Some disk utilities don't work correctly with FAT32, and using them under Windows 98 can result in data loss.

Summary

In most cases, you want to allow Windows to make its own Registry repairs. If you're having hardware problems, for instance, remove the device driver using Device Manager, and allow the operating system to redetect it. Problems with an installed program? Reinstall it. If documents open in the wrong application, use Windows Explorer's Folder Options dialog box to associate the filename extension with the appropriate program.

Removing a program from the computer almost always leaves artifacts behind. This hour showed you how to remove a program's entries from the Registry.

In addition to repairing the operating system and removing programs from the computer, this hour provided solutions for more specific problems. It showed you how to repair the fonts folder. It showed you how to fix a program's property sheets. It even showed you how to spoof the operating system's version number so that you can run applications that won't run in your particular version of Windows.

Q&A

Q I called the help line and they told me to reinstall Windows 98. Should I?

A After a support technician ventures beyond his level of competence, he'll usually tell you to reinstall Windows in order to fix the problem. This is a favorite line of support technicians around the globe, even at Microsoft. What happens when you reinstall Windows 98 depends on how you do it. In either case, the setup program treats your actions as an upgrade, so the same rules apply. If you start the setup program from within Windows, it migrates your settings from the existing Registry, redetecting all the Plug and Play devices. If you start the setup program from MS-DOS mode, it redetects all the devices on the computer, including legacy and Plug and Play. In either case, Windows 98 keeps most of your personal preferences, other than a handful that relate to Internet Explorer and the desktop.

All your applications work the same as they did before. Reinstalling Windows 98 just isn't necessary, as you can see from the preceding explanation. The only benefit that you might receive by doing so is that the setup program redetects your hardware, possibly rebuilding that portion of the Registry. Even that is questionable, however, because you can do the same thing yourself.

Q I heard about a new feature in Windows 2000 called Windows Installer. Will this be available in Windows 98 and what does it do?

A Yes, Microsoft will make Windows Installer available for Windows 98. Furthermore, Office 2000 installs Windows Installer. Windows Installer replaces the Add/Remove Programs dialog box. It adds additional capabilities to the operating system that enable administrators to publish applications on the server. More importantly to you, applications that use Windows Installer technology can be completely removed from the computer, leaving no artifacts behind. They can also repair themselves if important files are missing or become corrupt.

Workshop

The following quiz will enhance your understanding of the topics discussed in this hour.

Quiz

1. True or false? The Registry is the best tool for fixing most problems in Windows.

2. Which of the following does not help you associate a filename extension with a program?

   a. Registry

   b. Folder Options dialog box

   c. File Types dialog box

   d. Open With dialog box

3. Which of the following describes the relationship between filename extension subkeys and program identifier subkeys?

   a. A program identifier's ext subkey associates a program with a filename extension.

   b. A program identifier's default value contains the name of the filename extension with which it's associated.

   c. A filename extension's default value contains the name of the program identifier with which it's associated.

23

4. Which of the following class identifiers represent the My Computer icon in the Registry?

    a. {208D2C60-3AeA-1069-A2D7-08002B30309D}

    b. {645FF040-5081-101B-9F08-00AA002F954E}

    c. {20D04FE0-3AEA-1069-A2D8-08002B30309D}

5. True or false? Windows 95 disk utilities work in Windows 98.

Answers to Quiz Questions

1. False

   Use any other means possible to repair Windows 95 and Windows before resorting to the Registry. If the operating system doesn't provide a user interface to do what you need, by all means, try fixing the problem with the Registry.

2. c

   Windows don't have a File Types dialog box. The Folder Options dialog box does have a File Types tab, however, which you use to associate a filename extension with a program.

3. c

   Each filename extension subkey's value entry associates a filename extension with a program.

4. c

   {20D04FE0-3AEA-1069-A2D8-08002B30309D} is the My Computer icon's class identifier, which you can use to add commands to the icon's shortcut menu, and so on.

5. Trick question. Windows 95 disk utilities continue to work in Windows 98 if you don't convert the disk to FAT32. After converting the disk to FAT32, do not try using Windows 95 disk utilities.

Hour **24**

Deciphering Common Error Messages

In this hour, you learn how to interpret a variety of error messages, including those that you encounter when

- Starting Windows
- Editing the Registry
- Importing and exporting REG files
- Using the real-mode Registry Editor
- Working with Remote Registries
- Using the Registry Checker

Registry errors are less common in Windows 98 than in Windows 95, but they are still unsettling and sometimes indicate more serious trouble to come. This hour helps you figure out what the occasional error message indicates and whether there is anything that you need to do about it.

In most cases, these errors simply mean that you're trying something that you shouldn't and that you need to therefore stop. Continuing probably won't bring harm to the computer, but stopping prevents you from seeing the message again.

This hour is broken down into the following sections, which describe the error messages that you encounter when you are performing certain operations:

- "Starting Windows" describes errors that occur when you are starting the operating system.
- "Editing the Registry" describes errors that you're likely to see when you are editing the Registry with Registry Editor.
- "Importing and Exporting REG Files" and "Using the Real Mode Registry Editor" describe similar errors that occur when you are trying to import from or export to REG files.
- "Working with Remote Registries" describes errors that occur when you are using the Registry Editor with remote administration.
- "Using Registry Checker" describes errors that SCANREG and SCANREGW, the MS-DOS and Windows versions of Registry Checker, generate.

The following sections contain a number of paragraphs that each consist of an error message, a description of the error, and a solution for it. In many cases, an error message can end in several different ways. In such cases, you see a bulleted list describing each of the possible endings.

How did I figure out all the possible error messages? I didn't create errors to see what might happen; I'd never discover all the possible messages. Instead, I used a nifty program called Programmer's Assistant to display a list of all the text messages contained in EXE and DLL files such as Regedit.exe and Kernel32.dll. You can download a copy of Programmer's Assistant from http://www.hotfiles.com.

Starting Windows

Use the following general troubleshooting tips to fix Registry errors that occur as Windows starts:

- Make sure that you have a valid Msdos.sys file. If this file becomes corrupt or is missing, Windows can sometimes report Registry errors, even though such messages are erroneous. My Web site, http://www.honeycutt.com, contains an

Msdos.sys file that you can copy to the root folder of your boot drive. I named the file Msdos-sys so that it wouldn't be hidden in Explorer. Rename it Msdos.sys and copy it to the root folder of your computer's boot disk.

- Scan the Registry for errors using the DOS-based Registry Checker (SCANREG). You learned how to use this utility in Hour 22, "Fixing Errors in the Registry." In short, start the computer in MS-DOS mode (hold down the Ctrl key while starting the computer, and choose Safe Mode from the menu) and type `scanreg /fix` at the command prompt. After running SCANREG, restart the computer. If you're using Windows 95, which doesn't contain Registry Checker, use Norton's WinDoctor.

- Use one of the third-party tools that are available for fixing a corrupt Registry. A good choice is Norton WinDoctor, which is a utility that can fix a variety of Registry problems. WinDoctor is discussed in Hour 22.

24

> Some of the errors that you see when Windows starts are misleading—particularly if you see numerous messages, one after another. Address the most logical problem first, and the rest of the errors will most likely go away.

`Error Accessing the System Registry. You should restore the Registry now and restart your computer.` My experience suggests that you can sometimes get past this error message, eventually, if you keep restarting the computer when you see it. I have no explanation for this, but it's worth rebooting the computer a few times to make sure that you don't lose any settings. Otherwise, click the Restore button to restore the Registry and restart the computer. You'll lose any settings that you've changed between backups.

> The might see the following additional message: `Warning: Windows has detected a Registry/configuration error. Choose Command prompt only, and run SCANREG.` If so, click the Restore button; otherwise, restore your previous Registry using the DOS-based Registry Checker as described in Hour 22. This error is unique to Windows 98.

`Registry file was not found. Registry services may not be operative for this session.` Where are your Registry files? If you didn't intentionally hide them from Windows, you must restore the most recent backup using the DOS-based Registry Checker.

`Windows was unable to process the Registry. This may be fixed by`
`rebooting to Command Prompt Only and running SCANREG /FIX. Otherwise`
`there may not be enough free conventional memory to properly load the`
`Registry.`   In most cases, look for other error messages because low memory is not the
problem. If you really are running low on memory, consider freeing conventional memory by removing device drivers from Config.sys and Autoexec.bat or by relocating them
into upper memory. Otherwise, do as the message says and type `scanreg /fix` at the
command prompt after starting in MS-DOS mode. This message is slightly different in
Windows 95, omitting the reference to SCANREG.

`The windows Registry or SYSTEM.INI file refers to this device file, but`
`the device file no longer exists.`   This occurs for a variety of reasons, the most
common of which is an errant uninstall program or the manual removal of a program
from the computer. Hour 6, "Reducing the Size of the Registry," contains more information about locating and removing from the Registry references to files that no longer
exist.

`Registry File was replaced with backup copy. Changes made in last session`
`may be missing.`   Windows didn't give you much choice. The operating system took it
upon itself to restore the backup copy of the Registry, causing you to lose any configuration changes that were made between backups.

> I found the text for the error messages in this section within two files: Io.sys
> and Vmm32.vxd. Both files are critical components that Windows loads as it
> starts. Both are also in MS-DOS executable format, so the only way to
> extract error messages from these files is to open them in a text editor such
> as Notepad, ignore the binary garbage, and browse the file, looking for bits
> of text. Alternatively, you can view both these files in Quick View or any
> other text editor.

Editing the Registry

Most of the error messages that you see when you are editing the Registry have two
causes. The most likely cause is that you're trying to do something with a key or value
that another process has open or has already removed. If you're viewing a particular
branch in the Registry, for instance, and another program removes a key in that branch,
you'll still see the key in the Registry Editor window even though it doesn't exist anymore. When you try to do something with that key, the Registry Editor displays an error
message. To make sure that the key still exists, press F5 to update the Registry Editor's

display. Another likely cause is that you're trying to do something with a dynamic key or value, such as those in HKEY_DYN_DATA. The only thing I can tell you about editing dynamic keys and values is this: *don't*. HKEY_DYN_DATA is a dynamic key that the operating system doesn't enable you to edit.

 The Registry Editor enables you to remove an entire key that contains dynamic data. Windows rebuilds this information after you restart your computer, however.

24

Cannot create key: *error message*.   The cause of this error depends on the rest of the message:

- **Error while opening the key *name*.**—Either you don't have permission to edit this particular key, or you're trying to add a subkey to a key that another program deleted in the background. Refresh the Registry Editor by pressing F5 so that you can tell if a program did indeed remove the key.

- **Error writing to the Registry.**—If you try to create a new key under one of the dynamic keys in HKEY_DYN_DATA, you'll get this error message. Remember that you can't edit dynamic keys.

- **Unable to generate a unique name.**—It is unlikely that you will ever see this message. It means that the Registry Editor wasn't able to create a unique name for the key, such as New Key #1.

Cannot create value: *error message*.   This error message is similar to the one that you get when you are creating a new key. The *Error message* portion is Error writing to the Registry if you're trying to create a value in a key that no longer exists or that is dynamic. If you're not trying to create a value in a dynamic key, refresh the Registry by pressing F5 to make sure that the key still exists. As for Unable to generate a unique name, the same goes for values as for keys: The Registry Editor wasn't able to create a unique name for the value, such as New Value #1.

Cannot edit *name*: *error message*.   The meaning of this error depends on the rest of the message:

- **Error reading the value's contents.**—This error message indicates that a Registry key is in use by another process. To avoid this message, close the process that's using the key. Another likely possibility is that another process has removed the key, in which case you can refresh the Registry by pressing F5.

- **Error writing the value's new contents.**—This message implies that you're trying to write to one of many dynamic values—don't.

`Cannot open` *name*`: Error while opening key.`   The most likely cause is that you're trying to open a key that another process has removed. The fact that you see a key in the Registry Editor doesn't mean that another process might not have removed it. To make sure, press F5 to refresh the Registry Editor's display. Another possibility is that the key that you're trying to open is corrupted. The only plausible solution to this problem, if the key is indeed corrupt, is to use the Registry Checker to repair the Registry (as described in Hour 22).

`Cannot rename` *name*`: error message.`   The reason behind this message depends on the rest of the message:

- **`Error while renaming key.` or `Error while renaming value.`**—These generally mean that you're trying to rename a dynamic key or value—don't.

- **`The specified key name already exists. Type another name and try again.`**—This message means that you're using a name that already exists. Each subkey name within a key must be unique. Likewise, the message `The specified value name already exists. Type another name and try again.` means that you're using a value name that already exists within that same key.

- **`The specified key name contains illegal character.`**—This message implies that you're using a backslash (\) somewhere in the key's name—don't.

- **`The specified key name is too long. Type a shorter name and try again.`**—This error message means that you're trying to use a name that is longer than 255 characters. Use a shorter key name. Remember also that creating a key with no certainty that a program will use it is as senseless as it is useless.

`Cannot delete` *name*`: Error while deleting key.`   Remember that you can't remove dynamic keys from the Registry. Therefore, don't try to remove keys from `HKEY_DYN_DATA`. You also see this error message if you try to remove a key after another process has already beaten you to it. Press F5 to refresh the display, verifying whether the key exists. The message `Unable to delete all specified values.` is a reminder that you can't delete the default value entry for any Registry key. You can delete the default value entry's contents; or, if the default value entry is the only item remaining for the key, you can remove the key itself. You can't delete dynamic values either, so you'll see this error whenever you try to remove a key from `HKEY_DYN_DATA`.

`Cannot print:` *error message*`.`   The reason behind this message depends on the rest of the message. In either of the following cases, follow the instructions that the error message gives you in order to solve the problem:

- `Insufficient memory to begin job. Try closing down some applications, and try again. If you still see this message, try restarting Windows.`

- An error occurred during printing. Check your printer and your printer's settings for problems, and try again.

Registry Editor: Registry editing has been disabled by your administrator. The system administrator has disabled the Registry Editor using system policies. Hour 21, "Controlling the Desktop via System Policies," tells you more about using the Disable Registry Editing Tools policy. If you must unlock this policy so that you can edit the Registry, see Hour 16, "Other Customizations."

Importing and Exporting REG Files

Most of the problems that you encounter when you are importing and exporting the Registry come from two sources. First, the path and filename might be invalid. Second (and most likely), the REG file might be invalid, especially if you create it by hand. Look for these two problems when you get any error message during an import or export operation.

Cannot import filename: error message. The meaning behind this error depends on the rest of the message:

- **Error accessing the Registry.**—For some reason, the Registry Editor cannot access the Registry. Make sure that if you're editing a remote Registry, you have permission to do so, and make sure that the Registry files are in place if you're working with a local Registry. Otherwise, open the Registry Editor and inspect the Registry to make sure that it is indeed OK. If you suspect corruption, run SCAN-REG with the /fix option to repair the Registry. If you're using Windows 95, use Norton WinDoctor instead of SCANREG.

- **Error writing to the Registry.**—This means that you're trying to import data into a corrupt or dynamic Registry key. If you suspect that the Registry key is corrupt, run SCANREG with the /fix option. Remember that you can't import values into HKEY_DYN_DATA. If you're using Windows 95, use Norton WinDoctor instead of SCANREG.

- **Error opening the file. There may be a disk or file system error.**—First, double-check the filename. If you're importing a filename that contains spaces from an MS-DOS command line or from the Run dialog box, you'll see this error message when you forget to surround the filename with spaces. If the filename isn't the problem, try opening the file in Notepad. Also run ScanDisk to check the file system for errors. You might have to use a stronger utility, such as Norton Disk Doctor, to fix this problem, particularly if ScanDisk doesn't fix it.

- **`Error reading the file. There may be a disk error or the file may be corrupt.`**—This error is similar to the preceding one, except that the Registry Editor can open the file—it just can't read it. Try reading the REG file in Notepad. Can you see its entire contents in the editor window? Also run ScanDisk to check the file system for errors. If you can read the file using Notepad, but you can't import the file into the Registry, you have a more serious problem; a utility such as Norton Disk Doctor can possibly fix it.

- **`The specified file is not a Registry script. You can import only Registry files.`**—This means that you're trying to import a REG file that's invalid. If you're definitely importing a REG file, make sure that it's not damaged. Double-check Hour 18, "Scripting Changes to the Registry," to make sure that you're using the correct format for REG files. Also make sure that you have `REGEDIT4` on the very first line of the file and that the second line is blank.

`Cannot export` *`filename`*`: Error writing the file. There may be a disk or file system error.` Again, double-check the path and filename that you're specifying. Also make sure that you have enough space on the disk to create the file. Other than that, this error usually indicates a more serious problem that involves the file system. Run ScanDisk or Norton Disk Doctor to look for errors in the file system.

> If you suspect that a particular Registry branch is corrupt, back up the Registry, and then try removing that branch from the Registry. If you can export that branch to a REG file before removing it, that's even better. That way, you can restore the REG file after removing the branch. You might also consider optimizing the Registry using Registry Checker's /opt switch to recover any dead space before importing the REG file that you created as a backup. This and other creative techniques can usually help you salvage a damaged Registry, but in most cases you're better off restoring a recent backup copy.

Using the Real mode Registry Editor

Hour 4, "Editing the Registry with REGEDIT," describes the difference between the Windows-based Registry Editor and the DOS-based real mode Registry Editor. In short, you can run the real mode Registry only in MS-DOS mode. The only real use for the real mode Registry Editor is to import REG files into the Registry or to export portions of the Registry to a REG file.

Cannot open *filename*.   The REG file that you're trying to import doesn't exist or doesn't contain valid information. Make sure that the format of the REG file is correct (that is, make sure it starts with REGEDIT4, followed by a blank line). Also make sure that you're not missing any brackets ([]). Finally, be sure to double-check the filename. If the path contains spaces, enclose it in quotation marks.

Cannot import *filename*: *error message*.   The meaning of this error depends on the rest of the message. The messages you see when you are importing a REG file using the real mode Registry Editor are the same as when you're using the Windows-based Registry Editor. The preceding section describes these messages and tells you what to do about them.

Cannot export *filename*: *error message*.   The meaning of this error depends on the rest of the error message. The following two messages are unique to the real mode Registry Editor (the preceding section describes any remaining error messages that you might see):

- **Error creating the file.**—This error message suggests that you need to double-check the filename, making sure that you enclose paths that have spaces in quotation marks. Also, make sure that you have enough disk space for the REG file.

- **The specified key name does not exist.**—This message means that you're trying to export or delete a key that doesn't exist. Double-check the command line.

Error accessing the Registry: The file may not be complete.   The real mode Registry Editor reports this message if you try to import a REG file that's too big. There might not be enough memory available to import the file. Try freeing additional conventional memory by starting the computer with a minimal configuration. To do so, copy Config.sys and Autoexec.bat to backup files, and then remove them. After importing the REG file, restore both files.

Optionally, split the REG file into multiple REG files using a text editor, and then import each REG file separately.

The real mode Registry Editor reports a variety of error messages if you don't get the command line just right:

- Invalid switch
- Parameter format not correct
- Required parameter missing
- Too many parameters

24

In any of these cases, check Hour 4 or type `regedit /?` at the command prompt to make sure that you're using the correct command line.

DATA IS MISSING FROM THE REGISTRY

It's a common complaint: "I imported a REG file, but the data is missing from the Registry." The leading causes of this problem are that a REG file isn't using the correct format or that it has syntax errors. Refer to Hour 18 to make sure that you're using the correct format.

Here are some other notes to help you locate problems in a REG file. Make sure that you're not missing any brackets around key names: [HKEY_LOCAL_MACHINE\SOFTWARE]. Be sure to enclose each value name in quotation marks. Use @ to indicate the default value entry. Check the format that is used for string, binary, and DWORD values. Enclose string values in quotation marks, and prefix DWORD values with DWORD:.

Working With Remote Registries

`You cannot connect to your own computer.` This error message is self-explanatory. If you want to edit the local Registry, you don't need to connect to it by choosing Registry, Connect.

`Error Connecting Network Registry.` The Registry Editor reports this error message when it can't connect to the remote computer's Registry. This message is vague and applies to situations in which the other error messages don't apply. In general, double-check the same old things: Make sure that you have permission to connect to the remote computer's Registry; double-check that remote administration is enabled on the remote computer; and make sure that both computers are running the Microsoft Remote Registry Service.

`Unable to connect to` *name*`. Make sure that this computer is on the network, has remote administration enabled, and that both computers are running the remote Registry service.` Follow the instructions in this error message to fix the problem. Beyond that, make sure that your own network connection is working properly.

`Unable to connect to all of the roots of the computer's Registry. Disconnect from the remote Registry and then reconnect before trying again.` I've never seen this error message when connecting to another Windows Registry. I *have* seen it when connecting to a Windows NT Registry, however. This is just an indication that you don't have permission to connect to one or more of the root keys in that Registry.

`Unable to connect to` *name*`. Make sure you have permission to administer this computer.` As this message states, you probably don't have permission to connect to the remote computer's Registry. Double-check the remote administration settings on the remote computer. You might also double-check that you're a member of the appropriate administrative groups on the server.

Using Registry Checker

`Invalid command line parameter.` Take another look at Hour 22 to make sure that you understand each of Registry Checker's command-line options.

`The Registry file` *filename* `is damaged.` This doesn't necessarily mean that you need to abandon hope. Registry Checker reports this error when it detects a problem. It then restores the most recent backup copy of the Registry or tries to repair the Registry.

`Windows encountered an error accessing the system Registry. Windows will restart and repair the system Registry for you.` Each time you start Windows, it runs Registry Checker, which scans the Registry for errors. If Registry Checker finds any errors, it returns this error message. Then it restores the computer and runs the MS-DOS version of Registry Checker in order to repair the Registry.

`Unable to scan the system Registry.` If you see this error message or one that says `Unable to scan the Registry file` *filename*`.`, repairing the Registry is probably beyond hope. Your best bet is to restore the most recent backup copy and move on.

Program-Related Error Messages

This section helps you figure out a variety of Windows error messages, each of which has a solution in the Registry.

`Cannot find a device file that may be needed to run Windows. The Windows Registry or SYSTEM.INI refers to this device file, but the device no longer exists.` You get this error as Windows starts. All it's saying is that the Registry or System.ini is telling the operating system to load a device driver that it can't find. First, check the `[386Enh]` section for any entry that looks like `device=`*filename*`.vxd`, where *filename*`.vxd` is the name of the missing device driver. Either erase that line from System.ini, or, if you believe the file is necessary to run Windows, replace it from the CD-ROM (as discussed in Hour 23, "Fixing Program Errors via the Registry"). If you don't find the file in System.ini, search the Registry for the root filename, or look in `HKEY_LOCAL_MACHINE\System\CurrentControlset\Services\VxD` for it. Remove the key if the VxD is no longer required; otherwise, replace the file from the Windows CD-ROM. One other note: If Windows doesn't provide a filename in the error message, look for values named `StaticVxD` that don't contain valid data, and remove them.

`Your display adapter is not configured properly. To correct the problem,
click OK to start the Hardware Installation Wizard.`   Windows might have restored System.1st because it thinks the Registry was corrupted and it didn't find a suitable backup copy to restore. Restore one of your own backup copies of the Registry, or click OK to reconfigure the display adapter.

`Error occurred while trying to remove` *name*`. Uninstallation has been
canceled.`   You've already removed the program from your computer, but it still has an uninstall entry in the Add/Remove Programs Properties dialog box, and you tried to remove it. Remove it from the list as described in Hour 16 or by using Tweak UI as described in Hour 8, "Using Microsoft's Tweak UI."

`Properties for this item are not available.`   The cause of this problem is usually a bad `PropertySheetHandlers` subkey for a class or program identifier in `HKEY_CLASSES_ROOT` (see Hour 23). In addition, the attribute flag for this particular object might erroneously enable the Properties command even though a property sheet isn't available for it. Hour 14, "Files and Folders," shows you how to adjust this value entry. A better solution to this problem is to reinstall the offending application, allowing it to make the appropriate repairs.

Summary

Most of the Registry errors that Windows generates are benign, indicating that you're doing something wrong. If you see a Registry error as the operating starts, however, take it seriously.

The best way to repair most errors in Windows 98 is to use Registry Checker to scan and fix them. If you're using Windows 95, you don't have Registry Checker. The next best thing, then, is Norton WinDoctor. These utilities are discussed in Hour 22.

Q&A

Q **I just upgraded from Windows 95 to Windows 98 and now I'm getting Registry errors. Can I restore the last Registry backup I made before upgrading?**

A Absolutely NOT. Doing so prevents Windows 98 from starting properly and renders the computer useless until you reinstall the operating system. The best solution is to use the repair tools discussed in Hour 22.

Q **I'm getting a Registry error message that I don't see anywhere in this hour. How can I learn more about the message and how to fix it?**

A Search Microsoft's Online Technical Support for the error message. `http://support.microsoft.com` is the URL. If you don't find help there, shoot me a message at `jerry@honeycutt.com`. Aside from helping you with the error, I can include it in future editions of this book.

Workshop

The following quiz will enhance your understanding of the topics discussed in this hour.

Quiz

1. True or false? Windows 95 spits out more Registry error messages than Windows 98.

2. True or false? If Windows displays a Registry error message that tells you to reinstall the operating system, follow its instructions.

3. True or false? Most error messages that are displayed by the Registry Editor are user input errors rather than serious problems with the Registry.

Answers to Quiz Questions

1. True

   Windows 98 does a better job of ensuring the Registry's integrity. It also repairs many errors without the user ever knowing that there was a problem.

2. False

   Some error messages indicate that the solution is to reinstall the operating system. This is bad advice. When you see an error that indicates you need to reinstall the operating system, the first thing you need to do is make sure that you have plenty of free disk space for the operating system to make backup copies of the Registry.

3. True

   Virtually all the error messages that the Registry Editor displays are a result the user trying to do something he ought not to do.

INDEX

X-Y-Z